£8·95

# THE BRITISH WORKER QUESTION

# THE BRITISH WORKER QUESTION

## A new look at workers and productivity in manufacturing

Theo Nichols

Routledge & Kegan Paul

London

*First published in 1986 by*
*Routledge & Kegan Paul plc*
*11 New Fetter Lane, London EC4P 4EE*

*Set in 10/12pt. Sabon*
*by Columns of Reading*
*and printed in Great Britain*
*by T.J. Press (Padstow) Ltd.*
*Padstow, Cornwall*

*British Library Cataloguing in Publication Data*
*Nichols, Theo.*
    *The British worker question: a new look*
  *at workers and productivity in manufacturing.*
  *1. Labour productivity—Great Britain.    I. Title.*
  *331.11'8'0941        HC260.L3*
  *ISBN 0-7100-9779-4*
  *ISBN 0-7102-9850-2*

*For Rob,*
*for Jo*
*and for Claire*

# Contents

Preface                                                                                    xi

Part One:
**The mould of opinion**                                                                    1
1 Labour productivity, ideological divisions and the
  division of labour in the social sciences                                                 3
2 British workers, 'attitudes', 'effort'
  and the economists                                                                       39

Part Two
**Into detail: some comparative evidence re-examined**                                      53
3 British workers in the world of comparative statics (1)                                   55
4 British workers in the world of comparative statics (2)                                   74

Part Three
**Into context: productivity, productiveness
and social organisation**                                                                   95
5 'The difficulty' reconsidered (1): Quantity, quality,
  and the measurement of management and 'men'                                               97
6 'The difficulty' reconsidered (2): Different quantities,
  and another side to the quality of labour                                                112
7 'The difficulty' reconsidered (3): The social
  organisation of production and the British context                                       127
8 'The difficulty' reconsidered (4): A closer look at
  the social organisation of production in Britain                                         144

Part Four
**The difficulties resolved?**                                                             171
9 Enter Mrs Thatcher: The 'fear and anxiety' syndrome                                      173
10 The new 'realism' and reality: Workers
   and management                                                                          187

11 Productivity, productiveness and myopia in
   Britain today                                      215

   Three commentaries on productivity and
   the conventional wisdom                            241
   Notes                                              263
   Bibliography                                       284
   Author index                                       306
   Subject index                                      311

# Tables

1.1 Annual compound rates of growth 17
2.1 Studies of the motor vehicle industry 46
3.1 Industrial analysis of international productivity
    differentials 57
3.2 Summary of the causes of productivity differentials 58
3.3 Rules and practices of workers that might affect
    labour productivity to some degree adversely,
    compared on the basis of the UK and non-UK
    operations of international companies 68
4.1 Examples of overmanning in the British car industry 77
6.1 Fatality rates in Western European manufacturing
    industry 119
11.1 Manufacturing investment, 1979–84 236

# Figures

1.1 Typical 'restricted' output     27
5.1 R & D scientists/engineers per 10,000 of the labour
force by country, 1965–75     107
7.1 Net plant and equipment per worker in UK, West
German, US and French manufacturing     140
9.1 Output and productivity in manufacturing industries,
1973–83     174
10.1 The flexible firm     202
11.1 Working population and employed labour force,
1973–84     239

# Preface

> The solitude must have been disturbing me, because instantly, I broke into a run without thinking. I stopped and said to myself, 'You are not a shipwrecked mariner or a lost explorer. You are walking about in a factory in England and all things have a rational explanation.'
>
> Peter Currell Brown, *Smallcreep's Day*

Before I wrote this book I had long been accustomed to British society, its politics and culture. Quite simply, throughout my lifetime it had always been there, a sort of background music full of familiar melodies. One tune in particular had played on and on for as long as I could remember. Sometimes loud, sometimes a distant echo, it had always been accompanied by a more or less constant refrain – something about 'British workers and productivity'. This, I also knew, was a jingle so familiar that some people just could not get it out of their heads. The very mention of the word 'worker' was itself sufficient to impel them to utter other equally old and equally familiar phrases – 'don't work hard enough', 'laziness', 'restrictive practices' and 'British trade unions have too much power'. I had never sung along myself. Like a good many other people, I suspect, I had heard all this so often – it really was background music – that I had never really *listened* to the message that the words in the song conveyed. Then probably about 1977 or 1978, the music got turned up so loud that I too could not get it out of my head.

I began to listen. I listened to the industrialists. I listened to the politicians. Tory and Labour, they mostly said the same thing: British workers did not work hard enough. Reading around a bit, I came to realise that 'British Workers and Productivity' is one of the longest running shows in British politics. I started to pay more attention. I soon realised that the economists – the people who, it seemed, had now come to write the script for the entire performance – were not much troubled by the few discordant voices that were occasionally to be heard from off-stage (from those who asked 'What about the investment they put behind workers in other countries?' and so forth). For their part, those economists I spoke to were apt to acknowledge that there were of course other things to be taken into account, but then they too would break into the words of the old refrain. Sometimes delivered with a twinkle in the eye, sometimes with a barely stifled yawn, 'British Workers and Productivity' was, it seemed, part of their repertoire as well. Not only this, but I gathered that some of their fellow economists had actually set the notes in the tune to numbers. Since all the econometricians who had done this had reached a similar conclusion, that, it seemed, was that.

This, then, is how I was placed when I began to write this book. That is, I stood outside the particular academic sphere within which productivity had been researched, yet I lived in a society where the talk about British workers and productivity went on and on. I knew of no good theoretical reason why the workforces of different capitalist societies could not affect the productivity outcome to different degrees. In fact, I knew that some of those on the political left, as well as those on the political right, made just such an assumption about the adverse effects of British workers on productivity, and even relished it. On the other hand, though, I had my doubts about what the productivity situation in Britain really was, I felt that the question was too important to be monopolised by economists, and, on every front, I had become intrigued. To cut a long story short, I decided to have a look myself. I decided to concentrate on manufacturing, where the level of labour productivity was lower in Britain (something which is not disputed throughout this book: what interests me is with what justification it can be said that this is the 'fault' of British workers). For purposes of comparison I also decided to keep my eye on the situation in other countries, for the most part West Germany, France and the US and of course Japan.

What I have found has surprised me. For as I see it now, those tunes about British workers and productivity had seeped into my consciousness to a far greater extent than I should have ever allowed them to do. I have been driven to conclude that the British worker idea, which was so prevalent in the 1970s (and, as will be seen, long before that) lacks credibility, as do the new shrill noises about productivity that have emanated from the Thatcherites in the 1980s – for whom, of course, the British worker idea serves as an important 'historical' backcloth. In large part, indeed, I have come back to the position to which I had always been drawn instinctively, before the noise about productivity reached a crescendo in the mid to late 1970s. But now I feel that I have more than instinct to support me. I have tried to write this book in such a way as to suggest to the reader what this is and to save others treading the same road twice.

Briefly, the structure of the book is this. Beginning in Part One with a consideration of the ideological trappings of the British workers and productivity idea, I quite deliberately refuse to take the easy course and to counter one ideology with another. Rather, accepting that, in principle at any rate, an idea may be both ideological *and* true, I attempt from this point on to proceed step by step. To this end I sketch out (at first in an elementary manner) what evidence is required to assess the validity of the British worker idea, then examine in Part Two some of the evidence that has actually been put forward, and how adequate this has been. Following this, in Part Three, the task is begun of introducing evidence of a kind that has rarely figured in productivity research and of reinterpreting some of that which has been conventionally provided. Here, too, the shift is made to a different, much less 'mechanical' kind of analysis. This is carried over to a consideration of productivity in the present day, which is the subject of Part Four. By proceeding like this, I hope that the book can be read by anyone who starts out with a relatively open mind, and not simply by social scientists (to whom the following paragraphs are mainly directed).

I suspect that some sociologists will not find it to their liking that I harp so much on the 'evidence'. They may not take kindly to my refusal to invoke 'culture' and 'attitudes' lightly either ('empiricism', 'positivism' and all that). No doubt I have gone 'over the top' about attitudes in some places. I can only plead here that I have been driven to this in order to make clear, and then move away from, the quite inadequate way that some of the issues which concern me have so often been dealt with before. 'Culture',

I am happy to agree, cannot be reduced directly to the economic. But it is no free-floating miasma either. And especially since what has concerned me to an increasing extent in writing this book is how goods are actually produced, I have not allowed 'culture' to figure very much outside of this or a more general material context. In fact, rather than invoke 'attitudes', as the book develops I have tried to put the stress on how, in Britain, capital is organised and how manufacturing capital organises itself as well as labour. Rather than making 'attitudes' my starting point, or invoking them to give the appearance of greater weight and understanding where the evidence runs thin (a practice not simply of politicians, but, where productivity is concerned, of too many academics as well), I have come to prefer a different way of going about things, and to prefer also a rather different language – one that speaks in terms of opportunity and constraint, and in turn of the consequences of these, and, at all levels, of organisational capacities and of organisational process. It is, as I see it, these matters that need to be taken into account if we are to understand better some of the important determinants of productivity levels between different capitalist societies that are at a broadly similar level of development. Even the differences that pertain between such systems in the degree to which they intensify or otherwise exploit labour, and other differences of an allocative kind (e.g. in the mass or ratio of investment) are only one part of the answer. These things said, however, I am only too well aware that I must leave it to other hands than mine to push such work further by investigating in much more detail not only differences of an international kind but also those that pertain between different industries, regions and firms within Britain.

As for economists, my feelings about their work are mixed. I certainly hold the work of some of them in the highest esteem, and I hope that I have made this clear (so too my debt to some economic historians). But I must confess that I have been less than happy about the theory and methodological rigour that has informed some of the economics that I have read.

J.K. Galbraith once depicted the prestige structure of economics as a hollow pyramid or cone. At the base of the cone the sides were transparent and there were many openings to the outside. But towards the apex the sides became increasingly opaque and impermeable. It was here, at the top of the pyramid, that the economists lived who dealt with pure theory. These mathematically gifted formal economists were highly regarded in their profession. According to Galbraith those at the base of the cone were not held in such high repute precisely because they were closer to the outside world. I can only say that although Galbraith's imagery may have something to recommend it, it seems to me to be highly deficient in one respect. For as far as research into productivity is concerned, a truly remarkable feature of economics, both at the top of the cone and at its base, is that, where it *is* in touch with the outside world, it is overwhelmingly in touch with one small part of that world only. So close has the relation been with this small part of the world – notably with management – that our knowledge of the determination of productivity has long been flawed by substantial lacunae. That is, there has not only been 'bias' (economists, and others, who have conducted empirical research having been all too ready to view workers through a management lens), but by a supreme irony and with few exceptions, even in the performance of their explicitly or implicitly adopted role as management scientists these researchers have signally failed to produce a grounded analysis of management itself – how it is organised, what it does, and how well it does what it does.

That this vacuum in our knowledge has been allowed to persist for so long cannot be laid entirely at the door of economists. For the most part those of their fellow social scientists who are sociologists, and who should have had something to contribute on both the theoretical and the methodological side, have rarely bothered themselves with the question of how international differences in labour productivity are to be explained at all. Sociologists are apt to caricature economics as a science that considers only what comes out of the labour process, not what goes on inside it (production is a 'black box', etc). An element of oversimplification is involved in this, as we shall see. But as things stand now, it would not be too difficult for economists to turn such criticism back on sociologists, to charge that they have been concerned with what goes on in the labour process to the exclusion of investigating what comes out of it. Part of the justification for writing this book is that I find this situation rather absurd.

This book has been a long time in the making and many people – sometimes with different perspectives to my own – have given me helpful advice, opinions or information along the way, and have

xvi *Preface*

provided me with unpublished materials, draft manuscripts and so on. To be numbered among them are Huw Beynon, Paul Edwards, Tony Elgar, Leon Grunberg, Geoff Hodgson, Bryn Jones, John Kelly, Craig Littler, Ernest Mandel, John Muellbauer, Harry Scarborough, Sydney Smith-Gavine and Shaun Stewart. I am especially indebted to Terry Austrin, with whom I have spent many enjoyable and useful hours discussing related issues, and who read the entire manuscript in draft, and to Pete Armstrong and Bob Carter, who also read most of it. As for Nancy, no one could have helped me more than she did, and however odd it may sound to say 'thank you' to someone for being herself, I do. My sincere thanks also to Pauline Tilley, whose typing has been a magnificent help.

Figure 1.1 is reproduced from D.J. Hickson, 'Motives of Workpeople who Restrict Their Output', *Occupational Psychology*, 1961, p. 115, with the permission of the author. Tables 3.1 and 3.2 are reproduced from C.F. Pratten's *Labour Productivity Differentials Within International Companies* (1976a), pp. 13 and 61, with the permission of Cambridge University Press. Table 4.1 is reproduced from *The Future of the British Car Industry* (CPRS, 1975), with the permission of the Controller of Her Majesty's Stationery Office. Figure 10.1 is reproduced from J. Atkinson's. 'Manpower Strategies for Flexible Organisations', *Personnel Management*, August 1984, p. 29, with permission of Personnel Publications Ltd.

Theo Nichols
Bristol, March 1985

# Part One

# The mould of opinion

# 1 Labour productivity, ideological divisions and the division of labour in the social sciences

In the first decade of this century, in 1907, those employed in British manufacturing industry probably produced about half as much as their American counterparts. Investigations conducted over the subsequent period suggest that by the mid to late 1930s the Americans out-produced the British by a ratio of 2.2, and that by 1950 American output per worker was 2.7 times greater than in Britain (Phelps Brown and Browne, 1968; Rostas, 1948; Paige and Bombach, 1959). That American productivity in manufacturing has probably been between two and three times that obtained in Britain throughout this century, is confirmed by investigations conducted in the 1970s, which indicate that British workers in manufacturing produced only about one third as much as their US counterparts (Prais, 1981a; Smith et al., 1982). The shortfall in the level of productivity has been less sharply defined between Britain and other Western European nations. But Prais reports that West Germany's manufacturing output per employee was 30 per cent ahead of Britain's in 1975. Other research for the earlier 1970s also found West Germany to be ahead by a similar margin and the differential between Britain and some other industrial countries pointed in the same direction, France then being 15 per cent ahead, for example (Pratten, 1976a).

Few people who lived in Britain in the 1970s could have failed to hear that the level of British manufacturing productivity fell short of that in other major industrial counties – or that British workers did not work hard enough. It has in fact been the lot of British workers for several generations to hear that they work 'less hard'.

Go back to 1901. It's Christmas Day. Churchmen, colonels, industrialists, civil servants, politicians – in fact a cross-section of those who pretend to informed, responsible opinion – sit down for a post-prandial read of *The Times*. And what do they find on their letters page? No less than *five* letters on 'The Crisis in British Industry'. Back in November of that year the first of a series of articles had appeared under this same title.[1] The author of these articles, E.A. Pratt, had maintained:

> The injurious effect that trade unionism of the more aggressive
> or of the more insidious type may exercise on the trade of the
> country is a question of very great importance at a time when
> there seem to be so many difficulties in the conduct of our
> industries, especially in regard to the cost of production and
> foreign competition.

Particularly incensed by the practice of 'ca' canny' or 'restricting the output' amongst seamen, Pratt further maintained that 'socialist labour leaders' had it as their aspiration to make 'Go Easy' the 'policy of the British working man in general' – a policy which, he opined, had been adopted so generally already that it was 'eating the heart out of British industry'. In the building trades, the first of many industries Pratt was to refer to, he claimed that 'all the men' were 'tarred with the same brush in regard to doing less work for more money, especially where there is any lack of proper supervision'. The very next day a report to *The Times*, telegraphed in from Leeds, confirmed how bad the situation was in the building trades in that city, where 'if any one should wilfully attempt to carry eight bricks at a time the whole of his comrades would at once stop work'. Such was the public interest that correspondence about this and related articles ran on till March the next year. The industrialists, politicians and churchmen extended their congratulations to the author – who had of course related 'the crisis of British industry' to the practices of British working men and their trade unions. Congratulations were also offered by supporters of the National Free Labour Association, and with good reason; for such was the target of the *Times* articles that even a contemporary official American publication was to dub them a 'savage attack made on trade unions' (US Bureau of Labour, 1904, p. 731).

The articles advocated trade union reform. But the problem was seen to be such that mere legislation could not provide the whole answer. 'Evidence' was cited from 'an ironmaster' (unnamed) about 'districts where the people seem to care for nothing but betting, football and drinking'. Tales were reported of 'boys' getting together and 'deciding to have a holiday'. The author of the articles himself saw 'the decadence of the working man' being matched by 'a distinct degeneration on the part of the working boy' who, in some shops, was 'losing all sense of discipline' – so much so that this sparked his interest in 'an elaborate scheme for subjecting all boys to a regular drill', 'and girls, too', he added, 'up to a certain age'. In this he was out-done by an enthusiastic supporter. This particular gentleman, whilst agreeing 'about the organised idleness of our workmen', found 'the disease' – from which, he claimed, 'our Continental competitors suffer less than we do' – to be so deep-seated as to warrant military training *for managers*, 'as is done in Germany'. Comparisons with Germany and references to 'American methods' were in fact commonplace.

In his assessment of workers in the Boot and Shoe trade the *Times* correspondent claimed: 'they "go-easy" . . . there is no doubt that the output of the English worker is a good deal less than that of the American'. With reference to the Black Bottle trade, he sang the praises of a scheme to bring in German glassblowers and thereby to run 'an English factory on English soil with the help of German workmen following German methods'. Readers were left in no doubt that productivity would increase as a consequence of this.

Some trade unionists tried to defend 'the British working man'. The Webbs, for their part, wrote a lengthy letter. They claimed that 'the manual labour of this country (irrespective of the results of machinery)' was 'far more productive today than it ever was before'. 'Would any great employer', they asked, 'change his present workers for those of 1801?' They pointed out that 'in so far as the disposition to limit the amount of energy exists, it is incorrect to ascribe it to trade unionism . . . only five per cent of the population are trade unionists'. Above all, they drew on their historical researches to repudiate the view that 'the evil is worse than formerly and that it is increasing'. They reported that 'complaints as to diminished quality or energy at work, and of the tacit conspiracy to discourage individual exertion, occur with curiously exact iteration in every decade of the last one hundred years at least', and they backed this up with their own findings of 'exactly the same accusation of the bricklayers' limiting the number of bricks, and precisely the same belief that they were only doing 'half as much' as they did twenty years before, in the great strikes of 1833, in those of 1853, again in 1858–60, and again in 1871'. As the Webbs saw it, this only went to show that 'the employers felt the workman's constant attempt in all ages to alter the bargain to their own personal advantage'.

Since labour is always a potential problem for capital ('the trouble with industry is people'), it is no cause for surprise that, in Britain, the first industrial nation, the ideological castigation of workers can be traced back over a very long period indeed – right from the onset of the Industrial Revolution; right through the nineteenth century, as noted by the Webbs; and throughout the eight decades of this century as well. As far as British workers and trade unions go, it has also been a recurrent theme that things are getting worse.

Of course, the idea that things are worse than at some previous time carries with it the implication that once upon a time things were better. Some of the older generation of British politicians (and not least those on the Labour side), are given to looking back to the evacuation at Dunkirk in May–June 1940 as an example of just such a better time, and to invoke the 'Dunkirk spirit', which they see as having brought the whole nation together, including managers and workers in industry. An enquiry into British war production that was conducted in 1941–2 puts matters in a rather different light.

Based on conversations with over 1,000 workers, and with managers and others in about eighty firms, this rare piece of ear-to-the-ground wartime reportage contains a number of interesting observations. On British management: 'They feel less secure than ever before, they see all-round encroachments on their traditional rights'; 'we note a common assumption that managerial staffs must be recruited from a managerial class, and not upgraded from below'. On the conduct of the war, and the quality of war production: 'Much of the current comment on our generals is unprintable'; many people 'wonder about the weapons which so many of them have been making'. On the expectations of those in different classes: 'The strongest single expectation people have about the result of the war is that after we have won it there will be economic depression. This feeling is held by a majority in all groups but it weighs heaviest on the minds of those with larger capital interests or higher standards of living ... if everyone accepted the possibility of economic depression as something which would be equally shared out, the fear of it would not matter so much.' However, what the authors of the study had to say about what might be called the 'once upon a time' syndrome is, in retrospect, of particular interest. For whereas they acknowledge that 'in the much talked of period after Dunkirk . . . it was the people of Britain who rose up and fought in the factories'; they were equally clear, writing only shortly afterwards, that the 'momentum has been winding down', so that, as they put it, 'This is the problem that now faces us' (Mass Observation, 1942, pp. 57, 300, 303, 379).

It is as well to remember that the idea that the war years induced a deeply felt sense of solidarity, with everyone contributing as best they could, according to their station in life, was not one that was universally held at the time. Some thoughts put to paper by a works manager serve to underline this. 'Events like Dunkirk', he reflected in 1943, 'put a spurt into the nation which does not last'; and he went on to point to 'slackness on the part of the worker, as evidenced by absenteeism, lavatory-mongering, petty strikes, and manifested in other sections of the population in Black Market operations, evasion of quotas, illegal use of petrol, luxury feeding, and the like'. In addition, he quoted from a contemporary article by Stephen Spender in the *New Statesman and Nation* which ran:

> Men in the factories, the Army, the Civil Defence, work, but without a sense that they are sharing the responsibilities of war. On the contrary, their great consolation is to feel that they are not responsible. At a discussion on the loss of Malaya amongst firemen, the men talked with a certain satisfaction about the hopeless incompetence of the 'ruling class' and the 'bosses' . . . Convinced that they cannot do anything, they take the satisfaction of the impotent in the guilt, and indeed to-day, the punishment, incurred by the potent ruling class. (Mass Observation, 1943, Appendix, pp. 123, 125)

The works manager had thought this quotation 'worth recording'. From our standpoint it was. For quite apart from anything else, it gives pause for thought about the ideology of 'once upon a time', which, over the years, has informed so much public debate about 'Britain's problem of productivity'.

Once upon a time . . . Once, British trade unions were 'a model to many other countries by the[ir] steady commonsense methods, tempered by militancy, courage and self-sacrifice . . . All that lies in the past.' So wrote a British professor of economic history in 1982. In his view, British trade unions, by 'barbarising industrial

relations', had 'in a few short years . . . destroyed the moral basis
of trade unionism'. They had, in a well-worn phrase, become 'too
powerful'. As for the 'the British workman' (1982 version): 'he
will put his boot in'; will no longer work 'properly' – unlike
'Americans and Continentals' (Pollard, 1982, pp. 106–11).

'Organised idleness', 'decadence', 'degeneration' – such was the
language of *The Times* eighty and more years ago. The language
of this contemporary economic historian is not that much
different. What he had to say, in 1982, is not a carbon copy of the
earlier version. It was hardly open to him, at a time when British
workers' wages compared unfavourably with those in much of the
rest of Europe as well as America, to charge, as it was done in a
letter to *The Times* on 19 November 1901 – that 'idle scoundrel',
the British working man, will 'laugh in your face while he is
receiving the highest pay for his ignorant, wasteful blundering' –
but the ideological skein can be stretched to encompass even this
otherwise awkward circumstance. For, 'in recent years', Pollard
tells us – and most certainly he is not the only one to do so –
British unions 'have to be counted among the most irresponsible
and destructive unions in Europe'. And, of course, once British
workers and their unions have been counted as such, it is not a
long step to a further charge: that they 'have had a material share
of the responsibility for keeping down the incomes of their
members and other workers'

In short, variations on the theme that British workers work less
hard than those of other nations, and that they work less hard
than they used to, have been part of British society for a long time
now. What this means is that it is particularly difficult for anyone
who lives in Britain to consider 'innocently' the contribution that
British workers make to productivity. At the very least it is
necessary to hold our minds in check, lest they take us down all-
too-well-trodden thought-ways, for it is in just this manner that
ideologies are apt to have their way with us. They 'work', when
they do work, through reiteration to the point of familiarity, and
through the translation of what is familiar (what 'everybody
knows') into what is 'common sense'. As a consequence of this
'the facts of the matter' are too easily taken for granted.

It is of course the responsibility of social scientists to go beyond
the conventional wisdom, no matter how long established it might
be, and to provide logical and thoroughly researched accounts of
the reality it purports to describe. How far they have been
successful in this is something that will be considered shortly. But

so far, in stressing that certain ideas about British workers are indeed of long standing, it has only been possible to provide a loose introductory sketch of the conventional wisdom. Before considering the contribution that social scientists have made to the study of whether British workers work less hard than those elsewhere, it is therefore necessary to make some modifications to the general outline presented above.

'Productivity Has Never Been Higher!' That's the message that the Tory party put over to the British public at Christmas-time 1982 (Conservative Party BBC radio broadcast, 29 December). The first Thatcher administration made many such claims, of course, and much later on, in Part Four, an attempt will be made to assess their validity. At this point, however, there are two quite different reasons why we cannot yet put the above discussion of ideas about British workers and productivity behind us, even though in more recent times it has been claimed that British productivity has improved.

The first reason stems from the need to have a prudent regard to the future. There is, in short, no telling whether the good news about British productivity will continue to be broadcast, Christmas after Christmas. Indeed, the ideological currents already referred to have washed over British society for so long, and have run so deep, that, come another crisis, they will almost certainly rise to the surface again. Because of this a case remains even now for mapping out the ideological seascape, so that next time round the evidence can be better evaluated. (By the same token, there is also good reason to look again at the recent past: in particular to enquire into the evidence that actually was advanced about British workers and productivity during the 1970s, the period that immediately preceded what some regard as the Thatcherite transformation. It has been seen already that even the 'spirit of Dunkirk' may not have been all that it is sometimes assumed to have been in retrospect – or at least that production in British factories 'during the war' may not always have been deserving of the rosy lens through which it has frequently been viewed. This prompts the question whether the performance of British workers during the 1970s has too often been viewed through a lens that, far from being too rosy, has been unduly dark. Parts Two and Three are addressed to just this point.)

The second and quite different reason why some further

remarks on ideas about the performance of British workers are in order is, quite simply, that by concentrating so far on the mainstream view, some other crosscurrents have not received their fair share of attention. The trade union response is a case in point and some further consideration will be given to this shortly. But there is something else which has been neglected and which needs to be considered as well; namely a tradition in British social thought which, initially at any rate, seems to run plain contrary to some of the long-established assumptions introduced so far.

Essentially, this tradition of social thought is anti-productivist. 'Liberal humanism', as it might be called (though, as will be seen, it has a 'radical' variant, and can coexist with a deeply ingrained conservatism), has always cut across the left/right political divide. Part of a British intellectual tradition that stretches back at least to the end of the eighteenth century, its traces are to be found in William Morris, George Orwell and R.H. Tawney, and also in Burke, Coleridge and T.S. Eliot. In more recent times it imbued certain features of the work of F.R. Leavis. His acid comment 'Productivity – the extremely important thing – must be kept on the rise, at whatever cost to protesting conservative habit' could well be considered the leitmotif of liberal humanism generally (Gwyn, 1980, p. 15).

It is of course possible to trace an ambivalence towards industrialism and economic growth within the culture of the English upper and middle classes over a relatively long period (a task recently accomplished by Wiener, 1981). Even over the course of the last quarter of a century, however, the idea of economic growth has itself been directly questioned. The odd economist has popped up from time to time who has a bee in his bonnet about motor cars, and generally, too, it must be conceded that the advertising and packaging industries have always been good for a measure of criticism. That these ideas have some currency outside the ranks of those whom Wiener calls the 'elite' is hardly the subject of dispute. Indeed, they may even have a relatively new constituency, amongst certain segments of what is sometimes called the 'new middle class' or 'new petty bourgeoisie', whose number increased following the Second World War. A variety of occupational groups within this category are likely to be receptive to such notions – social workers, teachers, lecturers, some of those drawn to their work as a vocation (including some of those in the media, and a few in architecture and in medicine). One of their defining characteristics is that whilst they live off the surplus produced in industry, they do not have to extract that surplus directly themselves. Amongst their number are not a few who are given to dream, and talk to each other, of 'dropping out' (though by and large, they don't). Such people sometimes originate in the working class, but whether or not this is so they can often be seen in their present positions as in some respects marginal to the main class polarity. Not a few of those who make up the ranks of professional sociologists may be included here. Occasionally, a certain liberal disaffection surfaces in the writings of those who specialise in industrial relations, taking the form, in affluent times, of a 'little kite flying' to the effect that one way of overcoming boring work would be if management were to introduce 'deliberate inefficiency' (Klein, 1963), and appearing at times of crisis, in the form of a critique of 'the ideology of work' (Anthony, 1977). In sociology generally, in fact, with its emphasis on that which lies beyond the economic, there is always the chance that such ideas may manifest themselves via the underlying theme of 'not by bread alone' (Dahrendorf, 1976).

Now on one view all such signs of liberal humanism – whether as expressed in the writings of some of the country's major literary figures or from within the more mundane world of contemporary sociology – are merely further evidence of the failure of the British (English?) ruling class to drive through a complete bourgeois revolution. For those on the political right who incline to this view the anti-productivist tone of a critic like Leavis is anathema: it is nothing less than a 'high-culture' expression of the 'English disease' itself – a disease that racks the 'low-culture' of the British working class, and which, as far as the middle levels of society are concerned, is evidenced in 'more sympathy than sense' for the exponents of that low-culture in practice (i.e. for the British working class at work). From this standpoint, such ideas are to be eschewed and scorned for their antagonism/ambivalence towards productivity, growth and – in extreme cases – all things economic and industrial.

At this stage, though, we are not debating values, only seeking to map out some of those that exist, and, at this point, even speculation about the possible *effectiveness* of some sort of liberal humanist ideological demiurge in British industry and society would be premature. It would be premature because we have not yet investigated the facts about British workers and productivity, and there is clearly little point in invoking an explanation (in this case a primarily culturalist one) for a particular material outcome (in this case low productivity, as induced by British workers), if the facts of the matter in question have not been thoroughly investigated first. As indicated already, those facts will be investigated later. But for the present, liberal humanism is of interest to us because, *prima facie*, it seems to represent a competing strain of social thought to the general and persistent set of ideas that was sketched earlier. What has to be said now, however, is that though liberal humanism does differ from the recurrent themes of the conventional wisdom in one respect, it does not, in another respect, disturb the institutionally dominant view one whit. As will now be seen, this holds both when liberal humanism is considered in its more usual form ('liberal humanism proper') and when its less familiar 'radical' variant is considered as well.

It is the work of an American journalist, Nossiter, which perhaps best captures the tone of 'liberal humanism proper'. Nossiter's very title – *Britain: A Future That Works* (1978) – has a discordant ring when set against the dull peal of the many dismal post-war publications whose authors have bemoaned and wrung their hands over British productivity, and much else besides (*Suicide of a Nation* for example, and of course *The Future That Doesn't Work*). But upon closer inspection, the key difference between Nossiter's account and these others distils itself into a difference of moral evaluation. Instead of speaking the language of 'disease' and 'sickness', Nossiter speaks the language of health. In Nossiter's Britain, there is a sense of 'fair play and justice', which fosters a 'quietly confident sense of identity' and which, in turn, makes for 'a very stable society'. These *virtues* coexist with, and help to reproduce, something else which he envies – 'an attitude, a life-style, a choice . . . for leisure over goods'. Frequently, Nossiter tells us, Britain has been held up as 'a horrible example'. But 'a cooler appraisal' suggests (to him) that it is 'moving hesitantly toward a more civilised life'. Britain is 'a comfortable, decent, creative place'; 'by choosing leisure over goods, both as a style of life in factories and as a source of work, Britain has created a society that attracts many outside it'.

This point about a British preference for 'leisure over goods' is worth hanging on to. To see why, it is useful to put Nossiter's account alongside that of another American commentator, Allen, a consultant who came over in the 1960s, and who added to the *brouhaha* about British workers and productivity at that time. Heaping up examples such as 'for each person required to produce a ton of steel in America, three are required in Britain', it clearly followed for Allen, as for most other economic commentators, that a 'more appropriate rate of economic growth will not be possible until a number of industrial beliefs are critically re-examined, and, when found wanting, abandoned'. For Allen, therefore, it was a self-evident *criticism* that in Britain 'the work force takes a substantial part of its wages not in money but in leisure, most particularly [he added acidly] the leisure that is taken at the place of employment' (Allen, 1964). The point is that Nossiter is not in dispute with the main bones of such an analysis. Just as Nossiter accepts 'Britain's consistently low productivity' as something that is 'both measurable and indisputable', he *also* accepts that British workers 'are not stretched as they are in Turin, Detroit or Wolfsberg'. The difference is that Nossiter welcomes this state of affairs, since he chooses to celebrate the culture, civility, etc., of which he sees it to be a part. Far from disputing the facts of the conventional wisdom, Nossiter takes them as his starting point, and, in his appreciation of these same facts, he takes the productivist values through which they have so often been interpreted and stands them on their head. His 'cooler appraisal', in short, is largely a function of his own warm attachment to different values (Nossiter, 1978, pp. 85, 86, 90, 200).

Much liberal humanist thought tends to equate class with culture, and more particularly to hark back to an idea of real or supposed past community. The focus of interest is therefore either on some community that is supposed to have existed previously, but which has been ravaged by 'industrialism'/'materialism', etc. (which is to be decried); or it is on the vestiges of a former life-style that are to be found in modern Britain, a preference for 'leisure over goods', for example (which is to be welcomed). Nossiter's observation that in Britain 'one worker calls another "mate", an unconscious reflection of a genuine fraternity' (1978, p. 200) is but one small symptom of this. However, there is a variant of liberal humanism that, initially at any rate, does seem to mark a radical break from the general outline that has been put forward so far. Indeed, its very rhetoric is radical, for in the words of one of its exponents (Mann, 1976), it depicts the history of the British working class in terms of its exposure to, and effective counteraction of, 'the exploitation that is capitalism'. On further inspection, though, the break that such language apparently signifies – from a conception of class as cultural difference, to one of antagonistic class relations – does not amount to much of a departure at all; not, once again, in one vital respect anyway.

Mann himself is, for example, quite clear that the typifications of 'the British worker' that are to be found in the 'foreign press' (and *a fortiori* in the British press, it might be added) are *not* 'inaccurate stereotypes'. Quite the reverse, in fact. For the thrust of this 'radical' view, as of liberal humanism proper, is precisely that the British worker *does* 'experience a steadier and relatively less taxing workpace than the German, French or American worker'. Indeed, on this view, not only is it claimed that it is the 'inalienable right of British workers to work less hard than the workers of any other industrial power', but this is held up as the 'principal achievement of the British working class' (Mann, 1976).

Mann's particular line of analysis has not caught on. At any rate there are few articles and books in sociology that make such bold assertions. In a sense this is something of a puzzle, for what Mann said did touch the imagination of many of the 'silent majority' of British sociologists. In particular, his reference to 'Old Bert' (a British worker of whom it was said: 'You've got to hand it to old Bert. They can't put one over on him') had all the makings of a new 'type of worker' – the 'canny curmudgeonly worker', as he might be called – another one to add to the list of anti-heroic worker types that have had such a success already – 'affluent workers', 'apathetic', 'militant', 'bourgeois', 'instrumental' ones, and so on. That the 'the canny curmudgeonly worker' did not 'arrive' is probably accounted for by two reasons. First, Mann's depiction of 'Old Bert' betokened a certain romanticism: 'provided the working class sticks to the rules of the game', he argued, 'it is guaranteed security (even Bert)'. Untenable when it was first said, this has become yet more untenable with the passing of every year since, as several million unemployed will testify. Second, and this may not be the lesser of the two reasons, it is possible that Mann's 'Old Bert' did not make a special impact as the representative of another sub-type of British worker precisely because, for so many people, the canny, curmudgeonly British worker had not only 'arrived' already, but was in fact a symbol for the *whole* British working class. A 'curmudgeon', in the dictionary definition, is 'an avaricious, ill-natured churlish fellow'. Few people use the term today. They speak instead of the 'greedy' and the 'boody-minded'. There's no need for a survey to prove the point that, in British society, such terms are associated, above all, with *workers*.

Enough of 'Old Bert', however, and, for the moment, of sociologists too. The main point of substance that has to be made about liberal humanist views on the productivity of British workers is this: typically they do not dispute the main bones of the conventional interpretation, such as that put forward by Pratt at the beginning of this century; nor do they dispute the claims, of a factual nature, that have been repeated so often since. The radical variant of liberal humanism does not challenge the supposed facts of the matter any more than does liberal humanism 'proper'. In some of its forms it might well be called 'the romantic inversion of conservative rhetoric' (Hyman and Elger, 1982). Is there, then, any significant break in the dominant consensus?

Some recent survey material, collected in 1980-81, does point to one significant cleavage in the way in which the contribution of workers to productivity is viewed in Britain. It suggests, not surprisingly perhaps, that trade union leaders are different. For example, as many as 57 per cent of employers in a national UK sample cited a lack of workforce motivation or opposition to change by trade unions as a factor that inhibited growth – a view held by only 3 per cent of trade union leaders. Looking at matters the other way round, only 16 per cent of employers cited failure to invest in new equipment, compared to 65 per cent of trade union leaders. Such statistics tell us nothing about British workers or rank and file trade unionists, of course. But related survey evidence does suggest that British employees voiced opinions closer to those expressed by employers than to those of trade union leaders (cf. Sentry, 1981a, 1981b).[2] More recent survey data also suggests that between half and two-thirds of the population think it an 'important' cause of Britain's economic difficulties that 'people are not working hard enough' – and this whatever their social class or whether they are in trade unions or not (Jowell and Airey, 1984, p. 69, Table 3.4).

True enough, 'general' opinions, as solicited through surveys, may differ from the particular opinions – and the particular *practices* – of the same individuals as expressed in the context of their own workplace, and with reference to their 'own' job of work. Furthermore, what people think is often complicated and can shift over time (Nichols and Armstrong, 1976). But week in, week out, and over several generations, it has been the rule rather than the exception for British workers to hear that they and their trade unions impede managements in their pursuit of higher productivity. When confronted with a request for their opinion on such matters, it would not be an astonishing outcome if, not taking this to refer to them personally, British workers were to reiterate the view they had heard so often – a view that has been advanced by government spokesmen, by industrialists, and which, let it be said, has long been a persistent theme of the proverbial bar room fly (in the saloon bar and the public bar alike). For this reason alone, it is pertinent that any search for breaks in the consensus about British workers and productivity should pay special attention to those commentaries from trade union leaders and others who make representations on behalf of the British trade union movement which do not take the form of instant reactions to opinion polls. Here too, however, certain stock responses exist, and even a brief consideration of some of these serves to make clear that those who have resort to them must be particularly careful to circumnavigate the many pitfalls involved. A further look at the Webbs' response to *The Times* serves to illustrate one such difficulty (see pp. 5–6 above).

Just consider for a moment the context within which the Webbs' intervention was made. Briefly, the retardation of British industry had been a matter for public concern for at least a quarter of a century – and with some reason, for as can be seen from Table 1.1, the rate of growth of British industrial output had probably lagged behind that for Germany and America throughout the second half of the nineteenth century. At the outbreak of the First World War Britain's share of world manufacturing output had fallen to 14 per cent, compared to 32 per cent in 1820; by contrast, Germany's share had crept up from 13 to 16 per cent, and America's had increased from 23 to 36 per cent (Glyn and Sutcliffe, 1972, p. 17). Contemporary economic historians have disputed whether the climacteric of the British economy set in during the 1870s or the 1890s (Phelps Brown and Handfield-Jones, 1952; Coppock, 1956), but what matters here is that, at the time the Webbs wrote, the idea was certainly widespread that the British economy had run out of steam, and that other great industrial powers were on the up and up.

In 1894 that exceptional German-born British industrialist Friedrick Engels had noted in the third volume of Marx's *Capital* that over the past three decades 'many profound changes have taken place'; that 'the colossal explosion of the means of transportation and communication – ocean liners, railways,

Table 1.1 Annual compound rates of growth

| | Industrial Output | | | | | | Volume of world trade | |
|---|---|---|---|---|---|---|---|---|
| Great Britain[a] | | | Germany | | USA | | | |
| | % | % | | % | | % | | % |
| 1827–1847 | 3.2 | (–) | – | | – | | 1820–1840 | 2.7 |
| 1848–1875 | 4.55 | (2.7)[b] | 1850–1874 | 4.5 | 1849–1873 | 5.4 | 1840–1870 | 5.5 |
| 1876–1893 | 1.2 | (1.5) | 1875–1892 | 2.5 | 1874–1893 | 4.9 | 1870–1890 | 2.2 |
| 1894–1913 | 2.2 | (2.6) | 1893–1913 | 4.3 | 1894–1913 | 5.9 | 1891–1913 | 3.7 |

*Notes and sources*

[a] The construction industry is excluded from the figures for Britain in both the left-hand column and the column in brackets.
The former figures derive from Mandel (1980), Table 1.1, p. 3, and are based on Mitchell and Deane, (1962), following Hofman (1955). The figure of 4.55 per cent for 1848–75 reflects an error in Mandel's calculations, on my own calculations on the original Hoffman index, this should be 2.8 per cent.
The figures in brackets derive from the revision of the Hoffman index by Lewis (1978), which is an improvement on Mandel's own source. However, Lewis uses different time periods when making use of this data himself, and the figures in brackets are the result of my own reworking of his revision of the Hoffman index to make it compatible with Mandel's periodisation.[3]
Apart from the figures in brackets, all other tabulations above are reported directly from Mandel.[3]

[b] 1852–1875.

electric technology, the Suez canal – has made a real world market a fact', and that 'the former monopoly of England of industry has been challenged by a number of competing industrial countries'. Perhaps few people regarded some other matters to which Engels referred in quite the same light as he did – for example, the prospect of 'a far more powerful future crisis' and of 'a new world crash of unparalleled vehemence'. But there was lively debate about 'competition in the domestic market [receding] before the cartels and trusts', and about 'the foreign market [being] restricted by protective tariffs, with which', as Engels noted, 'all major industrial countries, England excepted, surround themselves' – and all this was allied to a general concern about the competitiveness of British industry, particularly as compared to Germany and America (Engels in Marx, 1972, p. 89). When, for example, in 1902 the British businessman Mosley, sponsored trade unionists on a visit to the States, even this had a precursor in other visits to American industrial areas which had taken place as early as 1853 and 1854 (Levine, 1967, p. 12). And when in 1905 Shadwell wrote in his seminal comparative study of industrial life in England, Germany and America, 'the nations which have "outstripped" us in industry . . . have done so by working harder', this too was not so much an original thought as a confirmation of what had often been held to be the case already – that workers in other countries *did* work harder (Shadwell, 1913 edn, p. 658).

But given this context, what was the logic of the Webbs' argument? They argued against the view that British workers worked less hard than they had done hitherto, and they challenged the view that employers would prefer the British workforce of 1801 to the workforce they had in 1901 – adding for good measure, of course, that it was in the nature of employers to complain about workers. What, by contrast, the Webbs failed to address was the comparative rather than historical charge that was laid against British workers. Even if the British could be shown to work harder than they had done hitherto, this still left the door open to the counter-argument that American and German workers worked harder still. Some of the stock responses of contemporary trade unionists can also run into this sort of difficulty.

In 1977, for example, Jack Jones of the TGWU, in seeking to rebut the argument of the school of thought he labelled 'The Buggers Won't Work', came up with the rival slogan 'The Bastards Won't Back Us' (the 'bastards' including people in 'the media' and 'some Boards of Directors'). However, as Jones developed his riposte to the 'bastards', he argued, as many trade unionists are wont to do, that British workers put in longer hours and had shorter holidays than their foreign counterparts, and that 98 per cent of manufacturing plants in Britain were free from strikes (Jones, 1977). There is no problem here about whether these assertions are true. They are. The problem is that, as a matter of strict logic, such observations once again leave intact an essential claim made by those who espouse the conventional wisdom: the persistently advanced view that British workers won't work and don't work as hard as workers will and do elsewhere.

In Britain, of course, the Labour Party has been regarded throughout this century as the 'political arm' of the trade unions. But whatever the Labour Party has done for British trade unions, one thing that it has not done successfully is to shift the blame for the country's productivity record from the shoulders of the British working class. Above all, the Labour leadership has failed to accomplish this when in office. Part of the reason for this is to be found in the ideology of 'Labourism' itself, since, for good or ill, the Labour Party is a reformist party. This is no big news of course, or should not be. But one thing that flows from it is the fact that the greater the instability of British capitalism, the greater the need that is felt from within the Labourist habitus to restabilise,[4] and that, when in office, the Labour Party leadership finds itself in the business of managing British capitalism within a competitive world economy, quite often in more than usually difficult circumstances. Again, there is no news in this. But what does need to be recognised is that Labour governments have certainly been as exercised as Conservative ones about 'the problem of productivity'. In fact, few governments have exhorted British workers to increase their productivity more than Labour governments did during the 1970s.

It should be perfectly obvious by now that such concern did not spring out of thin air. Between 1949 and 1952, for example, and arising from the aftermath of the Second World War, no less than sixty-six investigative teams crossed the Atlantic in an attempt to improve British productivity. Funded by the Marshall Aid Plan, and operating under the auspices of the Anglo American Productivity Council, their reports covered an A to Z of industries and processes, all the way from Ammunition to Zinc. 'If', it was argued, 'British productivity was as high as American, many (indeed, most) of Britain's domestic problems would disappear'

(Hutton, 1953, p. 18). But the 'promise of productivity', as it was called, was not fulfilled, and as the Second World War receded, the rise in the competitiveness of other national economies served only to provide further points of comparison against which the British economy, and British workers, were to be judged, adversely.

By 1977 the situation was such that an economic columnist could report of the then Chancellor of the Exchequer: 'Almost every time Mr Healey gets to his feet these days, he makes some allusion to one of the most baffling problems of Britain's economic performance . . . The problem is the clear difference between the productivity of comparable firms in Britain and in our main industrial competitors', and she followed this up with the assertion:

> Comparing British industry with that in the United States, or in West Germany, or even in France, there is striking evidence of differences in productivity for which neither the volume of investment nor the average age of machinery nor the industrial structure can account. (Cairncross, 1977)

So far attention has centred on productivity *and ideology*: on the persistence, right through this century, and before that, of the view that British workers work 'less hard'. It has been seen that even some of the ideological currents, which at first sight seem to support a different view, actually take it for granted that this is so. Latterly, it has been noted further that the exhortations to British workers to increase their productivity have emanated as much from Labour governments as from Tory ones, which has only served to reinforce the dominant consensus. At this stage, however, it is also apparent that some of the long-established stock responses of trade union leaders, and of others who seek to defend British workers and trade unionists, are open to dismissal on the grounds that they miss the point. And on first hearing, at any rate, it must be admitted that claims like those made in the quotation above – to the effect that the British labour productivity shortfall *cannot* be accounted for by investment, etc. – would seem to put the skids under *any* defence of British workers. Laymen can be forgiven if they take statistical data on 'labour productivity' to refer to the productivity of workers alone, taking statements to the effect that 'Company A (or Country X) has lower labour productivity than Company B (or Country Y)' to mean that the difference is not to be accounted for by differences in investment, machinery, etc. But in the context of the above remarks this commonsense interpretation comes very close to fitting the bill.[5]

This brings us to a point of some significance. For in so far as it is *industrialists* who complain that their workers' productivity is 'too low', no great leap of the imagination is required to spot that it might suit their interests to say just this (it would be cause for surprise indeed were they to complain to the contrary, and to insist that their workers work 'too hard'). During the 1970s, of course, there was no shortage of complaints from industrialists about the low productivity of British workers. For instance, at more or less the same time Mr Healey was expressing his disquiet, Mr Michael Edwardes (then with the Chloride Group though later to be head of British Leyland, and Sir Michael) made an influential contribution to a seminar at the Department of Industry on 'Manufacturing and Management'. He reported that at his Dagenham battery plant only twenty-eight of the forty hours the average worker put in were effectively used in working, compared to thirty-four hours in his biggest American competitor's plant. A senior man at ICI claimed much the same, and Edwardes himself went on to claim that in Chloride's own American plants, with the same techniques and equipment, and even with British management in charge, productivity was up to double as much as at home (Cairncross, 1977). However, these and other similar claims probably carried more weight than ever before – for now, to a much greater extent than hitherto, systematic academic and government research existed that could be cited to prove the same thing. What British *industrialists* had always said, and what had so often been repeated by politicians, what the newspapers, the radio and the television had so frequently told workers about themselves, was now being said by social scientists, inside and outside state employ, in the universities, in independent research institutes and in 'Think Tanks'.

In 1975, for example, a government 'Think Tank' report had made a major impact by asserting that with the same power at his elbow and doing the same job as his continental counterpart, a British car assembly worker produced only half as much output per shift. 'These weaknesses', it argued, 'basically arise on the shopfloor and it is on the shopfloor that they must be corrected' (CPRS, 1975). The following year saw the publication of what were widely regarded as two of the most thorough comparative studies of productivity by a professional economist in Britain (Pratten, 1976a; 1976b). These also invoked British workers as part of the explanation for lower productivity in Britain. Since that time further comparative research has appeared. A study that particularly caught the headlines at the start of the 1980s was an American Brookings Institute investigation of Britain and America which was conducted by Caves, and which was itself a follow-up to an earlier Brookings study. The more research that was conducted, however, the slimmer Britain's prospects appeared (so that whereas the earlier Brookings study had been entitled *Britain's Economic Prospects*, by 1980 a quite non-commital title was chosen, *Britain's Economic Performance* (Caves *et al.*, 1968; Caves and Krause, 1980)).

Today, as a consequence of such research the notion that the productivity of British workers was lower, at least in the 1970s, has gone into the social science literature as a staple empirical fact. And since most of the available recent research either refers to, or was conducted during, the 1970s, these years will figure prominently in later chapters – for given the existence of this social science research, it is clearly important to consider the evidence upon which it was based. Throughout this century, however, the social sciences have been subject to an ever-increasing division of labour. This has implications for the way different social sciences – economics and sociology, for example – have approached questions about productivity, which is the matter to which we turn now.

In beginning to discuss the division of labour in the social sciences as it bears on the question of productivity it is instructive to consider the following quotation:

> [M]ilitary science assumes the strength of an army to be identical with its numbers. Military science says that the more troops the greater the strength. *Les gros battaillons ont toujours raison* [large battalions are always victorious] . . .
> In military affairs the strength of an army is the product of its mass and some unknown X . . .
> That unknown quantity is the spirit of the army . . .
> The spirit of an army is the factor which multiplied by the mass gives the resulting force. To define and express the significance of this unknown factor – the spirit of an army – is a problem for science.

This problem is only solvable if we cease arbitrarily to substitute for the unknown X itself the conditions under which that force becomes apparent – such as the commands of the general, the equipment employed, and so on – mistaking these for the real significance of the factor, and if we recognize this unknown quantity in its entirety as being the greater or lesser desire to fight and to face danger.

This quotation, from Tolstoy's *War and Peace*, prefaces a book by Leibenstein, the economist who coined the term 'X-efficiency' (Leibenstein, 1976, p. viii). By means of this concept Leibenstein sought to capture the idea that production outcomes are not the result of the mere combination of (fixed) inputs – so much labour, so much capital, etc. – but that something else is involved – an 'X-factor', or in plain English, 'spirit', as Tolstoy, albeit writing about armies, had said. Confronted with this idea, no sociologist could fail to recall one of the founding fathers of their discipline, Max Weber, whose *The Protestant Ethic and the Spirit of Capitalism* was published in the first decade of this century. In fact, even the title of Leibenstein's book, *Beyond Economic Man*, has a Weberian ring to it. Of course, Weber was more concerned with the 'spirit' of capitalists than with that of workers, but, in part because of his very great influence, which stressed the importance of the subjective element in social life, this idea of 'spirit' – whether in the grand form of '*Geist*' or by way of more mundane references to 'attitudes' and 'orientations' – has long been implicit in much sociological thinking.

It might be supposed, then, that sociologists would look favourably on Leibenstein's view that a 'significant area in which X-efficiency theory is applicable is the analysis of intercountry productive differences'. Given his observation that post-war studies by economists have 'established that differences in physical capital explain very little of [these] differences in productivity', it might also be surmised that they would look with favour on a further suggestion that Leibenstein made: namely that 'the main differences can be explained by the motivations of firm's members during their work, by the motivational atmosphere they find on the job, and on the type of interactions and influences toward work and production that people have on each other as well as the attitudes they bring to the work context' (1976, p. 270).

In making his suggestion, however, Leibenstein offered no evidence for the part that 'X-efficiency' did play in international differences in labour productivity. As a consequence of this, 'X' serves only to mark a spot that remains untouched by the daunting power of econometric technique. If this really is the case – and whether it is will be considered in later chapters – it would follow that economics is in some important respects deficient. But the sad truth is that, as far as the study of the contribution of workers to international productivity differences is concerned, any such deficiency in economics pales into insignificance when set alongside a deficiency in sociology. For modern sociologists have neglected this question to a quite remarkable degree. Such is the deficiency that the reader who consults books with apparently promising titles, like *Productivity and People* (Sutermeister, 1963) or *Worker Productivity* (Macarov, 1982), will be hard put to it to find *any* discussion of international differences. This is doubly odd. For not only has Weberian thought been at the root of much modern sociology, but industrial sociology had its very origin in the study of restriction of output among workers, and might therefore have been expected to promise much in this respect. To consider why this particular promise of productivity has not been fulfilled it is necessary to retrace certain developments.

The major impetus to the development of industrial sociology was, of course, the research that Elton Mayo and his associates conducted at Western Electric's plant near Chicago between 1927 and 1933. The results of the so-called 'Hawthorne Experiments' have been relayed world-wide, not only to students of industrial sociology, but to managers, foremen, and sometimes workers as well. For some time, indeed, the results of these experiments were a standard feature of most textbooks in the area, a not untypical account running as follows:

> Dr Mayo decided to investigate . . . the 'bank-wiring' room, in order to discover as much as possible about the restriction of output by those employed in it. There were fourteen men employed on 'bank-wiring', which involves attaching wires to switches for certain parts of telephone equipment, and, of these, nine men attached the wires, three soldered them, and the remaining two were inspectors . . .
>
> The results of this investigation showed that this little group of men had developed spontaneously into a team with natural leaders who had risen to the top with the active consent of the group . . . Towards the financial incentives of the company the attitude of the group was one of complete indifference, and, although the incentive plan provided that the more work an employee did, the more money he received, neither more nor

less than 6,000 units were produced each day. Yet the group could without the least difficulty have produced 7,000 units daily . . .

It became clear that, in the 'bank-wiring' room, there existed a highly integrated group with its own social structure and code of behaviour – a code which conflicted not only with the intentions of management but also with the express purpose and social function of industry, which is to produce more goods. There are two lessons to be learned from this part of the Hawthorne research. Firstly that no collection of people can be in contact for any length of time without such informal groupings arising and natural leaders being pushed to the top. Secondly, that it is not only foolish but futile to try to break up these groups; a wise policy would see to it that the interests of management and workers coincided to such an extent that the collection of informal groups which makes up a factory would be working towards the same goals instead of frustrating each other's efforts. (Brown, 1954, pp. 80, 81, 82)

In the light of this it certainly cannot be maintained that sociological studies, broadly defined, have neglected labour productivity entirely. In fact, the Hawthorne Experiments were only the beginning (or the most publicised starting point) for a sizeable body of research that was to follow in their train.

The 1930s had seen the publication, again in America, of a study of output restriction by Matthewson, which caused a shock because it indicated how widespread this was among groups of unorganised workers. As Roy notes (in Matthewson, 1959, p. xv.), this was to become essential reading for all those who became involved in field studies of factory life during the 1940s. It also inspired Roy's own investigations of 'constricted exertion in the workshop', which appeared in the 1950s (Roy 1952; 1953, 1954). It can even be essayed that, by the 1960s, the academic study of the world of 'goldbricking', 'quota restriction', 'the fiddle' and 'the fix' provided a niche for some anthropologists and sociologists who had themselves once been manual workers (Roy in America, Lupton (1963) in Britain, for example). Indeed, this back-to-front process – of the natives 'going anthropologist' rather than the anthropologists 'going native' – is not the only intellectual curiosity to characterise the development of social anthropology at this time. For as undiscovered peoples abroad came into short supply, though for other reasons too, the anthropologists became more interested in hitherto largely undiscovered tribe on their own doorstep – the working class. However, in Britain the 1960s also saw the growth of sociology as an academic discipline, and of a relatively new group of academics in higher and further education, some of whom were busy developing courses in Business Studies, Management Science and the like. For them, teaching about the restriction of output by workers was an attractive option, if only because case study material was readily available. But although teaching and research about output restriction was well to the fore in industrial psycho-sociology by the mid-1960s, it is equally apparent that something then went 'wrong'.

What went 'wrong' can be exemplified by a remark made by Brown, an influential exponent of industrial psycho-sociology in Britain. Writing in 1954, and seeking to defend the Hawthorne Experiments against the charge of management bias, he blandly replied: 'The obvious reply to this is that no industrial psychologist has ever shown anything else' (Brown, 1954, p. 92). He was largely right. But this is not why he has been quoted here. For the point is that such criticisms were to become much harder to shrug off in the ensuing years.

The 'discovery' of small informal groups in industry had given currency to the idea that it would be 'wise' to channel their sentiments to the ends of management. It helped to spawn what became known as the 'human relations industry'. But by the 1960s an increasing number of social scientists, including a good many academic industrial sociologists, had become sensitive about charges of 'cow sociology' (the sort of sociology designed to milk workers better) and about approaches to shop floor behaviour that counterposed an 'elite' (management) to the 'aborigines' (those irrational primitives who lived on the shop floor). They came to favour more broadly based politico-moral criticisms of 'manipulation' and became hostile to what C. Wright Mills called 'illiberal practicality' (see Bell, 1947; Kerr and Fisher, 1957; Mills, 1959). Consequently, we find even the author of the major British study of 'restriction of output' actually refusing to use this term, because of its 'reprehensible connotation' (Lupton, 1963, p. 9). Other writers are also to be found who had eschewed an unproblematic acceptance of the management view and who substituted for this the chimera of value freedom. As one of these put it: 'the term "restriction"' has 'the inherent risk that the impartiality and objectivity that is the aim of the research viewpoint will be prejudiced by the overtone of disapproval which can be read into the word' (Hickson, 1961, p. 114).

By contrast, agonising about 'value freedom' is rather passé in sociology today – but so are studies of restriction of output. It is true that Roy's work in particular continues to be cited by sociologists as a model of ethnographic method; that the site of his research has recently been revisited (Burawoy, 1979a); and that reappraisals of the Hawthorne Experiments continue to appear. But if the sociological study of worker restriction of output is not stone cold dead, it is but a shadow of its former self.

An example of one of the findings of output restriction studies can be seen in Figure 1.1, where a group of workers engaged in what Hickson called 'typical "restricted" output' are shown to have set an output ceiling of 6,000 components per shift. Since numerous similar studies were conducted it cannot be maintained, as noted earlier, that sociology has entirely neglected the subject of labour productivity, even if such studies have now largely fallen out of fashion. For present purposes, however, such studies would have little to offer even if they were more up-to-date, and even if their authors could always satisfactorily counter changes of management bias. There are several, interrelated reasons why this is so.

First, the studies tended to take the form of single case studies. Even in Lupton's work, where two cases were considered at length, the investigator, on his own admission (Lupton, 1963, p. 199) could only posit a 'crude' linkage between what he called

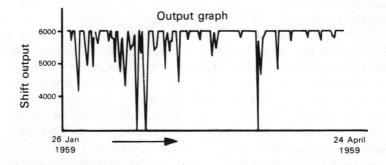

*Source*: Hickson (1961), Fig. 1(a) p.115.

**Figure 1.1** Typical 'restricted' output (Output of 3 men on successive shifts on the same machines, 3 months 26 Jan. 1959 – 24 April 1959)

'internal' and 'external factors' ('internal factors' included 'method of wage payment', 'productive system', 'sex', 'workshop social structure' and 'management–worker relationship', and 'external factors' included 'market', 'competition', 'scale of industry' and 'trade unions'). In the case of the more typical single case studies, the determination of causal relations between such factors was obviously rendered all the more difficult.

Second, in so far as these researches were one-off pieces of ethnography, or were even exercises in comparative ethnography, they lacked a historical dimension. If they stretched to an analysis of 'factors', they did not usually stretch further to an analysis of where these 'factors' came from. Because of this, workers were not typically situated within the historically evolved class relations of a particular social formation, nor were managers for that matter. (The same holds for many studies of the relation between productivity and 'leadership styles'/'participation'/'morale', which were themselves another spin-off from the early work at Hawthorne.)

Third, in addition to the fact that workers were studied in particular factories outside of class relations, and that the work practices of given national working classes were in no way a central concern, it was also a characteristic of such studies that they lacked an international, comparative dimension. As a function of this, whereas the authors of particular studies could indicate, say, that restriction of output occurred in an American factory or a British one, they were in no position to come to conclusions about differences in the extent and significance of worker practices in America as compared to Britain.

The relative demise of studies of restriction of output was followed by the expansion of industrial sociology, as judged both by the emergence of several different theoretical perspectives and by the broader but discrepant range of subjects that industrial sociologists came to investigate. It is a matter of opinion whether this theoretical eclecticism and the enlarged scope of subject matter spelt the flowering of post-1960s conventional industrial sociology or its intellectual collapse. But whichever view is taken – and since the subject now lacks a dominant theoretical or empirical focus, the second has much to be said for it (for a recent textbook see Watson, 1980) – it is more than ever the case today that conventional industrial sociology pays scant regard to productivity. Had our concern been with the sociology of (sociological) knowledge we could certainly have found more than a passing interest in the pre-1960s development of industrial anthropology (see Whyte *et al.*, 1955, preface; Burawoy, 1979b) and in the development of industrial sociology thereafter (Rose, 1975). But as far as labour productivity is concerned, conventional sociology certainly has less to offer than might at first seem likely. Some comparative work has been conducted (Gallie (1978) on France and Britain, for example, and Maitland (1983) on Britain and West Germany), and this will be introduced later. But it seems reasonable to suppose that if we are to learn anything from sociological approaches to labour productivity we are more likely to be rewarded by looking outside conventional sociology, towards those studies that were born out of a different, marxist tradition, which began to take hold in the early 1970s.

The modern point of impetus towards the development of marxist analyses of the labour process can be dated with some precision. It is marked by the publication of Braverman's *Labour and Monopoly Capital* in 1974. In this book Braverman sets forth a contemporary analysis, which draws heavily on Marx's *Capital*, and which gives short shrift to the intellectual and moral preoccupations of several cohorts of industrial psycho-sociologists. In his view, the history of work in the twentieth century is the history of its 'degradation', this degradation taking the form of 'deskilling'. In capitalist class society, so Braverman's argument runs, capital buys the human commodity of labour-power (the workers' capacity to labour), and, for the sake of capital accumulation, is driven both to cheapen this, as a commodity, and to control the variable potentiality that it constitutes in its necessarily human aspect. In Braverman's view, both these ends were served by the deskilling process, the deskilling of work itself having been a product of the application of the Scientific Management practices, associated above all with the name of F.W. ('Speedy') Taylor. Throughout his book Braverman remorselessly and single-mindedly pursues this theme, providing a wealth of concrete instances to back it up from a whole variety of sectors of American industry.

At the most general level, Braverman's analysis is predicated on the use of a 'reproduction schema'; that is, it takes the form of an analysis of how capital must act, if capitalist relations of production are to be maintained. It should be conceded at once that Braverman did not regard the reproduction of capitalist relations of production through the deskilling of the labour process as entirely unproblematic for capital. He noted, for example, the periodic complaints of employers about shortages of skilled labour. More importantly, he argued that deskilling resulted in the homogenisation of the condition of labour throughout the world of work – and thus (as he saw it) to the expansion of the working class. Following Marx, the deskilling of work was therefore seen as a mechanism whereby, in the long run, capitalism produced its own 'gravediggers'. Those workers outside the 'traditional' manual working class – clerical workers, bank clerks, those employed in the retail sector, even those who worked in the new 'advanced' technical sectors like computing – all these, as he saw it, were being progressively subjected to factory-like jobs and to a working-class-like 'condition' (see Nichols, 1979, pp. 162, 168). It is fair comment that Braverman left himself open to two main critical readings of his thesis, each of which ties back to the leap that he makes from an abstract generality (the capitalist mode of production) to one empirically particular practice (deskilling) and to the relationship he posits between them by his implicit resort to a reproduction schema.

According to one of these criticisms, this leap from the general to the particular meant that too little account was taken of working-class *resistance* to Scientific Management. Because of this, Braverman assumed too readily that Taylorism had *successfully* dealt with the fundamentals of the organisation of the labour process and of control over it, and he assumed too readily also that it *could* be successful – irrespective of the level of organisation and consciousness of the working class which, in his book, he chose deliberately not to investigate. According to the other main critical reading, Braverman's overwhelming stress on deskilling distracted attention from the possible existence of a whole lexicon of other management practices, and of the many historically forged contingencies that can bear on the working class and contribute to its exploitation – what, by shorthand, could be called the specific state of the international and national economies, their uneven development and internal differentiation. Clearly, to understand the labour process it is necessary to take account of state policy in the forms, for example, of legislation and wages policies; of attempts of diverse origin at trade union repression and incorporation; of 'participation' schemes, of attempts to elicit 'involvement', to heighten 'morale' and so on; of the use of sub-contract labour, internal and external, and of migrant labour; and also of the switching of production sites by multi-national corporations, etc., etc.

Both these sorts of criticism are well-founded. The fact is, of course, that the exploitation of labour, though a necessary condition of existence for a capitalist mode of production, always takes place in a particular historical situation, which *inter alia* has its own specific political and ideological components. The precise manner in which the exploitation of wage labour is aided, abetted, and frustrated, and the degree to which capital meets with 'success', cannot therefore be derived directly from a highly abstract model of that mode of production. By the same token, just one possible mechanism – deskilling – cannot be isolated out, with the inference that it constitutes an inexorably given and unilinear tendency of 'capitalism' (or of 'monopoly capitalism' for that matter).

Since both the above sorts of criticism of Braverman's work carry weight, it becomes appropriate to consider some of the more recent analyses of the labour process that have arisen from attempts by other writers to go beyond them, thereby to cope with the differential incidence of worker resistance in time and place, and to cope also with devices of capitalist control other than that of deskilling. But there is one final thing to say about Braverman before considering what light is thrown on the subject of productivity by these contemporary studies of the labour process. This is that though Braverman was very definitely concerned with the exploitation of labour, and with the way in which surplus value is extracted from the working class – through mechanisation, and intensification of labour, deskilling and stricter control – his book can be read in two ways: either as an account of how this occurred in the United States, or as a generalised account of how the working class is controlled at work, and labour cheapened, which applies to all capitalist societies. But whichever interpretation one takes (and though Braverman's examples come from the USA, he would seem to imply the latter), *Labour and Monopoly Capital* remains starkly deficient from our point of view, because it has nothing to say on the vexed question of differences between nations in labour productivity. This, quite simply, is something that Braverman did not consider.

It is frequently observed nowadays that marxists had badly neglected the labour process before Braverman wrote. This is true especially in America. But there were certainly marxists in Europe who took the labour process seriously: in France, for example, Gorz (1967) and Mallet (1975); in Belgium, Mandel (1975); and in Britain, not least with special reference to the productivity deals of the 1960s, Cliff (1970). Moreover in both America and Britain there were marxist analyses that stemmed from labour historians, which put the stress on working-class culture and struggle, on resistance and the battle for control in the workplace (in fact some of Braverman's critics were to refer to these – for example the writings of Montgomery (1979) – when advancing their argument that Taylorian Scientific Management was not uniformly imposed on labour and that it did meet with worker opposition). Also in America, research had begun on so-called 'segmented labour markets', it being found that urban blacks and other poor working people appeared to operate in a labour market different from that of urban males (Bluestone, 1970; Doeringer and Piore, 1971). In both Britain and America such research proved to be of interest to a significant number of academic economists whose faith in their own discipline was becoming somewhat shaky. They are mentioned here because one influential approach to the labour process that appeared 'post-Braverman' represents a coming together of ideas of this type with further ideas that derive from critiques of Braverman's thesis.

On the one side, this new approach stresses that workers are treated differentially (because economies themselves, and within them firms, are not undifferentiated entities, but have 'cores' and 'peripheries', and operate within different labour markets). On the other side, it takes its inspiration from the criticism advanced against Braverman to the effect that the 'direct control' of scientific management is not the only possible means by which capital can seek to manage labour in the workplace (which is something that the now old-fashioned 'human relationists' had also often believed, of course). The simplest expression of this approach is to be found in Friedman's work in Britain (Friedman, 1977).

Briefly, Friedman's analysis rests on two dichotomies. In the first dichotomy it is workers who are divided: there are those who are considered to be 'central' to securing long-run profit, because of their skill, knowledge, authority, or the strength of their resistance; then there are those who are considered 'peripheral'. In the second dichotomy, managerial strategy is divided: there is a 'direct control' strategy and there is what Friedman calls 'responsible autonomy'. ('Direct control' is of course a synonym for Braverman's 'scientific management'. 'Responsible autonomy' (after Trist and Bamforth, 1951) refers to the kind of relationship in which workers are allowed more scope, provided they act in a manner beneficial to the employer.) In the body of Friedman's analysis an affinity is posited between central workers and responsible autonomy management strategies, and between those workers who occupy a peripheral place in the labour market and the direct control management strategy. The dynamic of class struggle is introduced to account for which groups of workers are controlled in this way or that in particular historical conditions (conditions that Friedman seeks to illustrate in his work by reference to researches in the Midlands' car, ribbon and hosiery industries).

An American work (Edwards, 1979) is informed by a similar way of thinking. But Edwards' project is more broadly conceived to encompass the evolution of the structure of work in the US over the course of this century, and his penchant is for three-fold distinctions rather than dichotomies as with Friedman. The main bones of Edwards' analysis can be presented here in three stages. *First*, Edwards delineates three control systems: (1) simple control, which is epitomised by the 'one boss workshop', and which soon evolves into 'extended control' through foremen; (2) 'technical control', epitomised by Fordism; (3) 'bureaucratic control', which is evidenced in grading systems, disciplinary and promotion procedures, etc. *Second*, three labour markets are specified: (1) the secondary market, basically casual labour; (2) the subordinate primary market, including jobs in mass production and unionised clerical labour; (3) the independent primary market, including foremen, craft workers, professionals. *Third*, three fractions of the working class are proposed: (1) the working poor; (2) the traditional proletariat; (3) the middle layers.

Edwards' analysis, like Friedman's, rests on the basic assumption that workers *can* exercise some control within the labour process, and thus, in certain circumstances, can pose problems for management's authority, productivity and profit. Edwards treats the three control systems as 'representative' of particular historical periods, which are characterised, amongst other things, by the degree of heterogeneity/homogeneity of the working class, and its general and particular strengths. Accepting, like Friedman, that changes may take place with respect to the particular groups of workers who operate in more or less privileged labour markets, his book explores the interconnections between control systems, labour market segmentation, and the emergence of working-class fractions in a dynamic way.

In their concern with the way that management divides workers and applies different strategies in order to extract surplus from them, the segmented labour market/control system theories are quite evidently 'about productivity'. But Edwards, like Braverman before him, does not go into the question of possible differences in the level of productivity in different national economies, and this is so even though the whole gist of his work is such as to underline the fact that worker resistance *can* have material effects, so that it would not be outlandish to allow that such effects *might* be greater or lesser in different economies. Much the same can be said of Friedman, though at one point he does cite what he calls 'weak worker resistance' and higher productivity on the Continent as a factor in the decision of car manufacturers to shift plant there, and he notes that 'comparing productivity across countries is extremely difficult' (Friedman, 1977, pp. 258, 294). Just how difficult we shall see later. But thus far our purpose has been different.

An attempt has been made to uncover contributions to the study of international productivity differences from social scientists whose analyses might be expected to be 'sociological' – and both in the case of industrial sociology, and its traditional studies of restriction of output, and of marxism, and the new wave of labour process studies, the upshot of this enquiry has been that the contribution of such studies has been slight. It may well be true therefore that economists, for their part, have often been more concerned with what comes out of the 'black box' of production than with what goes on inside it. Leibenstein's work on 'X-efficiency' is important precisely because it promises to rectify this imbalance. But both industrial sociologists and modern students of the labour process are, it seems, vulnerable to the opposite criticism – that they have explored what goes on within the 'black box', and at its environs, to the detriment of what comes out of it. The 'labour process debate' that followed the publication of Braverman's work has travelled far and relatively wide in a short space of time, and some interesting comparative work on labour processes has been produced (notably by Littler, 1982). But even the latter research makes little reference to international productivity differences, and as far the productivity outcome is concerned, nearly all of the other sociological research has also failed to arrive.

The situation in marxism is not as bleak as in industrial sociology. In America, for example, Bowles and his colleagues have recently produced a historical account of the determination of productivity in that country (Bowles *et al.*, 1983). Similarly, the bargaining strength of the British working class figured prominently (alongside increased international competition) in a relatively early and influential study of post-war British political economy (Glyn and Sutcliffe, 1972). Work has also been produced in Britain by Kilpatrick and Lawson which is in consonance with this, and Hyman and Elger have, in turn, re-examined the productivity of workers in four British industries, thereby challenging the view of Kilpatrick and Lawson (Kilpatrick and Lawson, 1980; Hyman and Elger, 1982). Similar research has also been conducted on the British steel industry (Bryer, Brignall and Maunders, 1982; Manwaring, 1981).

At a theoretical level, too, persistent attempts have been made by Hodgson to stress to followers of Marx that, whether they strictly adhere to the labour theory of value or not, the notion that labour-power is variable should be central to their thinking, hence also the question of differences in productivity (Hodgson, 1981, 1982a, 1982b, 1982c). Although the case for a marxist 'technological determinism' has recently been restated (Cohen, 1978), this has not in fact been a popular stance amongst Western marxists for some decades, and to this extent Hodgson's argument is therefore likely to be well received.

In this connection it is perhaps worth noting that some modern marxists have argued that Marx himself, having set out to understand the interaction between the social relations of production and the development of the productive forces, ultimately forgot the dialectic between these, so that, with the advent of 'modern industry' (based on machine technology), he slipped into depicting workers as entirely dominated by the capitalist in the workplace (Lazonick, 1982).[6] This could suggest, of course, that Braverman's own fundamental error was that he followed Marx *too closely*, and that this – the fact that his was an authentic marxist analysis – was the source of his neglect of workers' organisational and ideological resources, and the way resistance (and compliance) affected capitalist control and strategy. There are things to be said to the contrary on this score, especially when the totality of Marx's writings is considered. Certainly it is a line of interpretation that can be pushed too far, even if some of Marx's work can be read in this way (especially the preface to *A Contribution to A Critique of Political Economy* of 1859).

In this book, though, we are not concerned with 'marxology', but with the contribution that marxists have made to the study of productivity. And about this two things can be said: first, that the renewed interest by marxists in productivity is to be welcomed; second, that problems remain – general ones, and particular ones too. Glyn and Sutcliffe, for example, sought to show that profits declined from the early 1960s as a share of the British national income, and they invoked the power of British trade unions to explain this. But in resorting to a wage-drive theory to explain labour's contribution to poor profits, they overlooked that it is not only by pushing up wages that workers can affect productivity, and also that, as Hodgson has argued, a direct effect on profits would not have occurred if productivity had increased sufficiently. To this extent, as Hodgson also argues, their analyses bypassed certain aspects of the question of productivity, despite first appearances to the contrary (Hodgson, 1981, pp. 152–4). Over and above whatever particular problems such studies may have when considered individually, however, they tend to share a common defect with the studies in industrial sociology that were mentioned earlier. For whereas most of the marxist contributions have been historically informed in a way in which the literature on restriction of output was not, they have not usually taken the form of *international* empirical investigations, either at industry or at factory level.

This is not really surprising, given the nature of some of these contributions, two of which were written very much as invitations to further debate (Kilpatrick and Lawson, 1980; Hyman and Elger, 1982). In any case, adequate original work on comparative productivity is costly, in terms not only of time but also of money. It is for just this last reason, though, that a further omission – in the literature of both marxism and sociology – is cause for surprise, and is to be regretted. To see what this omission is, it is necessary to retrace our steps a little, and to view the contemporary division of labour in the social sciences against the backcloth of public discussion about British workers and productivity.


It has been seen in this chapter that a dominant strain of thought about British workers and productivity has held sway throughout this century. That this is 'ideological' is clearly evidenced in the implicit or explicit assumption that British workers not only fail to work 'as hard' as others overseas, but that they do not work 'hard enough' and that they should work harder. Of course, it could be that such claims have been well founded (at least those of them that can be expressed as propositions of a factual kind). But it has also been seen that even the sub-stratum of alleged fact upon which the case against British workers has for so long been mounted has rarely met with direct challenge. Those who represent various strands of liberal humanist thought have not typically disputed the 'facts of the matter'; nor has the British labour movement had much success with its attempts at rebuttal, and the Labour governments of the 1970s, for their part, only added fuel to the fire. There was, however, as we saw earlier, a relatively new iron in that fire in the 1970s, namely the mounting number of empirical social science researches that appeared in that decade. These made the pronouncements of those who linked British productivity to the poor performance of British workers more credible, if only because they did not emanate from industrialists (an obviously interested party). It is in relation to this development that one of the unfortunate effects of the prevailing division of labour in the contemporary social sciences is to be seen. For it is remarkable that, despite some signs of a growing interest in productivity within the social sciences outside economics, these comparative empirical researches have not been the subject of sustained scrutiny by social scientists in other disciplines. This is so both with respect to sociologists, and with respect to those marxist students of the labour process and political economy who have taken the question of productivity seriously. As a consequence of this, the study of productivity – and most especially the empirically-based investigation of inter-national differences in labour productivity – has virtually become the property of economists.

This book is in part an attempt to rectify this. Our starting point is that this situation is, in one word, unsatisfactory. It is unsatisfactory because, in so far as economists draw adverse conclusions about the effort put in by British workers, these are of far from trivial importance; for they can be utilised to deliver a political clout aimed at the life-fate of millions of people. Judged much more narrowly, from within the social sciences, the situation is again unsatisfactory, since if, for example, economists tell us that British workers make 'less effort' – or that their 'attitudes' have bad effects on British productivity – it is perfectly in order for other social scientists to enquire how these things have been established. Given what could be at stake in the wider political arena, it might even be argued that it would be remiss of other social scientists not to investigate just this.

This brings us to Chapter 2, which begins with a consideration of what economists do say about such matters, and then moves on to consider how an evaluation of their empirical researches might best proceed.

# 2 British workers, 'attitudes', 'effort' and the economists

> Englishmen do not work as hard as Canadians or Americans: a
> multitude of witnesses in all walks of life are unanimous on
> this . . . All British families living in Belgium agree that
> charwomen work harder and longer for less in that country.

The last chapter featured the discussion in *The Times* in 1901,
which linked the then crisis in British industry to the alleged
relatively poor performance of 'the British working man'. The
above quotation might be thought to stem from this same source.
In fact, it is of much more recent origin: it comes from an article
on the efficiency of labour in the *Oxford Economic Papers*, which
appeared almost exactly fifty years later, in 1951 (Wiles, 1951).

Today, few economists would address themselves to the
question of international differences in labour efficiency by
stating, as Wiles did, that they wished 'to discover whether the
Briton is more or less idle than the Swede, Swiss or Belgian'.
However, if references to 'the Briton' being 'idle' are out (and so
too casual references to 'charwomen'), the question Wiles posed
remains of interest, at least to some economists. For not all
economists live exclusively in a world of theory, even though
many of their fellow social scientists are fond of charging that they
do; and despite the common criticism that mainstream (neo-
classical) economics regards labour as a fixed input, so that
questions about variations in labour efficiency do not arise, it is
not the case either that the economists who conduct empirical
investigations rigidly adhere to such a theory, or to any sort of
theory for that matter.

'Nothing will stop us from continuing to hunt for sophisticated explanations of comparative growth rates [but] the thought can never be wholly silenced that perhaps it is simply that Americans work harder.' Such was a British economist's view of the results of a major Brookings Institution enquiry into Britain's economic performance at the end of the 1960s (Worswick, 1969, on Caves *et al.*, 1968). It has been seen already that far from being 'wholly silenced' such thoughts have been voiced loud and clear throughout this century. They continued to be voiced in the 1970s by the economists who conducted empirically based international comparisons of productivity.

The major studies published in the 1970s not only found labour productivity to be lower in Britain than in the USA, West Germany and France, they also invoked 'attitudes' as part of the explanation for this. Thus Caves, the co-editor of a more recent Brookings Institution investigation, held that 'the difficulty' lay in 'attitudes of the workforce that sustain hostility to change and co-operation' (1980, p. 179). Pratten, the author of a study of labour productivity differentials in Britain, North America, Germany and France (1976a), also held to the view that in Britain 'there are widespread differences in efficiency attributable to different attitudes to authority and work' (1977, p. 24). And the 1975 Think Tank Report on the British car industry held to this same line – that 'the basic problem is attitudes' – although it did add, 'attitudes of both management and labour' (CPRS, 1975, p. v., para 4). Caves himself also went beyond pointing to the attitudes of present-day British workers as the sole source of the problem, asserting that 'the productivity problem originates deep within the social system': so much so that in his view 'one needs an optimistic disposition to suppose that a democratic political system can eliminate the problem' (1980, p. 185). But references to the 'attitudes' of British workers are a staple element of all these accounts.[1]

Yet to ask upon what evidence these conclusions about the attitudes of British workers were based is to discover this was so slender that it is surprising these authors felt able to say anything about attitudes at all. Not one of them attempted to study shop floor attitudes systematically; even Pratten, who was aware that techniques were available to do this, made no use of them himself, pleading lack of resources and expertise (1976a, p. 26). In short, the freedom with which these researchers felt able to generalise about 'attitudes' would seem to have been matched only by their confidence in dispensing with any need to investigate them. Whence, then, their common confidence?

Part of the answer may be found in the 'trained incapacity' of economists (as Pratten's frank admission suggests). But of deeper significance is the logic of enquiry that informs these investigations. First, 'economic' factors are examined (the level of investment in different countries, for example), then 'non-economic' factors are introduced, in an attempt to explain the differences that remain when the economic analysis is exhausted. By proceeding in this way 'attitudes' are, in practice, invoked *post facto* as a synonym for the extra bit (the 'X-factor', if you like) that the initial econometric analysis has failed to explain. Such a logic of enquiry runs the danger of failing to take seriously the fact that production is always social production, in each and every facet. It deflects attention from the fact that the 'economic' is always informed by social relations, neither the 'economic' nor the 'non-economic' existing independently of the other but interacting in complex ways.

The latter sort of considerations lend themselves to a line of criticism that is predicated on the belief that 'the totality' is the only fit subject for study. In its 'hard' form, such criticism amounts to a claim that the key method employed in productivity investigations (that of 'comparative statics') is, quite literally, totally invalid. When confronted with such criticism, however, economists are likely to protest that they *know* production is a highly complicated business, but that they are trying to make sense of it, not to explain every last thing, and still less to explain everything at one and the same time. Such defences of exercises in comparative statics are not to be lightly dismissed. For whereas they carry the implication that empirical economic research is, in fact, a matter of judgment and approximation, this has in turn to be balanced against the common observation that those social scientists who urge others to treat 'the totality' rarely make attempts to do so themselves. This conceded, however, two further things are to be noted.

The first is that any analysis which introduced social factors to explain the residual differences that persist after the 'economic' factors have been deemed to be the same (or 'held constant' or 'controlled for'), must make a very good job indeed of measuring these factors in the first place. (The validity of some of these measures will be considered later.) The second is that, even if it were to be conceded by these researchers that production *is* a highly complicated interaction of economic and social relations – and that their references to 'attitudes' signify precisely that they *do* understand that 'social' factors *are* important – this only serves to underline how important it is that these attitudes are systematically investigated in their own right. To seek to justify an empiricist research method is one thing, but if the pretence is to be made that, for 'practical purposes', the facts 'speak for themselves' – and that they are there to be collected (economic facts and social ones too) – there is no justification for conducting investigations in a way that leaves in its wake significant lacunae. If some facts are not collected and are not presented, they cannot 'speak for themselves' at all.

Of course, *were* students of international productivity differences to meet this much 'softer' requirement (that they systematically research the attitudes to which they refer), they would soon run into the difficulty that attitudes are not always good predictors of behaviour anyway. They would also run into the related problem that social relations are not reducible to 'attitudes'. But taking international productivity comparisons for what they are, and even without pursuing a 'hard' line criticism of their entire method, the point retains its force that these studies refer to 'attitudes' – and judged against conventional social scientific criteria there is small reason to place credence on what they say about them, for the evidence is lacking that these attitudes have been researched in the first place.


'Effort' is a term that is often used in connection with attitudes to work, and especially with reference to 'hard work'. In fact, 'effort' is often merely another term for the economists' 'X-factor'. Having criticised economists for their failure to systematically investigate attitudes, since despite the difficulty of such research their failure to do so leaves their claims unsupported, it does not follow, however, that they should be criticised for their failure to directly measure international differences in effort – though once again, this is something that they do not typically attempt to do. One of the leading researchers into international productivity differences has himself confessed that he found 'the quantitative importance of differences in the intensity of work . . . impossible to judge, much less to measure by any direct approach'. As a consequence of this he stated plainly that 'the most serious gap' in his own measure of labour input derived from his 'inability to answer the simple question – how hard do people work? and to compare different places and dates' (Denison, 1967, pp. 112–14). In our view, too, the direct measurement of 'effort' is so difficult as to be well-nigh impossible. In what follows, an attempt will be made to justify this claim. At the same time, an attempt will also be made to specify the sort of relevant criteria that students of international productivity differences *could* be reasonably expected to meet, after which it may appear that Denison and other economists may not deserve quite so much sympathy.

The scientific status of time and motion study has long been proclaimed in all advanced industrial societies. But few economists who are interested in productivity have looked to this for assistance in the measurement of effort.[2] This is just as well. For one thing, the actual practice of time and motion study can be affected by the relative strength of capital and labour in a given workplace at a given time (the strategies by which workers seek to win 'loose' times for particular jobs is a matter of common record in many of the restriction of output studies referred to in Chapter 1). But there is also considerable room for doubt about how reliable time study is, even when practised without the mischievous help of workers. The claim has been frequently advanced that specialists in this field can assess how long it should take a worker to perform a job, working at a 'normal' rate, and without 'undue' fatigue, etc., by a procedure that is accurate to 'about 3 per cent'. Controlled studies show time study assessments to be fourteen times more inaccurate than this would suggest (Cliff, 1970, pp. 101–4).

Turn to the social sciences other than economics, and the prospects for measuring effort are no better. The concept of effort is of course implicit in a good deal of the literature produced by industrial relations specialists and students of organisations, but it has remained ill-developed, even by those who have written with special reference to 'effort' and 'wage-effort bargains' (e.g. Behrend, 1957; Daniel, 1970). In sociology, the one outstanding, explicit, theoretical treatment remains that made over twenty years ago by Baldamus. In seeking a provisional definition of 'effort', Baldamus proposed that it be regarded 'as the sum total of physical and mental exertion, tedium, fatigue, or any other disagreeable aspect of work'. But having proposed that 'for theoretical purposes we may . . . define effort as the sum of these deprivations' (which he took to be 'impairment', associated with 'physical conditions'; 'tedium', associated with 'repetitiveness';

and 'weariness', associated with 'routines'), Baldamus himself was forced to add: 'but this definition is of no use for practical application because it ignores the instability of work feelings' (1961, pp. 29, 77). The truth is, of course, that the instability of 'work feelings' remains a problem whether one speaks of 'attitudes' or of 'effort' ('fatigue', for example, is both a physiological and psychological category, as is 'effort' itself); and just as 'attitudes' may prove poor predictors of behaviour, a similar problem also arises with 'effort' in relation to labour productivity.

The problem of relating effort to labour productivity would in fact remain, even if it were *not* the case that effort 'defies rigorous definition and is certainly unmeasurable', as Baldamus himself correctly concluded (1961, p. 30); and it would continue to beset any productivity comparison, even if this had successfully taken account of differences other than those of effort (differences in capital equipment, etc.). To see why this is so, it is only necessary to consider a case where workers, by dint of expending great 'effort', work very efficiently indeed, and bring great ingenuity to their task too – but where they perform this task on their own account in work time. Such an example brings to light the fact that managers are *not* interested in 'hard work' – or 'effort', or 'efficiency', or the development of human ingenuity *per se*. What they are concerned with is how workers produce *for them*. They are concerned with what workers *do*.

If the above point is accepted, the methodological prescription to be followed in studies of international differences of labour productivity is not that they should systematically investigate 'attitudes' or measure 'effort' directly – but that they should systematically study working practices. The narrow question that inevitably comes to the fore in Chapter 1 – do British workers work 'less hard'? – accordingly becomes transformed into the question of how British working practices differ from those elsewhere. Production being a social process, and productivity a social product, to ask this question is in any case more appropriate, for working practices can be considered a mediating link between individual workers (whatever their 'attitudes') and their output.

There are some theoretical, as well as practical, problems in conducting research into international differences in working practices. After all, working practices are not 'suspended in mid-air'; they can have complex origins, and complex socio-economic and political conditions can be required for their reproduction. But these problems are no more difficult than others that arise in comparative investigations in almost any field, and the problems of an international comparison that examined working practices would be far outweighed by the yet greater problems of one that failed to do so. Indeed, the sympathy extended to Denison (above) is rendered the less whole-hearted when this is taken into account. For whereas he was correct to warn us about the chimera of 'effort', and whereas he also quite properly revealed his own failure to answer the question 'How hard do people work?', he did nothing himself to look-and-see how people in different societies actually *did* work. How, then, do other studies fare when judged on this basis? How well, for that matter, do they comply with an ABC of elementary requirements for the conduct of productivity comparisons?*

A summary of research, produced in 1976, promises to help us begin to answer the above questions, for this was designed not only to deal with 'the measurement of labour productivity and the causes of differences in labour productivity' but to present 'a review of the large number of industry-level studies in the United Kingdom which have attempted, among other things, to examine the causes of international differences in labour productivity and the use of manpower' (Pratten and Atkinson, 1976).

In all, Pratten and Atkinson reported evidence from no less than twenty-five studies that were conducted between 1944 and 1975. Here, for ease of exposition, one particular industry is singled out – the motor vehicle industry. This seems legitimate, given that the five motor industry reports reviewed by Pratten and Atkinson tend to be of more recent origin than those for some other industries, and given also that during the 1970s this industry was often cited in support of the view that British labour productivity, in the

---

*The 'look-and-see' requirement – that international productivity comparisons should systematically report on working practices – is referred to below as *Requirement C*. But there is little point in this requirement being met unless other requirements are also met. Two of these are referred to below as *Requirement A* – that such studies specify whose productivity is being compared (and the quality and duration of their labour); and *Requirement B* – that the physical means of production (a term that will be critically examined later) should also be specified. Note that it is not assumed here that these requirements, if met, would allow for all possible variables to be controlled. On the contrary, they are introduced here merely as rock-bottom, very rudimentary requirements.

**Table 2.1  Studies of the motor vehicle industry**

| Report | Date of report | Does over-manning or ineffici-ency exist? | Sections or trades to which over-manning or ineffici-ency applies | Causes of overmanning or inefficiency | | | | | Other causes of low productivity | | | |
|---|---|---|---|---|---|---|---|---|---|---|---|---|
| | | | | Labour restric-tive prac-tices[b] | Union struc-ture | Strikes | Unsatis-factory man-age-ment union negoti-ating machinery | Man-age-ment failures | Scale differ-ence, size of plants, prod-uction runs etc[c] | Old vint-ages of capital equip-ment | Other differ-ences in capital equip-ment | Shift working restric-ted |
| Maxcy and Silberston | (1959) | | | | | | | | • | | | |
| Clack | (1967) | | | | | | | • | | | | |
| Beynon | (1973) | Yes | | • | • | • | • | | | | | |
| Ryder Report[a] | (1975) | Yes | General | • | • | • | • | • | • | • | • | |

*Source:* Adapted from Pratten and Atkinson (1976), Table 4, p. 574.

*Notes*

•  Indicates that the cause was mentioned in the Report.
a  Also the CPRS Report on the *Future of the British Car Industry*, HMSO, 1975.
b  Restrictive practices include demarcation rules, especially between crafts, and between craft and non-craft workers, and union rules involving the use of mates.
c  This heading includes differences in vertical integration.

common-or-garden sense, was comparatively low. A table presented by Pratten and Atkinson is partially reproduced as Table 2.1, since it concerns the five motor industry investigations.

The table apparently summarises a good deal of factual information from a number of authoritative 'reports'. But there are surprises in store for those who take the trouble to check back to the original sources. Take Requirement A, for example. In the case of two of the reports, those by Ryder and the Central Policy Review Staff, it is at least suggested that these covered all 'sections or trades', for these researches are presented as having demonstrated that 'overmanning or inefficiency' is 'General' (see col. 3). But, as far as the other studies are concerned, no information at all is provided that meets Requirement A. And no wonder: two of these studies (Beynon, 1973; Clack, 1967) were not even concerned 'to examine the causes of international differences in labour productivity and the use of manpower'. Clack's work, a case study, focused on the structure of the trade union organisation and industrial relations machinery in a Midlands car assembly plant. Beynon's work, another case study, took the form of an analysis of the formation, limits and possibilities of worker organisation and consciousness at Ford's Halewood factory. It scarcely needs to be added that, given the nature of Beynon's study and the one by Clack, neither meets Requirement B either. In the light of what some of these 'reports' actually are, it really is necessary to take some prefatory comments made by Pratten and Atkinson very seriously indeed. For those particular studies most certainly do 'lack . . . quantified estimates of the differences in productivity' and they most certainly do fail 'to quantify the causes of the differences'. A 'noticeable feature' of them quite definitively is 'the brevity of [their] comments about differences in manning and efficiency' (1976, pp. 574–5). What 'comments'? What 'differences'? one might ask.

Maxcy and Silberston's work is the first that appears in the table. Sure enough, to go back to Maxcy and Silberston (1959) to see what they actually did say, is to find that they *did* have their eye on productivity differences between the British and American motor industries and that they *were* interested in exploring 'to what extent different factors account for the considerable difference in productivity per head' between the two industries, albeit in the period up to the mid to late 1950s. As to their conclusions, they argued that 'the difference in scale of production, leading to greater mechanization and hence a high output per head' was 'a very important factor'. Conceding that 'other factors are certainly at work', they stated as 'an important one . . . the high level of labour costs in relation to machinery costs in the USA [which] gives rise to a substitution of capital for labour (and hence to higher output per head) in circumstances where it would not be justified on cost grounds in this country'. But in Maxcy and Silberston's account working practices are introduced only in a cursory way: 'Among other factors that might be mentioned', Maxcy and Silberston tell us, 'is the possibility that general management efficiency is greater in the USA or that operatives work harder. It is impossible to know what weight, if any, to assign to these factors. If some observers are to be believed, however, the possibility of greater managerial efficiency in the US motor industry cannot be ignored.' 'If some observers are to be believed' . . . This seems a rather slim basis upon which to enter a neat little black dot in the table, which suggests that Maxcy and Silberston (1959, pp. 211–2) have actually, and independently, established that 'failures' – in this case on the side of management, but the same would have to be said if workers' practices had been cited – are a cause of differences between UK and American performance in the motor vehicle industry.

There is a more general point to be made about Maxcy and Silberston's work, however. This is that it was pitched at the level of the industry *as a whole*. This – as they appreciated – made it difficult for them to compare like with like with respect to the types of vehicle produced in the US and the UK. This has some significance for further criteria that will be advanced for the conduct of international comparisons of labour productivity at the end of this chapter. For the moment, though, it is perhaps sufficient to note that their work did not match up at all precisely to our Requirement A, or Requirement B, and, not being based on the observation of shop floor working practices, nationally or internationally, it had no chance of meeting Requirement C either.

Of course, had Maxcy and Silberston employed a different method, they *might* have found evidence that overmanning and worker inefficiency were greater in the UK, or they might have been able to provide the evidence that, on further inspection, they failed to provide about 'managerial inefficiency'. We are looking for evidence though, not speculating about what might be; and so far the comparative evidence has not been exactly convincing, as an indictment either of British workers or their managers. Although represented in the part of the table reproduced from

Pratten and Atkinson as if it were 'evidence', some of it can hardly be dignified with that term at all.

The Ryder Report was commissioned at the end of 1974, to make an overall assessment of the British Leyland Motor Corporation. It warned that BL's success would 'depend most of all on the skills, efforts and attitudes of its [then] 170,000 employees'. But Ryder also reported that 'the most serious feature of BL's production facilities . . . is that a large proportion of the plant and machinery is old, outdated and inefficient' and that its 'record of underinvestment is the main reason for the low productivity of BL's workforce compared with say Fiat or Volkswagen'. Moreover, the Ryder Report made it clear that it did 'not subscribe to the view that all the ills of BL can be laid at the door of a strike-prone and work-shy labour force'; and it argued that interruptions to production had often been the result of factors 'outside the control of BL's labour force'. At one point Ryder did report that (according to BL management) 'comparing like with like, [BL's] labour productivity is often less than its competitors' '. But, on the other side of the coin, Ryder was also of the opinion that 'on labour productivity many of the comparisons made between BL and its competitors both in the UK and overseas are unfair and unreliable', and it criticised such comparisons for not taking into account the 'type and sophistication of vehicles produced . . . or the extent to which bought-in materials and components are used'. To cut matters short, however, the Ryder Report itself did not meet Requirements A, B or C; nor did it publish the like-with-like comparisons that BL management had apparently conducted, 'for reasons of commercial security' (1975, paras 8.11, 9.2, 9.5, 9.6; Summary paras 28 and 35). Here again, then, those little black dots in the table may be thought a little too precise in so far as they relate, this time, to the Ryder Report.

Even such a brief look at the studies collected together by Pratten and Atkinson on the motor vehicle industry is therefore sufficient to warn us that, for our purposes, a synoptic statement of other researchers' conclusions is not enough. It is not enough because in order to evaluate such conclusions, the methods by which they have been arrived at, and the evidence advanced to support them, must be made manifest and be investigated in detail. It can already be seen that out of the four investigations looked at above, the one by Ryder tended to minimise any adverse effect on labour productivity which stemmed from British labour, and was far from demonstrating such an effect anyway; likewise the study by Maxcy and Silberston. Moreover, neither of these two studies could be judged to have met Requirement A, B or C, which it is highly necessary that they should do if they are to help answer the question 'Do British workers work less hard?' Modify the form of this question, and make it refer to international differences in working practices, and these studies still do not provide us with an adequate and systematic basis for an answer. As for the studies by Clack and Beynon, although their findings tell us something about what went on in two British factories they still tell us nothing about how this compared to factories in *other* countries; in no sense at all could they be said to have 'controlled for' Requirements A or B, or provided an ordered assessment of C.

The starting point in this chapter was the observation that economists, whose property the international study of productivity differences has become, are apt to invoke 'attitudes' to explain lower British productivity. True enough, the attitudes to which they refer are not exclusively those of workers. But in Britain a great deal has been heard for a very long time about workers' attitudes, from industrialists, the media and, especially in the 1970s, from politicians. It is because of this that the question was asked earlier in this chapter: how has the existence of these attitudes been demonstrated? It rapidly became apparent that it had not. A discussion followed about the difficulties of measuring 'attitudes', and then about 'effort'. As a consequence of this, it was concluded that it could not be held against these researchers that they had failed to measure effort directly, but it was also argued that they could not be let off the hook so lightly as far as working practices were concerned. It was clearly important to consider what evidence was advanced about these, and how well other rudimentary requirements had been met. It was in this context that Pratten and Atkinson's synopsis of researches was introduced. A brief examination of this has now to put us on our guard about what, according to the conventional wisdom, international studies have shown about how British workers contribute to poor economic performance (and about how British managers contribute too).

To conclude that the studies mentioned above did not always meet the rudimentary ABC of requirements set down for productivity comparisons is one thing, however; to conclude, as a consequence of this, that the much-cited findings of empirically based research in this area should be rejected out of hand is quite another. Every field of enquiry is likely to encompass research of uneven quality. Having got our toe in the water, the next step must clearly be to consider those investigations that promise to be the best. This means specifying some further criteria.

One general criterion which has been implicit in the discussion so far is that measures of what people do are to be preferred to those which deal in subjective states or 'feelings' (hence working practices rather than attitudes). Other general criteria are that, since, from our point of view, the importance of productivity comparisons is that they have been held to produce factual information, (a) they should be conducted in such a way that researchers can be plausibly considered to be closely 'in touch' with the facts to which they refer, and (b) they should eschew ambiguous measures. It is in consonance with (a) that a study conducted by first-hand enquiry, when the researcher has taken the trouble to look-and-see for himself, is to be preferred to one conducted by telephone – an example that is not so far-fetched as it might sound: such studies exist and they have been cited uncritically by senior economists and politicians.[3] It is in consonance with (b) that studies which employ physical measures are to be preferred to those that use price terms, the latter adding a further level of complication. Even physical measures, of both input and output, require careful construction, for each of them has a qualitative as well as a quantitative dimension. But the problems with price measures are that much greater. They can be affected by different national accountancy practices, by the changing relation of international currencies, by the transfer pricing of international corporations and so forth. (It is as well to remember also, not only that price terms can bedevil the measurement of productivity but that the price mechanism can provide a route to profit for particular industrial capitals that owes nothing to their own productive efficiency. In the early 1980s, for example, it is reported that BP's world-wide currency trading exceeded not only the value of its own annual oil trading but that of the Bank of England; similarly, Volkswagen overshadowed most West German banks in the Eurocurrency market (Harris, 1983, pp. 66–7).)

Now these requirements – that researchers should get as close as possible to their facts and that they should eschew ambiguous measures – are obvious enough; indeed, they stem merely from an attempt to consider researches on international productivity differences as fact-gathering exercises. It is equally obvious that a key test of the validity of labour productivity comparisons is the extent to which they succeed either in selecting like-with-like situations, or in 'controlling' variables statistically, and, to go one step further, that studies which are based on like-with-like comparisons are to be preferred to those that depend to a greater extent on statistical manipulation, especially of aggregate national data. In the case of the British economy, for example, there is considerable difficulty in answering the apparently simply question 'How many people are employed?'[4] And if it is difficult to answer even this, it has to be appreciated that it is yet more difficult for international comparisons to take account of differences in the effects of state policy, in the role of banks and other financial institutions, in the structural composition of different economies, in differences in their levels of demand – all of which, and much else, it is pertinent to consider if any valid claims are to be arrived at about the differential contributions of national workforces to labour productivity.

All this has clear implications for how the best studies produced by students of international labour productivity differences are to be specified. For it now follows that since there really is so much else that can vary, the most promising studies would seem to be those that compare the operations of the *same companies* in different countries, and those that compare the *same manufacturing process* in different countries. By general repute, and on the basis of my own reading, Pratten's investigation into international companies is a leading example of the first type of research; the Think Tank investigation into the car industry (referred to in Table 2.1, but not signalled out for separate comment as yet) is a prime example of the second. In the mid to late 1970s these two investigations had the combined effect of strengthening the confidence of those who held that the UK had a particular problem with labour productivity – meaning, as laymen thought it meant, a particular problem with workers. Because of this, and also because equivalent studies of these two types have not been published since, there is every reason to consider them carefully. Pratten's study of companies that operated in the US, or Germany or France as well as in Britain is considered in the next chapter; the Think Tank Report in Chapter 4.

# Part Two

Into detail:
some comparative
evidence re-examined

# 3 British workers in the world of comparative statics (1)

Pratten's comparative studies of labour productivity were well known to professional economists in the 1970s. News of his research also reached a wider audience through press reports, through the article already referred to, which he wrote in the *Employment Gazette* (Pratten and Atkinson, 1976) and through another article he wrote in *Lloyds Bank Review*, in which he claimed, amongst other things, that in Britain 'there are widespread differences in efficiency attributable to different attitudes to authority and work' and that 'on average, the intensity of work is probably greater overseas' (Pratten, 1977, pp. 24, 25). It is even possible that his work directly helped to form the opinions held by Mr Healey and other Labour politicians whose concern about the British productivity record was reported in Chapter 1.

Pratten published two studies in 1976. One of these took the form of a comparison of labour productivity in the UK and Sweden and was conducted, on his own admission, with very limited resources (1976b, p. ix). The other, on which we will concentrate here, was much more wide-ranging. It took the form of three paired comparisons of labour productivity in the UK and North America, the UK and Germany, and the UK and France. In the present context a particular attraction of this study (1976a) is that it mounted its comparisons on the basis of the UK and overseas operations of the *same* international companies, Pratten following the logic that this helped to hold relatively constant a number of important factors that could affect labour productivity. To this same end Pratten also developed an extensive 'list of characteristics'. This included, *inter alia*, differences in scale (total output in each country, output at each site, size of plants, rate of output of products); product mix; rate of growth of output; rate of capacity utilisation; extent of vertical integration; labour (hours, quality, availability, etc.); material inputs (quality and wastage of materials, substitutions of labour by materials); plant and machinery (rate of investment per employee, production techniques, age of plant); manning of machinery, and of 'indirect' operations; utilisation rates for machinery; rates of output from machinery; rejection rates for products; and channels of distribution (1976a, pp. 25–6).

Briefly, as can be seen from Table 3.1 Pratten claimed to have found that on average labour productivity was higher in the non-UK operations of the international companies, whatever the industry compared. An average 'productivity differential' of 50 per cent was found in the UK-North American investigations (i.e. productivity appeared to be 50 per cent higher in the North American operations) and he reported 27 per cent and 15 per cent differentials in the UK-German and UK-French investigations. In practice these figures mask a wide dispersion of productivity differentials: differentials on UK comparisons with North American operations ranged from −15 to +200, UK-German differentials from −7 to +125 and UK-French ones from −40 to +50 (1976a, p. 7). None the less, Pratten did find productivity to be lower in the UK in the large majority of cases. His investigation into the *causes* of these differences, which is summarised in Table 3.2, also suggested that what he called 'behavioural' ones played a significant part.

Pratten's work has come to be regarded by specialists in the field as one of the building blocks in the pyramid of knowledge about the determinants of British labour productivity. As can be seen already, there is much to recommend it. The same companies have been compared internationally. A standard methodology, in the form of a check-list, has been employed. In the study itself, moreover, Pratten's causal analysis is often put forward cautiously: thus he states that 'the breakdown of the contributions to the productivity differentials is very tentative' and notes, for example, that 'behavioural forces' may have contributed to some differences in scale and investment and 'economic forces' such as slow growth to the 'behavioural' ones (1976a, p. 60).

However, the very first thing to strike anyone who is not a specialist in this field is that the determination of productivity outcomes must be a highly complicated business – so complicated and so difficult, in fact, that there is every reason to enquire further how this particular building block in the pyramid of

**Table 3.1 Industrial analysis of international productivity differentials**

| | Unweighted average percentage productivity differentials (number of observations in brackets) | | |
|---|---|---|---|
| | UK–N. America | UK–Germany | UK–France |
| Oil, chemicals, pharmaceuticals, soap and detergents | 67 (5) | 35 (6) | 8 (5) |
| Food, confectionery, tobacco and packaging | 63 (5) | 50 (3) | – |
| Engineering components | 90 (7) | 22 (8) | 16 (7) |
| Vehicles and allied trades[c] | 69 (4) | 25[a] (6) | |
| Machine tools and allied trades[c] | 29 (10) | 31 (4) | 42 (5) |
| Process plant engineering | 41 (4) | –[b] | |
| Domestic appliances, electronics and allied trades | 11 (4) | –[b] | –[b] |
| Textiles, clothing and furniture | 34 (6) | –[b] | –[b] |
| Other trades | 48 (5) | 16 (8) | 0 (7) |
| Average | 50 (50) | 27 (35) | 15 (24) |
| Metalworking trades | 48 (29) | 24 (19) | 28 (12) |
| Other trades | 52 (21) | 31 (16) | 2 (12) |

*Source*: Pratten (1976a) Table 3.3, p. 13.

*Notes*

[a] Including electronics.

[b] Included in 'other trades'.

[c] Trades allied to vehicles include earth-moving equipment and tractors. Trades allied to machine tools include textile, footwear and tobacco machinery.

**Table 3.2 Summary of the causes of productivity differentials**

| Cause of differential | UK–Germany (%) | UK–France (%) | UK–N. America (%) |
|---|---|---|---|
| Economic causes | | | |
| 1 Differences in rates of output of products and length of production runs | 5½ | 1½ | 20½ |
| 2 Differences in plant and machinery | 5 | 5 | (6)[a] |
| 3 Other 'economic' causes[b] | (2) | (2) | (6) |
| 4 Total | (13) | (9) | (35) |
| 'Behavioural' causes | | | |
| 5 Incidence of strikes and major restrictive practices | 3½ | 0 | 5 |
| 6 Other 'behavioural' causes[c] | (8½) | (5½) | (6) |
| 7 Total 'behavioural' causes | (12) | (5½) | (11) |
| 8 Average differential | 27 | 15 | 50 |

*Source*: Adapted from Pratten (1976a), Table 9.1, p. 61, who notes the contributions to the productivity differentials are multiplicative not additive.

*Notes*

[a] The figures in brackets are intended to indicate possible orders of magnitude.

[b] Other 'economic causes' include 'differences in product mix, the substitution of labour for materials (or better quality materials) capacity utilisation, and the availability of labour'.

[c] Other 'behavioural' causes are 'effectively differences in manning and efficiency'.

British productivity knowledge was actually constructed. This chapter considers Pratten's research from this point of view. It begins by considering how Pratten coped with some of the problems that arise from the business about 'attitudes' discussed in Chapter 2. It then goes on to consider how he measured productivity, and how he determined its causes. Then, following a rather broader discussion of certain institutional factors to which Pratten refers, the attempt is made to put his work in context, and to consider what issues he does and does not take up, and the adequacy of his conclusions.

Pratten refers to both 'attitudes' and 'behaviour'. The first point to be established about Pratten and 'attitudes' has already been noted in the last chapter – briefly, he made no systematic attempt to study them. However, it was argued in the last chapter that whereas the failure to study attitudes (or to directly measure 'effort') could be excused, the failure to investigate working practices could not. How, then, did Pratten come to know about these? This question is well worth asking, not least because, to the best of my knowledge, it is something that the economists who conduct international productivity comparisons have not felt it worthwhile to comment on at all. The answer is that Pratten gleaned his information about what went on in factories *from managers*.

Pratten refers to 'behavioural' causes and effects – but there is not a shred of evidence in his report to suggest that he actually observed the work practices that prevailed in a single British factory, let alone in a single North American one, or one in France or Germany. Judged on the basis of what he wrote, it is not even clear that Pratten so much as clapped eyes on a single British worker – again, let alone a single American or French or German worker. What primary investigation did take place was conducted by managers and relayed to Pratten, in a more or less 'hard' or impressionistic form, by the managers of the international companies concerned. The check-list referred to above was a check-list that Pratten used to interview managers. The information that it produced was in part a function of Pratten's judgment and in part a function of the judgment of the managers who answered his questions. He tells us that it 'was a long list of questions to put to managers', that 'no attempt was made to press for information . . . which seemed unlikely to provide a significant

part of the explanation for differences in productivity' and that he
'was forced to rely on [his] own judgement for selecting and
pressing questions . . . and upon the judgement of managers who
answered the questions' (1976a, p. 26). It is quite consistent with
all this that when we get down to the nitty-gritty of explanation
and consult three appendices on 'Explanations for Differences in
Labour Productivity' these also turn out to be 'synopses of the
explanations received from firms' – that is, these 'explanations'
are once again explanations advanced by managers (1976a, pp. xi,
28, Appendices 4, 5 and 6). Pratten tells us in his preface that he
'had conversations' with 'officials of trade unions' and this might
be thought to balance things up. But it appears that these trade
union officials were only five in number. By contrast, Pratten
conducted 119 'observations' (as he called them) into UK-North
American, UK-German and UK-French international operations.
The full significance of his statement that he 'obtained *most* of the
information for the study from the managers of the companies'
comes across all the more clearly when it is recognised that even if
he had made contact with only one manager in each of these
hundred-odd operations (which would give cause for concern
about the adequacy of their knowledge, and consequently his),
this would mean that in terms of his sources of information
Pratten's work was pretty well a 100 per cent management study
(1976a, p. ix, my emphasis).

On first hearing, Pratten's research sounds impressive. His
declared objective – to identify the causes of differences in
performance in a way that earlier attempts based on macro-
economic data could not – commands respect. But it is now
perfectly clear that Pratten himself conducted his research at
least one remove from certain vital elements of his subject matter,
and that for the most part he had to make the best sense that he
could out of what information he could get – from managers.

Pratten's fellow economists might find all this no cause for
surprise. They might not be worried that 70 per cent of Pratten's
informants were not only managers but British managers (1976a,
p. 78), nor about just how close the managers he interviewed were
to what went on in the production processes of their British (*and*
overseas) operation, which remains unclear in Pratten's account. It
is doubtful whether other social scientists would take such an
untroubled view. For there is considerable evidence that managers
and workers' representatives give different answers even to what
appear to be simple, objective questions (e.g. 'How many unions

are there with members among the manual workers at this establishment?'). An SSRC-commissioned review of surveys of workplace industrial relations found 'significant differences' in this respect (Abell *et. al.*, 1983, pp. 34, 37–40, Table 1). When the emphasis shifts from facts to opinion, and from description to explanation, there is every reason to think that such difficulties are compounded. (It is not difficult, incidentally, to guess the reaction that would greet an enquiry into productivity that rested pretty well 100 per cent on facts and opinions provided by workers.)

There is another problem, however, which concerns the way in which Pratten measures productivity. The conceptualisation and measurement of productivity is, of course, at the very heart of a project like Pratten's. Ideally, as was argued in the last chapter, labour productivity should be compared in terms of physical product per employee. From what he writes elsewhere, Pratten would appear to hold to this same view (1976b, p. 18). But in practice Pratten relied on the performance figures that companies (managers) had – whether these were based on volume, adjusted sales and value added, manning and machine utilisation or costs of production. Moreover, some of the measures of performance rest on nothing more than 'assessments by managers' (14 per cent of the UK-German comparisons, and 18 and 25 per cent of his UK-North American and UK-French comparisons rest on a non-quantitative 'method of comparison' which Pratten crisply refers to in this way: 1976a, p. 8, Table 2.4).

As noted already, the information and opinion that is the bed rock of Pratten's study derives in large part from British managers. There is no sense in which this is matched by information and opinion that has been gathered from British workers (or from those of any other nationality) – either on managers or on any other determinants of productivity. Indeed, to all intents and purposes, the attitudes and opinions of workers – as opposed to those of managers – play no part in determining the conclusions of this research at all. But to consult Table 3.2 is to see at once that – despite this overwhelming reliance on and interaction with managers – no formal entry appears for 'managers' under 'behavioural' causes. As Pratten himself reports on the question of there being international differences in management: 'Our methods of research were inadequate to determine whether such differences existed, but they were not referred to by any of the respondents' (1976a, p. 50). Given that these respondents were managers, it becomes a matter of speculation whether there might be good sociological reasons why this was so. But what stands out is that the methods employed in this research were ill-suited to determining whether such differences existed with respect to either managers or workers. In an attempt to cope with this difficulty Pratten tells us in connection with Table 3.2 that it would be an 'extreme assumption' to attribute *all* of 'the "behavioural" effects' to the labour force, and he then proceeds to the conclusion that – even on such an extreme assumption – 'the contribution of the labour force to national differences . . . is significant but not very large' (1976a, pp. 60, 61). On the face of it, this conclusion might seem a suitably modest one. But a few further observations suggest that, taking Table 3.2 as it stands, it deserves yet more modesty still, for there is a problem about how representative it really is.

'Strikes', for example, appear in the table, along with 'major restrictive practices'. But elsewhere in his report Pratten tells us: 'Strikes were not a cause of differences in productivity for the firms in our sample not in the motor industry' (1976a, p. 54). A similar problem arises with the four cases cited by Pratten where 'overmanning imposed by restrictive practices had substantial effects', for two of them would appear to be associated with printing unions. And as Pratten himself states: 'Apart from the firms subjected to widespread restrictive practices or strikes' (namely three in the vehicle industry, two in printing, and two in food and allied trades) only 10 per cent of the UK operations 'were affected by restrictive practices of indirect employees or inflexible division of work between operators and indirect employees' (1976a, p. 54). Clearly, the motor industry is no more a microcosm of British industry than print unions are of the British labour movement – even though these industries have been apt to figure disproportionately in productivity students' references to British industrial relations (as other authors have also noted: see Edwards and Nolan, 1983, p. 5). But there is a further reason for doubting the representativeness of Table 3.2, and indeed Pratten's sample as a whole.

To understand this it is necessary to consider what Pratten states is his 'most significant and firmly established conclusion'. This is that 'it is very difficult for even an international company to determine an efficient level of productivity', to which he adds: 'if these companies were readily able to do this, most of them would be able to make accurate comparisons of productivity for their operations, and assess the contribution of productivity differentials' (1976a, p. 62). It has been seen already that Pratten's *own* ability to make accurate comparisons, and his *own* assessment of the causes of productivity differentials, were based on the comparisons and assessments made by the managements of the international companies he studied. Judged in this light, the above conclusion is indeed a significant one. For it turns out that of the firms Pratten contacted initially, over 70 per cent failed to provide him with quantitative information, and a sizeable number – which might well have included firms that did not have adverse UK productivity differentials – apparently did not respond to his enquiry at all (1976a, pp. 74–5).[1] We were drawn to Pratten's research because his strategy of comparing the same companies internationally promised to yield superior results to those likely to be forthcoming from more macro approaches to labour productivity or from others that were largely based on what were regarded as inadequate means of investigation, like resort to correspondence and telephone calls (though even in Pratten's research twenty investigations were conducted in this manner – 1976a, p. 75). But it now appears that the whole investigation is in fact beset by an ABC of elementary flaws and faults, the consequences of which for his research generally could be profound. On the specific matter of the estimates of the causes of productivity differentials, however, it is appropriate to give Pratten the last word. 'These estimates', he tells us, 'are not statistics like those appearing in the *Annual Abstract of Statistics* . . . [and] are subject to a substantial margin of error because of errors of measurement and estimate' (1976a, p. 60). Of this at least there can be no doubt.

The logic of this enquiry has of course been to take the argument that UK workers have a disproportionately adverse impact on labour productivity on its own terms, to search out the evidence upon which such a view is held to rest, and to investigate how good that evidence is. Pratten's study, based on a number of 'snap-shots' refracted through a managerial lens, was static in form and he had little to say about institutional process. In true empiricist style he saw factors here and factors there, indeed 'economic' factors and 'behavioural' ones. But the world of work is not constituted simply of managers, with their particular 'attitudes' and 'behaviours', and workers, with theirs, plus 'economic' factors. The whole is itself enmeshed in institutional procedures, structures and understandings. For this reason it is important to note those ventures that Pratten did make into a level of analysis over and above that of the 'behavioural'/'economic' divide. Concerning such matters Pratten suggests amongst other things (a) that a low level of 'general efficiency' in the UK labour force was possibly more in evidence in larger factories (1976a, pp. 14–15); (b) that 'a feature of the behavioural differences was the marked differences within the UK between companies and regionally' (1976a, p. 57); and (c) that 'one of the more surprising features' of the results of his study, as it related to UK trade unions, was 'the loose control shown to apply within trade unions' (1976a, p. 59).

It is difficult to flesh out some of the above comments here because, with the relative exception of (a), which derives from a statistical analysis, they have little hard empirical grounding in the first place. Concerning (b) for instance, though six of Pratten's (anonymous) firms that operated in the Liverpool area reported to him that they had 'distinctly greater difficulty in achieving a good performance from their labour force' (1976a, p. 57), only the foolhardy would take this as justification for launching into a disquisition on 'Merseyside Militancy and the Scouse Mentality'. Other research suggests that the case for lower productivity in Liverpool – as compared to other cities, and bearing in mind the composition of industries – is difficult to sustain[2]. Even those given to invoking the notion of a 'Scouse mentality' are far from agreed about its nature: associated with 'mindless militancy' by some, for others it is a 'generalised apathy', with consequently different alleged effects on shop floor behaviour (Nightingale, 1980, pp. 20–1). And if Liverpool *is* different, this also, of course, makes for difficulty in any blanket generalisation about 'British workers', as compared to those elsewhere. Pratten's comment about 'marked differences between companies' points to a similar limitation.

Prais has done much to confirm Pratten's notion that there is a 'size effect' in the UK, where he holds that it operates with greater force than elsewhere, and Caves has arrived at a sort of composite explanation of the part played by labour relations in the UK in the determination of labour productivity, which combines the alleged reinforcing effects of size and location in the older industrial regions as well as other variables. Caves, however, was yet more removed from production than Pratten was, whereas Prais, who suggests that UK managements restrict their size of plant, and even relocate to avoid increases in established plant sizes, may inadvertently make the regional argument less plausible than it might be. To briefly explain why, it is necessary to appreciate that in Prais' own analysis the relation between plant size and strikes is most marked of all in the motor vehicle industry, and most particularly in car assembly rather than in the manufacture of components or commercial vehicles, for it is in car assembly that Prais finds the most disputes, and here that he also finds the largest plant sizes abroad.

It is certainly not a theoretical nonsense to entertain the idea that managements will steer investment away from labour 'trouble', other things being equal. The proposition is in fact no more outlandish than that they will prefer low-wage areas, or economies; or will prefer to invest in countries that are not marked by civil disruption. But what is the evidence that such considerations have governed the size of plants in British car assembly? And to be even more precise, what is the evidence for this in the period 1960–75, a time when, Prais tells us, the present substantial differences became evident between US and German plant sizes on the one hand and British ones on the other?

It is a matter of fact that during the 1960s new plants were built in Britain, that these were not of German or American proportions and that these new plants were built rather than expanding existing ones. But an earlier writer on labour relations in the motor industry (who incidentally could 'find no obvious association between the relative size of a firm or plant and its relative dispute-liability') reported that it was 'not clear' whether 'the major car firms expected the new areas to be free of the dispute proneness of the older car producing districts' (Turner *et al.*, 1967, pp. 328, 68) and Prais himself advances far from a cast-iron case. When it comes to it, his evidence is no more than an inference: 'in assembly, where leading plants abroad have about 40,000 employees, it is clear that a British plant of that size would have to expect an intolerable frequency of stoppages; and this, it must be inferred, is a major reason why British assembly plants have not grown to the typical size found in America and Germany' (1981a, p. 162). This, to repeat, *might* be so, but what Prais presents is no more than an inference, and to back this up with received wisdom of the kind that (some unspecified) managers (in some industries) have told economists that this sort of thing happens is not to make an adequate case. One reason why this is not adequate in this particular instance is that, quite apart from any role played by government regional policy, if managers can be cited as saying that plants of over a certain size are not built in Britain because of distinctive problems with British workers (who, so to speak, get even nastier when crowded together than workers in other countries do), they can *also* be cited as saying that they face particular difficulties with British labour in certain parts of the country – like Merseyside. And where were the new plants sited in the relevant period? The answer is that, aside from the Rootes plant at Linwood, Scotland, Ford went to Halewood, Vauxhall to Ellesmere Port, Triumph to Speke.[3] All on Merseyside . . .

Had Prais shown much more convincingly that the UK car industry has plants of the size that it does, and that it failed to enlarge its plants because it was fearful of a consequent size effect, and that the same applied in other sectors that he rates technically deficient in plant size, this would have constituted a very neat demonstration of the distinctive impact of UK labour on UK productivity, and a very important link would thereby have been established – from a low-productivity-inducing characteristic of the British workforce to the very structure of certain less competitive areas of the British economy. As it is, the size effect in Britain as compared to its competitor nations clearly merits further patient investigation, and in the meantime one is left to wonder both about the 'Scouse' mentality, its alleged peculiarities and, on an industry by industry basis, its extent.

As for the third of the points taken from Pratten above (c), it would appear that it was 'shown' to him that there was 'loose control' within UK trade unions by his other eyes and ears on British industry, the five trade union officials. In one respect such evidence is not all it might be. Trade union officials have their problems, and one problem, given their organisational role – and the fact that one important function they perform is to 'deliver the membership' to management – is the rank and file. Of course, this sort of objection does invite the response that 'really, we all know there is loose control in British trade unions'. But the problem is that we 'all know' that workers are a particular problem for British industry – that British labour productivity does not compare well with that in other countries because British workers do not work 'as hard'. This is precisely why the questions being asked insistently in this part of the book are: *How are these things known? And how well have they been established?*

Whether low British productivity can be readily linked to the structure of British trade unionism is something that will be discussed later. For the moment it should be noted that even though Pratten reports managers as saying that they found their UK labour force 'harder to manage', this was *not* simply because 'more of the UK labour force are members of unions, or that unions in the UK are more demanding or politically oriented', but because 'employees in the UK were simply less willing to co-operate', whether in trade unions or not (1976a, p. 59). This idea that the UK labour force is 'less willing' (meaning in effect less willing to change) can be exemplified by what Pratten was told by some of the managers of firms that operated in both West Germany and the UK. Specifically referring to 'the greater ease of introducing changes' in Germany, Pratten reports that it was 'relatively "difficult" to introduce changes in equipment in the UK'; that 'negotiations to obtain changes led to delays' in the UK, and that whereas 'in the UK, employees at many factories insisted on negotiating changes in pay when new machinery was introduced', this was 'not the case in Germany'. To this he adds: in Switzerland 'where co-operation between management and labour was very good, managements could put in machinery without negotiations' (1976a, pp. 55–6). Yet again, this raises some important issues that will have to be returned to in later chapters. But for the present it is sufficient to say that if British workers are 'simply less willing to co-operate' – and they have most certainly often been said to be so – Pratten's evidence that this actually is the case is slim. Indeed, his evidence on this, and on the working practices that might come to embody such unwillingness, is not presented in a detailed and systematic way. As noted earlier, however, Pratten does provide synopses of 'Explanations for Differences in Labour Productivity within International Companies' in the appendices of his study. One way to put what evidence Pratten did obtain from his managers on a more systematic footing is therefore to reanalyse this material using a simple check-list.

Check-lists of rules and working practices like the one presented in Table 3.3 do not usually appear in the works of students of international productivity differences. The twenty-five rules and practices it contains stem from a simple, and limited, four-fold distinction of how potential encroachment on the political economy of capital might be effected by labour. Items 1–5 are

**Table 3.3   Rules and practices of workers that might affect labour productivity to some degree adversely, compared on the basis of the UK and non-UK operations of international companies**

| Rules of practices | UK-France (N = 27) | UK-Germany (N = 42) | UK-North America (N = 69) |
|---|---|---|---|
| 1 Employment of apprentices | – | – | – |
| 2 Employment of supplementary workers | – | – | 1 |
| 3 Controls on part-time work | – | – | – |
| 4 Closed shop | – | – | – |
| 5 Controls on recruitment | – | – | – |
| 6 Manning | 6 | 8 | 13 |
| 7 Transfer between tasks | 1 | 2 | – |
| 8 Control on access to jobs | – | – | – |
| 9 Craft demarcation | – | – | 1 |
| 10 Controls on starts/stops | – | – | – |
| 11 Breaks in working day | – | 1 | – |
| 12 Controls on shift working | – | – | – |
| 13 Controls on overtime | – | – | – |
| 14 Controls on lay-off | – | – | – |
| 15 Pace of work | – | – | 1 |
| 16 Controls on standards of craftsmanship | – | – | – |
| 17 Controls on output | – | – | – |
| 18 Controls on job timings | – | – | – |
| 19 Payment system | – | 1 | – |
| 20 'Not working' | 1 | 5 | 4 |
| of which: | | | |
| absenteeism | (–) | (1) | (2) |
| quitting/turnover | (–) | (1) | (1) |
| strikes | (1) | (3) | (1) |
| 21 Machine installation, etc. | 1 | 3 | 4 |
| 22 Starting time | – | 1 | 1 |
| 23 Controls on machine operation | – | – | – |
| 24 Controls for health | – | – | – |
| 25 Theft, sabotage, etc. | – | – | – |

*Source*: Information derived from Pratten (1976a), Appendices 4, 5 and 6, pp. 83–118.

possible instances of rules and practices that might bear especially on the recruitment of the labour force; items 6–9 are possible instances of those that might bear on the allocation of tasks within the division of labour; items 10–20 are possible instances of those that might bear more directly on labour time, the cost, intensity, quality of performance and reliability of labour, and items 21–25 bear more directly on the physical means of production. This second look at Pratten's information on the basis of what is available from his Appendices is in reality of course a highly approximate affair.[4] First, Pratten asked questions of managers. Then he edited their replies. Now we are taking these edited replies as a source for the explanation of labour productivity with special reference to the part played by workers. Dependent from the word 'Go' on the say-so of managers, and mediated by unknown and diverse elements as this exercise is, Table 3.3 does make it immediately clear, however, that the incidence of reported UK labour practices that were claimed to be a problem by managers, and which Pratten thought it worthwhile to record in his Appendices, based on interviews with them, is remarkably low. Only ten of our check-list of twenty-five items receive any mention, and five of these only one. Looked at in this light the contribution of labour practices to UK labour productivity does not loom large: it 'looms small'.

At the very least, therefore, this sort of exercise serves to create an impression of the extent of restrictive working practices in Britain compared to other countries which differs from that which is conveyed when the usual method of presentation is followed: that is, when the 'economic factors' are considered first and – a quantified estimate of differences in output per worker having been cited – examples of British working practices (or just 'attitudes') are then instanced or simply alluded to, thereby creating the impression that these speak volumes, but without any real attempt being made to systematically compare or measure their volume. Of course, it cannot be concluded, even on the basis of this more detailed examination of the distribution of practices, what their significance is for productivity. The presence of a whole scatter of such practices might, for example, be less damaging to productivity than the existence of just one practice, if, say, the perpetuation of this was a particularly important impediment to management. Moreover, even if it were assumed that each of these practices actually was a fetter on management action, the table tells us nothing about how widespread each practice was within each firm. But the real problem with the table is a more fundamental one: it derives from the attempt to evaluate international productivity comparisons on their own terms, with the consequences that the table, like Pratten's research itself, fails to situate the practices of working men and women in the socio-economic process and context of which they are a part. Part Three of this book attempts to go some way towards rectifying this deficiency, which will involve amongst other things bringing to light the sort of evidence that many of those who investigate international productivity differentials are apt to neglect or fail to research adequately (including, it must be said, evidence about British managers). Here, by contrast, only two comments will be made, concerning particular aspects of process and context respectively.

Concerning process, if the table is viewed as a whole, and if it is borne in mind that the ten entries for item 20 relate to a more than usually polyglot category, it is interesting to see that the greatest incidences of reported practices fall into two groups. These are manning (twenty-seven references against item 6, nine of which, equally spread across the French, German and North American operations, relate to maintenance or indirect workers);[5] and controls alleged to be exercised by workers either over the transfer of labour between tasks (item 7, three cases) or over the installation, modification and up-rating of machinery (item 21, eight cases). Added together these two last items (7 and 21) only amount to eleven cases but, perhaps here, above all, there is some evidence to support the view that change is more difficult to introduce into British factories (or at least some of them), as Pratten suggests. The importance of this is, of course, that this could act as a drag on technological innovation, which is a great motor of the rate of productivity change and a most significant factor in the determination of the level of productivity as well. Clearly, to say more about this it would be necessary to say more about what was referred to above as 'context'. This is, indeed, absolutely essential if falling into the trap of a 'labour-led theory' is to be avoided – that is, the sort of theory in which labour is not only seen to be able to affect productivity outcomes, through the strength of its organisation, but is assumed to be actually in control, and able to determine the overall pattern of capital accumulation and investment as well. It is this sort of reasoning which, in its everyday usage, the very term 'labour productivity' conspires to invite. But taking a final look at Pratten's work, in which the information reported in his appendices is subject to a further secondary analysis, provides a useful antidote to this.

Pratten's managers of UK-American operations were reported in his synopses as making twenty-five references to working practices of all kinds. An examination of this same material for what the managers of these operations (the largest category in his sample) had to say about *other* determinants of labour productivity reveals, by contrast, that they made thirty-two references just to the larger output of North American plants, their scale of operation and production runs, which were sometimes held to have very significant effects. It reveals that they also made sixteen references to differences in product mix, to differences in the quality of products, to smaller batches and less standardisation in the UK; and nine specific references to greater North American mechanisation/automation. In addition, the managers of North American-UK operations had plenty to say about wages in the UK (i.e. *low* wages in the UK) as an explanation for low UK labour productivity. There are in fact a further eighteen references to this, which stress 'the effects of higher wages and salaries in the USA for justifying the introduction of more mechanisation', which claim that 'the lower level of UK wages ... reduced investment and hence labour productivity in the UK', and which make the point that a further contribution to higher productivity for indirect labour in the USA was 'the higher level of wages and salaries in the USA which had forced the company to economise on the use of clerical and indirect staff', etc. (1976a, case 2, p. 83; case 34, p. 95; case 68, p. 104).

Of course, North America is not France, and France not Germany. Of course, too, 'economic causes' do feature prominently in Pratten's own analysis of the causes of UK-North American differences (as can be seen in Table 3.2). None the less, to read carefully through Pratten's synopses of explanations put forward by managers of UK-North American operations is to gain an overwhelming impression about the importance of these basic differences, which owe little or nothing to the 'attitudes' of the respective workforces – unless perhaps, through some alienated logic, UK workers are to carry the can because, by virtue of putting up with low wages, they have failed to make their managers invest more. Such an assumption is not one shared by the present writer, nor, let me hasten to add, is there any indication whatsoever that it was shared by Pratten. Indeed, this is also an appropriate place to recall that much of Pratten's analysis is put forward in a suitably tentative manner. The problem is, however, that those looking for an account of the relative contribution made by British labour and other 'factors' to the British productivity shortfall have frequently made reference to Pratten's study. Worldly-wise as they may think themselves, and aware as the economists amongst them may be of the limitations of econometric science (though one sometimes wonders), there is very little indication in the literature that, given Pratten's methodology, it truly is the case that his findings should be regarded very tentatively indeed, especially as they concern the two key active agents in the production process: managers and workers. Pratten's study has been influential. As a piece of research it represents a sizeable endeavour. But it is insufficient to cite this research as if it were one of the building blocks of empirical social science, the sum of which points to the conclusion that British workers do contribute significantly to lower produc-tivity – qualifying such an appreciation, if at all, only with respect to Pratten's finding that productivity was higher in nearly a quarter of his British observations (Cairncross *et al.*, in Matthews and Sargent, 1983, p. 172) or with a note to the effect that his analysis of the causes of productivity differentials was a 'guestimate' (Caves, 1980, p. 145).[6] It is insufficient to evaluate his research in this way because Pratten's investigation was significantly limited by what was available for him to work with (by his reliance on those firms which did provide information, and the information that they supplied) and, partly related to this, by his dependence throughout on management.

It was seen in Chapter 2 that some economists have a penchant for invoking 'attitudes', especially towards hard work – so much so that in commenting on a fellow economist's analysis one of them was led to say that 'the thought can never be wholly silenced that perhaps it is simply that Americans work harder' (above, p. 40). In our view, Pratten's research does little to substantiate this particular proposition, though he too is in the habit of invoking attitudes, as are others who refer to his research. But his research does call to mind another, quite different thought which, because of the manner in which his investigation was conducted, is also one that 'can never be wholly silenced'. This is that British workers – who Pratten signally failed to study – may have been beset by similar difficulties to those that Pratten himself experienced: what was available for them to work with, and their dependence on British management.

# 4 British workers in the world of comparative statics (2)

Such was the troubled state of the car industry in Britain in the 1970s, and such was Government concern, in particular about BL, that the report by Lord Ryder, which was referred to in Chapter 2, was followed within four months by another report on the motor vehicle industry, the Fourteenth Report of the Trade and Industry Sub-Committee of the Expenditure Committee. Like the Ryder Report, this held to the view that 'inadequate investment and the lower productivity of old plant have been the greatest contributors to poor profitability on the mass production of the car side of the industry' (Expenditure Committee, 1975, p. 34). By contrast, the Government Think Tank Report (CPRS, 1975) which appeared in the same year, took another view, and it is this that has held sway in public discussion since. The Think Tank not only claimed that productivity per man in the British car industry was 'far below' the level in the EEC, and that, though British wage rates were lower, they were not low enough to compensate for this; it claimed 'inadequate capital equipment' to be 'only a minor cause of low productivity'. It claimed that 'to improve productivity, investment alone is not enough'; and it declared – in a phrase with which the reader will be all too familiar by now – 'The basic problem is attitudes' (CPRS, 1975, p. 87, para. 45; p. v., para. 5). True enough, the CPRS found the 'attitudes' of both labour and management wanting. But its references to 'politically motivated militants' did much to focus opinion on *workers*. So, above all, perhaps, did the startling, highly quotable and much-quoted assertion that 'with the same power at his elbow and doing the same job as his continental counterpart, a British car assembly worker produces only half as much output per shift' (1975, p. v, para. 3).

The key importance of this study here, of course, is that it is a leading example of research that compares the *same* industry in different countries. Indeed, as stated in Chapter 2, it is probably the best example of this method of comparing productivity differences and their causes. The CPRS noted, for instance, that 'comparing output per man in different countries is beset with difficulties'. It drew particular attention to problems associated with differences in the model mix (i.e. the balance between different sizes and types of vehicles within the total produced), to variations in the extent to which producers rely on 'bought-out' components and to differences in the way plants are laid out and equipped. Moreover, in actually making comparisons, it took account of man-hours, thus controlling for duration of labour. Yet more impressively, having made the claim that 'we are particularly bad in assembly', the CPRS went into finer detail. It held that British 'labour requirements for assembling the same car, even with *identical capital equipment*, are nearly double' – and it based this claim on information obtained on the man-hours required to assemble the Ford Cortina and Escort, BL Mini and Marina, Fiat 125, Vauxhall Viva and Opel Kadett ('identical' Cortinas and Minis being assembled in Britain and Belgium; Escorts in Britain and Germany; and the remaining models being held to be 'comparable in all major respects'). We are assured that, apart from obtaining data from manufacturers, members of the CPRS team, including two engineers, examined all the plants involved in assembling these models to ensure that production facilities, including capital equipment, age of equipment, and plant layout, were comparable; that differences were taken into account when calculating the indices; and that in the opinion of the CPRS the margin of error did not exceed 'plus or minus 10%' (1975, p. 78, para. 36, p. xi, para. 12, p. 74, para. 37).

It was on the basis of a comparison of the above 'identical' or 'comparable' conditions that it was claimed the man-hours required in Britain to assemble a car were on average almost double those required on the continent, and the CPRS advanced further and yet more specific claims about the hours required in powertrain assembly (i.e. that of gearboxes, engines and rear axles). Comparisons of 'identical powertrain components' were held to indicate that '50–60% more labour is required in Britain than on the continent' (1975, p. 81, para. 39).

Now, essentially, the CPRS argued that 'the direct causes' of low labour productivity in the British car industry fell into three categories. These were: overmanning; failure to reach the levels which men and equipment should be able to achieve, even when production lines were manned at correct and competitive standards; and underinvestment in capital equipment (1975, pp. 82–4, paras 41–3). Such is the methodological rigour that appears to have informed the CPRS Report that the evidence on these three 'direct causes' is well worth reviewing in detail. It is to this task that we now turn, considering first overmanning, then what for convenience will be referred to as 'underproduction', and finally underinvestment.

According to the CPRS there was 'clearly an overmanning problem in many parts of the (UK) car industry'. It illustrated the 'scale of the problem' by three examples. Taken as a whole the standard of presentation that characterises the CPRS Report is outstandingly high, and the way these three examples were presented in a table (reproduced here as Table 4.1) is certainly eye-catching. At the time the Report appeared it neatly presented the evidence for the charge that the UK car industry was overmanned, in a way that could be readily digested by busy politicians and newsmen. Considered one by one, however, the three examples presented in the table are not as convincing as they might appear at first glance.

Example 1 takes the form of a comparison for work on trim, final assembly and engine dress. The actual numbers given are for direct and indirect UK manning per shift at capacity, as compared to what is referred to as 'Competitive Manning Level' (i.e. direct and indirect manning at capacity 'on the continent' for 'identical models with identical equipment'). The extent of overmanning in the UK is put at a very precise figure – 41 per cent. But to dig a little deeper is to discover that the actual data upon which this comparison was conducted is confidential, that it is not made clear how or from whom it was obtained, that in the case of this example no information is provided about plant layout, and that there is certainly no lengthy examination of the difficulty of establishing whether the equipment *was* 'identical'. It is not even clear from the Report whether the 'comparison between plants in the United Kingdom and on the continent' had as its base only a

**Table 4.1   Examples of overmanning in the British car industry**

| Operation | Actual number employed per shift | Competitive manning level | % overmanning |
|---|---|---|---|
| Trim, final assembly and engine dress | 940 | 665 | 41 |
| Plant maintenance employees | 900–1,200 | 550–650 | 69–78 |
| Wet deck sanding of car body before painting | 18 | 12 | 50 |

*Source*: CPRS (1975), Table 14, p. 82.

single pair of plants or more than this, nor which country or countries on the continent were involved. No comment is made on whether the trim, final assembly and dress operations that were singled out for comparison were representative of other such operations within the companies chosen – or on how these companies compared to others in the same country, which might be relevant, since the CPRS itself reports that 'differences of up to 80%' existed in Britain in the man-hours required to assemble 'similar' British cars (1975, p. 82, paras 40 and 41, and Table 14).

Example 2 compares the number of plant maintenance employees per shift in the UK and 'on the continent'. Again the particular countries which were compared on the continent is not stated, though we can infer that the comparison is based on two or more cases because two sets of figures are provided for the UK and the continent and two figures, '69–78%', are given for the UK overmanning. The report does tell us that if a multiweld machine broke down in Britain, six maintenance men would be required, as against two men on the continent – one mechanical and one electrical maintenance man accomplishing there what in Britain would involve an electrician, a jig fitter, a pipe fitter, a mechanical fitter, a tool man and a repair man. But even this may not be such a straightforward matter, for it cannot be assumed that in the UK the training given for these various tasks is such as to allow ready interchange between them (a point taken up later), and even if it were assumed that training was solely determined by UK trade unions the reasons for this would have to be gone into. Moreover, in this example – in which the claim is only that the plants are 'similar' in size, production equipment and capacity – there is no information on how similar they are, or in what respects they differ. No information is provided on the age of plant, though this might well have implications for the amount of plant maintenance required, and for the number of maintenance workers.

Example 3 concerns wet deck sanding of the car body before painting. The actual number employed per UK shift is given as eighteen; the 'competitive manning level' as twelve. This puts the UK 'overmanning' at 50 per cent. But something lies behind this 50 per cent figure which, once again, is far from making it a simple fact. For on further inspection it turns out that this comparison is not one of international differences in productivity at all. The actual basis of this '50% overmanning' is a comparison of the actual number employed on wet deck sanding at some (unspecified) UK plant and a 'standard calculated by industrial engineers' (CPRS, 1975, p. 82, para. 41, Table 14, n.3).

Taken together, all three examples point in the same direction. They suggest that – other things being equal – more workers are required in the UK. But there remains room for doubt on the extent of the differences reported, about whether other things were equal, and about whether and how far responsibility for this state of affairs could be laid at the door of workers and their trade unions in the UK car industry.

'Underproduction' was held by the Think Tank researchers to be an even more 'critical problem' than overmanning. In their view, output in British plants failed to reach the levels which men and machines 'should be able to achieve' and they found that British production lines produced less, even when they were 'manned at correct and competitive standards' (CPRS, 1975, pp. 82–3, para. 42).

'Correct and competitive standards' – this distinction is one that should not be glossed over. As has been seen, some of the CPRS evidence on overmanning was based on actual international comparisons: some of it on standards deemed to be 'correct' by engineers. Shortly it will be questioned whether it can be taken on trust that the engineers were 'correct'. Already a number of doubts have surfaced about whether the actual international comparisons that were mounted really were based on 'identical' or 'similar' cases and even about which plants of which British companies were compared. However, the CPRS advanced four 'underlying causes' for underproduction in the UK: slow work pace; shortage of materials; the high incidence of quality faults; and poor maintenance. Let's review the evidence for these as it appears in the Report.

*Slow work pace*: a CPRS comparison of 'planned and actual output per man on identical equipment in British and European plants' was used to examine slow work pace with particular reference to body framing lines on which the manning levels were, we are told, without further explanation, neither 'similar' nor 'identical', but 'virtually identical'. Actual output per man in Britain was held to be well under half that on the continent. A further piece of evidence took the form of a comparison of the output of '*identical* door assembly lines' in British and continental plants. It was shown that more doors were produced per hour in the continental plant (CPRS, 1975, p. 83, para. 42, i).

*Shortage of materials*: here 'British car manufacturers' were cited as saying that about 40 per cent of the production lost due to stoppages was attributable to labour disputes or to poor internal management, and suppliers' failure to meet delivery dates was said to account for some 25 per cent of lost production (CPRS, 1975, p. 84, para. 42, ii).

Even if British car manufacturers were correct in what they said, considerably more evidence than this would be required to firmly implicate British workers rather than their managements. Clearly, in the absence of further enquiry, the failure of suppliers to meet delivery dates cannot be laid at the door of their own 'labour problems' – after all, it could be, in certain cases, or to some extent, a function of their own 'poor internal management'. Similarly, if we consider the main car firms themselves, 'poor internal management' might have some causal relation to the frequency of labour disputes, just as dispute duration, and the amount of production 'lost', could be partly determined by customer demand.

*High incidence of quality faults*: we are simply told here that 'plants in Britain require up to twice as much rectification time as do continental plants' and that 'if the standard of care and of "house keeping" in paintshops is poor' cars will have to be painted twice before the finish is satisfactory (CPRS, 1975, p. 84, para. 42, iii). This little example, of a hypothetical kind – 'if' the standard is poor – is an interesting one. It is interesting because at

BL Cowley there really was a paintshop which was almost incapable of producing an unblemished finish – it was then already over a quarter of a century old. What, precisely, one wonders, *was* the level of output that men using such equipment 'should be able to achieve'?

*Poor maintenance*: the claim is made here that despite the fact that British manufacturers employ 50–70 per cent more plant maintenance personnel than their continental competitors, mechanical breakdowns resulted in the loss of about twice as many production hours in the UK as on the continent (CPRS, 1975, p. 84, para. 42, iv). Since the reference here is to mechanical breakdowns resulting in the loss of about twice as many production hours 'on identical equipment', this would seem to block off a rather obvious explanation for underproduction in Britain – namely that British and continental plant was *not* of the same age and reliability. Does it, though? And are there other explanations for the various symptoms of 'underproduction'? Trade unionists, for their part, have argued that there are, and in some instances they have supported their case with the sort of shop floor detail that does not appear in the CPRS Report. It is worth considering this and other evidence before proceeding further.


One British union reports, on the basis of its members' actual experience, that whereas it was true that at the time of the CPRS research Ford's formal quality specifications were the same in Britain and Germany, at certain times when the pressure for peak production was on, Ford management in Britain passed the word to lower the standard. The same, it was conceded, also occasionally happened in Germany, but it was held to happen much more frequently in Britain for two reasons: first, because there were more hold-ups in production in Britain and therefore more need to catch up (once more, it is difficult to suppress the thought that this could be related to differences in plant, layout, and scheduling), and second, because the British company was under greater pressure from Detroit to meet profitability targets (TASS, 1976, pp. 14–15). For its part, the CPRS itself attached only slight weight to the possible significance of 'poor internal management' and 'poor scheduling'. But here, too, other evidence points to a different conclusion. A joint management-union enquiry, carried out at BL Cowley in November 1975 (the same year that the CPRS reported), suggested that poor internal management was a very important cause of low productivity levels. It referred to congestion in the stores area leading to a situation where materials were often dirty by the time they reached the production line. It also attributed serious production problems to a failure to replace automatic tools quickly and to malfunctions of plant (*Labour Research*, 1976, p. 35; *Financial Times*, 26 June 1975).

Then again, it is not quite as clear as the CPRS Report implied – indeed, often unequivocally asserted – that like was being compared with like as far as plant was concerned. After all, identical models do not mean identical production facilities, and TASS reports that even in the allegedly 'identical' manufacturing conditions of Ford Britain and Ford West Germany there were substantial differences in, for example, track layout and man-oeuvring room. (It also notes that 'industrial engineers the world over will marvel at the talents of the wizard in the Think Tank' who, on the basis of a short study, could justify the claim that there was a margin of error of 'plus or minus 10%' in estimating differences in production facilities!)

The very idea that a comparison of Mini 1000 production at Longbridge, Birmingham, and at Seneffe, Belgium, could be a comparison between like and like is also open to challenge in view of the (then) not inconsiderable difference in the age of these plants. At the time of the CPRS Report, Longbridge was using equipment which was introduced when the Mini was first produced in the late 1950s. Around 85 per cent of Seneffe plant capacity was built after 1969.

Another dimension of the comparability problem, which again bears on 'underproduction', comes to light when it is realised that the bulk of the CPRS investigations were conducted between January and May 1975. The rapidity with which the whole investigation was mounted – taken in conjunction with the apparent exactitude of its conclusions – is, as others have noted, itself some cause for wonder. But the point here is that this was not a 'typical' period. Looking at Ford's international operations, for example (and Ford must have been an important company for the CPRS because it produced models both in Britain and on the continent), Ford UK sales were down on the previous year, and those for Ford West Germany were on the up – and the CPRS itself argues that when men see their plants are underutilised they seek to slow production and create extra work (*Financial Times*,

26 June 1975; *Labour Research*, 1976, p. 35).

This last admission of a general point – that management decisions, conditioned in part by a particular economic context, can themselves condition workers' responses – is greatly to be welcomed. But it has to be remembered also that management decisions can exert a *direct* effect on what workers actually produce. Obvious enough to UK workers, this is obvious enough to their continental counterparts too – even to West German workers who work for Ford. At the beginning of 1981, for example, Ford Fiesta production at Dagenham was only 70 per day. After a couple of months it picked up to 200 a day. By mid-summer production was running at 350 a day. Citing these figures, Herman Rebhan, a trade union member of a Ford Supervisory Board in West Germany, asked: 'Had British Ford workers miraculously become five times more productive over a six-month period?' Clearly, they had not. The answer, as he said, 'lay in a management decision'. But neither UK nor West German workers were given any say in the CPRS Report – nor were they usually given any say in the many other, more popular comparisons of British car workers and those in other countries that followed in its train. When their views are reported, however – not their 'general attitudes' but their informed, detailed judgments – it is remarkable how other facets of reality come to the fore, and how other questions arise. To quote Rebhan again (who was replying to one of the many articles on Ford UK's poor worker productivity that appeared in the British press after the CPRS Report, in this case in *The Times*, 18 October 1981): 'I would like to have far more details on the Saarlouis-Halewood comparison before automatically falling in with the one-off figure supplied by the Ford public relations department.' The same goes, it might be added, for the one-off and two-off examples that so often served as the basis for making inferences of a causal kind in the CPRS Report.

Moving now from the CPRS and other evidence about British car workers and underproduction to the CPRS view on the importance or otherwise of investment, it must be conceded that if a German and British plant were part of the *same* multinational, which might be expected to want high productivity in all of its plants – and if an important key to this is further mechanisation and better capital equipment – some explanation would be needed for why, say, Ford Germany was more automated than Ford Britain. Bhaskar (1975, chap. 5, pp. 115–16) presents us with an interesting example in this connection, which concerns the conversion of rolls of steel into body panels. His sketch of the process at Ford Saarlouis or Ford Cologne is simple enough. Steel is fed into a continuous process, cut to length, and fed from one press to another automatically. By contrast, at Ford Dagenham he presents a situation where the roll strip was first of all cut out; then handled by fork-lift truck, then stored; then fork-lifted to a first press; then manually loaded, then pressed; then transferred to a conveyor track; then manually loaded into the next press; and so on. In looking to explain such a difference in the degree of labour process mechanisation, Bhaskar raises the possible significance of wages (the *lower* British wages we have come across before): for the higher wages of German workers would make the potential savings (the amount of wages saved by further mechanisation) higher in Germany than in the UK. At the very least this sort of possibility merits thinking about. It cautions against the ready acceptance of another interpretation – namely, that lack of modern equipment in British industry itself results from the 'underproduction', slower work pace, etc., of British workers, which, relatively speaking, does not make investment in better plant worthwhile. It was of course the latter sort of view that was favoured by the CPRS researchers, according to whom British car workers not only affected British productivity directly, through overmanning and underproduction, but, by virtue of this same overmanning and underproduction, affected it indirectly as well, by making British managements disinclined to modernise plant.

In principle, it is beyond dispute that the productivity outcome can be determined by both direct and indirect effects. But, in practice, the CPRS seems to have been over-keen to indict workers, whether directly or indirectly. At one point, for example, concerning BL, its authors even found it necessary to remind their readers that it 'should *not* be taken to suggest that new capital equipment . . . is unnecessary' (CPRS, 1975, p. 87, para. 45, emphasis in original). This is a statement that bears repetition, for the 1975 claim by the CPRS that inadequate capital equipment was only 'a minor cause' of low productivity has to be set against the reality of BL, a company which had such a protracted history of underinvestment that when Michael Edwardes got there, in 1977, he was to refer to what he called 'Dickensian facilities at most of our factories' (Elgin, 1982; Edwardes, 1984, p. 19). Such was the situation that when it came to build the AD088 (later the

Metro) as a replacement for the Mini, the 'Body in White' area of the Longbridge West Works was found – by management – to be not only too small but decrepit (though it was still in use for producing the Mini and Allegro). According to an internal management document:

> The W. Works body build plant was erected 50 years ago and is not capable of taking a new model due to the buildings being extremely congested, not suitable for modern BIW assembly, with the building fabrics in poor condition, with wooden roof structure. Further, the building is on 3 levels, environmental conditions extremely poor, with inadequate services and facilities. (*AD088 Programme Submission, Executive Summary*, Section Five).

No wonder the CPRS found it necessary to put it on record that it 'should *not* be taken to suggest that new capital equipment is unnecessary'.

To sum up on 'underproduction': there is a real element of doubt concerning much of the evidence that the CPRS advanced about the slow work pace, the shortage of materials, the high incidence of quality faults and poor maintenance – not least if this is to count as evidence of what, in Britain, 'the men', rather than management, have failed to achieve. The CPRS considered underproduction to be a yet more critical problem than over-manning. It may have been a more critical problem, but, if it was, it must be recognised that CPRS failed to establish where the balance of responsibility for underproduction lay. Some further remarks are also in order about how the question of investment and capital equipment were dealt with in the CPRS Report.


As has been noted already, the CPRS saw inadequate capital equipment as 'only a minor cause of low productivity' in the UK car industry. But the authors of the Report were so careful about what evidence they would permit as relevant to the whole question of whether investment was adequate that their height-ened caution in this respect deserves comment in its own right. They tell us that 'in analysing investment in plant and equipment and in making comparisons of levels and rates of investment between companies and countries great care must be exercised', which is true enough. The preference they express for a physical measure is to be welcomed. But what is so interesting is the sheer amount of difficulty raised by the CPRS when investment and capital equipment are concerned. In fact, the methodological difficulties come thick and fast when these matters are at issue, and they loom inordinately large as compared to the difficulties that are raised when the CPRS team discusses 'overmanning' and 'underproduction', both of which are commonly, and often almost automatically, attributed to the 'labour side'. Five reasons are put forward why the use of standard ratios to determine whether the British car industry suffers from underinvestment is 'often misleading' (CPRS, 1975, pp. 85–6), para. 43). It is worth going into these reasons in some detail to appreciate the extent to which the CPRS stresses the difficulty of comparison – when it is investment that is concerned.

One of the reasons advanced is that at least 60 per cent of capital expenditure in the car industry is directly related to the introduction of new models, which 'has little or no effect on productivity'. However, whereas the Report points out that it would be misleading to make comparisons which overlooked the fact that capital expenditure might be higher in one company than in another simply because it had introduced a new model range, this does not mean that the introduction of new models can be assumed to take place with no significant change in capital equipment and production organisation and with no subsequent contribution to productivity. The view that new models are not introduced along with changes in capital equipment which can affect productivity, is one that requires empirical verification, and the CPRS chooses not to provide this.

A similar reluctance to actually enquire into the specifics of the situation when investment is at issue – substituting for this a more general cautionary comment about how difficult it is to draw hard conclusions – is evident in the manner in which a second reason is advanced: that ratios involving sales as a denominator 'fail to take account of the degree of vertical integration or the product mix'. Why, one wonders, could account not be taken of 'companies producing more sophisticated cars' or 'operating their own steel mills and glass works'? Is this really so difficult? And, more pertinently, if it is, was it by comparison so *easy* and unprob-lematic, in compiling evidence on manning levels and under-production, to control for either differences in integration or indeed for 'the way plants are laid out and equipped'? And was the latter *really* so easy that two engineers and other members of the CPRS team (including how many experienced car *workers* –

none?) could estimate 'production facilities' – the productive potential and actual efficiency of capital equipment, and plant layout – within a margin of error of 'plus or minus 10%'?

The remaining three reasons do little to make it more credible that the difficulties of estimating the part played by capital equipment, on the one hand, and overmanning and under-production, on the other, have been set forth in the CPRS Report in an even-handed way. The three reasons are: (1) that 'demonstrating that total assets or value added *per employee* are lower in one company or another is of dubious value unless manning levels are comparable'; (2) that 'while age of machinery is one useful indicator of the adequacy of capital equipment, it is inappropriate because not all old equipment is inefficient or requires replacement'; (3) that 'any ratio involving comparisons of total assets in different countries is valid only if the accounting conventions employed are comparable and the effects of inflation are adequately taken into account'. Valid as each of these propositions is, it is still difficult to see why allowance could not have been made for differences in manning levels (access to which seems to have been no problem, as judged by other parts of the Report) or why accounting conventions should totally defy standardisation or why inflation could not be taken into account. In fact, one gets the impression that when it comes to investment and capital equipment, the CPRS Report 'doth protest too much'; and that the conclusions of the Report as a whole are partly a function of a touching faith in the abilities of engineers, combined with a reluctance to place much faith at all in the abilities of accountants. This relative estimation of the general difficulties that the members of these two professions face in this field may merit some sympathy. But there would seem to be room for doubt about the validity of this relative assessment in the specific context of the CPRS Report itself. The CPRS team does not seem to have even visited the Chrysler UK plant, for instance; those plants which engineers did visit do not seem to have always been compared to continental plants; and one wonders about the accuracy of the physical comparisons that were made. In short, physical measures should be superior, but in this research they are too often employed without detailed, patient qualification – and yet do much to implicate British workers in overmanning and under-production. When it comes to investment, by contrast, method-ological kerfuffle reigns. There are no descriptions of physical plant, and no handsome photographs to set against the neat tables either – certainly not of plants that were a quarter of a century or half a century old.

The CPRS, as has been seen, conceded that BL had an investment problem, but it probably underplayed the possible consequences of investment difficulties and more general related deficiencies and it was probably also uneven-handed in the way it introduced and qualified its evidence about the importance of investment. After all, a common factor underlying each of the four basic causes of underproduction cited by the CPRS – slow work pace; shortage of materials; quality faults; poor maintenance (and even to some degree the overmanning claimed in maintenance) – could very well be that British plants were older, were less spacious, and were poorly planned. On the specific question of investment, an accountant has noted that at the time that the CPRS was reporting, 'over 50% of UK car making capacity had an investment problem'. In his opinion, too, 'continental and UK plants are not directly comparable [because] the UK plants are older, less spacious and not as well planned as their European counterparts . . . this, in turn, is a direct result of the failure to invest capital in new plant and equipment throughout the UK motor industry' (Bhaskar, 1979, pp. 61, 63).

It is possible, of course, that this investment problem was partly a function of government demand management policies. Between 1950 and 1975, for example, there were nearly fifty changes in consumer credit restrictions, rental deposits and tax levels, which particularly affected the car and consumer durables industries (Maunder, 1979, p. 142). These may have made for difficulty in long-term investment placing and in marketing strategy, as well as leading, when the measures were reversed, to resort to imports (as argued by Aldcroft, 1982, p. 42). Whatever weight is accorded to these disruptions, however, it is difficult to gainsay that investment is a management responsibility – or that, in one way or another, its importance was played down by the CPRS.

In Chapter 2 a table was presented which contained several reports that were claimed to be investigations of international differences in labour productivity in motor vehicles. At the end of that chapter it was said, by way of anticipation, that the CPRS study was the best of the bunch, at least as far as the investigation of a possible labour contribution to differences in labour productivity was concerned. Confirmation that this is so is given by the fact that the CPRS investigation comes closer than Pratten's to meeting Requirement A (that the same groups of workers be compared), though, as will be discussed in Chapter 6, there are in fact considerable difficulties in meeting even this requirement in international productivity comparisons. It also went much further towards explicitly recognising and seeking to meet other rudimentary requirements set down in that chapter – attempting 'experiments' with 'similar', 'identical' and 'virtually identical' cases. Even so, the CPRS Report fails to convince in the claims it makes of having actually met the sort of criteria outlined in Requirement B (about documenting and 'controlling for' the physical means of production as ordinarily understood), and it fares very badly indeed when judged against Requirement C (that working practices be observed and systematically reported).

It is plainly insufficient, with reference to an alleged slower British workpace, for example, to simply associate this with 'slower line speeds, late starts, frequent stoppages between shifts, and delays in correcting mechanical problems' (CPRS, 1975, p. 83, para. 42). Just how and why these things have come about – as well as systematic evidence that they have done so – requires accurate reportage, and throughout the CPRS Report this sort of evidence, based on the actual observation of work practices, is given short shrift. The Report states emphatically: '*Heavy capital expenditure simply increases production costs* unless manning levels and work practices change.' It stresses: '*Productivity will not improve* unless there is a willingness to accept new manning levels and work practices', and it adds: 'There is not the slightest prospect of the British car industry becoming viable at any level of production if the present constant interruptions of production, reluctance to accept new methods of working and capital equipment, and readiness to accept sub-standard quality continue' (CPRS, 1975, p. 119, para. 33, iv, p. 120, para. 34, and p. 119, para. 34, i). Clearly it is important for the CPRS argument that evidence is put forward on these matters – especially, for example, on the British reluctance to accept new work practices, new capital equipment and changes in manning levels – which goes beyond the Report's claim (on the say-so of managers) that continental plants have a lead of up to three years over British plants in introducing sophisticated new equipment to raise productivity '*simply because* of the problems of gaining acceptance of new manning levels and work practices in Britain' (CPRS, 1975, p. 120, para. 34, iii, my emphasis). But the nearest the

Report gets to providing appropriate evidence is the following passage:

> During this study, members of the CPRS team have visited six production plants in Britain and five on the continent. It is usual in the British car plants for production lines to start late, stop early, and stop between and during shifts for reasons other than materials shortages or equipment breakdowns. During visits to continental plants, the line was never seen to stop during the working day and at shift changes the relief shift was invariably waiting to take over before the time for the change, so the entire production line never stopped operating. In all cases we were assured, and have no reason to doubt, that what we saw was typical and in no way exceptional. The failure of the workforce to accept established grievance procedures is another factor which leads to constant interruptions to production. All British car plants have standard procedures for transferring men between jobs to overcome sickness or absenteeism, but in every British car plant we have visited there are continual disputes over transfers, leading to loss of production on a daily basis. Most of the interruptions are later settled by Senior Shop Stewards according to the agreements, but the interruption should never have occurred in the first place. (CPRS, 1975, pp. 119–20, para. 34, i)

These claims at least have the virtue of stemming from the observation of what actually happens, even though they relate only to interruptions in production, and one is left uncertain how carefully the observation was conducted, where, for how long, etc. Generally, though, given the claim of the Report that the 'severe weaknesses' of 'poor quality, bad labour relations, unsatisfactory delivery record, low productivity and too much manpower ... basically arise on the shopfloor' (CPRS, 1975, p. v., para. 3) – and given also that to the extent that the Report does concede that lower British productivity has something to do with inferior British capital equipment, even this inadequacy tends to be traced back to *workers* – the analysis of what actually happens on the shop floor is slight.

The casual reader who glanced quickly at some of the tables reproduced from the CPRS in this chapter and from Pratten in the preceeding one might very well gain the impression that the studies under review had conclusively demonstrated that British workers had a greater adverse affect on the productivity outcome in the 1970s than their counterparts in other countries. Both studies do point towards this conclusion. Both of them point to overmanning in Britain, which would clearly have a direct effect on the level of productivity; both of them also suggest that working practices were less flexible in Britain, which might be thought to make for a similarly adverse consequence through retarding the rate at which managements could introduce change. In the 1970s, however, the notion that the productivity of British workers was lower than elsewhere was a commonplace, not just in Britain but in America, Germany and France. In particular, of course, the idea was current that Britain was 'strike prone'. This idea remained prevalent, despite official statements that 'the UK's reputation abroad has probably suffered more than the time lost through strikes in comparison to other countries would warrant'; that 'British industry in general is certainly not widely or continually affected by industrial action, it is not "riddled" with strikes'; and despite the finding of the Donovan Report that in terms of striker-days 'the United Kingdom's recent record has been about average compared with other countries', and also despite many analyses conducted by British industrial relations experts (Ministry of Labour, 1965, p. 41; C.T.B. Smith *et al.* for Department of Employment, 1978, p. 88; Donovan Report, 1968, p. 96). Indeed, the current of opinion that runs against British workers is so strong in Britain that over half of trade unionists, let alone non-trade unionists, readily slip into agreeing with statements to the effect that most trade unions are 'controlled by a few extremists and militants' and that 'trade unions have too much power' (MORI Surveys, 1980, 1982). Given the ideological climate of the 1970s, and the generally adverse conception of 'the British worker', which as we saw in Chapter 1 goes back many decades before this, it really would have represented a turning of the tide if British workers had come out of these investigations scot-free. For this reason alone it is as well to be on our guard. Quite apart from this consideration, though, and over and above the sort of detailed doubts and criticisms raised in this chapter so far, it must also be appreciated that the methodological strength of the CPRS Report was also a weakness – in the sense that it took the form of an enquiry into one (representative?) industry only. (Pratten's investigation was not subject to this particular limitation, of course. But whatever it did or did not plausibly suggest about the *causes* rather than the extent of the British shortfall in productivity, it failed to establish that there was a shortfall across all the companies compared, which also makes for difficulty in generalising about 'the British worker').

There are other considerations to be taken into account when assessing the findings of these investigations. Not the least of these is their unbalanced analysis of the contributions of workers on the one hand and managers on the other. It is perfectly true that the CPRS Report, for its part, acknowledged that the British car industry was beset by certain fundamental problems which were 'the responsibility of management' – 'too many manufacturers, with too many models, too many plants, and too much capacity' – and it was in no way blind to the importance of the restructuring of the world car market that had taken place and the exposure of the British industry to the (then) new chill winds of competition. However, in both the Pratten and CPRS studies managers are much more in evidence in their role as informants and mentors to the productivity researchers than as subjects of enquiry in their own right. Indeed, whereas in the case of workers ideas tend to be floated which implicate them in the productivity shortfall, either directly or indirectly, in the case of management little information is reported, even on how they directly perform their duties.

In the process of examining the evidence put forward in the studies reviewed in this and the last chapter it has frequently been necessary to indicate that this situation is unsatisfactory. And so, indeed, it is. The tendency of investigations of the sort reviewed above to rely to a disproportionate extent upon management, and most heavily of all on *British* management – for their factual information, for the supporting opinions that they adduce, and even for the provision of hypotheses to test (most especially so perhaps in the work of Caves (1980), to which attention is drawn in the next chapter), is in fact a particularly important reason why it would be undesirable to let matters rest simply because, whatever their individual limitations, investigations into British labour productivity seem to point in a similar direction. The moulding of opinion, and, no less important, the building of confidence in what can be taken for granted, is a subtle and complicated business, and taken for granted assumptions are the very ones that merit the sharpest critical evaluation. If, therefore, we find that productivity researchers operate within a mutually reinforcing circle of opinion, of which management is also a part, it is best to stand firmly outside that circle and to adopt a critical stance when seeking to evaluate the claims produced from within it about workers.

There is of course an obvious counter to this last comment, namely that, as far as productivity is concerned, management is in the possession of the relevant facts, and that, compared to workers, it truly is the case that management 'knows best'. As far as certain facts are concerned this is doubtful. In a machine shop, for example, workers will often know, on the basis of hard-won experience, that some machines are better to work on than others, even if management regards all the machines in the shop as 'similar' or even 'identical'. Extend this example to encompass layout, the flow of work and production facilities more generally and it is still worth considering that workers are better placed than managers to spot the differences that render the work they do easier or more difficult (or hazardous). The higher the position that British managers occupy in the corporate pyramid the more likely it is that this will be the case, for at the very top of the British corporate pyramids are men whose upward path has only brought them into contact with manual workers in a minority of cases – the majority having risen through sales, marketing or finance (Fidler, 1981, p. 252). In any case, whether or not managements 'know best' about the conditions in which production takes place, there is good reason to doubt whether what British management knew about productivity in the 1970s was good enough. For instance, it now appears that in the 1970s BL management had 'no breakdown of cost information model by model'. Michael Edwardes was to describe 'this mammoth defect' as 'unbelievable'. 'On inspection' though – and how important such closer inspection is – he also found it 'quite explicable'. 'Accountants', as he remarked, 'can only work on information provided to them', and the truth about BL was that the 'organisation, including that at factory level, was a shambles' (Edwardes, 1984, p. 54).

'Unbelievable', 'mammoth defect', 'a shambles' – there is no trace of such language in the CPRS Report, nor, of the reality to which it related. Nor is there in other professional productivity investigations. But British management does not figure at all largely in most of these reports either – let alone the idea that BL was 'a classic case on a massive scale, of faulty executive appointments' (Edwardes, 1984, p. 58). Leaving the particular case of BL behind us, however, it also has to be remembered that the apparently sensible proposition that management 'knows' about productivity was hardly confirmed by Pratten's research. A significant number of his cross-section of companies could not provide him with reliable and relevant productivity data – for the simple reason that they had not collected this themselves in the first place.

Part Three

# Into context: productivity, productiveness and social organisation

# 5 'The difficulty' reconsidered (1): Quantity, quality, and the measurement of management and 'men'

Micro studies of international productivity differences should be better placed than macro ones to explore what actually happens in production. It is for this reason that such studies have figured so prominently so far, to the relative neglect of research that rests on larger aggregations of data (for instance the many investigations of Maddison or the influential work of Denison, 1967). Yet over the course of the last two chapters, it has become apparent that micro investigations into labour productivity themselves suffer from certain deficiences. Broadly speaking, it is useful to distinguish two sorts of deficiency: (a) those that arise because such firm- or industry-based investigations do not do what they could do sufficiently well, and (b) those that arise because they are not suited to accomplishing particular tasks anyway. An obvious example of the former sort of deficiency is evidenced in the widespread practice of viewing industry through a managerial lens. That the views of workers scarcely figure at all in international productivity comparisons simply cannot be excused on the grounds of time or cost, both of which could be minimised by resort to sampling techniques. That many studies do so little to establish the qualifications of managers – let alone their quality – cannot readily be excused either. Type (b) deficiencies are, however, of a different order. They arise because international productivity comparisons tend to adopt a particular method – that of comparative statics. In reality the social scientist's 'factors' or 'variables' are no more than summary measures of what are often highly complex social processes, and it is an in-built deficiency of the method of comparative statics that it is ill-suited to the analysis of quality rather than quantity and to the exploration of social process.

To shift the emphasis from quantity to quality and from social statics to social process entails situating the alleged worker-induced problems of British manufacturing production within the web of relations of which they are a part. In Part Three an attempt is made to move in this direction. We have not quite finished with the quantitative side of things yet, however. In fact, this chapter is prefaced by a brief consideration of one further international productivity comparison precisely in order to underline the extent to which such investigations are characterised by both type (a) and type (b) deficiencies.

This investigation, namely Caves' contribution to the 1980 Brookings Institution study, echoes a view that we have now heard many times before: that 'the difficulty' (as Caves calls the British productivity shortfall) lies in 'long-standing attitudes of the workforce that sustain hostility to change and co-operation' (1980, p. 179). But it is also important to refer to Caves' work for two further reasons. First, as Caves sees it: 'The economist's first job is to test whether the institutionalist explanation in fact holds up.' This promises the sort of analysis that we have not come across to any significant degree before. Second, Caves' most significant statistical result was that 'a British industry's productivity falls as the industry's need for managerial sophistication rises' (1980, p. 170). This suggests that Caves has applied his econometric technique to just some of those matters that the above remarks indicate require attention – the institutional context in general and the quality of management performance in particular.

In considering Caves' work, however, it is as well to remember that the formal and informal, substantive, procedural and disciplinary rules that make up industrial relations clearly involve two sides – management and labour – for in Caves' work a slippage occurs when he uses this term (or the analogous one 'labour relations'). It tends to become a synonym for workers – for what they do to management and for what they prevent management from doing. This is symptomatic of a wider imbalance in Caves' analysis, for whereas his most quoted claim is almost certainly that the British productivity problem 'originates deep within the social system' – which might suggest that both British workers and managers may have inherited a set of institutions that is not necessarily of either of their choosing – he is much less critical of what the evidence will bear in the case of managers than of workers.

Caves prefaces his consideration of British management's own possible contribution to the British productivity shortfall with the statement that productivity could be low 'either because management really is ineffective or because management cannot triumph over hostile forces that have gone undetected by the investigator' (1980, p. 153). Considered by itself this is quite reasonable. But an equivalent hesitancy does not characterise Caves' approach to British workers and to what has or has not been firmly established about them. Here, by contrast, Caves asserts straight away not that a great deal may have gone undetected by the investigator (or himself), but that 'Britain's system of industrial relations in the workplace, rooted ultimately in class and social attitudes, has been found to impair industrial productivity in a manner of ways'; and he follows this up by referring to four matters that he claims 'have been quantified and subjected to some international comparisons' – strikes, restrictive rules, policy overtime and the costs to management of dealing with labour relations (1980, p. 143). Indeed, whereas Caves seems to miss few opportunities to suggest that the practices of British workers directly or indirectly impede British management, even in quite subtle ways, his analysis of how British management enters the equation is altogether less extensive and more cautious, and not a few leads are unnecessarily neglected that might have pointed to management's door. Here, two examples serve to indicate Caves' seeming reluctance to follow up clues that might implicate British management.[1]

The first example is simple enough. It concerns marketing. Caves implies that worker-induced uncertainties about output rates leaves UK companies unsure how much they will have to sell, 'thereby reducing the effectiveness of the resources . . . allocate[d] to marketing activities' (1980, p. 147). Logically, this is a possibility. If UK workers are more likely to disrupt production than American ones this *could* have such an effect. But quite apart from the fact that such a proposition requires evidence about American workers to be furnished too (and Caves makes no attempt to provide this), the real oddity of this little example is that Caves fails, either at this point or as far as I can see anywhere else in his account, to consider whether UK management *are* up to scratch on marketing activities. Caves makes much in his contribution of what 'business executives' have told him. Perhaps they were not inclined to point to their own defects? Or perhaps

Caves simply found it too difficult to establish whether British managers were competent in marketing or not? It is even possible that they *are* proficient in marketing – though it is not difficult to find the contrary view being expressed, and there is indeed some evidence to support this (e.g. Connel, 1979). The point is, though that Caves implicates British workers in the productivity shortfall via the complex route of 'marketing activities', without considering how proficient British managers are in the performance of this function, or how proficient they are when compared to managers in the US.

A second example concerns Caves' claim that differences between British and American manufacturing performance cannot be accounted for in terms of differences in the capital goods themselves (1980, p. 170). As was noted in Chapter 1 it was just this sort of generalisation that lent credibility to the idea that British workers were responsible for the country's poor productivity record during the 1970s. As was also observed earlier, the credibility of such claims is likely to be given an extra boost when they derive from social scientific research. This makes it all the more important to take a careful look at how Caves substantiated this particular claim, which brings us immediately to the work of Bacon and Eltis, whose research on US and UK machine tools was important in moulding the opinion of politicians, economic journalists and their fellow economists in the mid to late 1970s. (For a particular example see the quote from Cairncross at p. 20 above.)

Caves himself was doubtless influenced by this research and the climate of opinion it helped to create, but he was also directly indebted to it since he actually made use of Bacon and Eltis' data. To go back to this original research is to find, however, that not only did it take the form of an analysis of the *vintage* of machine tools in Britain and America – so that its results were not incompatible with there being more machines in America, nor with some American machines being technically superior – but that Bacon and Eltis themselves took particular note of these possibilities. There is, in fact, room for debate about how this research should be interpreted. But just as Caves does not go into this, he also (together with a long line of other commentators) fails to follow up another possible management lead arising from this study. For Bacon and Eltis entertained the idea that the US/UK difference in performance might be accounted for in terms of a combination of three elements: (1) higher manning levels in the UK, (2) a higher utilisation rate in the US, and (3) some technical superiority in the US capital stock (1974, pp. 31–2). Concerning (2) they also entertained the idea that US *managements* might be 'more technically skilled in some firms and therefore better able to plan and organise production runs which maintain high utilisation of plant'. Bacon and Eltis later went on to explore pastures new (Bacon and Eltis, 1976), but it is worth noting that support for this last idea was in fact forthcoming from one of the managers whom Pratten interviewed, who had experience of both the US and the UK. 'It is my observation', he said, 'that productivity overall is often less in the UK, *primarily* because of less management attention to methods, systems and capital utilisation' (Pratten, 1976a, p. 52, my emphasis). Caves does not cite Pratten's managers' opinions on this point, though he does cite their evidence as it relates (adversely) to British workers, which is quite consistent with the general stance that he adopts throughout. For as Caves sees it, 'the hypothesis that poor management causes low productivity is essentially unsatisfying. It leaves the entrepreneur to carry the residual burden of opprobrium' (1980, p. 53).

Of course, the hypothesis that poor management causes low productivity *is* essentially unsatisfying – if, that is, it is not supported by evidence, since then it *does* leave the entrepreneur to carry the residual opprobrium. But what Caves does not make clear is that most of the literature on international differences in labour productivity suffers from a parallel, but quite different, defect: it leaves the British worker to carry the residual opprobrium – by failing to accord any equivalent weight to the investigation of management.

In so far as Caves takes his supporting evidence about British management from the existing professional literature, his own inadequate treatment of management is perhaps understandable. For example, despite the quotation cited above from Pratten's study, even some managers who had the chance to read a draft of Pratten's book were apparently led to comment on 'the omission of references to "administrative efficiency" ' (1976a, p. 52). It could also be the case that it really is more difficult to rank managements on a country-by-country basis than to demonstrate practices on the part of workers, as other writers have recently suggested (Cairncross *et al.* 1983, p. 75). To the extent that this is so it would be wrong to single out Caves for his one-sidedness. But this makes things worse rather than better, for it only serves to strengthen the suspicion that such a deficiency is one that is general to the literature and that professional students of international productivity differences are less than adept at investigating efficiency, especially the efficiency of managers.

In practice, there is reason to believe that British management does not score highly with respect to its ability to plan and organise production. That this might be important for the productivity outcome is obvious enough. It opens the way to an explanation of how British productivity might be lower, even when the capital goods *are* the same (a proposition, incidentally, that sits uneasily with another one – that British workers retard the rate of technical change – though it is not uncommon to find both ideas expressed in almost the same breath). We will bring some evidence together that bears on the planning and organisational record of British management in later chapters. At this point it is simply being maintained that, in Caves' own treatment of workers and managers, there are innumerable small ways in which he points the finger of suspicion in the former direction rather than the latter.

True enough, Caves allows that evidence from comparisons between foreign affiliates and domestic companies 'seems' to 'support the hypothesis of inferior UK management performance', though he then adds immediately, 'but not conclusively'. True enough, too, at one point he does tentatively advance the view that managerial ineffectiveness 'should probably take some blame' for UK productivity, but he prefaces this with the further assertion that 'low capital productivity *can be* partly attributed to labour practices'. It is indeed quite in keeping with the general tone of his discussion that whereas he relates UK capacity utilisation to 'idleness from strikes', rather than make any specific reference to deficiencies on the management side he refers only to a 'variety of other constraints on management's ability to utilise its plant' (Caves, 1980, pp. 153, 155, 169).

There are other difficulties in Caves' work that merit attention, and these stem from the method of analysis that he employs. From our standpoint it is a limitation of his study that it is conducted in price terms rather than physical ones and that it takes the form of an analysis of differences between industries rather than companies. But over and above this, there is Caves' habit of transforming the complex world of industry into 'variables'. Some indication of what this amounts to is that he develops not one but three variables of labour force gender composition. That Caves

calls these measures 'FLAB 1', 'FLAB 2' and 'FLAB 3' says little
for his credentials as a sensitive analyst of social structure; that he
reports he was mindful that 'business executives' had 'frequently'
suggested to him that ' "bloody-mindedness" . . . is much greater
in industries with largely male labour forces' is also testimony in
its own way to the marriage of econometric technique and
business opinion that permeates his work more generally. But
Caves only arrived at his statistical conclusions after what he calls
'a good deal of experimentation', which he concedes he was
'forced to do' (1980, p. 167). This suggests, as far as the 'labour
relations variables' are concerned, that some measures ('variables')
have been selected to work with rather than others, according to
whether they yield statistically significant associations, and that
interacting combinations of variables may well in turn have been
selected on the same basis. It could be that the statistical results
that Caves ends up with will prove to be reliable and that they are
indeed valid, but those sceptical of the higher empiricism may well
reflect that if enough variables are fed into a computer something
'significant' is likely to come out at the end. In any case, though
the term 'variables' sounds scientifically precise, it is always as
well to enquire exactly what it is that a particular 'variable' stands
for.[2]

We have already encountered the difficulty of supposing that
Caves' measure of the age of machine tools (on which,
incidentally, he lacks data for more than half of his industries:
1980, p. 170n) is a satisfactory measure of technical inferiority or
superiority. To consider the measure of 'quality of management'
that he employs is to encounter a similar difficulty. For in addition
to its being a feature of Caves' general discussion that circumstantial evidence about management deficiencies is not followed
up with alacrity, his own measure of management quality – which
does *appear* to implicate British management – is constructed in
such a way that it does not, and cannot, serve as a test of quality.
Briefly, Caves finds a statistical association between his dependent
variable (VPW) and his measure of management quality (MGRS).
But in order to decode the possible meaning of this it is necessary
to appreciate not only what VPW is – and actually it is a measure
of the value of net output per person employed in the UK industry
(summed over 1963, 1968 and 1972) divided by the value added
per person employed in the US counterpart industry (summed over
1963, 1967 and 1972) – but what MGRS is as well, and MGRS is
'managerial and kindred employees as a percentage of total

employees, US counterpart industry, 1970'. In other words, it is arguably not a measure of management quality but of management *quantity*. As such, Caves' statistical association suggests that the trouble with British industry on the management side is that there are not enough managers; that there are 'Too Few Chiefs'. This makes for a neat reversal of the old British shop floor adage about 'Too Few Indians; Too Many Chiefs', but it also opens the door to the interpretation that bigger management teams may themselves be more common in one particular circumstance – when the poor bloody 'Indians' produce sufficient surplus to maintain them. This line of thought has been long rehearsed in some of the literature on the theory of the firm – for example Williamson (1964) or Galbraith (1967) – but Caves does not refer to it.

In Caves' work, then, despite initial appearances which suggest the contrary, further support is forthcoming for the view that management lacks detailed scrutiny in international studies of the determinants of labour productivity, and this despite, if not because of, the close association that those who conduct them are apt to have with managers. This is clearly of some importance: it has implications for the implicit or explicit claim that must underpin all such studies – that they are in fact comparing like with like or that all things have been considered. Sometimes, of course, it is possible that management has been considered, but that as a result of such deliberations any deficiencies discovered have not seen the light of day in published reports (the Think Tank report may well be an example of this). But where management is concerned it does seem that an acute inspection of what the evidence will bear has not always been the order of the day. At one point, for example, Caves, taking his lead from Pratten, plays down the likelihood that there would be significant differences in the qualifications and performance of managers in international companies. But he fails to observe that this might sit awkwardly with another view that Pratten advances on the very same page: namely, that 'improvements in labour productivity after changes in management . . . showed that management can have quantitatively dramatic effects on productivity' (1976a, p. 51). He also omits to make clear that Pratten reports: 'I did not make a survey of the formal qualifications of managers, at any level.' Nor, needless to say, did Caves. This raises the question of whether international differences in management may contribute more to productivity differentials than is commonly supposed. After all, if you don't look you don't see. In Caves' particular case it also suggests that the available evidence has not been accorded the weight it might deserve, and this despite his statistical evidence on VPW and MGRS (a category that of course includes 'kindred employees', of whom more later).

Since Caves claims to have demonstrated a statistically significant association between his measure of management quality and his main dependent variable, it may be that he assumes it to be obvious that British management *is* implicated in the poorer economic performance he finds in Britain compared to the US. It would be highly improbable that management did not have some influence on the relative success or failure of an industry, however. The question is therefore one of degree. And simply because the 'variables', as Caves call them, will in all probability interact in highly complex ways, and there are limits to the sensitivity of quantified information, a good deal of the analysis of this matter of degree must rest on inference: about which social processes are explored or speculated on in which connection, and which are explored the most extensively. What is being maintained here is that Caves makes more inferences about the way British workers are linked into 'the difficulty', and that he does not follow up a number of leads that might be interpreted in such a way as to link in British management. Even if there were no significant differences in UK/US manufacturing investment, for example, and even if the quality as well as the vintage of machinery were to be the same in both countries, it could still be possible that the actual organisation of production differed; that there were different linkages on the management side between research and production, that marketing expertise was more highly developed in one country than in the other, etc. Caves does not go into these questions, the investigation of which might have tipped the balance the other way. This much said, however – and Caves' work having provided a number of examples of type (a) and (b) deficiencies, as well as a conclusion about the lack of sophistication of some British managers that, formally speaking, his own evidence cannot bear – what *is* the quality of British management?

In 1835 Richard Cobden wrote after a visit to America that 'our only chance of national prosperity lies in the timely remodelling of our system, so as to put it as nearly as possible upon an equality with the improved management of the Americans' (cited in

Barnett, 1975, p. 7). Three-quarters of a century later, by which
time several enquiries into British technical education had already
been conducted, Shadwell even dared to hope that Britain was set
to match the technical education then provided in Germany
(1913, p. 640). Yet a century and a half after Cobden, the leading
stars in the firmament of British industry have been none other
than Giordano, an American, at British Oxygen; a Scots
American, MacGregor – first at British Leyland, then at British
Steel then at the National Coal Board; and of course a South
African, Edwardes – most notably at BL, but before that at the
Chloride Group and afterwards at ICL and Dunlop. For some
commentators, among them Sampson (1982, p. 430), the presence
of men like Edwardes only serves to underline the lack of business
acumen, drive, industrial spirit, among England's own 'ruling
tribes'. There may be something in this idea that outsiders have a
better chance of cutting through the many layers of British 'class'
and culture. In any case it is quite refreshing to find 'class'
discussed in a way that does not get automatically reduced to
workers; to what *they* feel, to what *they* think, and to what *they*
do or do not do. But what people can do – any people, workers or
managers – is in part a function of their technical capacities, and
the quality of management is not reducible to matters of self-
presentation and style; in some of its aspects it involves technical
ability too. It is this technical aspect of the quality of management that is of interest here.

Now such is the inclination of many economists to put a price
tag on everything, that they sometimes use wages as a measure of
the quality of labour, with the implication that this reflects skill
(Raimon and Stoikov, 1967). Some international productivity
comparisons also take average compensation per employee as a
'surrogate indicator' of comparative labour force quality (Smith *et
al.*, 1982, p. 49). The not unreasonable assumption that the value
of the work an individual can perform can be affected by his or
her education sometimes also leads students of international
productivity differences to ask themselves decidedly weird
questions – 'Is a college graduate to be counted as the equivalent
of 1½, 2 or 3 elementary graduates?' (Denison, 1967, pp. 79, 82).
The reader will be spared the pursuit of further such oddities here,
for as far as the formal qualifications of British managers go, there
is no need to seek out surrogate measures.

The fact is that today the number of members of the working
population with a university degree or professional qualification in

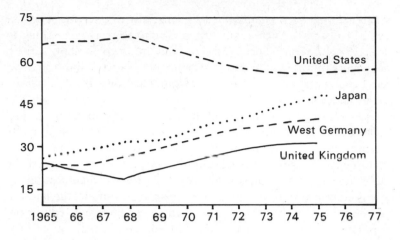

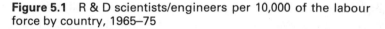

*Source*: Schott (1981), Fig. 3, p.15.

**Figure 5.1** R & D scientists/engineers per 10,000 of the labour force by country, 1965–75

engineering or technology is about 40 per cent lower in Britain than in Germany, and the gap rises to about 75 per cent if only degree holders are compared (Prais, 1981b, p. 50). To look further afield, to Japan, is to discover that in 1978 nearly 80,000 engineers graduated in that country, compared to about 10,000 in the UK – four times as many per head of population (NEDO, 1982b, p. 8). Moreover, whether the comparison is drawn with Japan or West Germany or the US the indications are that throughout the 1970s more of those so qualified found their way into R & D than was the case in Britain (see Figure 5.1). It's much the same story as far as production managers are concerned. In 1977 a Department of Industry enquiry found it 'disquieting that there is evidence that industrial managers in Britain, particularly those concerned with the production function, tend to be less well qualified in academic and vocational terms than their continental counterparts'. Looking at the academic qualifications of British managers in manufacturing, it considered that 'most of the evidence suggests they have not caught up with their competitors and that there are fewer technical people at the higher levels in Britain than elsewhere' (Department of Industry 1977, pp. 1, 4). The authors of a survey of British managers were to reiterate this view in the early 1980s: 'it is hard to avoid concluding that British managers are relatively undereducated and certainly less well qualified than their counterparts in some other countries' (Poole *et al.*, 1981, p. 49). Such a conclusion *is* hard to resist: according to the 1981 Labour Force Survey, out of two million British managers only 116,000 had first or higher degrees, and over two-thirds of a million had no formal qualifications at all (*Employment Gazette*, April 1983).

A quantitative measure such as a head-count of formal qualifications is by no means an exact measurement of what really matters for productivity – quality of performance. But official reports *also* suggest deficiencies in this respect – even amongst the minority of those in Britain who do hold formal qualifications at the graduate level. The Finniston Report, for example, the latest in a long line of enquiries into British engineering education, reported in 1980 that engineering graduates 'usually have little experience of engineering tasks as they occur in practice' (Finniston Report, 1980, p. 84). It is all of a piece with this that when Finniston asked his research staff to look at all previous reports – going back to 1852 when Sir Lyon Playfair had first described the superiority of German engineers – he realised that none of them had been followed by effective action (Sampson, 1982, p. 223). All of this makes for a different sort of account from those that assume that management can be treated as a constant in international comparisons – and from those (the great majority) that hark back to explanations that are couched in terms of 'attitudes', especially of workers. For if British managers tend to lack academic or vocational qualifications, if this weakness is particularly evident amongst production managers, if Britain produces fewer engineers, and these are not strong on practical application – and if all this has been so for several generations – it is not at all difficult to conclude that British management may well have played a significant part in the productivity shortfall. Though such a situation may well have been aided and abetted by British attitudes to technology and industry, it can also have effects in its own right.

Of course, the quality of management, and especially of production management, cannot be measured in purely technical terms – 'man-management', as it is sometimes called, is also involved and so, at this and higher levels, is organisational skill. For the moment, however, my point is simply that there is much to suggest that British management is relatively lacking in technical ability, and that this is something that the more micro investigations into the determinants of British labour productivity have typically neglected.

Relatively micro comparisons of the determinants of international labour productivity of the type reviewed in Chapter 3 and 4 generally had very little to say about differences in the technical composition of management. However, with the exception of one particular investigation (Prais, 1981a), their authors have also tended to leave us to assume that the technical capacities of different labour forces can be disregarded in international comparisons – hence in part the stress on attitudes and motivational elements in their discussions of international differences amongst 'the men'. Remarkably enough, a similar omission characterises a good deal of marxist-inspired research into the labour process. For despite the central importance it accords to labour-power this has also generally failed to investigate possible international differences in the technical capacities of advanced capitalist labour forces. In this respect it might be said that much marxist analysis has been deficient in its analysis of what goes *into* the labour process – as well as giving little consideration to international differences in what comes *out* of it, as was argued in Chapter 1.[3]

As far as international investigations into the determinants of labour productivity are concerned, the signs are that this omission may have been an unfortunate one. It is sobering to realise that in 1980 German employers were making over six times more apprenticeships available than British employers had done, even in the early 1970s, and this for a school population not much greater than that of the UK (Dixon, 1984). In fact the UK–German difference in 'intermediate qualifications' (apprenticeships, City and Guilds certificates and the like) is yet more pronounced in favour of Germany than are the differences that pertain to management. In German manufacturing Prais found the greater part of the workforce to have such intermediate qualifications – a whole 60 per cent, compared to 30 per cent in Britain; and *pro rata* there were more people with intermediate qualifications in Germany in each and every one of the dozen manufacturing industries he compared (Prais, 1981b, p. 47 and p. 48, Table 1).

When British management's technical qualifications were considered it was necessary to concede that quantity did not of course necessarily spell quality of performance. The same holds for craft and technical qualifications. But Prais also indicates that – as with management so with labour more generally – the breadth and nature of the skills conferred by the German qualifications is

superior (Prais, 1981a, 1981b). This makes all the more plausible
his further contention: 'It is clear that output per employee for the
past two decades has been higher in Germany, and has been rising
more rapidly, than in Britain' and that there seems 'little doubt
that the higher level of qualification of the German labour force
has made a contribution, and probably a very important
contribution, to that outcome' (1981b, p. 57). Subsequent
research by Katrak, which indicates that the 'skill intensity' of the
manufacturing goods exported from Britain in the 1970s rose less
rapidly than that of the basket of goods imported, and that this
shift was much greater for Britain than for Germany, or for the
US, gives a yet sharper edge to Prais' comment that Britain is
behind in this respect and lacks a technically trained and
technically adaptable labour force (Prais, 1981b, p. 57; Katrak,
1982, pp. 38–47.

Another and no less significant consequence of general deficiency in technical skills may well be, as Prais has also argued (in
Carter, 1981, pp. 32–4), that British management lacks technical
support on the periphery of its own ranks – the engineer thus
being 'like a skilled surgeon trying to work without adequate
nursing help'. This, too, suggests that British manufacturing's lack
of technical manpower may have had direct and indirect effects on
the level and rate of change of UK productivity – and that it
would have probably done so if UK workers had been just as
hard-working and co-operative as we have been told so often that
workers are elsewhere. The point of this chapter has been to draw
attention to this and of course to the related point that for the
most part those who conducted micro productivity comparisons
in the 1970s scarcely bothered to investigate international
differences in labour-power at all.


Of course, even if it is the case that British industry is relatively
deficient in the technical quality of its management and its 'men',
the claim has often been made that British manufacturing is
overmanned, especially in auxiliary functions. This same message
comes across in all of the major 1970s productivity comparisons –
from Pratten on Britain, America, Germany and France; Prais on
Britain, America and Germany; the Think Tank Report on the
British car industry and its continental counterparts; and of course
from Caves on Britain and America. The consensus is such that
the automatic reaction is likely to be that it must reflect the

reality. The counting of heads is itself by no means always a simple matter, however, and a particular problem arises with sub-contract work – that is, with work that goes towards a given employer's final product but which is not performed by those who are formally in his employ. The next chapter therefore starts out by considering the possible significance of this. In an attempt to set the labour-side determinants of British productivity more firmly in context, consideration is then given to some further aspects of international differences in quantity and quality that were often given much less prominence in studies of the type reviewed in earlier chapters.

# 6 'The difficulty' reconsidered (2): Different quantities, and another side to the quality of labour

'The Japanese have a particular ability to work at high speed on the production line with no problems: their devotion to the job is very different from most other nationalities'' – that's what a spokesman for the Society of Motor Manufacturers and Traders told a House of Commons Select Committee in 1980. It is what an awful lot of British workers have been told in recent years as well. But the public noise raised by British employers about the exceptional devotion to work of Japanese workers has rarely been matched by public displays of the concern that some of them have clearly experienced about the rather exceptional structure of Japanese industry – even though, according to one account (Fryer, 1982b), a confidential document was circulating in the EEC Committee of Automobile Constructors in 1982 which claimed that the secret of Japan's success lay in an underworld of tens of thousands of small suppliers. The document implied that many of these supplier-firms were 'sweatshops', which in turn was held to explain how Nissan could buy in components at 30 per cent cheaper than BL or Ford. Other research conducted in Japan amply confirms that the structure of its car industry is different, and that the eleven major Japanese vehicle assemblers – which, it might be said, truly are 'assemblers' rather than manufacturers – each stand at the top of a more or less closely integrated pyramid of thousands of primary, secondary and tertiary sub-contractors (Smith, 1983; Dodwell, 1983).

Various forms of sub-contract are well to the fore in other Japanese industries. In the steel industry, for example, it is common practice to contract out a large share of maintenance work as well as raw materials handling and the actual shipment of finished steel products. In a number of instances 80 per cent of maintenance is contracted out. Cases are on record where almost half a workforce of 7,000 has been supplied by outside contractors (Hogan, 1972, p. 87). Much was made of the high productivity of other country's workforces in the public debate about the British steel industry at the end of the 1970s, the British rates being variously cited at between 100 and 140 tonnes per annum, compared to 200 to 250 tonnes for German workers – with startling figures of 400 and 500-odd tonnes per worker being cited for Japan (Upham, 1980, p. 17). It is pertinent therefore that a recent Japanese researcher has been able to demonstrate that the so often cited labour productivity figures for steel in his country drop dramatically when allowance is made for sub-contract workers, in one case down to 210 tonnes per man-year (Matsuzaki, 1980). Similarly, the authors of a recent financial analysis of BSC would seem to have every reason to insist on the need for 'matched plant comparisons' (Bryer, Brignall and Maunders, 1982). It is to be welcomed that several researchers have now helped to put the Japanese steel productivity miracle in context as did the Iron and Steel Trades Confederation (see, for example, Manwaring, 1981; Blewitt, 1983; ISTC *Sense or Nonsense; Steelworkers' Banner*, No. 6).[1]

As far as maintenance in particular is concerned, there is reason to believe that contracting-out has also been less common in Britain than in countries other than Japan, and that this may have been the case with a number of other 'indirect' functions as well – indirect functions having been the very ones that were found to be overmanned by all of the 1970s productivity investigators. A recent NEDO report on the food and drink industries is relevant here. Having collected together a number of international comparisons it prefaced its review of them by pointing to the stress they placed on 'indirect labour' – 'variously defined' (it stated advisedly), 'but normally including maintenance, catering, laundry and medical services, quality control, building repairs and security'. Noting 'greater differences between the UK and other countries in terms of output per indirect employee than in terms of output per direct employee', it concluded: 'these differences largely appeared to stem from a greater amount of sub-contracting of indirect operations overseas'. It suggested also that 'in the USA the use of sub-contractors was more cost-effective than doing such tasks "in house" ', this, in turn, being attributed to 'the greater availability of such contractors' in the US. The NEDO Report relates to one industry only. It has technical limitations, and it also cites specific instances of demarcation and lack of work flexibility in UK maintenance operations (Food and Drink Manufacturing EDC Report, 1982, p. 11, para. 3.7ii, pp. 33-4, paras 5.33 and 5.34). What is being suggested here, however, is that this is probably something more like the full picture than, for example, Caves' summary that 'the fact that overmanning often occurs in auxiliary functions (maintenance, canteen services and so on), where craft unions are important, seems to signify restrictive labour practices' (Caves, 1980, p. 145).

Once comparative statisticians have shown overmanning to exist (at least to their own satisfaction) they often seem to feel little need to do more than allude to restrictive practices on the part of workers. The problem here is not simply that the actual level of British manning may have been overestimated, though this could be the case if, for example, sub-contract was not carefully allowed for – but that, by proceeding in this way, the full significance of differences in manning levels may be lost from view. For instance, it is quite commonly held that overmanning exists on the maintenance side in British industry because of craft demarcations and the employment of craftsmen's mates, these being unknown figures at some continental plants. But to look at an industry in some depth – as the NEDO did with another industry, chemicals – is to bring to light something also glimpsed in the last chapter: that more workers on the continent are *trained* to a higher level, thus enhancing their efficiency, individually and collectively (NEDC, 1973; Taylor, 1982, p. 90). Indeed, as Prais suggests (1981b, p. 57), certain organisational differences between Britain and West Germany may to a large extent reflect the need to make the best use in Britain of skills that are relatively scarce – British industry being reluctant to engage qualified craftsmen on production when they are more urgently needed at higher levels, or need to be shared out to provide general services. Clearly, such an absence cannot be solely attributed to trade union restrictive practices.

The greater resort to sub-contract in other countries, at least up to the end of the 1970s, poses questions about how firmly the extent of overmanning has sometimes been established, and thus about the extent of 'the difficulty' that is to be accounted for. Taken in conjunction with the probability that the (technical) quality of the British labour force may compare unfavourably with that in some other countries, and that British management itself appears to be technically deficient, this serves to caution against any tendency to automatically attribute a productivity shortfall to curmudgeonly British workers. It is possible, however, that the composition of the British labour force has been less than ideal (in capitalist terms) in quite another respect, so that for much of the post-war period there were not only too few workers who were relatively well qualified technically, but too few workers who were relatively underqualified as citizens as well – that is, too few who were sufficiently *vulnerable*, inside production or out of it, whether because of legal constraint or social disadvantage as induced through other means.

This other side of 'the problem' of quality in the composition of the British labour force is something that many productivity researchers seem reluctant to spell out. In discussing differences in general efficiency, for example, Pratten tells us that in Switzerland managements could put in new machinery 'without negotiations' and that 'co-operation between management and labour was very good', but he fails to relate this to the extensive use of immigrant labour in Swiss manufacturing, which might contribute to such an outcome (see Pratten, 1976a, pp. 55-6, and on Swiss immigrant labour, Wicks, 1983). This sort of thing is typical of much productivity research. Again and again instances are to be found where important facets of social structure are referred to, but not situated in their context, where certain leads are followed up with alacrity and others not, a superficial and in some respects misleading understanding being fostered as a consequence of this – misleading because it fails to make plain where 'attitudes' *come from*. The closest Pratten himself gets to explaining this is in a footnote on German 'guest workers'. Reporting that their performance was generally said to be 'satisfactory', he does at least add here that 'the need to renew their contracts provided a means of maintaining discipline' (1976a, p. 57n).[2] The authors of another comparative study (Smith *et al.*, 1982, p. 51) also report with reference to German 'guest labour' that 'there are grounds for believing that, in terms of effort and application and the amount of labour derived per worker, the quality of this, perhaps compliant labour force, is especially high' – but they too fail to say anything about the quality of *life* that these workers 'enjoy' or about the conditions of their existence that might make them 'compliant'.

'Do foreign workers work harder than German workers?' The

German mass circulation *Bildzeitung* was asking its readers this
question as early as 1966. There is reason to think that they did
'work harder'. German 'guest workers', who were recruited on
unequal terms to sustain Germany's post-war growth when the
country had exhausted other pools of labour – the large number
of post-war unemployed, the seven million expellees from
territories lost to the Eastern Bloc and refugees from the GDR (on
which see Castles and Kosack, 1974, 1980) – experienced social,
economic and at times legal and political disadvantages. Some
multi-nationals made extensive use of such labour, both in West
Germany and in other Western European countries. In 1976, for
example, migrant workers accounted for about 70 per cent of the
production line workforce at Ford Saarlouis, 90 per cent at
Cologne, with some three-quarters of all production line work in
Ford's German, French, Belgian and Dutch operations being
performed by migrant workers from Turkey, Spain, Italy,
Morocco and so on (CIS, p. 35). The compliance of such workers,
like that of any other oppressed group, is not guaranteed for ever
of course (as was to be made plain in the 1980s, most notably in
the Renault and Peugeot car plants in France). But in the 1960s
and into the 1970s it was likely that such workers were more
'compliant', because they were more vulnerable. In the mid-1970s
the so-called 'minority' labour force in Britain stood at about 7
per cent of the total: in France and Germany and Switzerland the
figures were higher, at 8, 11, and 26 per cent (the proportions in
all Western European countries being more pronounced in
manufacturing and building). Despite some convergence in more
recent years between British state policy and that practised in
other Western European countries, and even despite the settlement
of some immigrants in these countries, migrant workers in other
countries had been, and to a significant extent still are, subject to
yet greater disadvantage than the very real disadvantage that has
been experienced by many immigrants and non-whites in Britain
(Castles *et al.*, 1984, p. 128 and *passim*).

During the 1970s Ford Britain often made use of the 'Cologne
yardstick'. But in Ford management's hands this did not stretch to
take in the context in which work was performed in Cologne or in
many other of Ford's Western European plants. And so it is
generally with most of the accounts that productivity specialists
have provided of their *bête noire* British industry, cars. As we saw
in Chapter 4, in the 1970s British workers in this industry were
held to be the cause of a whole number of difficulties. By contrast,

international differences in the constraints that beset different car industry labour forces (or significant parts of them) generally went unremarked or got lost behind the cover of talk about the peculiarities of British 'industrial relations'. It was rare indeed in the 1970s to find accounts that gave due recognition, not just to British 'full employment' (such as it was as the decade progressed), but to the *other side* of this – the past experience of poverty and near poverty and the enduring vulnerability that characterised significant parts of many manufacturing workforces elsewhere (the sort of places where, *à la* study of international productivity differences, 'co-operation' might have been termed 'very good'). An account by Dunnett paints a very different picture, precisely because he does take the context seriously. He makes plain that an 'important sociological factor common to the labour force of the other major car-producing countries but not the UK' was that 'all other countries had access to a labour pool attempting to escape from immediate poverty'. 'The labour force in Germany, France, Italy and the USA had similar characteristics. All the European car factories employed many "guest" workers from southern Europe and North Africa, whilst much of the labour on Detroit's production lines were first generation black immigrants from the South' often with 'a first hand experience of real poverty' (Dunnett, 1980, pp. 144, 182). In Japan, Brazil, and of course in the newly industrialising countries in the South Pacific, it is commonly acknowledged that social and economic deprivation is an important ingredient in economic 'success', as in some cases is outright political repression. When it comes to our own doorstep, many authorities seem less than eager to speak the language of social, political and economic disadvantage. Such important sociological considerations do, however, help to put all allusions to 'morale', 'attitudes' and 'spirit' into proper perspective.

The fact is that such real disadvantage can have real effects, not simply in terms of lower labour costs but in terms of higher costs *to labour*, and not only in newly industrialising countries either. For example, a matched plant comparison between two Chrysler subsidiaries at Ryton in the UK and Poissy in France showed that, in 1976, the French plant, in which about 40 per cent of the labour force and 80 per cent of the assembly workers were foreign (with nothing comparable to this situation existing at Ryton) produced the same C6 car in twenty-nine man-hours as compared with thirty-six at Ryton. In this case, as in so many others, it has to be taken on trust that the engineers had taken account of all the factors that might have flawed the comparison, like the older machinery and shorter production runs at Ryton. But in this instance there are two considerations that add credibility to the view that the differences in productivity were the result of a greater intensity of work. First, there is the French union the Confédération Française du Travail (CFT),[3] which in the view of the French management adopted an 'attitude of co-operation', but which, according to several other accounts, was manifestly weak, and which has been typified, amongst many other things, as 'a right-wing company union' (Grunberg, 1983; Linhart, 1981, Trehel, 1982). Second, there is the fact that Chrysler France could decide whether the migrant workers' one- or two-year contracts would be extended. In the light of this, we can well believe a manager's claim that 'there are few problems in their work attitudes'. It is indeed only by taking account of such things that we can begin to find some of the key elements for an explanation of how it has come about that, in the words of an industrial engineer, whereas when 'the work process is being changed, the British union demand negotiations', at Poissy the workers 'are just told what to do'. At Poissy it would seem that it was not only workers who were 'told what to do', however. A doctor, dismissed for speaking out, reports that the medical staff were directed: 'don't interfere with production'. That there was a need to speak out is confirmed by the more dangerous work practices at Poissy – an industrial engineer claiming that operators there were 'sitting on the side of presses with absolutely no guards and with the presses coming down inches away from their heads', whereas, at Ryton, a man could not operate a press without a guard. As he put it: 'In France they [management] get away with much more.'[4] At Poissy, as a consequence of this, not only productivity but also the accident rate was higher (as Chrysler's own statistics showed – see Grunberg, 1983).

Of course, the interpretation of international data on industrial accidents is subject to difficulties of a similar order to those that bedevil productivity comparisons. But what evidence there is suggests that the fatality rate, which for obvious reasons is likely to be the most reliable index, was lower in Britain in the 1970s than in France, Germany or Switzerland, as can be seen from Table 6.1. Other evidence points in the same direction. In 1974, for example, the year before the Think Tank enquiry, figures for industrial accidents per 10,000 employees in the British car industry were as follows – Vauxhall 142, Chrysler 110, BL 138

**Table 6.1 Fatality rates in Western European manufacturing industry**

|      | UK    | France | W. Germany | Switzerland |
|------|-------|--------|------------|-------------|
| 1975 | .037  | .103   | .160       | .092        |
| 1976 | .034  | .091   | .140       | .088        |
| 1977 | .034  | .090   | .130       | .091        |
| 1978 | .031  | .083   | .140       | .071        |
| 1979 | .029  | .071   | .130       | .098        |
| 1980 | .027  | .071   | .120       | .100        |

*Source*: ILO (1984) Table 29.
*Note*: UK figures are for reported accident rates per 1,000 wage-earners; West German figures are for compensated accidents per 1,000 man-years of 300 days each; the French and Swiss rates are for compensated accidents per 1,000 wage-earners.

and Ford 228; in West Germany for the same year the figures were higher – Ford 237, Adam Opel 350, Daimler Benz 769 (*Labour Research* 1976, p. 35-6). Those who specialise in international productivity comparisons have signally failed to take such facts into account. In this, once again, they have followed management's lead. Throughout this century British managements have berated their British workers with facts and figures about the higher productivity of foreign competitors. In the last two decades those who manage multinational companies have harped on this same theme with respect to the higher productivity of those of their plants that operate outside Britain. But managers have never gone out of their way to illuminate some of the objective conditions that may have contributed to such an outcome, and, especially as far as questions of safety are concerned, the consequences of adopting these practices for those they urge to produce more in Britain. Workers face an uphill struggle in piecing together such information for themselves. But some have, as at Ford's Halewood plant – and having discovered that in West German press shops over ten times as many arms, legs, hands and feet were amputed as in Britain, such workers have learned their lesson: fight against 'on-line' maintenance, insist on proper guards and safe working procedures, and, as the *Halewood Worker* put it in 1981: 'next time management starts quoting "PRODUCTION" figures for other countries, ask them to produce the accident figures as well . . . also ask them [about] immigrant workers' (cited in Beynon, 1985, pp. 376-7).

Were productivity researchers to concern themselves more with such for the most part hidden facets of the 'quality of labour', it is likely that they would not use such mild expressions as that the performance of (disadvantaged) labour is 'satisfactory'. Perhaps then we would not be treated to so many vague generalities about the possible significance of (apparently free-floating) national 'attitudes' either – a tendency that, unfortunately, is not confined to the ranks of economists. Recent research into international differences in the 'work ethic' is a case in point. This found the work ethic to be at a low level in both the UK and West Germany – a surprising finding in the light of the British stereotype of the Germans as hard working. But the researchers held that this did not translate into lower productivity in Germany in the same way that it did in the UK because German employers reacted to the morale problem with 'strategies that defuse[d] the impact of negative work attitudes on productivity'. They did this, we are told, by 'replacing people by machines' (which is clear enough), and by 'making special efforts to hire workers least affected by the self-expressive values' (which is not clear at all – but which would seem to refer in particular to 'foreigners', 'mainly Yugoslavs and Turks'). Again, then, the reality that lies behind this aseptic and convoluted jargon is that German employers had found themselves a vulnerable and disadvantaged workforce. As we have seen, to a greater extent than in Britain, so had employers in other Western European countries (Yankelovich *et al.*, 1984, pp. 62, 72, 75).[5]


Now, if it is held that the greater vulnerability of workers in some other countries helped employers achieve higher levels and rates of change of productivity – though at a cost to workers themselves, especially where migrant labourers and those on sub-contract were concerned – it might seem that it could equally well be argued that it was the relative lack of vulnerability that lay behind the frequently alleged lower productivity of British workers. Such an argument has much to recommend it, provided of course that a whole host of *other* possible determinants of productivity are taken into account (some of which are considered in Chapters 7 and 8). The line of enquiry that we are seeking to open up is a little more complicated than even this would suggest, however.

First of all, there are two faces of the 'quality of labour', not one, and it is their *combined effects* that have to be considered. As far as quality in its technical sense is concerned, it is only fair to concede that comparative research between Britain and other Western European countries is less well developed than is the case for Britain and West Germany. But Prais claims that 'the "German system" [of vocational training] also operates in adjacent countries, though with local modifications' and also reports that 'the systems of training in many other European countries (the Netherlands, Switzerland, Sweden and, more recently, France) have become increasingly similar to that of Germany' (1981a, p. 29; 1981b, p. 59).[6] Given this, and what has also come to light in this chapter – that many other Western European economies *also* had a significant pool of vulnerable labour available – the British 'labour problem' can be more accurately specified in terms of a *double* problem of labour force composition: the lack of higher technical ability in the one part being compounded by a lack of a disadvantaged pool of labour in the other. In other words, vulnerability (or the lack of it) was not the only difficulty that faced British employers on the labour front in the mid to late 1970s. But there is yet another twist to all this.

The UK itself was far from lacking a disadvantaged workforce in the 1970s. The increasing number of women who entered employment after the war, and in particular those of them in part-time work, fell into just such a category.[7] What is noticeable here, though, is that unlike migrant labour in Western Europe (which, when employed on such contracts as those at Poissy, was yet more vulnerable than Asian and West Indian immigrants in Britain), these women were heavily concentrated in 'services' – in distribution, insurance, banking and finance, public administration, etc. In short, with some notable exceptions, like food, drink and tobacco, and textiles and clothing, they worked outside manufacturing; in 1975 about 90 per cent of those employed in the motor industry were men, for example. On the labour front, therefore, part of the problem, for manufacturing capital, was not simply the *lack* of a vulnerable workforce in the UK, but a comparative disadvantage in the technical composition of the manufacturing workforce, and the concentration of a potential pool of relatively disadvantaged workers in *other* sectors of the economy.[8]

So far as the comparative disadvantage experienced by workers in different nations is concerned, it is of course true that British manufacturing capital in general was relatively less well placed *vis-à-vis* its labour force as it came out of the Second World War. In the US, where the labour force had long been divided and re-divided by successive waves of immigrants, the overall labour market was further swelled during the post-war expansion both, as in Britain, by an influx of married women and also by a shift out of employment in agriculture (the Japanese peasantry also constituted a notable labour reserve, and a similar shift from the land was evident in much of Western Europe). Not only this, but the German and French labour movements had *also* been severely set back by fascism (the repression of trade unions and workers' organisations also having been felt in Spain and Italy, and of course in Japan). By contrast, the labour movement in Britain came out of the war stronger than it went into it, wartime Britain having witnessed a greater degree of state planning than ever before or since, official unionism having worked closely at national level with the state machine as part of the war effort, and shop floor unionism having played an integral role too. That the new (majority) Labour government proceeded to dismantle many state controls and was content to leave the internal control structures of the industries it nationalised largely unchanged is testimony to the nature of the politics that held sway within it and to the nature and rather limited extent of the challenge that British unionism actually posed, especially to profitable segments of British capital. But despite this, after the war the balance of advantage to capital was more pronounced in many countries outside Britain.

Not only did British trade unions come out of the war intact, but the structure of British trade unionism remained somewhat distinctive too. Thus the organisations of the skilled workers lived on (including those of the craftsmen in maintenance). In the immediate post-war years something else lived on, however – the fear of unemployment. Widespread during the war years (see pp. 6–7), this had also been widespread in the period between the two great world wars, and had indeed formed part of the context within which the British form of scientific management (in the guise of the Bedaux system) had been introduced. That scientific management was most marked in those industries that had not been established on a craft basis, had helped the organisations of skilled workers to survive. But that it had come late to Britain, as compared to the (then) main competing nations, Germany and the US, has a further significance. For whereas it is doubtful that scientific management has ever been sweet music in workers' ears anywhere, in Britain it may have had a yet more hollow ring than in other countries, where it was introduced in more expansionary times and where it could be accompanied by a vision of progress and prosperity (Maier, 1970). As Littler observes, scientific management was introduced to Britain 'amidst the stench of unemployment' (1982, pp. 115, 141, 144).

Taken in combination, these elements – in particular the absence of fascism, the long-standing fear of unemployment and the particular circumstances in which scientific management was introduced – make a reasonable *prima facie* case for the view that British trade unionists might be less 'compliant'. But to slate British trade unions as the key 'variable' in the post-war productivity shortfall is a rather more difficult task than such a brief review might suggest. Part of the difficulty arises from the fact that, just as in Britain there is no *one* trade unionism – the NUM could not be mistaken for the EETPU for example – so, in France, the union referred to earlier, the CFT, is not to be confused with the Confédération Général du Travail (the communist CGT). As far as the overall structure of trade unionism is concerned, a game of 'spot the missing factor', which points only to the enduring importance of craft unionism in Britain and its relative absence elsewhere, is also of limited value. Internationally, trade unions can and do differ with respect to their coverage, their internal structures and degree of centralisation, but they also differ in yet other respects – according to whether they are organised on religious and political lines, for instance, which is often the case in other parts of Western Europe. Moreover, the fact that, say, British unions tend to be more decentralised does not necessarily afford them greater leverage. As has often been noted (Maitland, 1983; Stephens, 1979) a more centralised system might make for greater leverage. Similarly, increased flexibility in task performance – or the rise of the so-called 'polyvalent worker' – might not necessarily divest workers of control at shop floor level but might bring with it a potential for them to control and negotiate their labour as a co-ordinative activity, a possibility that has already been given some consideration by Italian trade union activists (Murray, 1985, Chap. 2).

The determination of international differences in union power, and of the opportunities and constraints which these may bestow on employers in different countries, is made all the more difficult by the different strategies that trade unions may pursue in different countries (in so far, of course, as trade unions in different countries do pursue only one strategy). The actual strategies pursued by managements are also pertinent here. A 1970s comparison of industrial relations in French and British oil refineries suggests, for example, that the French management's tendency to control work practices by fiat was not based on a simple calculation that their labour force was 'weak'. Rather the French management's practice was informed by the belief that the French unions posed more of a long-term political threat than was the case in Britain, the actual industrial relations system that had eventuated thus being in good measure designed to provide a bulwark against the ideologically radical French unions, which, especially with a leading role being played by the CGT, constituted a 'substantially more radical union movement'. By contrast, British unions (for the most part in this study the TGWU) were not so difficult to integrate and were more willing to legitimate decisions. They gained more influence on the shop floor through Britain's 'semi-constitutional system', but they *also* 'gave management a certain degree of help in controlling the workforce' (Gallie, 1978, pp. 310, 312, 313; for a broader treatment of British and French class consciousness and action see also Gallie, 1983; Lash, 1984).

The above are only some of the difficulties that arise in attempts to invoke the strength of British trade unionism as the key factor in the post-war shortfall in productivity, however. At the heart of a much more profound difficulty is the fact that British workers did not wish unemployment upon themselves in the inter-war period (nor later) and that German and French workers did not wish upon themselves the repression that fascism brought in its train, and which, as a political economy, was fundamental to its very purpose. To switch to a somewhat less vivid setting, it was no more the case that it was British workers who single-handedly, or even for the most part, determined the tardy onset of monopoly and scientific management. Moreover, even if it is plausible to suggest that some of the customs and practices of an earlier craft unionism were both perpetuated and to some degree diffused in Britain, so that traces of them are still to be found today, these also need to be placed in a wider historical context – a context that, on the side of employers, takes in the opportunities available to them (or which once were available) and the constraints they have experienced over and above those that stemmed from workers. To neglect this wider context is to attribute too prominent a role to the British working class and its organisations, which is something that some authors would seem to come perilously close to doing in their attempts to account for Britain's long-term economic decline (see Kilpatrick and Lawson, 1980, and for a corrective Aaronovich *et al.*, 1981).


In the previous chapter it was suggested that both British management and the labour force it manages may be relatively deficient in technical quality. In this chapter attention has been drawn to the other side of the 'quality' of labour in some competing nations, as it has been affected by the employment of sub-contract and migrant labour and, beyond this, by some major political and economic circumstances. It has been suggested that a problem for British manufacturing has not only been that the composition of its labour force has been comparatively deficient in technical terms but that, at least up till the 1970s, manufacturing capital failed to benefit from even that great mass of dis-advantaged labour that was available in the economy as a whole.

True enough, if it could be shown that it was British working-class men who single-handedly kept women out of manufacturing, a whole new way would open up of explaining how it really is the case that the British working class (or the male part of it) has been at the bottom of the productivity shortfall. No such view will figure here, for the ideology, politics and economics that structure the position of women in British society are much more complicated than this would suggest and women's employment has to be seen in its full context. What must figure, however, is a further consideration of the context in which production takes place, for the more the dessicated measures of quantity and quality that characterise productivity comparisons have been prodded and probed, the more apparent it has become that a good deal tends to be missed out in these investigations – not just management, but how industry is organised, and the historical balance of constraint and opportunity that British employers themselves have faced.

Clearly, since what is of key interest to us at this point is how productivity in the common or garden sense was determined in the 1970s, and in particular how far the conventional wisdom's attribution of the shortfall to the British working class was merited, a full-blown historical analysis of the British economy and polity would be out of place (quite apart from which it would far out-strip my competence). It may prove helpful, though, to now reconsider the problem of how productivity is determined. To this end Chapter 7 starts out in a highly general way, by setting down some of the main features of the circuit of industrial capital. By beginning in this general manner it is hoped that some further specificities of the British context will be rendered more visible than has been the case thus far.

# 7 'The difficulty' reconsidered (3): The social organisation of production and the British context

$$M - C_{MP}^{L} \ldots P \ldots C' \ldots M'$$

In the above circuit of industrial capital M represents money, C a commodity, L labour-power, MP means of production and P production. The circuit clearly differs from another one, $M - C - M'$, which is compatible with the sort of mere money-making that results from buying cheap and selling dear. Industrial companies sometimes engage in such activities, of course. But the circuit of industrial capital makes plain that the distinctive feature of the industrial capitalist mode of production is very much bound up with $C_{MP}^{L} \ldots P$.

Marx understood the circuit of industrial capital in terms of the labour theory of value, a point which is of no concern here, though before we go on, the marxist origin of the above equation does call for a few words about possible differences in the approach to productivity adopted by marxists as compared to conventional economists. On this it is necessary to recall something noted earlier – that economists who conduct empirical studies are not always bound by the mainstream theoretical assumptions of their discipline (p. 267, note 5). Whereas it is therefore perfectly in order to stress that 'marxists regard production as a social as well as a technical process', it may be going too far to claim, as Glyn does (1982, p. 49), that it is always a 'fundamental difference' that, for marxists, 'work is extracted from workers under certain hierarchical relations of production. The balance of power and thus the intensity of labour . . . leading to a change in productivity as conventionally measured . . . technology itself, and the workplace organisation of the work [being] directed to maintaining and increasing labour intensity.'

On the other hand, we have seen that it was not firmly spelt out in the reports economists produced in the 1970s that some of the 'difficulties' attributed to British workers had another side in the greater vulnerability of some workers elsewhere. Such features of their work are not to be lightly dismissed, and to the extent that economists plead that they are concerned with labour only as an 'input' (albeit a *variable* one), and not with the condition of those who labour, this tells us something about the nature of their discipline.

By contrast, a great virtue of marxism is that it is a political economy of an entire mode of production. It therefore not only encompasses (or should encompass) an analysis of the dynamics of the variable potential of living labour, represented in its commodity form by L, as well as of both the determinants of this within production and the conditions of work experienced, but also of the wider political, economic and social context through which people are more or less successfully transformed into sellers of labour-power and which endows them with greater or lesser degrees of individual and collective productive potential. However, the sub-equation $C_{MP}^{L} \ldots P$ not only directs attention to the social and political context within which workers contribute to productivity, which, inside production and outside it, may differ in time and place. It also demands that attention be given to $C_{MP}$ – the accumulation of means of production being, as Glyn puts it, 'the primary determinant of the level of labour productivity'. (To understand the massive historical importance of the technical composition of capital it is only necessary to consider the potential productivity of workers engaged in building cars with hand tools, rather than in a highly automated factory, for as this suggests there will be limits to the 'competitiveness' of some workforces, even if they are paid peanuts and are literally worked to death.)

These things said, two further comments are in order. The first concerns the fact that the circuit of industrial capital is a *whole* circuit, and not just a matter of $C_{MP}^{L} \ldots P$. The second is that $C_{MP}^{L}$ itself stands in need of further explication, especially when the question at issue relates to the determination of the relatively small productivity differences that pertain *between* broadly similar social formations (for our purposes other highly industrialised capitalist countries) in which, on most conventional accounts, the technical composition of capital is held to be much the same.

We shall get to the terms $C_{MP}^{L} \ldots P$ shortly, but first it is useful to consider those parts of the circuit that lie to each side of the important process that these terms denote. In now turning to these – starting at the beginning of the circuit – the opportunity will also be taken to introduce certain 'macro' historical considerations that set the context for the more 'intermediate' and 'micro' levels of the British case that figure more prominently later in this chapter, and also in Chapter 8, which goes into finer detail.

No one simple generalisation is sufficient to summarise the relation between financial and industrial capital and the significance of 'the City' for UK manufacturing. Indeed, the very terms 'finance capital' and 'financial capital' are currently the subject of debate (Ingham, 1982, Ingham, 1984; McDaid, 1983). However, economic historians of the late nineteenth century have long debated whether domestic industry was 'starved' of funds or whether British industrialists saw no need for them. A similar debate rumbles on with reference to the present day.

In the case of the banks, for example, their critics charge that they are 'a decisive factor' in Britain's low productivity, and bankers themselves resort to the long-established defence that 'the demand for investment has to be present if the available supply is to be taken up' (cf. Lever and Edwards, 1980a and b; Leigh-Pemberton, 1980). Both views are compatible with the observation that British industrialists have a preference for short-term profit (Spurrell, 1980) and the argument is in fact difficult to resolve – not least because it throws up a classic 'chicken and egg' problem. If industrialists become habituated to a poor response they may desist from making further entreaties. But even this complication directs attention to only one possible consequence of the way in which British financial capital and industrial capital have developed historically and to the institutional residue of this. The early established pattern of world trading links and colonial markets was such that on the eve of the First World War Britain owned a huge 43 per cent of the world's stock of overseas markets (Kirby, 1981, p. 14). As we shall see, this probably had long-lasting effects on British industrialists. The related fact that by the end of the last century the London capital market had become primarily an instrument of external finance (King, 1936, p. 271) has also had enduring effects on domestic British manufacturing.

The 'quality' of finance may not only differ with respect to whether it is available on a short- or long-term basis, however. It can also differ with respect to the market and technical intelligence which informs it and which it may bring in its train. There may also be differences in the degree to which financial-industrial capital relations are firmly integrated. In short, there is a host of ways in which the 'M' at the start of the circuit of industrial capital may be further specified, and the signs are that Britain does not have strong institutional links to support the long-term finance of domestic industrial innovations, at least as compared to Germany and France. The relation between industrial and financial capital developed differently in Germany, and as a consequence financiers are represented on the supervisory boards of industrial companies; in France the Crédit National operates as a 'lead bank', channels government financial assistance and absorbs part of the risk – and in Japan, of course, group banks are closely involved in the strategic decisions of their operating companies (Hu, 1975).

Even if a relative lack of strategic planning by industrialists in Britain can be linked to some features of British financial institutions, however, this still leaves the role of government out of account. In Britain well over half of research expenditure is provided by government, £1,650m out of £3,500m according to a recent official enquiry (ACARD, 1983, p. 7, para. 3.9). Moreover, just as international differences in the nature of the supporting infrastructure have to be considered with respect to private finance-industry relations, so it is with government support for research. A measure of quantity is not enough, for in Britain the brute fact is that the government's R & D 'spend' is heavily biased towards defence – £1,060 million being put to this end according to the latest available official triennial survey (a figure that is in turn swelled by some additional private sector funding, of course). Such is the situation indeed, that among OECD countries it is only in America that *per capita* expenditure on defence R & D is higher than in Britain, the British figure of £18 a head in 1978 clearly outstripping those of £12 and £4 in France and West Germany, with nothing at all being contributed in Japan (ACARD, 1983, p. 7, para. 3.10).

It is sometimes argued that the sheer amount of British resources allocated to defence may be too small (in capitalist terms), because were even more to be spent it would help keep industries at the technological frontier, in much the same way that it is claimed to have done in America. It is also sometimes assumed that defence expenditure will in any case tend to have spin-offs for commercial development, and if it is considered that much of the defence R & D budget ends up in the British engineering industry there must be some potential for this. But not only is there no automatic guarantee of commercial application, there is reason to conclude that work on defence has represented a relatively easy option for British industrial capital, both historically and through a certain elasticity of price in the more contemporary period, and that it has retarded both structural change and new commercial product development – this leading to what Kaldor nicely describes (borrowing the term from Landes, 1969) as the 'mummification' of the British manufacturing economy (Kaldor, 1980). Moreover, to the extent that R & D expenditure in Britain is heavily skewed to defence, and this is not the most productive application for it, any adverse consequences are compounded by the fact that this also represents a significant drain of technical manpower (which, as seen in Chapter 5, is in any case in relatively short supply in Britain).

More will be said about R & D in Chapter 8. Some further repercussions of financial capital/industrial capital/state relations will also figure below when the 'end part' of the circuit of industrial capital is discussed. But even at this point attention has had to be drawn to the important extent to which the structure and performance of the modern British economy has to be related to Britain's 'early start'. To be reckoned here are the overseas ventures which allowed money to be made available to early industrial capitalists on a personal basis so that a financial-industrial infrastructure was ill-developed; the fact that the economy as a whole came to have an international orientation through investment overseas, to the possible neglect of domestic manufacturing; and, amongst other things, the peculiar twist whereby the weight of resources devoted to defence, as a legacy of the imperial role, may now drag Britain lower in that same free world that its industry is disproportionately geared to protect.

It is quite clear of course that trade unions *also* have to be situated in the context within which capitalism developed in Britain. In due course we will attempt a further consideration of $C^L_{MP} \ldots P$ (the 'centre' of the circuit) and, before that, of the 'end' of the circuit, $P \ldots C' \ldots M'$. But this is a convenient point to switch attention from some of the specific features of the organisation of capital in Britain to some features of the development and nature of organised labour.

The idea that British craft unions pre-existed and survived the advent of the monopoly phase of capitalism in Britain was introduced at the end of the last chapter. An argument that stems from this has been widely rehearsed elsewhere (persistence of craft controls and the diffusion of craft-like practices to other sectors making for more restrictions on British capital, etc.). But over and above craft (and going back beyond this, artisanal labour) there are other elements which may be invoked to suggest why British workers might have developed certain 'peculiar' attitudes. Some of these were also introduced in Chapter 6, with special reference to the last half-century (e.g. the absence of fascism, the strengthening of the labour movement during the war years, and before that the particular conjuncture of mass unemployment and the advent of scientific management). To go further back is to find yet further circumstantial evidence that might point to a similar outcome. But again, much else has to be considered too, as can be seen if we first go back to the turn of this century and then further back again.

Briefly, the Taff Vale judgment of 1901 meant that trade unions risked crippling damages if they struck. According to a recent account by a leading British economic historian, the choice that was presented in ruling circles at that time was 'a singularly narrow one', to put shackles on the trade unions or to leave them to operate outside the law – and in hindsight he sees the reversal of Taff Vale, in 1906, to have had adverse consequences (Phelps Brown, 1983). He notes that as early as 1893 the miners, through forming the Miners Federation, had found a way of securing greater leverage by mounting an industry-wide stoppage – but that, at the same time, they had also found a means of bringing in the government to help secure a settlement, since the disruption they could cause had wide repercussions for the whole economy and society. In this view, then, the legal status of the trade unions was being decided at that time on the basis of inappropriate assumptions. The potential of trade unionism had changed. The character of trade union members had changed also. The London dockers who struck in 1889, for example, were a different kettle of fish from the old trade unionists. Hitherto, as Phelps Brown puts it, they had been regarded as 'inherently uncouth and disorderly', but they now constituted the advance guard of a movement among the unskilled labourers of the cities, and among the semi-skilled who worked alongside the craftsmen in industry but who had been excluded from their societies. By then, too, literacy had brought access to ideas, so that 'currents of trade unionism and socialism mingled', and in the cyclical depressions from the 1870s onwards this new unionism had become just as insistent as the old – even, Phelps Brown suggests, following Marshall (in Pigou, 1925), perhaps more insistent – in protecting employment through restrictive practices. In these changed circumstances, which in part as a consequence of Taff Vale also saw British unions grow their 'political arm' in the shape of the Labour Party, the legal standing accorded to trade unions in Britain by the overturning of Taff Vale was misconceived (from a particular point of view, of course, it was, and not least perhaps that of what was then Lloyd George's Liberal Party).

However, it is necessary to go back further in time to understand how British unions had arrived at the position they had by the first decade of this century. Phelps Brown's account is also important here, for though he personally is of the opinion that British industrial relations have been 'harmed' by the failure to adopt a statutory code, and though he most certainly makes much in his work of 'the characteristics of the British people', he goes much further than most commentators to ground his understanding of these characteristics in their historical, legal and political context. A consideration of such matters is very much to the point. For example, part at least of the traditions of British trade unionism had been formed before British manual workers had the vote. Prior to what Phelps Brown regards as 'the watershed' of 1867–75 – when the vote was first extended to many skilled workers, the TUC was founded and Parliament freed unions from legal taint – a meeting between trade unionists and employers was, in his words, 'a confrontation between men deemed not fit to be entrusted with a vote and members of the ruling class' (1983, p. 281). This made manifest the opposition of 'us and them'. But a sense of independence (and the reality of it) had also been threatened by the use of the law to repress trade unionists in an earlier period, as evidenced, for example, in the now legendary seven-years transportation meted out at Tolpuddle in 1834, and, before that, under the 1799 and 1800 Combination Acts, which resulted from ruling-class fears about 'Jacobinism'. The delayed and hesitant enfranchisement was therefore but one factor that contributed to the notion that law was of other men's making, and which led law to be identified with directly opposed classes and interests – and but one part too of the explanation of how it came about that what British trade unionists typically want most from the law is that they should be free of it.

But there is also another aspect to be considered. This has some bearing on the origin of the liberal humanist variant of popular thinking about the curmudgeonly British worker as sketched in Chapter 1 – in which, of course, 'the British worker' is apt to be invested with a staunch, but essentially likeable, character. Phelps Brown argues that in so far as the early unions were friendly societies they needed members of steady habits; that the lead in them was taken by 'men of character and ability'; that they were recognised by their employers as good workmen, by their neighbours as good citizens, and that on all of these personal counts trade unionists earned the approval of other ranks of society – some features of the early history of the unions in this way contributing to their acceptance in Victorian times. (Clearly, even if this was the case in the 1860s and 1870s such a positive evaluation of trade unionism has not fared well in the 'new Victorianism' that dawned at the end of the 1970s – though it is interesting that this 'new Victorianism' often has as its backcloth a concept of what 'proper', 'responsible', 'moderate', etc., trade unionism should be like, and which, 'once upon a time', it supposedly was.)

It is important to remember, of course, that the unions experienced a sharp, if short, reversal in 1901 and that, even before that, engineering workers had come under heavy attack during the employers' offensive of 1897–8 (Wigham, 1973; Zeitlin, 1983). However, in earlier years British workers had won a certain respectability. Phelps Brown notes that British unions had not been formed or controlled by a political party. Moreover, they operated informally – as 'clubs', as the Minority Report of the 1867 Royal Commission put it – their informal operation both contributing to an acceptance that they should be free to exercise their functions outside the law, and also contributing to another outcome that has been much remarked in more recent times, on which Phelps Brown also has something to say: namely that 'the headquarters may be under control but the membership is not' (this making for 'too much local spontaneity' for his liking: 1983, p. 282).

So far we have taken in some of the leading elements that may have combined to forge a distinctive British trade unionism. That reliance has been placed on Phelps Brown's work to introduce these should not be taken to mean that his analysis goes no further than this; it is rather because (as well as much else) his account provides the outstanding contribution to their understanding. But the time has now come to give due emphasis to some further considerations, which lead back to certain matters alluded to in earlier pages.

Briefly and bluntly, our starting point here is that British manufacturing, through its 'early start', enjoyed relatively easy profits. The (traditional marxist) theory of the labour aristocracy, according to which British workers were 'bribed' with crumbs from the imperialist table, is difficult to sustain for a whole number of reasons, including the non-coincidence of the imperialist phase and the existence of a labour aristocracy as such (Moorhouse, 1978). Discounting that particular theory, the fact remains, however, that the general assumption upon which it was based has much to recommend it: the development of British trade unionism has to be understood in terms of the opportunities of British employers and, in finer detail, in terms of their particular interests, and the relations that held sway between them.

The 'early start' facilitated a tendency for British manufacturers to stick unadventurously to traditional established markets, products and plant (Hobsbawm, 1969; Landes, 1969). The early fragmented state of the British ownership and industrial structures (of which more below) also had important consequences. The interests, often family ones, that helped to perpetuate these also helped to postpone the advent of the monopoly phase in Britain, the emergence of professional management and, indeed, its chosen instrument, 'scientific management', for the habits of yesteryear did not budge readily. As late as 1913, for example, a writer in *The Engineer* was protesting that he had 'yet to learn that British works managed on American lines have paid higher dividends than British works managed on British lines'.

Some economic historians have argued that it was not profitable for British employers to adopt American methods because, compared to America, the wages they paid were so low (just over half the American ones in 1913). Others have claimed that it was not worth it because the British work pace was slower (Lewis, 1978, pp. 123-5). But according to Hobsbawm, up until the Great Depression British employers were still apt to measure the degree of labour utilisation by custom, and British workers had not entirely broken with custom either (1964, chap. 17). If British workers themselves had not by then completely learned the 'rules of the game', and also relied on custom rather than demanding what the market would bear, this would certainly have helped sustain such practices by their employers, as did the fragmented structure of ownership and product market conditions. Indeed, recent research indicates that in some cases the latter conditions facilitated the perpetuation of craft controls right through the late nineteenth and into the early twentieth century (Elbaum and Wilkinson, 1979; Zeitlin, 1983; Lazonick, 1979, 1981). If low wages benefited British employers, it is arguable also that a slow work pace may have done them little immediate harm. Given an absence of imports, they could afford to feel 'at home' with some of the remnants of the artisanal tradition.

To point to the fact that the early British employers did not have to face the same degree of competition from imports as other countries which developed later and that, confronted with a different situation, these other countries had resort to different strategies for development, is of course to glimpse the further possibility that these 'usurper' nations may have benefited from their initially disadvantageous position in the longer term – the Germans going for monopoly and rationalised production, with all that this entailed for technical education and the financial infrastructure, the Americans going for standardised production (made possible by a large domestic market) and, much more recently, the Japanese aiming to catch up, amongst other things, by setting great store on the commercial application of technology and by taking the planning and co-ordinative aspects of management (and not just 'man management') very seriously indeed. This, however, is to begin to sketch out the beginnings of a much broader explanation for measured differences in labour productivity, whereas what is of concern here is a much more limited proposition: that British employers were comparatively content to 'live and let live', were loath to combine, even for the most part to launch collective offensives against labour; and that the relative absence of external competitive pressure on selling prices provided a material base for the acceptance of trade unions in Victorian society.

British industry has never been uniform: where external pressures impinged, in shipping and the exporting coal-fields for instance, employers were more than usually actively hostile to unions (Phelps Brown, 1983, p. 205). The opportunities for British industrial capital that helped open the door to British trade unionism did not last forever either; the rise of America and

Germany saw to that. But even in much more recent times complacency about markets was a characteristic of the British motor bike industry before it was ravaged by the new competition from Japan in the 1970s (Boston Report, 1975). Part of the difficulty with British car production in the same period was once again partly a function of long-standing complacency about its traditional markets. Indeed, it is difficult to resist the conclusion that in the 'live and let live' world that several generations of British industrialists inherited, organised labour was, to an extent, let live too. It may be in part as a consequence of this that practices which some economists are only too ready to slate as 'restrictive' have not always been so regarded by industrialists themselves. To the extent that such practices survived, or even gained wider currency in the 1950s and 1960s, and were still evident in the 1970s, it is therefore necessary to do more than point to the strengthening effect on labour of full employment. Not only did some of those 'restrictions' carry advantages to capital but what was practicable was itself likely to have been understood against a particular historical backcloth – one, moreover, that British employers had not been exclusively constrained to weave by workers.[1] On this view, in short, it becomes inappropriate to attribute the leading role to British trade unions. British trade union 'attitudes', like the very structure of British trade union organisation (for the early origins of which see Holbrook-Jones, 1982), have been shaped by the contours and particular inner dynamics of a social organisation that was not of workers' or their trade unions' making, and by a mode of operation with which British industrial capital had some reason to be complacent, once.

Clearly, such an account lacks sufficient substance unless supported by further, more recent material considerations. Wartime cost-plus contracts, and the role played thereafter in some sectors by defence contracts, go some way to provide this. But a good deal more also needs to be said about the specifics of British industrial organisation. It is for this reason that in later parts of this chapter, and much more so in the one that follows it, attention is given to various further facets of British industrial organisation in the more recent period, and to the possible effects of these on productivity as they extend *beyond* union-management relation. But before these are considered it is necessary to go back to our own point of origin in this chapter, the circuit of industrial capital, and to consider the 'end part' of this, P . . . C' . . . M', and of course its 'middle' $C_{MP}^{L}$ ... P. Since we are partly concerned to suggest a possible interrelation between the 'middle' and the 'end' of the circuit in the recent British case it makes sense to discuss them together, and since some relevant considerations that relate to the 'end' part of the circuit have made an appearance already (in the guise of markets) our discussion will be relatively brief.

The guiding assumption in this chapter is that though the relations within the circuit are general to the industrial capitalist mode, they – in this case P ... C' ... M' – can take *specific* forms in *different* social formations. Given this, we now need to ask: were there, as late as the 1960s and 1970s, any particular factors at work in Britain that related to the 'end part' of the circuit which had direct implications for productivity? To give an affirmative answer to this question it is only necessary to appreciate that production decisions are not only mediated by market intelligence (both the availability of information and the perception and evaluation of it entering in here), nor even by undulations in the world economy, but that within a given economy state economic policy can play a part too – a specific feature of the British state being given by its relation to industrial and financial capital.

The industrial capital/financial capital/state nexus is something that we have come across before, in the discussion of the beginning of the circuit. It might seem, indeed, that it is out of place to introduce it again here, but this is not so. Throughout much of the period after the Second World War, British governments felt fettered in the 'Go' phases of their recurrent 'Stop-Go' cycles by short-term panics about the balance of payments, and inflation – as mediated to them through the Bank of England and that remarkable home from home of Britain's financially orientated oligarchs, the Treasury. 'Stop-Go', in short, can be seen as a specific and quite recent consequence of the historical tendency of British financial capital to focus on investment abroad, and of the rise to prominence of London as a financial centre that this, the early trading contacts (and the booty brought home from other lands) brought in its train.

The argument is sometimes put forward that 'the City' has 'robbed' British industry of investment funds. In many ways this argument is difficult to sustain – not only because the argument that British industry is 'starved' of funds is itself difficult to establish (as we saw earlier with particular reference to the banks), but because many of the City's activities are not concerned with investment, and a considerable mass of the different sorts of capital that flow through the city are not British anyway. What is being suggested here by contrast is (1) that state policies in the form of 'Stop-Go' were shaped (as much else has been: Smith, 1981) by the fear of endangering income and interests that did not depend on the domestic manufacturing; and (2) that (following Pollard, 1982, 1983)[2] this probably had adverse knock-on effects – more accurately, knock-down effects, for British productivity. A situation in which industrialists became accustomed to believe that each 'Go' would have its 'Stop' did little to encourage them to get down to long-term planning; their habituation to the idea that each 'Stop' would have its 'Go' provided a reasonable justification for them to hold onto labour, this in return helping to institutionalise the comparatively high manning levels (responsibility for which is of course usually laid exclusively on British trade unions). For captains of industry to let go the tiller makes little sense. For them to follow this up by weighing the boat low in the water makes little sense either. But in a situation in which neither industrialists nor politicians had sufficient command of the ship of state these things can be more readily understood.

Public appraisals of the role of the City make much of its important contribution to the British economy through invisible earnings. Its consequences for British manufacturing deserve more prominence, not least because, from the standpoint of an exclusively domestic segment of British industrial manufacturing capital (in so far as this still exists), the problem, on the labour side, of a 'misplaced' disadvantaged labour force may be complemented, on the capital side, by the 'misplaced' political influence of that capital which is oriented more to world and financial matters than it is to the development of the British manufacturing base. But we must now get to the centre of things industrial – to $C_{MP}^{L} \ldots P$.

To briefly explicate the terms $C_{MP}^{L} \ldots P$ it is useful to consult the data reported in Figure 7.1 on international differences in net plant and equipment per worker. On the face of it, this would seem to indicate that there is no problem in British manufacturing as far as MP is concerned. In practice of course price measures are not the best guide to differences in the physical means of production. Then again, *per capita* measures require the most

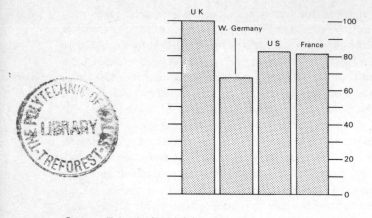

*Source*: Kaletsky (1984a) (as derived from OECD and Treasury data)

**Figure 7.1**   Net plant and equipment per worker in UK, West German, US and French manufacturing

careful qualification as to whose heads are being counted. Moreover, aggregated data, such as that presented in Figure 7.1, gives rise to further difficulties. For the sake of exposition, though, let it be assumed that the above data really does rule out that MP is inferior in UK manufacturing. For the moment, let us also close our minds to the other ('outer') parts of the circuit of industrial capital (even though there is reason to believe that these, and the influences that impinge upon them, may have important effects on the through-put of production, the degree of long-term planning that goes on with respect to product development, decisions to open up new markets, and so on).

Where does this lead us? Given the assumption that MP does not vary to the disadvantage of British manufacturing (to make things easier, let it be treated as an international constant), the above data invites us to use a new equation in order to fathom why British productivity is lower – namely, $C^L \ldots P$.

There is reason to believe that such a line of thinking is implicit in many micro productivity comparisons of the sort considered in earlier chapters. Such an assumption also lay behind the rudimentary requirements that were set down for the evaluation of such investigations in Chapter 2. At that point, though, the objective was to evaluate such investigations in their own terms. If their authors told us MP was not inferior in British manufacturing, we asked how they had reached this conclusion – whether, for instance, they had even clapped eyes on the physical plant that they generalised about. It was indicated then, however, that the term 'physical means of production' would have to be critically evaluated later, and that time has now come.

To consider $C^L$ ... P is to realise, looking to the real world, that something is missing (other, that is, than MP). Most obviously of all, what is missing is *management*. Indeed, if we look at the circuit of industrial capital in its desiccated algebraic form it is patently obvious that no little 'm' for management is to be found anywhere. Superficially this might be taken to imply that the circuit is deficient precisely because of this, but this is not so. The circuit is the circuit of a particular, class, mode of production, the capitalist one. Class relations infuse its every facet, and management, as an agent of capital, can therefore hardly be overlooked. Management was not overlooked by Marx, nor has it been overlooked by modern marxists. For example, when Glyn (see pp. 127–8) points to the importance of 'the intensity of labour' as a determinant of productivity, he tells us in the same breath that 'the workplace organisation of the work [is] directed to maintaining and increasing' this, as, he adds, is 'technology itself'. Glyn also makes it quite plain that work takes place under 'certain hierarchical relations of production'. There is room to quibble when it comes to the class location of managers who occupy different places in this hierarchy, for 'management' is a very broad term. But there can be no sliver of doubt that Marx, and subsequent marxists, have always placed a central stress on the 'hierarchical relations of production' (referred to by Marx in terms of 'the labour of superintendence' and the 'despotism of the factory'). On this score, in short, all is well and good.

It has been seen already, however, that labour-power, represented by the L in the equation, can vary with respect to more than its intensity, for the technical capacity to labour can also differ. What has to be taken into account now is that whereas 'hierarchical relations of production' most certainly link MP to L – and equally clearly link both MP and L to P – only a limited understanding of MP or of the relations of production can be derived from a stress on the hierarchical dimension.

Simply put, capitalist relations of production have two major dimensions, not one: a 'vertical' one that has figured already, which is embodied, within the factory, in the relation between 'management and men' and which, in its wider setting, is based on the separation of workers from the means of production; and a 'horizontal' one, which, most obviously of all, is based on the legal separation between capitals. But if our purpose is to distinguish between *different* capitalisms, it is necessary to go into finer detail. One way of doing this is to specify the 'macro' relations between different sorts of capital and between these and the state, as was attempted earlier – but a further elaboration of the 'horizontal' dimension, both at the 'intermediate' and 'micro' levels, is also in order.

The degree of integration can vary between different capitalist societies. It can vary both as judged by the degree of centralisation and concentration of legally defined production units (atomistic to monopolistic) and in terms of the linkages between them; and it can vary within firms, according to the degree to which production is integrated both as a production process narrowly defined, and with respect to other adjacent functions (e.g. R & D, marketing). To consider MP only in terms of 'physical' means of production is to neglect the possible differential effects of such co-ordination. For whereas MP has a physical presence – so many retorts, cooling towers, machines, robots – in actuality these will count for little as far as productivity is concerned, if the operation of such plant and machinery is not planned and co-ordinated; and other things being equal, the better the planning, integration and co-ordination, the higher productivity will be, even if MP is apparently the same in any two cases in its physical aspect (or of course as judged, less certainly, in price terms).

Students of the labour process are apt to dwell on the capital-labour relation. Writers on productivity in Britain, as we have seen, are apt to dwell on the (alleged disruptive) influence that *workers* may have on planning and on the flow of the production process, this often leading in practice to a one-sided account. But despite this bias, it might well be said (although it seldom is) that both productivity researchers and students of the labour process have much in common – at least in the sense that neither of them have typically made much of an attempt to marry an analysis of the ('vertical') capital-labour relation to a serious analysis of organisational forms (including 'horizontal' aspects). By contrast, it is fundamental to the view that informs this chapter that it is precisely this – something, incidentally, that goes beyond the usual passing reference to the fact that there are more unions in Britain than in other countries – that needs to be developed if our knowledge of some important determinants of international productivity differences is to progress. Just as $C_{MP}^{L}$... P cannot be reduced to $C^L$ ... P, nor L reduced entirely to a question of the intensity of labour, so even $C^L_{MP}$ ... P is only the *beginning* of the story when international differences are considered. Any adequate comparison has to take in not only possible differences in organisational capacities on the side of wage labour (in particular different trade union structures and strategies) but differential organisational capacities and qualities on the capital side as well. For this a literally *physical* concept of MP is of no help. And it is for just this reason, to cut a long story short, and to go back to our earlier question – 'if MP appears constant in physical terms where does this lead us?' – that where it should lead us, amongst other places, is to an investigation of how British industrial capital is *organised*.


The formal bodies that exist to advance the interests of employers represent only the most obvious example of a possible international difference in capital's organisational capacities, and as Phelps Brown observes it is 'surprising that we hear so little about employers and their associations, in comparison with the trade unions' (1983, p. 99). To recognise that these formal organisations have probably not played such a prominent role in Britain as in some other countries, is, however, to glimpse only the tip of a deeper reality. In Chapter 8, therefore, the attempt is made to explore some further facets of this and to put some flesh and blood on some of the rather more theoretical points put forward so far, beginning at an intermediate level, and then funnelling down to the shop floor. Such a procedure is highly necessary if we are to go beyond a physical concept of MP. But to consider 'intermediate' forms in their own right is also to be preferred to jumping from a consideration of 'macro' to 'micro' – or from the 'nineteenth century' (or earlier) to the 1970s – filling the space between with well-worn references to 'culture', 'institutional sclerosis', 'attitudes' and 'spirit'. Spirits have no material supports. They know nothing of constraint. Economically, politically and organisationally the 'attitudes' of workers and managements did not originate, and have not been reproduced, in any such void.

# 8 'The difficulty' reconsidered (4): A closer look at the social organisation of production in Britain

The retardation of British industry in the latter part of the nineteenth century affords an example of the possible effects of one particular facet of industrial organisation. It might be said to provide the classic example of this. British industry developed early. As was seen in Chapter 7, in part as a consequence of the 'early start' a multitude of independent competing firms survived, each pursuing its own largely separate interests. In Germany and the US, by contrast, large manufacturing units came to the fore sooner, an outcome that was facilitated in the one case by technological developments and the emergence of a particular financial infrastructure, and in the other, amongst other things, by the facts of geography, but which in both cases, had real effects on economic performance. Payne, an historian of British entrepreneurship in the nineteenth century, has suggested that such a 'structural' type of explanation for the onset of retardation has more merit than the notion that there was a general decline in British 'entrepreneurial ability' (1974, pp. 55-6). This is our view too. Certainly, such an explanation is superior to those interpretations (by non-sociologists) that are apt to invoke 'sociological laws' – according to which the enterprising founders of industrial dynasties are seen to be followed by a spiritless second and third generation who are almost inevitably seduced by the 'corrupting influence of fortune' or by the attractions of the ermine robe (see Burn, 1940, pp. 300, 303, on British iron and steel for example). It is as well to remember in this connection, perhaps, that Benjamin Franklin – who for Max Weber was the quintessential embodiment of the Protestant spirit – was himself far from adhering to the 'strict avoidance of all spontaneous enjoyment of

144

life', and that he retired from business at forty-two to escape its 'little cares and fatigues' (Kolko, 1961).

A problem that is general to the 'three generation thesis', and to others like it, is that scant regard is apt to be paid to the material opportunities available to enterprises and to changes in organisational circumstance. A consideration of such matters as they apply to the British case suggests that the early lead can no more be accounted for in terms of enterprising *individuals* than the beginnings of its demise as an industrial power can be attributed to a lack of them. Not the least part of the difficulty with arguments about the enterprising personal qualities of capitalists, and the lack of these in their offspring, is that 'individualism' had another face. The significance of this other face of individualism, which was to be seen in an overall structure of relatively small and typically family-owned enterprises, was brought into sharp relief by a Board of Trade investigation into the shipping and shipbuilding industry as late as 1918: 'Whilst individualism has been of inestimable advantage in the past,' it reported, 'there is reason to fear that individualism by itself may fail to meet the competition of the future in Shipbuilding and Marine Engineering, as it failed in other industries. We are convinced that the future of the nation depends to a large extent upon *increased co-operation* in its great industries' (cited in Payne, 1974, p. 56, my emphasis).

There is no dearth of other such instances where the early-developed atomistic structure of British industry had long-surviving consequences (on the tinplate industry see, for example, Minchinton, 1957). Here, given the general point that the monopoly phase came late to Britain as compared to Germany and the US, and that the small enterprise continued to dominate in the older industries like coal and textiles and in engineering till the turn of the present century, one further example must suffice – that of the 'silly little bobtailed carriages used in British goods traffic', which, as Thorstein Veblen noted facetiously in 1915, 'much impressed' American and German observers. To go back to this period is to find that the colliery owners, who owned these freight carriages, knew that it was possible to use carriages twice the size, and that this would make for greater efficiency. But – and here the other face of entrepreneurial 'individualism' enters in – they themselves were divided, and were not keen to invest money that would benefit the general business operations of the railways. The railway employers had a similar lack of concern for the interests of the colliery owners. Indeed, such was the drag exerted by the particular form of capitalist social relations that held sway in these industries that modernisation had to wait on the intervention of the state, with the nationalisation of the coal and railway industries in 1947 (for a general account see Hobsbawm, 1969, p. 189; for Veblen's comments see Saville, 1961, p. 54).

The sheer number of British trade unions,[1] the absence of the early development of a united employers' body or, at any time, of a TUC that has been stronger than the sum of its parts, can all be indirectly traced to the long-term effects of a pioneer production system that was composed of small independent enterprises. Add to this the relative absence of external competitive pressure on selling prices, and a dislike of price-cutting (and of mergers), and a possible link can be made to the origins of a distinctive form of British trade unionism too – British capitalists having tended to opt for accommodation with organised skilled workers, rather than confrontation, while the nineteenth-century boom allowed profits to be made, with rather more shop floor 'control' possibly being conceded in Britain than elsewhere as a consequence of this.

The above observations serve to highlight the potential significance for productivity of different structural forms. But any conclusions to be drawn about the importance of British industrial organisation for productivity in much more recent times have to be advanced with extreme caution. The truth is that any simple 'historical' formulation is likely to run into real difficulty if it simply superimposes on the present particular structural constellations that were dominant in the nineteenth or early twentieth century.

As far as the most obvious feature of the structure of relations between production units is concerned, for example – the degree of concentration – developments have been such that what was the case in 1870 was quite definitely not the case by 1970. By that date the largest 100 manufacturing enterprises accounted for 41 per cent of UK manufacturing output, almost twice the proportion that they had accounted for in 1949 (Prais, 1976). Moreover, in more recent times British manufacturing concentration has been high by international standards. The notion that a particular pattern of industrial specialisation has been consistently unfavourable for many decades does not wash well either. True enough, back in 1907, the old established staple industries (textiles, coal mining, iron and steel, general engineering) employed one in four workers and accounted for roughly half of industrial output – the first three of these industries accounting for 70 per cent of British export earnings, which were in turn concentrated in a narrow range of Empire, South American and Asian markets (Kirby, 1981, p. 3). But as Williams, Williams and Thomas argue, though British manufacturing may have been over-committed to export staples like cotton and shipbuilding in the 1920s and 1930s, this was no longer so by the 1950s and 1960s, when the pattern of industrial specialisation was more favourable (1983, p. 15). Indeed, reliance on these industries is even less evident today. To look to differences in the forms of enterprises that have existed in countries outside Britain as a possible explanation for the 1970s productivity shortfall is to run into similar problems.

Initially, the large 'modern' enterprises that belatedly emerged in Britain in the 1920s and 1930s took a different form than did those that had developed earlier in the US. The onset of 'big business' in America had been associated with the incorporated enterprise that directed control from a central office. In Britain it was associated with the industry-wide holding company. But the American model has not been the only one. The Germans had favoured cartels. After the Second World War the French were to favour the industrial group held together by financial holdings (Chandler and Daems, 1980, pp. 3-4). Here too, though, there have been changes. According to Chandler and Daems by the 1970s the centrally controlled, incorporated operating enterprise had become the 'normal' organisation of big business in the US, France, Germany, and in Britain.

However, conventional measures of 'intermediate' organisation may conceal almost as much as they reveal about other aspects of 'intermediate' and more 'micro' organisation. Because this is so – and despite what has just been said about concentration, specialisation and the form of enterprise adopted – we should not yet be prepared entirely to dispense with the notion that the early start, and the traditionally atomistic structure that derived from it, has had some long-term consequences, including some consequences even for the 'big business' that manifestly dominated the British economy in the 1970s. Appearance is sometimes a poor guide to reality in this field and, as will be seen later, organisational forms can also sometimes have long-term effects, which are relayed to the present only through highly complex and lengthy chains of decision-making.

The 1960s British 'merger boom' is a case in point. This led to a form of growth through the addition of other enterprises – a process which itself probably owed more to financial than industrial logic, and which has to be understood in the context of British financial institutions (on which see the previous chapter and Williams, Williams and Thomas, 1983, chap. 6). Growth by addition, rather than through internal development, also sometimes led to an organisational shambles. Not least was this to be seen at what was to become BL, the 'shambles' at which has been noted already (see pp. 92–3 above). There, following the delayed devaluation of the pound in 1967 (a delay which once again reminds us of the significant effects of City interests), the government had supported a merger between Leyland and BMH, the actual timing of this being partly governed by the hope of taking advantage of an anticipated cheapening of British exports. As a consequence of this merger, the newly created BLMC management had to wrestle, amongst other things, with the legacy of the BMH empire, which on the one side had its origin in a progressive agglomeration of household names like Jaguar, Daimler, Guy Motors and Coventry Climax Engines, and which on the other side – through what had previously been BMC – also had an extensive genealogy of private family trees behind it, which eventually had led on to W.R. Morris and, a little later on, in the first decade of this century, to the Austin Motor Company. Given the mish-mash of internal organisation that resulted from this, it is hard to resist recalling the directions given to the man who got lost in the Irish bog: 'Don't start from here.' But the problems that were to beset BL management right into the 1970s can hardly be understood without going back to the atomistic structure of the British car industry in the early twentieth century, which were to have long-term effects of their own, and this despite the apparently 'big business' characteristics of BL.

Corporations can *change* their internal structure, of course. In recent years business historians and behavioural theorists of the firm have paid increased attention to just this possibility and to the effects of such changes on company performance. A leading contribution has been made by Chandler (1977). A remarkable feature of Chandler's analysis of the development of US business is that he puts the emphasis on 'the visible hand' (which determines enterprise structure and policy, or which can seek to do so) rather than upon the role played by capital markets or government (through public policy on tariffs, etc.) or entrepreneurial 'spirit' (or enervation) – or indeed worker organisation and action. When set against the backcloth of so much public discussion, and also some academic discussion, this last feature of his analysis is extremely refreshing. It is also to be regretted. Chandler most certainly does not fall into the trap of constructing a 'labour-led' theory, but through this omission he comes dangerously close to advancing a 'capital-led' theory, or more precisely a theory that is 'management-led'. As for the approach adopted here: following an attempt to evaluate the evidence that empirical investigations adduce on the contribution British workers make to productivity, our stress has increasingly been on how such history as they have made has not been made in circumstances of their own choosing, but has to be understood in relation to a history the shifting contours of which have largely been laid down already. In this way the attempt has been made to avoid a labour-led theory. Moreover, although the view has been advanced that intermediate organisational forms most certainly merit attention, the attempt has also been made to indicate the importance of the fact that these themselves exist within the context of other 'macro' forms. In this way it is hoped that we have steered clear of a simple, and seemingly 'free-floating', industrial capital or management-led theory as well.

'Macro' forms (the state, the city) have of necessity already intruded into the above discussion, even though its main purpose is to draw attention to intermediate forms (to the way industry itself is structured and to some general features of industrial organisation). But it is important to appreciate that capital's organisational capacities may also differ internationally at the more 'micro' level, and it is to the more micro aspects of internal organisation that we must turn now.

To start with, it is appropriate to consider one particular type of 'internal' corporate information and control structure, the so-called 'M-form'. The origin of the multi-divisional structure is usually traced to America. For example, an earlier work by Chandler points to its existence at Du Pont during the 1920s and at General Motors under Alfred P. Sloan Jr., who was later to record his experience himself (Chandler, 1962; Sloan, 1967). At first glance, the 'M-form' would seem to carry particular advantages for modern big business, for it is usually held to be a response to two major problems that firms are likely to run into as they expand: a loss of cumulative control and the confounding of strategic and operating decision-making (Williamson, 1970, 1975). Both difficulties are held to be lessened by the creation of semi-autonomous divisions, with clearly defined objectives set down by a Head Office, which has responsibility for strategic decisions and monitors and seeks to control their performance through internal audits, the manipulation of incentives, etc. Econometric research has been conducted in both Britain and America which suggests that the 'M-form' of internal organisation has a statistically significant association with firm performance (Steer and Cable, 1978; Teece, 1981). Given hard evidence that British manufacturing long delayed the introduction of the 'M-form', this might therefore be thought to constitute an example of how one particular 'micro' organisational form (or more accurately the lack of it) made a contribution to the British productivity 'difficulty'. By 1970, however, it would seem that something like three-quarters of the top 100 British companies had adopted an essentially multi-divisional form (Channon, 1973). Any straightforward argument that a contributory factor to lagging British productivity during the 1970s was to be found in the failure of British management to implement 'best practice' organisational design is therefore difficult to sustain – at least as far as the 'M-form' is concerned. None the less some further consideration is called for. As has been noted already, appearance is sometimes a poor guide to reality in this field.

The first matter to be considered has been implicit in some of our discussion already, but a distinction between units of legal ownership and production establishments may help to make the point more explicit. Typically, throughout much of the nineteenth century, the legal entity that was the British capitalist firm was small, both as judged by the size of its capital and as judged by the numbers employed. Today, by contrast, the dominant legal entity in British manufacturing commands huge capital resources and employs a large workforce. As we have seen, one reason for this is that whereas (relatively small) British firms had for a long time been apt to jealously guard their independence, in the 1960s especially, the monopolies (or oligopolies, as the economists say) had given full rein to the opposite tendency, through merging with each other. When they merged with each other, however, the 'big fish' often swallowed up flotillas of little fish in the same gulp. As a consequence of this, the situation that pertained at BL was also to some degree in evidence more generally. For during the 1960s the typical giant firm was burdened with an increasing number of small plants, thereby, despite appearances to the contrary, reproducing the characteristically smaller size of British plants and some feature of the (historically) typical atomistic *structure* of British manufacturing – though now within a single corporate legal shell.

In 1958 the 100 largest firms owned an average of 28 plants, each employing 750. By 1972 the number of plants had risen to 72, and the number employed in each plant had fallen on average to 430 (Prais, 1976). As Williams, Williams and Thomas have put it: in Britain there was 'no rise of the giant plant parallel with the rise of the giant firm' (1983, p. 91). The reproduction, though now on an 'internal' basis, of an atomistic type of structure that had characterised the 'external' relations of British manufacturing up to the First World War (and which persisted to some degree thereafter) is really quite fascinating. But so is a further parallel that can be drawn between the 1960s and the inter-war period, the time when monopoly began to take hold and scientific management came to the fore. Then, 'scientific management' was 'clipped on' to existing managerial structures (Littler, 1982, p. 115); in the 1960s and 1970s, when resort was once again had to an 'American' model, and an attempt was made to refashion managerial structures themselves, these in turn were to be 'clipped on' – to an existing set of internal production relations.

Of course, outside of a fresh start, any new management information and control system has to be applied initially to what exists 'on the ground', wherever it is introduced and at whatever time. But, in Britain, in the 1960s and into the 1970s the organisational terrain in many manufacturing companies was such as to make the implementation of the 'new' information and control systems an uphill job. Indeed, the full force of attempts to flatten the 'lumpy' internal structures of many big companies was often not made manifest till later on, when, with deepening recession, 'flattened' became precisely the right word – parts of the plants, whole plants and entire factories (some of which had had their origin as family firms) being quite literally rased to the ground. That a particular factor behind this later development was that the state was then governed by a political party that delighted in the rhetoric of 'individualism', and which touted the virtues of 'good old-fashioned British competition' (and of the family), is not without irony.

The internal structure of large corporations does not consist solely of relations of an inter-plant type, of course. But nor, despite the inordinate amount of attention that these attract in Britain, are demarcations within corporate structures confined to those practised by *workers*. Institutionalised demarcations within management can also exist (between sales and production, for example). When considering the organisation of industry, the co-ordination and relative development of different management functions has therefore to be considered too.

It was seen in Chapter 5 that the assumption that the technical capacities of management can be treated as a constant in international comparisons was undermined as soon as the facts of the matter were gone into. But there is no good reason to rule out that the organisational capacities (and performance) of managements may also differ internationally.

Investment is an important case in point. In the last chapter the question was left open as to whether MP actually was inferior in British manufacturing. This was because the attempt was then being made to open up a wider argument, to the effect that it is inadequate to have exclusive resort to strictly formal allocative categories (so much labour, so much capital) in order to explore the different performances of more or less similar enterprises or capitalisms. In that context, indeed, it was even helpful to pretend for the sake of exposition that MP was an international constant, for this brought out all the better the need to explore *other* differential processes and relations. In practice, however, it is quite possible that the UK data that was cited in Figure 7.1 was distorted by the relatively high price of British investment. Since the higher the price of that investment is, the lower the *real* volume of investment, it might therefore follow that, comparatively judged, the level of British investment has been insufficient in quantitative terms – in short, that there has *not* been enough of it. But what concerns us here is not so much the quantity of investment as its quality. Recent research on the UK, West Germany and the US suggests that the difference in manufacturing output per unit of capital stock between Britain and these other two countries is so pronounced that it can be regarded as significant, notwithstanding the usual price-related difficulties. If, for example, UK output per unit of capital stock stood at 100 in 1980, in West Germany the appropriate figure was 195 and in the US it was 210 (OECD, 1985, pp. 17-18 and Table 6). Faced with such differences it is only reasonable to suppose that British *management* has contributed to them, either through making investments of inferior technical quality or through failing to make use of that investment efficiently by virtue of its own organisational incapacities and/or inept performance.

British manufacturing's relatively poor performance with respect to annual stock-turn is open to a similar interpretation. Recent research on stock-turn puts Britain towards the bottom of the league table – its 4.5 figure lagging behind those for Japan, the US and West Germany, respectively estimated at 9.0, 7.3 and 5.8 (Kransdorf, 1984). Of course, *other* factors must also be considered, like the way large Japanese companies have 'exported' stock-holding to their suppliers, also the role played by different product mixes and so on. Moreover, it is just as hazardous to generalise about 'the British manager' (on the basis of these or other figures) as it is to advance far-flung claims about 'the British worker'. But, confronted with this sort of data, there really is no warrant to immediately invoke British labour to explain the poorer performance. Indeed, the above investigation cautions against this. It found that Sweden – in British eyes the legendary home of good industrial relations – had a stock-turn of 3.5, which was lower than the figure for Britain. That it may be inadvisable to link such outcomes to the effects of British labour relations has not of course prevented such linkages being proposed,[2] but then it has to be remarked that the mere existence of information that points to deficiencies in the organisational competence of British managements (and to the organisational problems that may have brought these about) has been no guarantee of their prominent reportage either. Part of the job of this chapter is to correct this situation.

Some further detailed information which points to organisational deficiencies on the management side is forthcoming from research into forty West Midlands engineering and metalworking firms that was conducted over the years 1968–72, and from a further series of case studies into forty-five companies that was conducted during 1970–74. These studies indicate that neither labour nor plant was employed on directly productive work for more than an average of 50 per cent of the time available. Whereas workers were found to be responsible for a 10 per cent loss in labour utilisation, through waiting time, management was also held to be responsible for a further 5 per cent loss through waiting time. The rest of the loss incurred by 'non-productive' use of labour time represented about another 30 per cent of the working day and was attributed to attending, handling and servicing activities. As the author of the study concluded, it would seem that the time taken up by these latter activities represented 'a strong case for low cost automation equipment, which could reduce this time and thus release more man hours for productive work' – and it might very well be thought that this pointed to further management failing. Data on the 'productive' and 'unproductive' utilisation of machines during the working day implicated management yet more clearly. Management was held responsible for 45 per cent of the total machine time when machines were idle, as against 5 per cent attributed to workers, with only a small further proportion of total machine time being accounted for by other 'unproductive' activities (setting 4 per cent, tool adjustment 2 per cent and maintenance also 2 per cent). Subsequent investigation also suggested, as might be expected, positive statistical associations between effective modern costing systems, planning and control techniques and levels of efficiency as measured on a range of indices (Dudley, 1975, pp. 3-50).

As Prais and Wagner state: 'Smoothness and timeliness of production depend upon proper stock control, availability of materials and parts, grouping of production, progress-chasing, correct recording and book-keeping' – in general, on a high standard of 'good housekeeping' (1983, p. 56). This applies both to management proper, and within the supporting infrastructure, which it is of course a management function to control. The 'micro' productivity investigations that we looked at in earlier chapters neglected such matters. It now seems that in doing so they may have reflected a similar neglect within the ranks of British management. In fact, the more we search out information, the more likely this appears to be. Other detailed research points to the same conclusion.

In 1973 a British engineering company, Stone-Platt Industries, bought a US manufacturer of spinning machines, Saco-Lowell, and found that, though Saco-Lowell was selling its machines on the world market at roughly the same price as Stone-Platt's own subsidiary, it was achieving up to twice the sales and twice the added value per man-hour and paying about twice the British wages. Stone-Platt called in the consultants Urwick-Orr and Partners to explain how the American company could do this. Possible differences in equipment were investigated. But it was found that in the American operation 61 per cent of machine tools were more than twenty-one years old, compared to only 45 per cent of those in Britain, and that only 15 per cent of the machine tools in the US were less than ten years old, whereas 28 per cent were in the British operation. The answer did not therefore lie in the equipment, at least as judged on a vintage measure. Batch sizes were compared, but there proved to be more small batches in the US operation. The answer did not therefore seem to lie in any obvious differences in economies of scale. So: no disadvantage to the British plant in terms of the capital goods employed, and exceptionally for British-American comparisons, in this case there was no disadvantage because of economies of scale either.

Judging by what happened in the productivity investigations that were reported in the previous chapters, the stage was now set to wheel in British workers, their 'attitudes' and their lower levels of effort. Sure enough, Urwick-Orr proceeded to test the proposition that British workers made less effort. They sought to do so by making spot-checks on workers in the British operation, on their counterparts in the US, and in Saco-Lowell's Spanish operation as well. Subjective as these tests were, to Urwick-Orr's credit they were attempted none the less. The point, however, is that the consultants failed to demonstrate that British workers made less effort (their level of individual effort being rated on a par with that of the Spanish workers, and the US effort level being rated markedly lower).

The key factor accounting for the American company's much better productivity was found to lie elsewhere — in its skill in designing a product to the lowest cost. Two types of machine, each made on both sides of the Atlantic, were compared. For the first American machine the direct labour required was estimated at 70 per cent of the man-hours needed for the British design, for the second the American figure was 48 per cent of the British. As a commentator on the study has put it: 'It appeared that years of operating in a high income economy had forced the US management to put the stress on economic design' (Colchester, 1977). The comments of Edward Smalley, Stone-Platt's managing director, are no less pertinent: 'one of the first things we had to do' he explained later, was 'to re-educate the design department', and 'the most important thing was to get it established in the minds of our British management that we had a problem'. Perhaps, as suggested earlier, it is because British managers did not think in terms of this sort of thing as a problem in the 1970s that comparative researchers into British productivity, who frequently reported British managers' opinions (on workers), so infrequently stressed the design aspect? Whatever the case, the lesson of the Stone-Platt enquiry is that it is highly necessary that social organisation should be investigated, and not simply with respect to the hierarchical aspect of work relations but in its other aspects too.

Every few years debates about 'technology' recur in British society. A common theme is the separation between the knowledge produced outside industry, in the universities, and the gap between such externally generated scientific advance and its subsequent application in industry. In its own small way the investigation into Stone-Platt suggests that, whatever validity this particular point may have, the social processes at work *inside* manufacturing industry may play a part too. At times, indeed, the report on Stone-Platt brings to mind an image of US industry as a purposefully planned social organisation, as compared, in the British case, to a more *laissez-faire* form of organisation. To quote Smalley again: 'the tendency in Britain is to design something and then to hand the design to the production side and let them make it. In the US something is designed and then costed and then redesigned to lower the cost, and this might be done several times before a design is finally adopted.' Colchester comments that 'management control systems were better conceived and operated in the US'; that 'systems for controlling production and stores, involving the use of computers, were much better developed in the US'; that the American worker was 'presented with his task in a way which allows him to complete it with speed and efficiency'.[3] Stone-Platt's finding 'that the jigs used to hold components during manufacture were more carefully thought-out in the US to make the handling of components faster and easier' is quite in line with this. And these differences all point to a greater stress on planning – indeed, on the conception, integration and execution of production in the American case. In two words: better organisation.

As against all this, Urwick-Orr also found that under the piece-work system that applied in the British operation foremen *did* spend time sorting out rates for the job when they could have been employed on other tasks, smoothing out bottlenecks and so on. But by the 1970s the trend in Britain was towards measured day-work systems (not that some British managements had thought out the implications of these for their supervisory systems) and piece-work itself can hardly be claimed to have been the sole creation of British workers. Indeed, such payment systems are (literally) all of a piece with some of the other *laissez-faire* features suggested by this enquiry: that the design people were left to get on with the design; that the production people were left to make it; and that the workers, as under piece-work is more substantially the case, were left to get on with their job – a job, in the instance under review, that was not, it seems, 'competitively' planned in the first place.

Stone-Platt is of course just one company. There is reason to believe that, as far as its greater length of British production runs was concerned, it was rather exceptional. But to consider even this one case is again to raise the question of whether the degree of internal integration was adequate in British manufacturing in the 1970s and to ponder what the implications of any such deficiency might have been. The signal fact is that this issue has been severely neglected in most investigations into Britain's comparative productivity. In its stead, we find airy references to the British 'social system', to 'long-standing attitudes', etc. For the most part, the nitty-gritty of how production is organised goes by the board. Management, as an active process, is too often neglected. It is instructive, though, that when researchers do get down to detailed enquiry, deficiencies should so often come to light in resource control, budgets, planning objectives and in other quite fundamental *co-ordinative* aspects of the management function.

It is difficult to arrive at anything like a firm conclusion about international differences in the degree of integration between different functional specialisms. A recent British and West German comparison of the impact of computer numerical control machines is none the less suggestive. The authors of this (Hartmann *et al.*, 1983), having noted that the British workforce they studied had a 'more polarised qualification structure', and that there was also a greater separation between technician and worker apprenticeships in Britain, linked this to another of their findings – that CNC programming and operating were also more likely to be separated in this country. Indeed, according to this research German companies also 'distinguished less than those in Britain between specialised functions and departments for production management, production engineering, work planning and work execution functions'. A great deal is heard in Britain about lack of shop floor co-operation. But Hartmann *et al.* also suggest that whereas in Germany foremen are 'deeply involved in CNC expertise', they are 'largely by-passed' in Britain; that in small-batch turning in Germany operators are more involved in planning; and that 'in all cases, British companies used CNC in such a way as either to maintain planning departments control and/or autonomy, or to segregate the NC operations from other sections'. In short, CNC organisation in Germany not only differed because workers were more fully integrated in that country. There was less differentiation of management function, and CNC organisation linked 'foremen, chargehands, workers, and planners'.

The above investigation serves to remind us that corporate and departmental strategies, and the existing production, engineering and organisational procedures, and manpower policies, can all vary between countries. But, as these researchers also note, they can vary within a country as well. This puts difficulties in the way of generalisations about international differences in the structure and performance of management functions. Moreover, even if a sufficient number of *detailed* studies were to demonstrate that the degree of internal functional differentiation was greater in British companies, the effects of this on productivity would need to be documented. Given the present state of research, perhaps the best that can be said is that a higher degree of functional integration might well be a better recipe for higher productivity, and that the apparent lack of integration between planning and production indicated in the above study is indeed suggestive. However, any manufacturing economy will be likely to lag behind if, compared to those economies that operate in similar societies, it fails to stay at the technological frontier (other things being equal, of course). This suggests that the co-ordination of the R & D functions could be particularly important and that we might get a little further by now considering this in more detail than was attempted in Chapter 7.

On the face of it, if we go back to 1964 and compare the share of GDP going to research and development in the main competitor nations, Britain was not faring badly. Although behind the US, which had the highest share at over 3 per cent, Britain's 2 per cent plus percentage put it ahead of France, Germany and Japan. By 1979, however, although Britain was still ahead of France, it was not only behind the US but had been overtaken by Germany and Japan, and even these figures flatter British industry's perform- ance. One reason for this is that Britain's GDP has itself grown slower; another is that the above figures combine expenditure by both private firms and the public sector. When spending is considered in absolute terms, and for the private industry only, it becomes yet clearer that in the decade and a half up till the end of the 1970s, Japan surged right past Britain, that US spending was six times greater than that in Britain, and that British expenditure had stagnated, whilst that in France threatened to overtake it by the end of the 1970s, as Germany had already (NEDO, 1983, pp. 38-9).

Britain has an exceptional record for making radical break-throughs. But some of these have resulted in financial loss or required massive state support (like Concorde). What is probably of greater importance is that Britain lags behind where the improvement of existing technology is concerned. On one estimate, over the two decades 1953–73, only about 4 per cent of Britain's R & D effort was put to such use which, although it is more mundane, is probably of a lower-cost, higher-return nature. The comparative figures for France, West Germany, Japan and the US were 12, 36, 38, and 41 per cent respectively (Franko, 1983, p. 32, citing Hudson Research Europe). In fact, there are a whole number of different reasons for thinking that, commercially speaking, the R & D function is out of kilter in Britain. Numerous academic investigations and government reports in this crucial area testify to the persistent failure to make scientific advances count commercially, both in defence work and in the civilian sector. They stress that more *planning* is required, both long-term and in depth; that there is a need for greater *collaboration* between companies; and, at the 'micro' end of our continuum, they point to the need for research, design, production and marketing to be more firmly *integrated* (NEDO, 1981, 1982a; on product design see Corfield, 1979; on production process improvement, Bergen, 1983; for a sample of the academic research see various contributions in Pavitt, 1980, and Henwood and Thomas, 1984). What all this suggests is not only that Britain's R & D resources are insufficient, and that their deployment has been inappropriate to yield the best result – but that those resources that are available are not as profitably utilised as they are in some other competing nations. As was indicated in the last chapter, the way the British economy is skewed to defence may play a significant part in this. But as the above suggests, a lack of planning, and integration – both of an 'external' and, again, an 'internal' kind – would *also* seem to have played an important part.

British cultural history is threaded through with a number of themes that help to make sense of the above situation, at least in a very general way. The alleged British preference for liberal rather than practical education, for example, an antipathy towards science and its application to industry, and the low status of the engineer, have all been related to the role of the public schools and Oxbridge, to the social base and character of the civil service and so on. Allusions that have their origin in a different neck of the intellectual woods – which point to the early fusion of a rising bourgeoisie with the aristocracy, and the failure to develop a 'real' bourgeois revolution – can be interpreted as pointing in the same direction; so, too, can less grandiose statements about the lack of 'thrusting', 'aggressive' managements, 'the cult of the amateur', and the notion that the British way is to 'muddle through'. In one way or another, all this has been said a thousand times (for some of the more recent leading accounts see Roderick and Stephens, eds, 1981, 1982; Barnett, 1975; Wiener, 1981; see also Anderson, 1964). It has something to recommend it – provided it does not lead to a psychologistic harping on 'the British character' (which really, if it is to be found anywhere, is of course English), that the facts are got right, and, above all, that a consideration of 'culture' is combined with a consideration of those worldly issues that relate to constraint and opportunity (Thompson's comments on what Anderson has to say about the very early period are not without significance here: see Thompson, 1965).

How remarkable it is, though, that commentaries of this kind are often so very far removed from what actually goes on in British companies and factories. So much is this the case that one sometimes wonders whether the authors of some of them would want to avail themselves of an obvious defence – that not only is there an 'English disease', but that it is so insidious that even they are unable to escape its grip. Apart from anything else, however, it is essential, in mounting an argument which seeks to link 'British culture' to manufacturing performance, to show how this culture has been produced and re-produced, and not just outside industry but also inside it. As Carter argues, the experience managers gain *inside* industry is likely to have a significant effect on them (1981, p. 30). True enough, the novice manager does not enter a cultural void when he takes up his first job. When he starts work with a company, his very selection may depend on the real or supposed possession of certain diffuse qualities. There is in fact little to quarrel about here (Nichols, 1969, p. 119 and chapter 11). But to point to these particular facets of 'socialisation' is not to go far enough – not if we want to explore a possible link between management culture and performance anyway. More is involved in the socialisation of British management than arguments which point to the reproduction of a stratum recruited from particular social origins would suggest.

Much of the discussion in this chapter has been informed by the view that the structure and degree of integration of production relations has an important bearing on the organisational capacities of particular managements – but what has to be appreciated also is that these structures and relations also confront the new manager as a social fact in their own right. If, for the sake of an example, a young manager were to become habituated to a working environment in which 'the layout of machinery was chaotic' and 'inflexible', some of it being 'related to pre-1900 activities' and where 'each shop was generally related not to the product but to the machines' – and where the management functions were themselves physically split up and poorly integrated, so that 'contracts and purchasing only talked to each other by memos from behind mahogany doors' – it is difficult to surmise that this would inculcate a high degree of organisational competence. Such instances do not get much publicity, of course, except when a new man comes in, and then points to his achievements, as Michael Edwardes did at BL, or as in our example, was done by the chief executive of Vickers Defence Systems Division. (The above being his description of the Elswick West, Newcastle plant, as late as 1982: cited in Garnett, 1983a). In the 1970s, however, such cases were probably still quite widespread, and the general point to be made is that the immediate work environments in which generations of British managers have worked may have been such as to provide them with a less than optimal experience of coherent, efficient administration – these work environments clearly consisting of old bricks and mortar and old machinery, and their internal social organisation often showing the effects of some of the 'macro' and other constellations of social and economic organisation considered already (in the Vickers case, two world wars' worth of government defence work, and the perpetuation of this linkage thereafter).

Several elements of the above discussion indicate that the particular part of 'the difficulty' in British manufacturing productivity that stems from a long-standing deficiency in technical skill may be further compounded by the hidden costs of poor co-ordination. But to permit that poor co-ordination may exact a cost on productivity is to glimpse a further possibility. It may be further speculated that this in turn may have yet further adverse consequences via a more complicated route: workers habituated to a lack of organisational proficiency on the part of their managers begrudging that they are the ones who have to live with deficiencies which they see to be of others' making; managers, for their part, being resentful because it is not necessarily their competence as *individuals* that lies behind the cock-ups (even if this usually appears to be the case to workers), and thus becoming more than usually distrustful of workers, their motives, attitudes and judgment. Interestingly enough, even that modern 'Dunkirk', the 1974 three-day week, is testimony to how loath some British managements have been to encourage workforce participation, and to build on what support *has* come their way. Finding that workers had gained confidence and benefit from the increased communications that the emergency had forced upon both sides, the official enquiry into this unusual episode also notes the 'embarrassment' that some managements experienced when they wanted more.[4]

If 'participation' is to be taken as an index of British mangement's willingness to integrate its *workforce* it has to be concluded that the record has been far from good. In more recent times the reaction to the EEC Vredeling proposal and fifth directive was notable, above all, for the alacrity with which, with the Engineering Employers Federation well to the fore, the line was adopted 'We have our own arrangements, thank you.' According to a recent survey (Daniel and Millward, 1983) about a third of workplaces in the private sector have consultation committees. But it is symptomatic that this finding was rapidly pounced upon by some employers (with the EEF in the lead again) in an attempt to show that legal compulsion is unnecessary in Britain – even though, as an anonymous writer in *New Society* noted (15 September, 1983), further data contained in this report 'casts doubt on whether advances in participation can be left to the perceptions and whims of managers'.

It has been necessary to dwell on the theme many times in this book that the 'perceptions' of managers are not to be relied upon and that at the very least it is advisable to check them against the perceptions of workers. But the very notion that British management has been keen on participation is itself put in doubt by other research. For instance a study which followed up nearly 2,000 people outside their place of work in 1979 concluded that, in practice, the 'amount of involvement in decision making at work is astonishingly low', and that 'this applied to all levels up to quite senior management'. As one of those associated with this investigation has noted, though there was a growth in consultative committees in the 1950s, 'we also know that most of them died from inertia and a lack of worthwhile tasks a decade or so later' (Heller, 1983). Such participative ventures as there have been in Britain have in fact rarely lasted long, and the social distance that characterises the hierarchical relation of 'management and men' in this country is indeed so obvious as to require no further comment here. But whether or not the British manager's continental and American counterparts really do distance themselves *less* from their workforces – and whatever the real substance of the participation their workers enjoy – the possibility is also well worth considering that there has been relatively little 'vertical' participation in Britain within managements' own ranks. So is the possibility that British management may have lacked integration in its 'horizontal' dimension. This is something to which it has been necesary to draw particular attention above, in small part because the great weight of industrial 'participation' research has dwelt exclusively upon the hierarchical or vertical aspect (and particularly on the 'vertical' social integration of workers). And as we have seen, there is reason to suppose that British manufacturing has been lacking in horizontal integration, both within the ranks of company management and at other levels. Such a lack of integration could most certainly have implications for levels of productivity and their rates of change.

A brief pause here for some 'technical' comments. It was argued in Chapter 7 that the above features of industrial capitalist organisation are largely obscured if we consider MP separately, and even more so if it is treated only in its physical aspect – for then, even though MP can be considered (though in practice this is often attempted in a less than adequate manner), and even though L can also be considered (though, again, in practice, this is often attempted in a less than adequate manner), the exploration of the processes and relations that give a particular unity to MP and L, and which actually define important features of P, is all too likely to go by the board. It is a staple of marxist thought that what

passes for the (neutral) *co-ordination* of different 'functions' in the
literature of administrative science is often simultaneously the far
from neutral exercise of *control*, since it actually entails the
control of other people's labour. The implications of this for
productivity (and exploitation in its political dimension) are clear
enough – indeed, as we have seen, even empirical productivity
researchers are quite happy to recognise at least the *effects* of such
political relations. But both they and marxists are weak on the
horizontal dimension of management integration (for marxists
understandably so: this is not where the class war is at). Once the
focus shifts to the competitive performance of different com-
panies/countries, however, it becomes less excusable to fail to
consider the possible impact of such horizontal integration on
productivity, along with much else, of course. An extension of
conventional economic models to take into account that differential organisational capacities exist on the *labour* side of the
capital-labour relation is not likely to illuminate these. But certain
underlying tendencies in the so-called 'X-efficiency' theory are also
likely to lead to their neglect. For whereas 'X-efficiency' theory
does extend the insight that workers may be more or less 'X-
efficient', so that this also applies to managements, it tends also to
reduce everything to 'motivation'. In this way it not only
perpetuates the pretence that the circumstances of management
and workers are sociologically equivalent – which cannot be
borne out by any serious consideration of the hierarchical
component of capitalist relations (class relations in the workplace:
co-ordination/control) – it also invites an account of international
productivity differences in which a leading role is given over to
speculation about different national managerial motivations,
'growth-motivated' ones and so on (see, for example, Frantz,
1980). Such a tendency, which is reminiscent of earlier theoretical
work in another sphere – the 'n-ach' theory, as applied to
underdevelopment (see McClelland, 1961) – is likely to suffer
from the same defects. For a trenchant criticism of the latter, some
features of which have clear implications for this sort of
speculation about motivation, see Frank, 1971.


Recently it has become fashionable to point to the important
extent to which management has been neglected in the literature of
the social sciences. Thus Clegg asserts that 'the truth of the matter
is that the study of management in industrial relations is in a

primitive state', and Storey points out that industrial relations textbooks 'lavish detailed attention on the intricacies of trade union structure, government and finance . . . probe and prod the shop steward to reveal his intimate secrets, [but] blithely ignore the other half of the equation – i.e. managers and employers' (Clegg, 1979, p. 164; Storey, 1983, p. 75). As these quotations suggest, however, to a large extent academic criticism has focused upon the lack of attention paid to management *in the conduct of industrial relations*. By contrast, the authors of a recent study of Japanese firms in Britain point to a yet more glaring omission – one, moreover, that cuts across the entire division of labour within the social sciences, as well (in our view, as indicated in previous chapters) as also having serious implications for those empirical investigations into productivity which are usually conducted by economists. This 'curious and fundamental gap in our knowledge', as they call it, is that 'workers' views on the effectiveness of British management have not been the subject of systematic research' (White and Trevor, 1983, p. 12).

That this omission is a major deficiency is not open to doubt. Indeed, it is highly interesting that these authors, who are amongst the very few to have pointed to this omission, proceed immediately to speculate along similar lines to those we began to explore earlier on. Noting that in Britain 'the ineffectiveness of working practices has almost invariably been connected with the issues of work-place industrial relations and union power', they observe: 'It has not seriously been considered that cause and effect operate in the reverse direction: that ineffective working practices undermine respect for management, and hence lead to a deterioration of industrial relations.' When placed within the context of industrial relations this reassessment of what is cause and what is effect might seem to echo the idea that 'weak management makes for strong unions', with the further implication (in some right-wing versions) that managements who have been 'weak' in the past, deserve all 'the trouble' they get thereafter. In fact, though, even with respect to this narrow (industrial relations) context it is necessary to permit that managements may find it convenient to negotiate certain settlements, or leave matters undisturbed, given a certain balance of other constraints and opportunities – something that makes historical sense in the British context, where the conveniences of yesteryear have sometimes come to be experienced as constraints when circumstances have altered, with established markets coming under threat, etc. – and not merely because of increases in union organisation. Accepting, however, that the accommodations that managements arrive at with workers at one time may prove a source of difficulty later, and that deficiencies in the actual handling of industrial relations matters may have 'boomerang' effects for management, it is now relevant to ask once again whether management failings – *in the performance of their wider co-ordinative and planning work* – may also have indirect effects on worker productivity.

The investigation that White and Trevor conducted into Japanese companies in Britain suggests this may well be the case. It reveals that workers in British-based Japanese companies rated them more highly than British ones for organising work more efficiently, and for the thoroughness of their planning. Indeed, it was the view of *British workers* that these firms gained 'a great competitive advantage' from their well-organised, smooth-running production (1983, pp.32, 128–9). A further conclusion arrived at by White and Trevor is no less interesting. They found that there was greater resistance to Japanese methods amongst British managers than there was from manual workers.

There is a dearth of the sort of detailed comparative work conducted by White and Trevor, whose study is all the more valuable because it relates to foreign (in this case Japanese) companies that operate in Britain. The time is long overdue for an extensive and detailed investigation into how British workers evaluate their managements, not simply with respect to the 'style' they adopt, as it concerns matters of hierarchy and 'participation', but also with respect to the other organisational aspects referred to above. What other research exists, slim as it is, appears to be quite consistent with White and Trevor's findings, however. Take the studies of output restriction amongst British workers that were conducted during the 1950s and 1960s. As was made plain in Chapter 1, such studies (e.g. Shimmin, 1959; Cunnison, 1963; Lupton, 1963) are not suited to use for strictly comparative purposes, but they do nevertheless help put the performance of British workers in its micro (British factory) context. In these researches British workers are also to be found criticising British management for its inability to run production smoothly, and for failures in scheduling, progressing and materials controls. As White and Trevor put it: 'This merely hints at how much more might have been learned through a direct investigation of workers' perceptions of management methods' (1983, p. 12).

Systematic survey evidence is of course of limited value for the determination, in context, of actual management methods. For this, as has been argued so often in this book, it is best for the researchers to see for themselves, and only then, on the basis of first-hand information, to produce a grounded report. But systematic survey evidence can produce a snap-shot of workers' perceptions. And, here again, data is forthcoming that supports the insights reported so far. One such survey was conducted for the Department of Employment in 1973. Based on nearly 3,000 informants in 450 workplaces, it indicated that in 52 per cent of all situations 'employees thought that the work they did could be better organised and arranged'. Apart from pointing to the need for more or better use of staff, suggestions for improvements mainly concerned 'more planning of the work as a whole' and 'better communication between departments' (Office of Population, 1973) – both pointers to organisational failings on the management side, and a further indication that students of British productivity might have accorded a more prominent place to administrative (in)efficiency had they looked more closely at social organisation (or, as in this case, even asked the opinion of those who had to perform the work so organised).

The finding that Japanese companies operating in Britain were more highly rated by British workers for their organisational proficiency also fits well with some of the findings arrived at in Gallie's earlier French–British comparison. Gallie distinguished between criticisms workers made of management according to whether they were 'relational' (i.e. concerned with what workers felt about how authority was exercised) or 'technical' (concerned with management efficiency). His systematic data survey amply demonstrates that amongst the British workers 'technical criticism was the dominant type'. The verbatim reportage of workers' views in Gallie's study also does much to qualify the usual implications that international productivity investigators have drawn about maintenance as a key site of the British difficulty. Both operators, and understandably yet more so craftsmen, pointed to 'the pitiful way in which maintenance work was organised'. It was claimed that management gave 'the impression that it couldn't care less whether things get done or not'. There were complaints that 'management doesn't iron out unnecessary delays by getting the right crafts on the spot or the right time, or even the right equipment' and that 'we've got planners here that couldn't plan a light'.

Gallie concluded that the British workers 'were not seeking to displace management': they 'were urging management to do their job better' (Gallie, 1978, pp. 107–12). But on his account, and as judged by the other indications pieced together above, it does seem that British managements have not been doing their job very well. This is not exactly surprising in view of the numerous unpropitious combinations of relations and processes – macro, intermediate and micro, vertical and horizontal – that have shaped the immediate contexts within which many British managers have had to operate, and perhaps given also the relatively easy ride that some of their predecessors had. A comment by one of Gallie's British workers underlines a possible result of this: 'The average bloke does what he's told, but he has just given up now' (1978, p. 112) – an outcome that is also compatible with other, more recent survey evidence, according to which, compared to the US, Sweden and West Germany, the UK stands out as a country where the level of job commitment is lower and job expectations are also low (Yankelovich *et al.*, 1984, pp. 18–19, though see below, p. 275 n. 5).


It has been seen that there is a tendency at work amongst students of labour productivity to implicate British workers in deficiencies that could sometimes just as well derive from management. High inventories are attributed to strikes. Lack of planning is attributed to the amount of time British managements have to spend on the shop floor; low investment, to an anticipation of what British workers might do in future, and to the idea that their level of effort does not justify the cost of further outlay. We have come to look at things differently: to suggest that British workers give like for like, inefficient management fostering less than helpful workforces. At the very least, it really is high time this possibility is given something more like equal prominence, and also the proposition upon which it depends, that British management may be as deficient in its organisation – in the work of co-ordination, in planning, and in its functional integration – as it tends to be in some respects on the technical side.

Mere allusions to 'spirits' and 'attitudes' are insufficient to direct attention to the existence of such deficiencies. 'Attitudes', of which so much has been heard in this book, always have to be understood in their context. Given a change in context they can all too readily evaporate, like other ghoulies and ghosties – and as far as the productivity literature is concerned, it would be far the best thing if they ceased to go bump in the dark recesses of the night. Moreover, it really is not sufficient to fall into thinking that managers abroad (Japaneses ones, to take the favourite modern reference point) relate to the worker as a 'whole person', etc., and that a principal reason for the Japanese success is to be found in 'significant meanings, shared values and spiritual fabric' (Pascale and Athos, 1981). This will not do — amongst other things because there is much more to management than 'man-management'.[5] But it will not do either — to again briefly revert to a wider, theoretical issue — because the choice that confronts us in seeking to explain international productivity differences is not one between a theory of 'spirit' like Leibenstein's (attitudes, motivations, effort, X-efficiency,) and a theory of the 'big battalions'. Arguments from 'spirit', even as applied to armies, are all too apt to overlook the fact that real armies have courts martial, and, as applied to industry, that the workforces of different countries can differ in their vulnerability, and indeed in the disciplinary mechanisms to which they are subject, not least through reserve armies of labour. For their part, arguments of the 'big battalion' type are also apt to fail, in that they concentrate on quantity, to the neglect of quality, whether the quality of labour power in all its aspects, or the quality of means of production in its social one. In the (giant) space between these two paradigms there is most certainly space for another — one that has as its hallmark the view that social organisation matters, and that the macro context in which it exists, and out of which the social processes and relations of which it consists have developed, matters too. In one way or another the whole theoretical gist of these last five chapters has been to say just this, and it is hoped that the contribution of British workers to productivity may be viewed somewhat differently as a result.

If, however, the discussion of the contribution of British workers to productivity is to continue to be viewed through a clouded lens of 'culture', as it may well be — in part because econometrics remains so inexact a science, with resort to hazy references to 'attitudes', etc., always being a temptation to illuminate those facets that the computer has not yet reached, even though it operates at the speed of light — it might be a good thing if, in future, far more attention was paid to the very language that has kept British working-class culture alive from one generation to the next. 'It's a right Fred Karno's', 'Like a bloody circus', 'Couldn't organise a piss-up in a brewery', 'Couldn't organise a brothel in a troopship' – these are all stock phrases. No doubt the workers of all nations have their own stock phrases too, and in itself such 'evidence' is therefore worth little. But all these epithets do convey a form of criticism that, in Gallie's terms, is 'technical', and year in year out they have been directed at British management. For anyone wanting to construct a 'culturalist' explanation of the British productivity shortfall they might prove a good place to start. They might signpost a few clues for those who specialise in productivity research too.

Part Four

The difficulties resolved?

# 9 Enter Mrs Thatcher: The 'fear and anxiety' syndrome

In 1980 unemployment soared. In this same year the number of industrial disputes fell to a post-war low. The proportion of manual workers in manufacturing who were in trade unions, which had climbed from about 60 to 80 per cent over the course of the previous decade, also fell (Buiter and Miller, 1984, p. 347). Beginning in 1980, male absenteeism on the grounds of ill-health also appears to have fallen (*General Household Survey*, 1984, p. 125, Table 6.40). That the British trade union movement fell from the plateau it had occupied for four decades and more is of course very largely accounted for by mounting unemployment. So severe has the impact of this been that employment in British manufacturing fell by a quarter during the course of the 1979–83 Conservative administration. But whether consideration is given to the fall in trade union membership or to the very marked decline in the extent to which official trade unionism had the ear of government, it is not difficult to argue that at the outset of the 1980s the trade unions had been weakened.

Mrs Thatcher first took office in May 1979. There is room for doubt about how far the policies her government pursued actually derived from a strict reading of a particular (monetarist) school of economic theory. There is room for discussion about how far the rhetoric of Thatcherism has been a good guide to some of its practice, and even about whether some of the seeds of the new economic policies may have been sown by previous Labour administrations. There is room for debate about a number of other matters as well: whether the Thatcherites merely allowed unemployment to mount; whether they deliberately engineered some part of the massive increase, and if so how much of it; whether they actually underestimated the extent to which

173

unemployment would rise, and so on. The view taken here is that the harsh monetary policy was adopted to control inflation *and* in the expectation that its consequences would cow trade unionists, and that, despite some similarities, the policies adopted by the Thatcher administrations have been qualitatively different from those pursued hitherto. Some of these issues will be returned to in the final chapter. However, in the context of this chapter three points are of crucial importance. (1) In Thatcherite Britain a condition for success touted by several generations of vulgar Tories – 'What this country needs is three million unemployed' – was actually met. (2) The official figures on manufacturing productivity suggest that a significant transformation soon took place (see Figure 9.1, which plots their course from 1973 through the first Thatcher government, i.e. up to June 1983). (3) There is the conclusion that has so often been drawn, that the brute facts of unemployment have done their work.

All three of the above points make for a particular sort of

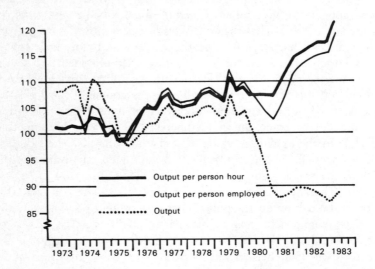

Source: *Employment Gazette*, July 1983, 516, 1.8.
*Note*: Seasonally adjusted. 1975 = 100.

**Figure 9.1**  Output and productivity in manufacturing industries, 1973–83

account of Thatcherism – an account that can be embellished to take in its triumph as an ideological force, and to take in also the changes that have been instituted in employment legislation. But the main lines of such an interpretation are clear to see. Mrs Thatcher – by boldly denying responsibility for bat, ball or wicket – achieved what had never been accomplished before. She made British workers find out the hard way what the game was really about. It was this, the new Thatcherite 'realism', that helped to change the 'climate' in which British industrial relations were conducted, which made British workers 'see sense', which got it into their heads that there really was no alternative and which (at last) led to a widespread change in their attitudes. On this interpretation, the productivity figures are the proof of the pudding – they are testimony to the fact that Thatcherism has worked. *Has it?* In what respects? With what consequences? Beginning with this chapter Part Four seeks to begin to answer such questions.

As early as November 1981 Mrs Thatcher was claiming recognition for what had been achieved with productivity. Opening the debate on the Queen's Speech she claimed: '*In the manufacturing industries, we have seen productivity per man-hour rising at a rate that is reminiscent of Germany or Japan.*' She claimed further '*Reforms of labour practices that should have taken place decades ago have been achieved in a matter of months . . . Many firms have found new scope for co-operation between management and employees.*' On top of this she drew attention to the fact that all this had been '*achieved in the teeth of a world recession – at a time when increases in productivity are rarely achieved*'. Other ministers kept the good news coming. In 1982 Sir Geoffrey Howe claimed in his Mansion House speech that Britain had 'earned respect in the international community . . . *in achieving dramatic improvements in productivity*', as evidence of which he cited an improvement of 12 per cent in 1981 alone. The same message came across in party political broadcasts: '*Productivity has never been higher*' (see p. 9 above). Such claims were well to the fore in the run-up to the 1983 election. They have continued to be made since – so much so that few in Britain can have failed to hear of the Thatcher success story with manufacturing productivity, nor failed to grasp who had brought it about, or how.

Sir Douglas Wass, the former head of the Treasury, got right to the heart of this particular matter – about how it had come about that things had changed – in an interview he gave upon his retirement in 1983 (*The Times*, 31 March). Considering changes in 'shop-floor behaviour' he quite clearly put these down to 'fear and anxiety'. That so much had been accomplished in this way had, he said, come as a 'surprise' to him. But, in no way confusing Mrs Thatcher's reference to '*scope for* co-operation' with co-operation itself, he made no attempt to disguise what he thought was really going on. In his view: 'What has emerged in shop-floor behaviour through fear and anxiety is much greater than I think could be secured by more co-operative methods.'

Given that the British trade union movement has been weakened, and given also the view that was put forward in Chapter 6 – that in so far as British labour could be said to have contributed to 'the difficulty' with British manufacturing productivity, a key factor was that British workers were not vulnerable *enough* – the explanation for the rise in productivity does look blindingly clear. A new regime that trades in the politics of fear has claimed its due reward. Evidence in line with such an interpretation was forthcoming as early as 1981, when a panel of business respondents was already reporting 'very realistic changes in outlook' and frequent references were made to a 'steady improvement in labour attitudes and productivity' (Wenban-Smith, 1982, pp. 58–9). Further evidence of a change in climate was forthcoming from a survey conducted by a British management journal in 1984, which reviewed progress over the previous eighteen months, by which time, on Mrs Thatcher's own thinking, the new realism should have had yet greater effect (back in 1981 she had staked her personal reputation on the forecast that the sacrifices of the previous two and a half years would be rewarded in the coming year: *Guardian*, parliamentary report, 5 November 1981).

This survey reported a number of changes that some companies had recently introduced – including 'tightening discipline and timekeeping, with much less abuse of tea breaks, washing-up time and the like; wiping out all, or most, unjustified overtime and "one in, all in" practices; eroding demarcation, horizontally between jobs and vertically between skill levels, and improving work flexibility; rationalising – in many cases, eradicating – special payments for heavy or dirty work, unmeasured work and samples; cutting out bonus for unexceptional performance (by tightening standards, for example); and tightening production and quality targets, often while introducing automation or more productive equipment'. 'We're not talking about screwing down the workers', the author of the survey stated, 'simply getting back to sensible working arrangements' (Chambers, 1984, p. 18). He passed off some 'more extreme examples' – in one case 'cutting holiday entitlement by 25 per cent, reducing standard times by 2½ per cent, and eliminating all unpaid leave and pay for overtime' – by noting that whilst 'these seem excessively tough . . . they have been justified by management and accepted by employees'. He similarly conceded that another arrangement, whereby 'the productivity bonus . . . is now tied to attendance' – so tightly that an employee would lose it 'if he is four minutes late' – might 'seem unduly harsh' (as well it might, since in this case the bonus represented *one third* of total earnings). But this too was excused, on the grounds that it was 'all part of a package', with 'tough discipline rigorously applied but also higher rewards – which the company could now afford since it has fewer employees doing more work'.

'For twenty years [managers] have had a buffeting and bashing from government and unions . . . we have an opportunity now that will last for two or three years . . . So grab it now. We have had a pounding and we are all fed up with it. I think it would be fair to say it's almost vengeance.' Such were the words of Mr Len Collinson, a consultant and director of several companies, and the man who, once upon a time, was briefly the chairman of the KME workers' co-operative (*Financial Times*, 5 January 1981). Collinson's words, and in particular his reference to 'vengeance' have been widely cited as symptomatic of a new hard line in British management (Storey, 1983, p. 1; Littler and Salaman, 1984, p. 114), and as we have seen there were certainly some managements who were fully prepared to drive home their advantage.

Nowhere, of course, has this tendency been more remarked upon than at BL, a company whose improved performance has attracted almost as much praise in the 1980s as its poor record did in the 1970s. Amongst Mrs Thatcher's admirers, indeed, BL is often regarded as the brightest jewel in her productivity crown. And, sure enough, productivity at BL *has* improved. For instance, man-hours per car in Body-in-White at Longbridge dropped by almost half between May 1979 and May 1983 (Willman *et al.*, 1985, chap. 8, and p. 153 Table 8.2). Whether or not some of the changes wrought on BL's shop floors have been inspired by 'vengeance', they certainly had much to do with 'tough discipline rigorously applied', and this particular feature has figured as much in left-wing accounts about what happened at BL as in those from the political right. As a writer in *New Left Review* pointed out in 1981: 'the Tories have been keen to advertise the Edwardes style of management as the epitome of the proper way to take a hand in the restructuring of British capitalism' – 'using closures and mass redundancies to "thin out" the workforce' (especially, as he noted, 'the militants': 'Red Robbo', the Longbridge convenor Derek Robinson, had been sacked in November 1979) – 'while intimidating the survivors into quiescence and higher productivity'. Describing the situation that applied where he worked, at BL Rover, Solihull, where productivity had also increased by 50 per cent since the summer of 1979, his account went on to make it quite clear that 'there is no doubt that the shopfloor has suffered a set-back' (Ahsan, 1981). An account that appeared the next year in *Militant* (23 April 1982) provided further details on the sort of changes that had taken place. With the focus this time on what had happened at Longbridge, it reported: 'In the past management wouldn't shift you without the agreement of the union: now it's done without consultation . . . In the old days the target was set by timing the operator, now the target is based on the "gross potential" of the machine, that means they set the machine as fast as possible, the only limit being quality, and you have to keep up with it. They . . . check your counter every hour; blokes have been suspended for failing to have an adequate explanation of why they haven't reached their target.'

There clearly was a transformation at BL. In general terms, the industrial relations system was restructured and the number of bargaining units for hourly-paid workers decreased. The large number of local agreements that were once negotiated at sectional level, yet which were put in writing and could be held up against management – thus tending both to restrict mobility between different areas and ensuring the close involvement of shop stewards – have gone. The number of stewards has also been reduced. Those remaining have sometimes found themselves refused facilities. Mutuality – a principle that goes back to an engineering agreement in 1922 whereby it was agreed that times and prices should be fixed by the mutual agreemenet of employer and worker – has also gone (BL broke from the Engineering Employers' Federation in June 1980). 'Flexibility' is in. If full team working has not been achieved, the degree of multi-trade manning in maintenance has been noticeably lessened. Since 1978, indeed, the corporate strategy of rationalisation, contraction and increased productivity has had as its complement a hard-line industrial relations policy. Aimed at the eradication of trade union influence in production other than on terms favoured by management, it has clearly met with a significant degree of success. The 'participation' scheme of 1976, such as it was, was soon dispensed with as part of the shift.

The above account should leave no doubt that the changes that occurred on the labour side at BL contributed to increased productivity.[1] Some further points need to be borne in mind, however. For a start, the Body-in-White man-hours per car figures cited above are a little misleading. Had we taken as our base for comparison not May 1979 but May 1977, the improvement would have looked more like 40 per cent than 50, for the man-hours per car performance had been almst 10 per cent worse in the month that Mrs Thatcher came to power than it had been two years earlier. Of course the difference this makes still permits the conclusion that productivity increased substantially. But it serves to remind us that the choice of base point can have an effect on the extent of the productivity change recorded, which has implications for any assessment of the Thatcherites' success. As can be seen from Figure 9.1, the official data on labour productivity was moving downwards in the second half of 1979. Then again, despite the changes in work practices, which did enhance flexibility – so that by 1983 the Metro line was being planned for output at the most efficient rate, and when the weekly output target was met men were transferred to other work, either direct or building up stock – it is important to remember that the Metro, work on which is included in the Body-in-White man-hours figures cited above after 1980, had a massive investment of £275 million behind it. In fact, the whole project had been planned to cut down on labour input. There was new plant. In the New West Works body shop two sets of robots substituted for the labour of about 200 workers on the main lines. Multiwelders dispensed with the need for another 134. Such a degree of automation was without parallel, at least as judged by BL's historic standards. Such was the contrast, indeed, that a journalist reporting on the new body shop in 1982 felt it necessary to preface his account of such technical advances by reassuring his readers that it was '*still dependent on humans*' (Fryer, 1982a, emphasis added).

It is hoped that the last few remarks will help to put the reader in a critical frame of mind. For despite the undoubted importance of changes on the labour side at BL, and of those other changes that have been reported from elsewhere, and despite the self-congratulating proclamations of the new Tory 'realists', it really is all too easy to leap to what on the face of it is the obvious conclusion about Thatcherism and productivity – in a nutshell, that there has been 'vengeance'; that the fruits of this came quickly; and that as far as managements are concerned, they have been sweet indeed. In this connection, it is instructive to go back to what Collinson said, and to report his comments a little more fully. To do so is to see that he not only spoke of 'vengeance'. He also warned his fellow managers: 'take your revenge carefully'. We too must be careful: both about assuming that a new hard, abrasive and confident managerial style, the very echo of the 'Iron Lady' herself, has gained currency throughout British management, and about the idea that it is this that has delivered the goods to a widespread and significant degree. To go back to the management survey that was quoted earlier, and to consider this rather more fully, and not simply for the examples it affords of the savage measures that some possibly smaller employers have adopted, is also to underline the need for caution. For although this survey of what forty works managers and directors had done to improve working practices did conclude that 'nearly all have taken action', it emphasised also that their achievements had been partial ones only, and that, as the author of the report saw it, 'the most wasteful work practices still exist'. It quoted managers themselves as pointing out: 'We're stuck with the traditional fitter and electrician'; 'Over the last 18 months little has been gained by changing work practices. In fact, we gave away an extra holiday at one negotiation in order to reach agreement'; 'A joint management–union working party is trying to increase flexibility, but the problem is every move is expected to have a price tag' – and so on (Chambers, 1984, p. 18).

These further comments by managers were not reported earlier, for the simple reason that due recognition had to be given to the fact that *some* managements *have* grossly exploited the weakening effects of anxiety and fear. By beginning as I have done I hope to have made this clear. But such is the potency of the 'new realism' *as an ideological force* that it always threatens to lure us into accepting simplistic assumptions. Prominent among these is the idea that there was one shop-floor world before Thatcher and that this was subject to a radical transformation thereafter – the change being such that, according to Thatcher herself, and Howe, even by the years 2T and 3T the changed work practices and effort-levels on Britain's shop floors had already translated into dramatic improvements in labour productivity. To retrace our steps one more time, this time to revisit BL, is to see some further need to pull back from such an interpretation.

Although this is often forgotten, the man who is popularly thought to have worked the miracle at BL, Michael Edwardes, was of course appointed by the Callaghan Labour government, which, judged in narrow party political terms, does somewhat melt the icing on this particular Tory celebration cake (so, reading between the lines, might Edwardes' own evaluation of the people he dealt with in Labour and Tory administrations, on which see Edwardes, 1984). It is worth remarking also that workforce ballots, a favoured Thatcher recipe, were an important ingredient in BL's labour relations strategy as far back as 1977, again before the Tories came to power. Of larger significance, however, is the fact that changes were underway on British shop floors during the 1970s, most especially so, as far as labour intensification goes, from the mid-1970s. It is in fact from this time that a shift in emphasis from technological renewal to changing the balance of power between labour and capital has sometimes been dated (Massey and Meegan, 1982, p. 207).

Looking to government economic policy, a number of commentators have concluded that the shift away from demand management also occurred in the mid-1970s – Healey's 1975 budget and Callaghan's 1976 Labour Party Conference Speech being the most cited dates for this (Brittan, 1983; Riddell, 1983). The OECD would seem to be of the same opinion: 'Although the change in approach was gradual, its clearest indication came with the 1975 Budget when the Chancellor [Healey] introduced a deflationary Budget at a time of falling output and rising unemployment' (*United Kingdom Economic Survey*, January 1984). Of course, the fall in output under Labour in no way measured up to what was to follow nor the unemployment – and anyone who wants to argue that there is 'no difference' between the Labour and Conservative parties will find this more than usually difficult following the rise and rise of Mrs Thatcher.[2] To make it plain, this 'all the same' view is not adhered to here. Nor, indeed, to anticipate, is it going to be denied in later pages that working practices have undergone some further modification during the Thatcher years. What is being urged at this point, however, is (1) that the politics of fear, even as they have been stridently proclaimed in recent years, and with what has all the appearance of ample material support, may not have translated into radical and quickly effected changes in higher productivity on Britain's shop floors to the widespread extent that is often supposed; and (2) that it is also necessary to draw back a little from the assumption that might have been thought to be implicit in the observations made at the outset – that it was from the weakening of British trade unions at the end of the 1970s that the early productivity improvement came (reforms in labour practices having been 'achieved in a matter of months', etc.). Both considerations suggest that it is necessary to exercise caution in evaluating the results of the 'Thatcher experiment'.

It has been argued repeatedly in this book that the drag on measured productivity that can be properly attributed to British workers was often overstated in the 1970s, and that a whole number of *other* determinants of productivity – over and above British workers' attitudes and the effort they did or did not expend or the peculiarities of British trade unions – were all too often neglected. The opposite, but logically quite consistent, point now has to be made as well: that increases in measured productivity in the 1980s cannot be automatically attributed to workers either. If common-or-garden labour productivity really has increased at BL, for example, investment has increased also (and this, as we shall see in the next chapter, is far from the whole story). Take another favoured Thatcherite productivity miracle, the one at BSC, and again it is necessary to consider the whole picture, not just one part of it: to concede that if labour productivity has increased, massive scrapping has taken place as well, much of it under the Callaghan government as it happens, and that production has *also* been concentrated into a smaller number of relatively modern plants.

In due course the Thatcherite record will be re-examined in the light of what progress has been made to improve British manufacturing productivity on fronts other than the labour one. But for the moment there is one particular consideration that merits attention which has been entirely neglected thus far. It relates to the other end of the Thatcherite productivity rainbow – that is, not to the evidence that shop-floor behaviour has changed, but to the extent to which the official data actually confirms that productivity has improved.

What, then, of the official statistics? And what in particular about the rapid take-off in productivity that they indicate took place in 1981? It is helpful to discuss these two matters together, because to do so is make more credible the most obvious of all explanations for this sudden surge – one that is unlikely to be accounted for by British workers suddenly having had a 'change of heart'. This most obvious of all explanations (which differs sharply from the one that was held out by Mrs Thatcher herself) is of course that as the recession bit deeper, more plants, factories and companies went to the wall. Since those companies and parts of companies that survived were likely to be the most efficient, the impression given by the national productivity figures – that common-or-garden productivity was improving – was largely a statistical illusion. On such an interpretation the statistics were not testimony to the alacrity with which workers had reacted to Mrs Thatcher's refusal to take responsibility for bat, ball or wicket. To explain what had happened quite another cricketing analogy is called for – that of 'the cricket team that improves its batting average by only playing its better batsmen' (Buiter and Miller, 1984, p. 358). Does such an explanation hold water, though?

As it stands, such an explanation is not entirely convincing. As can be seen from the collapse in output depicted in Figure 9.1, the shedding of plant was at its most drastic in 1980. So devastating was this collapse that from the end of 1979 to the end of 1980 manufacturing output dropped by a sixth – more than it had even during the inter-war years. But, on the official data, the productivity breakthrough was most in evidence through 1981.

In practice, however, this lack of correspondence between the output and productivity figures does not confound the interpretation that led us to consider them in the first place – that rather than British labour having been *shook-up*, thus heralding a new era of 'co-operation', it was the *shake-out* of British manufacturing plant that had created the statistical illusion of the sharp productivity increase. Two independently conducted sets of research into productivity are relevant here. One of these, the work of Mendis and Muellbauer, has resulted in the construction of an index, the object of which is to remove the main short-term cyclical elements from data on output per head.[3] It has been suggested at various points in this book that British managements may have been deficient in making use of the labour which is available to them, and that the work produced by that labour may well have gone to waste because of a lack of organisational proficiency. But, clearly, what workers can produce – no matter how hard they work – is in part a function of the work that is put to them by management. It is this kind of determinant of labour utilisation (or labour hoarding), and its cyclical undulation, that Mendis and Muelbauer have sought to capture. An early upshot of their investigation was that when the data in Figure 9.1 was corrected for short-term cyclical utilisation, the take-off point for productivity growth moved back, to the beginning of 1980, the steep downward path of output during that year thus having as its complement a steep upward rise in productivity.

This conclusion of Mendis and Muellbauer's not only does much to confirm the shake-out thesis, it also finds further support in the earlier utilisation of labour index developed by Smith-Gavine and Bennett. The close correspondence in the results of these two investigations is all the more impressive because they employed different methods: the Mendis and Muellbauer research taking a mathematical form, Smith-Gavine and Bennett monitoring a number of manufacturing firms and making direct use of management's own work measurement techniques. On the basis of an early comparison conducted by Mendis and Muellbauer (1983, p. 29) both investigations found an annual rate of cyclically corrected labour productivity of 1.8 per cent for the period 1971:3 to 1979:4; they varied very little in their estimates of the extent of the breakthrough that they both suggested began in 1980:1 (Mendis and Muellhauer put 1980:1 – 1981:1 at 11.0 per cent, Smith-Gavine and Bennett put it at 8.7 per cent); and they were also in agreement on 1981:1 – 1982:4, each of them coming up with an increase of only 1.3 per cent.

The validity of Smith-Gavine and Bennett's work is enhanced by the association it would seem to reveal between investment and 'technological productivity' (a term which for our purposes can be briefly described as the difference between their index of the utilisation of labour and measured productivity). Their data indicates that technological productivity rises following a rise in gross fixed investment in plant and machinery. Thus, when investment peaked in 1970, a rise in technological productivity followed; after a rise in investment in 1973–4 it rose again in 1974–5. Investment also increased in the last years of the Labour administration, however – and a further rise in technological productivity once again followed – in 1980–81 (Smith-Gavine and Bennett, 1982, Chart 12). It would appear, then, that at the very same time productivity was apparently improving, but in large part because of the massive destruction over which Mrs Thatcher presided, she might also have reaped the benefit of some real increase – though on the basis of investment that had taken place earlier on. To the extent that the Smith-Gavine and Bennett technological productivity measure reflects changes in working practices, it would seem that the groundwork for these had its origin in the pre-Thatcher years as well.

The idea that the most dramatic part of Mrs Thatcher's 'success' with productivity had a different explanation to that claimed for it is made more plausible when it is remembered that although the 1970s research into British productivity showed labour productivity to be lower in the large majority of cases, considerable differences were also shown to pertain *between* and *within* UK industries (see pp. 56, 77 above). The output figures confirm that since 1979 labour-intensive, low-productivity industries (like clothing, textiles and footwear) contracted rapidly.[4] This, in conjunction with the greater difficulty which low-value-added operations in any industry faced in coping with the effects of a high exchange rate, is almost certainly sufficient to explain a significant part of the 'breakthrough' of 1980. The notion that this was the time when some of the less efficient parts of the production units that were added together in the earlier merger boom went to the wall might also fit here (see pp. 147–51).

If, in the light of the above, the Thatcherites' own explanation for why (officially measured) productivity improved in the first Tory administration lacks credibility, the notion that such increases in productivity are 'rarely achieved' in recession also stands in need of correction. Such productivity 'miracles' have in fact been replicated in other countries that have been subject to high unemployment. During 1973–81 Belgium's productivity growth ranked second only to that of Japan amongst the major OECD countries, with unemployment rising from 2.8 per cent in 1973 to a massive 14.8 per cent in 1983. Again, the Netherlands, with 15.5 per cent unemployment, has also witnessed a productivity boom (Sachs, 1984, p. 371). If a recession is severe enough such increases in measured productivity are a likely result. (For the record, Howe's claim about a 12 per cent improvement in productivity during 1981 was also ill-founded. As Kellner has pointed out (1982b, p. 7), in making this claim Howe contracted an eighteen-month growth in productivity into twelve months.)

To prick the self-congratulatory bubble that surrounded Mrs Thatcher's early and supposedly dramatic success with labour productivity is one thing. To go on from this and to deny that labour productivity has undergone any real improvement at all is quite another. It has been seen that cyclically corrected figures for 1980:1 – 1981:1 correlated so closely with the collapse in output as to make the early claims that the Thatcherites advanced highly dubious, and that their claims were yet more dubious in some cases because they did not get even the official data right. But more recent estimates allow us to consider cyclically corrected data over a longer time period, both going back to an earlier starting point and following through nearer to the present. These suggest the following rates of annual productivity growth: 1955–73 3.4 per cent; 1973–9 1.4 per cent; 1979–80 −0.3 per cent; and 1980–3 2.9 per cent (Muellbauer, 1984).

The above figures are scarcely testimony to 'dramatic' achievement. If anything, indeed, the truly dramatic feature of this series is the *fall* in productivity in 1979–80, which suggests that the Thatcherites actually presided over what was in all probability the highest level of 'overmanning' in British manufacturing in living memory – an overmanning induced by the inability of employers to shed labour fast enough to match their falling order books. It can be seen also that even the 2.9 per cent rate for 1980–83 still falls below that for 1955–73. On the other hand, though, the 1980–83 figures do indicate some improvement on those for the immediate pre-Thatcher years – an improvement which is unlikely to be explained by exclusive resort to a simple shake-out thesis, though 'slimming' has of course continued since 1980. This makes it necessary to ask: was it a change on the part of British labour that lay behind this increase in the more recent period?

# 10 The new 'realism' and reality: Workers and management

Taking care to avoid generalities of the 'hearts and minds' variety, and placing particular stress on the fact that 'British labour' is not a homogeneous entity, in this chapter an assessment is attempted of change and continuity in three particular (albeit somewhat overlapping) spheres: in legislation, in industrial relations and in work organisation. Since the reportage of Parliamentary debate and trade union responses to the new legislation has seen to it that it is this that has made the greater clatter in the public ear, it is the new Employment and Trade Union Acts that are considered first, along with possible changes in industrial relations practices. Following this, the nature and extent of changes in work organisation are considered at rather greater length, with 'work organisation' itself being defined in a broad manner for reasons which will become apparent shortly. Finally, the attempt is made to highlight certain developments on the management side.

The general intention of the 1980 and 1982 Employment Acts was to delimit the legal sphere in which British unions operate. The new legislation confined the range of legitimate trade union action to employer-specific relations. It did this through outlawing many forms of industrial action such as solidarity strikes or blacking and 'union only' clauses in commercial contracts, and it sought to undermine closed shop agreements, to make it easier to sack strikers, and to make picketing unlawful almost anywhere outside the plant where a dispute was taking place. For example, picketing is now unlawful at an employer's head office, at the employer's other site, at companies that trade with the employer and at companies to which the employer transfers work.

As a consequence of the 1982 Act, unions now face the threat of crippling damages under civil law for each unlawful industrial action in which they engage, ultimately facing bankruptcy through fines for contempt if they do not comply with court injunctions. All this has been served up in the name of 'freedom'. What it actually amounts to is a concerted state offensive on organised labour on behalf of employers – and the new legislation has met with some 'success'. In the 1983 dispute between the NGA and Shah's *Stockport Messenger*, the TUC held back its support and the union was forced to stop its secondary picketing. The POEU was also defeated in its fight against privatisation at British Telecom, a Court of Appeal injunction on behalf of the private firm Mercury raising the odds too high for the union to continue in its refusal to connect that firm's network to the BT one. Legal actions also made an appearance in 1984 in the miners' dispute, though notably as initiated by haulage firms and 'working miners'. The NCB itself held back from resort to legal remedy, however, and the Tory government, in line with a plan formulated as early as 1978, preferred to mount a massive policing operation, its new legislation thus remaining for the most part so many words on sheets of paper, despite extremely heavy picketing. In fact, it is the apparent reluctance of so many British employers to resort to the law that has been the most remarkable feature of the new legislation to date.

Of course, section 3 of the 1982 Employment Act only came into force in November 1984. According to this anyone sacked for refusing to become a member of a union which has a closed shop agreement with the employer has an automatic claim for unfair dismissal, unless a secret ballot in the previous five years has demonstrated very significant support for this arrangement (closed shops now require between 80 and 85 per cent approval depending on the case, and if ballots are not held dismissal for non-union membership will be automatically unfair). The effects of the 1984 Trade Union Act, which provides for ballots before strikes, for the election of members of union executives, and on whether workers want their unions to have a political fund, also remain to be seen, both within production and on national politics, though it would seem that the Thatcherites learned their own lessons from Taff Vale and its reversal (cf. pp. 132–3). In seeking to put the clock back to the beginning of the century their objective would appear to be to attempt, this time, to cripple the unions *and* the Labour Party.

If British employers continue to be reticent about taking direct advantage of the legal offensive launched on their behalf, however, they will be running more or less true to historical form. This may be in part because – and here we find another historical echo – British industrial capital has not formed itself into a more highly co-ordinated and coherent body. Early on in the Thatcher years, for example, not enough employers were prepared to pay the high premiums required to launch a CBI German-style plan for strike insurance, the interests of industrial capital as a whole thus being thwarted by the reluctance of individual companies. A further token of the continuing lack of co-ordination within the ranks of industrial capital in Britain is that, as Batstone suggestively puts it, British employer organisation may have declined more rapidly in the recession than union organisation has, rather more employers choosing to go it alone. In 1978, 71 per cent of plants were affiliated to employers' associations; by 1983 the figure had dropped to 57 per cent. A similar thing happened in the inter-war years when there was a fall in both the membership of the largest employers' body, the EEF, and in the number of Joint Industrial Councils (for further discussion see Batstone, 1984, p. 208; Soskice, 1984, pp. 316–18; Brown and Sisson, 1984, p. 24).

True enough, there are some signs of change within industrial relations systems. To be counted here are possible (pre-1984) developments concerning the closed shop. Whereas, for example, the most thorough research shows that the number of those covered by the closed shop dropped from 5.2 million in 1978 to 4.5 million in 1982, which is broadly in line with the fall in employment, the closed shop, which is particularly evident in older industries (e.g. printing), can hardly be said to have got a very secure foothold in the expanding electronics sector. Things could change in time, of course, but a 1984 survey found that only 18 per cent of electronics companies had a closed shop, non-unionisation itself being a notable characteristic thus far, though with regional variations. In the South-East 73 per cent were non-union, in Wales less than 40 per cent, with a similar proportion in Scotland (Gennard and Dunn, 1984; ELF, 1984).

Other possible developments in industrial relations include a move towards the decentralisation of bargaining, the rather faltering emergence of some longer-term contracts, and in some cases a possible tendency to push unions into pay bargaining more closely tied to productivity within profit centres, and in parallel with *ad hoc* or other arrangements to communicate with the workforce more directly on other issues, and on a consultative basis only.

There are three things to be weighed in the balance here, however. First, all was not static pre-Thatcher, as can be seen from BL (see above). Second, it would be foolhardy to overlook the fact that even if some of these developments were to become generalised they might prove mixed blessings to capital. It is no more the case from capital's point of view than it is from labour's that there is any such thing as a perfect industrial relations system: decentralised bargaining can open the door to disputes about parity; two- or three-year contracts, which are actually precious few in number, are in themselves no guarantee of strike-free production; strikes called through the ballot could prove yet more solid; and single union agreements (discussed later) could strengthen the hand of labour in the longer term – as indeed could more flexible working arrangements (also discussed later). Pushing this line a little further, it is also perfectly clear that the legislative changes, through directly implicating the state, could backfire, Thatcherite economism having as its reward a politicisation of industrial relations. What is at issue here, though, is the question of whether the changes that have *already* taken place in industrial relations are likely to have contributed to the improvement in productivity, easily overstated as this itself may often have been. The third thing to note, therefore, is that with respect to each and every one of the developments referred to above there is evidence of *some* movement only.

Superficially, it looks as though the 1980s provided the employers with the opportunity to change the structure of British industrial relations *radically*. But that new developments are as yet limited is something upon which industrial relationists themselves are almost unanimous (see for example Gennard and Dunn, 1984; Goodhart, 1982; Groom, 1984a; IDS, 1983, 1984c, 1984f, 1984g; Kelly, 1984; Marsh, 1982; Rose and Jones, 1983; Soskice, 1984; Terry, 1983).[1] Batstone, who in 1983 conducted a survey which compared the industrial relations situation that pertained then to that discovered in earlier surveys, in particular the 1978 Warwick study, also concludes: 'up to the present what is striking is not the efficacy of market forces, but their limited effect upon those plants which survive' (1984, p. 310). In fact Batstone suggests that change has been very limited indeed. He tells us, for example, that the closed shop has actually *increased*, that there has been no significant change in non-recognition of unions in plants with manual union members, and that there has been little decline in shop steward density. However, Batstone's discussion of working practices is based on data that he admits to be 'crude' and which, as he states, needs 'to be treated with considerable caution'.

Unfortunately, there are several other reasons why Batstone's entire project has to be evaluated with considerable care. These extend beyond those which derive from the fact that his small postal survey was 'a very blunt instrument', and they are worth noting here in order to alert the reader to some rather different lines of interpretation presented later. First, Batstone's survey was limited to large plants, whereas what he calls 'macho' management may be more prevalent amongst smaller employers. There are in fact good reasons for expecting that the brunt of the recession has been borne by particular firms and (disadvantaged) groups of labour (Rubery, Tarling and Wilkinson, 1984). Second, his survey excludes the public sector, whereas it is possible that some of the most marked changes have occurred in this sector where the government could make its influence felt more directly, for example at BL (although it is perhaps indicative of Batstone's general stance that even when he refers to this company he seeks to minimise what change has occurred). Third, when considering both Batstone's and other surveys it is necessary to bear in mind that it does not necessarily follow that the effects of the recession on the working class are to be judged exclusively with reference to changes in 'industrial relations' as conventionally approached by industrial relationists; nor only with reference to changes *within* on-going work organisation. It is possible, in short, that Batstone would have found more to surprise him had he considered more closely some developments taking place outside of the surviving 'core' employment relationships upon which he concentrates – developments such as sub-contract, to which he appears to devote a mere paragraph, and then, once more, only to arrive at a no change/insufficient evidence verdict (see Batstone, 1984, pp. 191, 193, 195, 208, 211, 212, 214–15, 242–5, 295, 310, 313). Some such developments will be considered further below, along with other features of work organisation.

Turning now to work organisation, it is clear that our consideration must take in possible changes in *how the labour process is organised*. Obviously enough, this entails reviewing the evidence on such matters as a possible decrease in craft demarcation and a consideration of whether flexibility has increased more generally. But when industrial organisation was considered in earlier chapters a very definite attempt was made to apply that term in a very broad sense, so that our usage corresponded to something that might be better referred to as the organisation *of* industry – a term that both permitted and invited us to consider a very broad spectrum of relations, micro, intermediate and macro, including those that formed the industrial capital/financial capital/state nexus. Such an interpretation was adopted precisely because it was believed that the determination of productivity can only be partially understood in terms of a model that is confined to the direct employer-employee relation. Now, following a similar logic, a similar course will be followed with respect to the more limited sphere denoted by the term 'work organisation'. This term is quite deliberately used here to refer to the organisation *of* work, and again necessarily so because there is more potential variability in the organisation of work than a 'task model' would suggest.

The task model, in which pride of place is given to the 'task master' (manager) and to those who perform the tasks set in his particular factory, is most certainly of value for an understanding of productivity, but, equally certainly, it requires elaboration, and it also needs complementing with a broader analysis, one which forces us to raise our eyes from changes in the specification of tasks and the intensity of task performance within the given shop floor or factory. This, to cut a long story short, is why in what follows the temptation to jump straight into a discussion of the evidence of changes in *how* work is organised with respect to increased flexibility of job tasks, etc., has been resisted. Instead, it is 'spatial' and 'temporal' elements that are first considered – that is, possible changes in *where* production takes place, and *when*. Following this, attention is switched to possible modifications in *the basis of which labour is bought and sold*, that is, whether through the direct purchase of labour-power or through other means. Reliance upon a simple task model tends to deflect attention from such possible variations, especially if it is applied to the monitoring of the work and industrial relations practices of on-going labour forces in particular workplaces – which is of course the very basis upon which the still relatively modest amount of social scientific research into change during the recession has been conducted.

Relocation is clearly one important aspect of *where production takes place*, and relocation to greenfield sites is equally clearly one important mechanism through which changes in work organisation have sometimes been effected. When the cigarette manufacturer Rothman International shifted to Spennymoor in Durham, for example, there is little doubt that one key consideration was that this would allow the company to escape what management had come to regard as the unwanted effects of long-established working practices (Rees, 1984). Other examples of such moves being made to facilitate greater flexibility, sometimes through the introduction of 'group working', have also been documented (for Rothmans at Spennymoor, Trebor at Colchester, Whitbread at Magor, South Wales, and Fisher Body at Belfast, see IDS, 1984c).

Lane has argued: 'we can be quite sure that a new rural plant belonging to a multi-plant firm has been provided with carefully designed labour processes. Equipped with supervisory workers long experienced in the habits, ruses and dodges of urban workers, firms can establish from scratch their ideal job descriptions and work rhythms' (1982, p. 9). Lane is of course quite right. It is no mere coincidence that in the North-East, where many multi-plant firms have outposts, there exist also a considerable number of single-union agreements – an estimated 250 in 1984, mainly with GMBATU (previously GMWU), the TGWU and AUEW (*Financial Times*, North-East Supplement, 18 September 1984). That the much-remarked 'enterprise unionism' of the EETPU has been partly encouraged by the emergence of new production sites, or sites that have undergone a change of ownership – and not least Japanese ones, which have sometimes brought with them no-strike agreements and 'pendulum' arbitration agreements – is equally relevant.

It is in fact arguable that the most decisive impacts of the recession on labour have been at the *points of entry to* and *exit from* the labour process. Typically, the managements of on-going operations not only rely on their unions on a day-to-day basis, they are implicated in working arrangements made with their consent. At the 'exit point' from the labour process, by contrast, workers who have seen so many operations collapse elsewhere are likely to be constrained by the belief that their operation really must shut too, their ability to fight closure thus being clearly weakened, even if, up to this time, they have sought to hang onto what they've got. Similarly, at the point of entry to the labour process, starting afresh – and often vetoing jobs for stewards and others deemed 'awkward' – provides management with greater opportunity and less constraint.

The extent to which greenfield relocation may account for an improvement in productivity during the 1980s is rather less than the above might suggest however. The greenfield site, and the shift from densely populated 'traditional' urban areas, was evident in the 1970s, and many such moves had their origin before that, in the 1960s (as did the branch plant economy of the North-East, which was considerably stimulated by government grants). The notion that the sorts of agreements that the EETPU had made with Hitachi at Hirwaun, South Wales, and with Toshiba at Plymouth are evidence of a new 'enterprise trades unionism' in Britain also needs to be held in check. Of course, if, as seems likely, the AUEW gains sole negotiating rights at the new Nissan car plant at Washington, Tyne and Wear, its leaders will be well pleased, and they will be yet more pleased if they do not have to commit themselves to a formal no-strike agreement in the process. The North-East is burdened by high unemployment. Tyne and Wear needs work. It lost about one-third of its manufacturing jobs between 1979 and 1984. And in a recession unions need members, and revenue. No doubt other unions would have been equally well pleased to get recognition at Nissan for just these reasons. But it scarcely follows that all this testifies to a new enterprise unionism. The developments with which the EETPU is associated reflect a combination of elements – not only new sites opening up, particularly in an industry (consumer electronics) which is undergoing some changes in the technical composition of the labour force, but also that union's distinctive politics. It is difficult to think that a TUC-affiliated union would apply to join the CBI, for example. But the EETPU did, unsuccessfully, in 1984.

In short, then, if greenfield site development clearly can contribute to improved labour productivity, care still has to be exercised before assuming that this has been a particularly pertinent factor in the 1980s, and about associating a secular transformation in British trade unionism with it. Yet heavier qualifications are in order if the relocation of industry *outside* the UK is considered from the standpoint of indigenous trade unionism. Some shift in the balance of employment between the British and overseas operations of UK-owned multinationals was in evidence in the early 1980s. In round terms between 1977 and 1982 the forty-five leading manufacturing companies had cut their

UK labour forces by over 300,000, and increased the number employed overseas by almost 40,000. Some sectors such as Food and Textiles, which also reduced the number employed overseas, still reduced employment within the UK by an even greater amount (*Labour Research*, May 1983). Such shifts of employment have possibly fed through and shown up in increased measured productivity in some cases. But the plain fact is that British workers and their unions have never carried much clout in the formulation of location policies. These and other strategic decisions have nearly always taken place behind closed management doors. The shift to production overseas has certainly played its part in further devastating a number of areas (on the West Midlands see Gaffiken and Nickson, 1984), but effective resistance to such moves has always been extremely rare.

As for *when production takes place*, the two most obvious things to consider (apart from short-time working) are overtime and shift-work. Concerning the first, it seems probable that managements who have been shaken out of an habituation to Stop-Go government policies, and who have recently experienced a massive collapse in output (Stop-Stop?), will be disinclined to hoard labour, and, having less need to keep workers sweet, because of the threat posed by unemployment, they will in any case often be in a better position to demand whether overtime is worked or not. The other side of this is that, come an up-turn, managements may be inclined to resort to overtime rather than recruit new labour, a tendency that is to be expected if they have been badly shaken in the past and still lack full confidence in the future. Briefly, such an interpretation would seem to make sense of what has happened.

It is unclear to what extent shift-working has actually increased in manufacturing during the 1980s. In any case, to explain any such increase it would clearly be necessary to take into account a greater perceived need by employers to work their capital more efficiently – generally because of tighter markets and in some cases because of the introduction of new technology – and not only a reduced resistance on the part of workers to sacrifice domestic arrangements. What does seem to be the case is that there has been more experimentation with different shift-work patterns (IDS, 1984b). Evidence is lacking about whether the move from four to five shift working (as at ICI and Metal Box) has actually made for greater reliability in manning and more stable shift-teams, but if it has, and if the need for cover arrangements and other costs have been reduced, this too should have made some contribution to measured productivity improvement.[2]

What, though, of possible changes *in the basis on which labour is employed*? British industrial capitalism was substantially built on sub-contract labour, which was most certainly a prominent feature of the construction industry well after the Second World War (Littler, 1982; Austrin, 1980). In this sense it is perfectly true that sub-contract is nothing 'new'. It has to be conceded also that labour sub-contract is not necessarily disadvantageous to particular groups of workers. In the 1960s, for example, draughtsmen in some areas found themselves in a labour market that was short of their skills and benefited from such arrangements for a while. A similar situation may pertain amongst some sections of the labour force in electronics in the South-East today. For the main part, though, labour sub-contract spells casualism and vulnerability. It is precisely for this reason that such possible changes in the capital–labour relation merit comment here.

It has to be said straight away that both the investigation and discussion of any such changes has been sorely lacking as far as the British working class and manufacturing is concerned, and that developments in other sectors and at other levels have commanded much more public attention. On the one hand, for instance, the appalling conditions and pay rates of those who work for sub-contract cleaning firms, and who perform other ancillary functions in the NHS and the state education sector, have become a focus of interest and, rightly, of condemnation. On the other hand, the development of so-called 'linked sub-contracting' has quite often been celebrated and idealised by the mass media. But this particular interrelation of self-employment and labour sub-contracting – whereby those who were hitherto directly in the employment of a particular company are then taken on as independent contractors, so allowing the employer to reduce overheads in the form of social insurance, rates, rent, heating bills, parking facilities, etc. – has once again been more marked in services than manufacturing. Indeed, the 'new homeworkers', as they have been called, are more evident in professional, sales and advertising work than amongst manual workers (Upton, 1984). Another modification in a different dimension of the employment relation, in the form of part-time work, especially by women, has also received a fair amount of public attention. So has the shift from male to female labour, which is particularly evident in some regions where the demise of heavy manual work (steel, mining) has been complemented, though in no sense equalled, by the influx of women into light assembly and other operations (see Austrin and Beynon, 1980; Massey, 1984). But this has not, of course, usually meant the direct incursion of women, whether employed part- or full-time, into hitherto male preserves. Moreover, the entry into the labour market of (often part-time) women continues to be concentrated in services. (One particular ironic feature of this development is of course that as part-time women have added to the number in work, the number of unemployed has not fallen, in part because the government did not count such women as 'unemployed' in the first place.) To concede all this, though, is not necessarily to follow the drift of opinion amongst industrial relationists, which would seem to be that, as far as *manufacturing* is concerned, nothing much is happening at all.

Batstone concludes, for example, that part-time employment has gone *down*, that home-based work has *fallen*, that what sub-contracting does occur is *not new* and that work that is put out is largely put out to '*large employers*' anyway (Batstone, 1984, p. 313). The account of changes in the organisation of work that has been briefly presented in the previous pages of this book has also tended to play down the extent of those changes that have taken place, and with some reason. After all, the American 'born again' worker syndrome, where a section of the labour force is re-employed on disadvantageous terms and conditions to their fellow workers, is not yet a notable development in British manufacturing. Batstone's complacency about changes in the employment relation in manufacturing is not endorsed here, however. Historically, mass unemployment has made for a nexus of disadvantage – casualism, 'self-employment' and sub-contract – and, in the contemporary context, Batstone's reference to sub-contracting to 'large employers' is perhaps itself sufficient to put us on our guard that more is happening that he concedes. In services, for example, firms like Pritchard Services and OCS have been well to the fore in the scramble for privatised NHS laundry service contracts, but they are far from small, employing over 10,000 and 20,000 people respectively. And, turning back to manufacturing, if, as Batstone observes, the British situation does not compare with that in Japan, it is none the less true that most large employers depend upon a network of smaller companies, within or on the environs of which casual, turn-on turn-off labour is likely to be more prevalent, as is 'self-employment'. In such firms unionisation is also less likely. Casual and indeed 'off-the-cards' labour has always been a feature of annual maintenance work in many British industries. Everything suggests that, in recession, this type of labour will have increased more generally.

That the restructuring of the employment relation in manufacturing has not figured prominently in 1980s academic industrial relations commentary is not exactly surprising. For one thing, the official employment statistics are unlikely to be an adequate guide to the full extent – and still less to the possible significance – of such changes. For another, whereas research into on-going operations might, in principle, pick up some such changes in the employment relation – consider for example the case where a main employer re-engages hitherto formally employed lorry drivers on a self-employment sub-contract basis – in practice it rarely seems to have been designed to this end. Moreover, if we are concerned with the advantages that employers may derive from the restructuring of the employment relation, it is important to appreciate that this sort of relatively clear-cut change (and some examples of lorry drivers being re-engaged in this way can be found) in no way exhausts the possibilities. For instance, main employers can 'slim' or shut their own operations, then contract the work to other capitals, which in turn depend on labour sub-contract, casualism and non-union labour (or which simply employ labour on relatively disadvantageous terms). Then again, a main employer can sometimes benefit indirectly from casualism, labour sub-contract or the sale of labour-power on disadvantageous terms, simply by tightening the price he is prepared to pay for bought-in goods and services. All that is required for a main employer to reap such advantage is for these types of employment relation and disadvantage to exist further out in the web of production and exchange relations at the centre of which his firm is located.

Given that such webs of relations exist, to rest content that nothing is happening to the employment relation in British manufacturing in the 1980s or that certain sections of the British working class are not being further or more extensively disadvantaged – a parallel development that merits simultaneous recognition – might therefore prove very complacent indeed.

In Britain today an unemployment-induced, casual, and thus more *vulnerable*, peripheral labour pool exists. The Thatcherite propaganda about the need for people to 'price themselves into work' does not alter this one whit. It merely suggests the lengths to which these 'new Victorians' may be prepared to go. That some industrial relationists do not seem to be aware of the implications of what is happening already may be a function of their talking too much to personnel managers in large firms[3] and spending their time considering what has happened to their on-going industrial relations systems. But not only does the nexus of casualism, sub-contract and 'self-employment' exist, to consult other official data – not on employment but on industrial accidents – is to see the consequence of such disadvantage at work.

The shift away from direct employment and towards contract work – in electrical maintenance and repair, catering, transport and machine servicing and so on – was noted by the Chief Inspector at Factories in his 1981 Annual Report, which appeared in 1983 (Manufacturing and Service Industies, 1983a). Whether production of the report was delayed because this particular policing agency is understaffed and under-resourced I do not know. (However, the 1974 Health and Safety at Work Act added an extra 8 million working people to the 12 million already covered by the Factory Acts and other legislation; to deal with this the number of field inspectors was increased to 1,098 from 703 in August 1975, and even this inadequate level of provision was cut back to 915 in April 1984, each inspector thus being responsible for an average 700 workplaces, and the average workplace only seeing an inspector once every seven years.) What is quite certain, though, is that by the time the 1982 Annual Report appeared (also later on in 1983) the Chief Inspector was not only noting that an increased reliance on outside contractors had gone hand in hand with a reduction in maintenance manning levels, he was also expressing disquiet about *safety*. Such was the situation that a special 'Black Spot' enquiry was announced, one-fifth of all notifiable fatalities having been found to occur in maintenance, and the provision of information about the risks to outside contractors having been found to be 'often casual and dis-organised' (Manufacturing and Service Industries, 1983b, chap. 7). A further aspect of changes in the employment relationship, which may also have led to some increase in productivity, though again sometimes at a cost to workers themselves, is to be found in the trend to smaller businesses. This development is also referred to in the 1982 Report. And, once more, with good reason. A survey conducted by the Inspectorate of industrial estates found half the factories in one area to be unregistered – employees having been found on some of these premises who were experiencing conditions of work that gave a quite special meaning to the Chief

Inspector's Foreword ('This report on 1982, written in the 150th year of HM Factory Inspectorate contains much that would be familiar to the first Chief Inspector of Factories who was in post a hundred years ago').

The official data on industrial injuries during the 1980s is at present difficult to interpret. Although some of this data is compatible with the hypothesis that reductions in manning levels have brought about an increase in work intensity and thus a higher accident rate, a closer inspection also suggests that this process has been an uneven one, both between industries and over time.[4] There is, however, a mounting body of evidence which underlies the extent of the disadvantage suffered by those *who do not work in the predominantly unionised medium/big capital 'centre' or who do not do so on a direct employment or regular basis.*

What the Chief Inspector of Factories had to say in his Report for 1983 makes sober reading as far as the latter part of the labour force is concerned. It merits quoting here to emphasise the important point that 'fear and anxiety' have not been evenly spread among those involved in different employment relations. In the context of a review in which small enterprises figure prominently, as does sub-contract (especially in the guise of the 'visiting contractor'), the Chief Inspector suggests, for example: 'The extent of the fear of the loss of one's job may perhaps be gauged by the parents who offered to pay for damage to a conveyor when their 17 year old son jammed his shovel into it to stop it after his arm became trapped at the tail drum. They offered to waive their claim for compensation if only their son could continue to work.' He notes further: 'It is training and supervision generally that are the first to go. The raw recruit [in small enterprise] is set to work almost immediately.' Of course, he points out – as well he might – 'strong trade union organisation is not to be found in new small enterprises . . . The subject matter of complaints [about small enterprises] is dominated by concern for health and, perhaps surprisingly in the 1980s, the inadequacy of welfare facilities. And yet it is not so surprising if one considers how many new enterprises are established in old factories which have been sub-divided with inadequate regard to the need for a proper scale of washing and sanitary facilities, adequate heating and ventilation. Similar problems can arise even with speculatively built factory units.' And again, referring to the 'unpalatable fact' that 'certain economic and industrial trends . . . have continued in 1983, and each tends to militate against competent management of health and safety', he tells us: 'Most notable among these trends is the continuing slimming, if no longer so often the disappearance of major companies and the growth in many parts of the country of small new enterprises often funded on redundancy money. And these are not only engaged in manufacture but also in sub-contracting, *serving the continuing trend towards the "flexible firm" which depends increasingly on peripheral units and contractors to provide components and services, which the "core group" no longer does.*' Here, in a few words, the main bones of the developing centre/periphery structure are laid bare, as are its implicit productivity, and manifest human implications (Manufacturing and Services Industries, 1984, p. 1, my emphasis).

Sub-contract, linked sub-contracting, part-time work, twilight shifts, etc., can all be construed as a form of 'numerical flexibility' (which permits manning levels to be changed rapidly). To this can then be added yet other forms of flexibility – the 'functional' (to facilitate the more efficient deployment and redeployment of labour through the broadening and blurring of job definitions) and the 'financial' (to tie pay more tightly to the supply and demand for labour and productivity, as may be facilitated within M-form organisations through profit centre decentralisation and the imposition of divisional and operating unit cash limits). Given such an all-encompassing definition (for which see Figure 10.1 and Atkinson, 1984) it can be said with some justification that in the 1980s 'flexibility' has become a managerial *'cause célèbre'* (Groom, 1984c). It is, however, so-called 'functional flexibility', which clearly relates very closely to *how work is organised* (as narrowly conceived in the traditional industrial relationists manner), to which we must turn now. And, to anticipate, the story here, at least within the 'core', is a familiar one: some signs of movement, but, as yet, no clear and general break.

The unskilled in British manufacturing have always tended to be subject to 'functional' flexibility, the semi-skilled less so. But in the 1970s there were clear signs of a move towards greater flexibility for the semi-skilled. Productivity deals were struck then, and indeed earlier, often in the context of new grading systems and somtimes with much ill-founded talk of 'job enrichment', which led machinists to perform minor maintenance tasks or sweep up round their machines, and which generally took the form of

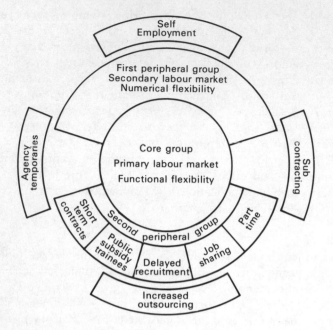

*Source*: Atkinson (1984), p. 29.
*Note*: On this model, the *core group* is subject to functional flexibility. It is composed of full-time 'career' employees and includes not simply managers but possibly maintenance workers and others whose skills are firm-specific and cannot be bought-in readily. The *first peripheral group* also includes full-time employees, but without highly developed or firm-specific skills (in clerical and assembly work for instance). They have less job security and are subject to greater numerical and financial flexibility. The *second peripheral group* combines the 'advantages' of numerical and functional flexibility, and is seen as supplementary to the first group – as Atkinson puts it, 'maximising flexibility while minimising the organisation's commitment to the worker's job security and career development'. In Atkinson's view *Outsourcing* – via agencies, sub-contract and self-employment – is likely where jobs are not at all firm-specific, either because they are very specialised (systems analysts) or very mundane (office cleaning). The general idea is clear enough: 'As the market grows, the periphery expands to take up the slack; as growth slows, the periphery contracts. At the core [workers are] insulated from medium term fluctuations of the market, whereas those in the periphery are more exposed to them.'

**Figure 10.1**    The flexible firm

adding a requirement to perform yet further routine tasks to those performed already (for examples see Cotgrove, Dunham and Vamplew, 1971; Nichols and Beynon, 1977). Such attempts to broaden the tasks that semi-skilled workers actually performed, or to enable management to direct them to perform a wider range of essentially similar tasks, have to be distinguished from other increases in flexibility, however – those that override craft distinctions and those which blur the yet more marked distinction between manual and white-collar work.

During the 1980s more British companies have made formal agreements for increased craft flexibility. Moves in this direction have not been confined to greenfield sites and consumer electronics, or to BL. They have taken place at BSC (Groom, 1983), at Scottish and Newcastle Breweries, at Mobil Oil, Coryton, at Esso, Fawley (which was incidentally also in the van of those productivity-related changes in working practices that were instituted way back at the start of the 1960s), and even within the *locus classicus* of British demarcation, shipbuilding (IDS, 1984c; Garnett, 1983c). To the extent that such agreements represent a clear break from the past, and do not simply represent attempts by management to take the opportunity to formalise practices that actually occurred before, or, when they are new, they are actually worked, they should increase productivity. But here again there is need to exercise some caution.

First, the much-celebrated 'polyvalent worker' is still probably more likely to be performing at best only two hitherto separately defined job skills – fitters doing some welding jobs or pneumatics, engineering craftsmen doing some electrical work, and so on. As the IDS put it: 'our impression is that in those companies where agreements have been reached, it is much too early to be confident about what effect they will have. And even in these companies, the increased flexibility negotiated thus far falls some way short of creating "dual trade" or "multi-skilled" craftsmen' (IDS, 1984d). Second, not only is it the case that 'Jack-of-all-Trades' workers are often masters of no more than two, or even one and a bit, but those agreements that have been reached are not always on a company-wide basis. New beginnings help, of course, as can be seen by the changes brought about at Pilkington's new Greengate glass works at St Helens, which started up in 1981. At Greengate the distinction between mechanical and electrical craftsmen was broken down. There were other initiatives too – the introduction of a simplified pay structure, the collapsing of what had hitherto been a dozen glassmaking operative jobs into one, staff status for all, and local plant negotiations. But this craft flexibility did not proceed so rapidly at Pilkington's other plants, where change on other fronts also appears to have been slower (Garnett, 1983b).

Managements themselves have often favoured a step-by-step approach, not simply because they have felt it prudent to get the thin end of the wedge in first but also for reasons that have little to do with craft union resistance. The introduction of new technology may seem to provide an ideal opportunity to restructure job specifications. In certain circumstances it can render old craft skills less important (as in printing) or make maintenance a less skilled task (Child, 1985). But the introduction of new machines, not to mention a whole new technology, is often itself a piecemeal affair. Moreover, even the introduction of two-trade maintenance can require extensions of craft competence which require training, and this can take time (as was discovered at both Pilkington and BL). In any case, whereas it by no means follows that craft workers will necessarily resist change as such (despite the folklore) – especially if it brings them better conditions of employment – managements need to prepare the ground carefully so as to cope with demands from elsewhere. Where non-craft workers constitute a majority of a bargaining group they are unlikely to give positive encouragement to proposals that increase differentials, for example (IDS, 1984c, pp. 5, 6). These and other considerations all mean that the contribution of craft flexibility to national level increases in productivity cannot be inferred as readily as it sometimes is.

The contribution that has been made by increased manual/white collar flexibilities is yet more limited. The 1980s have seen a continuation of an earlier trend towards the 'harmonisation' of the benefits enjoyed by white-collar and manual workers, notably staff status (IDS, 1982). But flexibility in task performance across the manual/mental divide remains slight. The sort of three-year deal signed between the EETPU and Toshiba, which has received a lot of attention, has some relevance here. As part of the package, not only are all employees monthly-paid salaried staff, who wear the same company coats and use the same car park and dining room, but, according to the EETPU's publicity-conscious national officer, Roy Sanderson, all employees *also* agree to do any work asked of them, so that 'someone can be in administration one day and on the shopfloor the next'. What is interesting about this, however, is that when similar deals have been offered to British consumer electronics companies – who might have been expected to be equally interested in flexibility, for they also have to keep up with the rate of technological and product change in that industry – they have turned them down. Not, it seems, because of resistance from the powerful craft-workers of British low-productivity legend, but because management did not want *other* parts of the package, like external arbitration (no outside interference, thank you) *and* because the office staff in these companies did not want equality with manual workers (Groom, 1984b; Thomas, 1984). The lesson to be learnt from this, yet again, is that all the barriers to what is often regarded as sane and reasonable and touched with the beginnings of a new collectivism in work, have not been erected by British manual workers. (It is perfectly plain, too, that as far as relocation is concerned, an analysis of its determinants on the labour side (generally defined) is not exhausted once it is conceded that some companies have relocated to escape the unwanted presence of organised manual workforces. The social appetites of technical/ managerial personnel can also enter into such equations as a 'pull' factor, as city and regional planners are very much aware).

Further to the question of change on the part of craftsmen, it is also worth recalling that the most systematic research on flexibility came to the conclusion that their responses can differ markedly, even when there is only one union on a particular site (IDS, 1984d). But it is no less important to appreciate that their response will in part be a function of how secure they judge their jobs to be.[5] It has to be remembered, of course, that where job security exists to any marked extent in the advanced capitalist world, in Japan, it is most certainly not extended to everyone, and also that the major recent attempt to grasp this particular nettle in America, in the form of the deals that GM and Ford made with the UAW in 1984, which did promise greater security, were so different that they made the headlines in the US. They also had a number of other features – including tying pay more closely to performance, and the widening of skilled/unskilled differentials (Dodsworth, 1984). British managements, for their part, might encounter a number of impediments in any attempts to make flexible working more attractive through offers of increased job security. Existing payment systems could prove a problem, also differentials. But then again, so could Mrs Thatcher, and the policies for which her governments are famed. After all, compared to their American counterparts, in the 1980s British managements had little reason to be so confident of rising demand.

In considering changes in work organisation in the 1980s, then, there are at least two points to bear in mind. First, it would seem that new developments – when they are new – have been unevenly spread. Of course, unemployment has tended to set some sort of floor under the power of employers. It is also the case that union leaderships, for their part, have had their commitment to militant action weakened through reduced memberships and revenues. But, within on-going production operations, the employers' power base is itself unevenly contoured, because of differences in product markets and so on. If the large trend has been towards the intensification of labour (through 'slimming'), it by no means follows that such intensification has been uniform. Nor does it follow that those workers in manufacturing who are party to what in post-war terms would count as a 'normal' employment relation (still the great majority, of course) have experienced changes that have taken them beyond the situation in other countries. For example, some of them have been exposed more sharply to the direct discipline of the market via 'self-certification' whereby they can be held more readily responsible for the quality of their work. Buy a Raleigh bike nowadays and you get the name of the bloke who built it, and his photo! There are other such cases (IDS, 1984a). But, in this case, as in others, it is as well to remember that instances of the same thing have been documented in other countries, both earlier on and in the contemporary period (see, for example, Pignon and Querzola, 1976). Flexibility of the 'functional' sort, when it has increased, has also been unevenly spread, even within companies, and is an often exaggerated tendency (and one, it should be noted, that can also reduce the number of *other* factory personnel, like inspectors, and so add to productivity in that way).

Second, some of the most significant developments that have accentuated the vulnerability of those who labour cannot be comprehended in terms of a model that concentrates upon changed work practices *within* the established and still on-going 'core'. Market forces have bitten all right, and British manufacturing workforces have been very substantially 'slimmed'. Between 1977 and 1983, for example, employment fell by between 25 and 30 per cent at British Shipbuilders and Lucas; by over 30 per cent at Vauxhall, ICI and Massey Ferguson; by 50 per cent or more at Courtaulds, BL, GKN, Tube Investments and Dunlop; and by over 60 per cent at British Steel and Talbot (Owen *et al.* 1984, p. 2). A whole mass of less well known medium and small firms collapsed entirely. And whereas a few companies survived these years more or less intact, like GEC, which lost 'only' about 10 per cent of its labour force, even this company had made its own contribution to the dole queue earlier on, the memory of what happened at Woolwich and other consequences of Weinstock rationalisation still lingering in the memory of many older engineering workers. No section of the population has been more severely disadvantaged by market forces than the large and still mounting body of those who are not employed at all, however, and in discussions of productivity in the 1980s those who gain only a tenuous hold on employment, and who form an emergent and vulnerable periphery – so that even when they do get work they are more likely to remain outside of established protective structures – merit special attention. Although it has been no means fully accomplished, a shift towards the casualisation of labour is underway.

Since the changes in work practices that have taken place have been unevenly spread and often limited, it is doubtful whether a major (post-statistical illusion) Thatcherite-induced increase in productivity can be claimed to have occurred, or that a deep-seated transformation has taken place in the hearts and minds of many of those shop floor workers who have continued in employment. But it could be the case that an as yet unquantified, and in some respects unquantifiable, contribution has stemmed from the wider restructuring of employment relations. Various forms of sub-contract and of 'self-employment' are relevant here, including the sort of 'off the cards' work that contributes to output, but does not add to employment in the official count.

Let us now look to the longer term and speculate a little further. On the periphery it may well be that a 'grab-now-do-anything' world is coming into being. Within the 'core' manufacturing firms, and perhaps most especially in the core within that core that is largely composed of skilled workers, it is difficult to see that Thatcherism will do much to substantially transform a 'hang-onto-what-you've-got' world, however – though the resentment arising from what incursions have been made could have long-lasting effects. It would also seem that an American-style 'underclass' (a part of the working class that is subject to extra disadvantage) is unlikely to work 'as well' in Britain as in America, given the survival of some important features of the welfare state. Inadequate as it is, this still provides some real measure of support for those out of work. In any case, there is more to the American labour model than an 'underclass'. Important though the American underclass is, the technical composition of the American workforce is also important, and thus far British market forces have shown little capacity to generate an equivalent productive potential in this respect. Then again, for Thatcherism to decisively restructure economic relations it will also be necessary for it to forge an enduring realignment of political blocks. Wage demands from the skilled could prove troublesome here. And on top of this the Thatcherites have to retain their middle-class electoral support. The British middle class benefits considerably from its relation to the state (mortgages and insurance tax relief, grants for higher education, etc.). Much as the Thatcherites might yearn for a society of self-reliant enterprising individuals, the great majority of the 'comfortable' will experience a deal of discomfort with any notion that they too should be rendered blue in tooth and claw.

Some of the issues raised above belong more properly to a more general discussion of whether Thatcherism is working, which is postponed till Chapter 11. But for the moment it is necessary to consider something that has been totally neglected so far – something which once again underlines the need to qualify the simple notion that the increase in productivity can be accounted for exclusively in terms of the unemployment and 'slimming'-induced changes in the practices (or 'hearts and minds', if you wish) of those workforces that have survived the Thatcher years. To see what this is, it is helpful to have another look at BL.

That an increased flexibility of labour made some contribution to increased productivity at BL is beyond dispute. Referring to the much-cited article in *Militant* p. 178), Armstrong, Glyn and Harrison tell us, for example, that one Longbridge worker had been transferred to five different departments in one year, and to ten different jobs in one department in three months (1984, p. 396). But more has changed at BL than this – more than is implied by the bar-room Tories who chortle at how 'Edwardes sorted out the workers'. More, too, than those on the left have been apt to imply when they in turn have been driven to expose what this has meant for BL's present workforce, and for the tens of thousands of others thrown on to the dole. The changes introduced at BL also go beyond the fact, noted earlier, that the company has (at last) put more power at its workers' elbows.

At BL there has most certainly been 'slimming'. The intensity of labour *has* increased. Shop floor unionism *has* been subject to severe constraint. In Thatcherite newspeak, 'scope for co-operation' *has* improved, temporarily at any rate. But another thing that has happened is that management has improved – at least as judged technically, if not in terms of human reasonableness, which is quite a different matter. Planning has improved, also the application of industrial engineering techniques, also costing and scheduling.

An account provided by Fryer (1982a) helps to show what some of those changes have meant. Hitherto, he reports: 'It was not uncommon for the tracks to stop every half-an-hour, and these intervals were a cause of aggravation in themselves. When the line "went down" some men would sit back and read a newspaper until it restarted. Others, however, would work their way back down the line completing their tasks while the line was stationary, so they could have a rest afterwards . . . With a team of men on each car, one working during a stationary period could cause friction. An operator accustomed to fixing a component by leaning through where the windscreen goes would become annoyed if one of his colleagues had fitted say, a steering wheel, thereby thwarting his normal method of entry.'

This is, of course, precisely the sort of detail that did not figure at all sufficiently in 1970s productivity investigations. And Fryer's report is worth sticking with for a moment because stoppages of this type – caused by 'poor scheduling of components and bodies' – had not only been a cause of tension and disaffection amongst workers, they also had direct affects on productivity. Up to autumn 1980, for example, the transfer of bodies from the Longbridge paintshop to the assembly line had been, in Fryer's words 'far from smooth – with often cataclysmic repercussions'. The forty men working at the transfer point had to try to match the arriving bodies with the requirements of the assembly tracks. Often bodies of the wrong specification would arrive, causing chaos for the man who had to issue a sheet of paper, with twenty copies, to colleagues in the assembly area telling them the building sequence. If bodies of an unexpected colour or design arrived, he had little time to forewarn assembly workers. Wrong bodies had to be manhandled through into 'sidings', where there was space for only twenty-five. Managers, who themselves were never sure what models would come down the line for final trim and assembly, had to man-up, willy-nilly, for the highest labour content cars (those with sunshine roofs, etc.). In short: 'the control point – the axis on which Longbridge's output performance depended – was cumbersome, slow and inefficient. It was simply inadequate for a modern factory.'

Now, by contrast, there is a new computerised painted body store, which stocks nearly 300 bodies. It checks incoming bodies against the sales programme every forty-two seconds, and determines that the correct components are available. Since it is now possible to precisely control the flow of materials to the assembly tracks and to ensure that the bodies flow down the line in the correct order – hardly an outstanding achievement, you might think, but at BL it was – it really is no surprise that, to quote Fryer again, the impact on trim and assembly – the most labour-intensive part of car building – has been 'enormous'.

Here, then, in an attempt to begin to locate *other* changes in British manufacturing that may have contributed to an increase in productivity, we are led back to a maxim developed in Chapter 8 with reference to the 1970s: that organisation – planning, design, co-ordination – *matters*. Even as far as flexibility is concerned, good product design is important. To switch attention from one part of the Leyland empire to another – to the bus assembly plant at Workington – is to see something of what this means. Workington's productivity record has featured in the financial press, along with its flexible working practices – and, true enough, from the beginning Workington had one 'obvious' ingredient for success, few time-served craftsmen being recruited, and the workforce having come out of the local steel plant, coalmines, nearby shoe-factories and farms. But, another important factor is that some of the vehicles they work on are well-tooled, jig-built, easy-assembly models – that is, they are designed in such a way as to lend themselves to the semi-skilled nature of work of Workington (Garnett, 1984).

Of course, it was seen earlier that some of the changes at BL occurred prior to 1980, and it also has to be said loud and clear at this point that the idea that the turn of the present decade marked a clear watershed in British management practice probably has no more merit than the idea that there was a universal transformation in the practices of on-going workforces. In 1984, for example, a thousand directors and senior managers in British manufacturing were surveyed to discover what use they were making of computers and automated machinery. It was found that 30 per cent of them had done nothing to measure the results of their performance against project objectives. The investigators concluded that once the money had been approved 'these people see that as the end of the battle'. (Three-quarters of these companies were using government grants: Wyles, 1984, p. 31).

The fact is, though, that it is not just workers' practices that determine the productivity outcome. Management proficiency has to be considered as well. And it is also important to recognise that during the recession British management had more on its plate than an understanding based on stereotypical notions about curmudgeonly British workers would suggest. The remedies managements resorted to also ranged far and wide beyond mounting offensives on British labour. The larger picture can be glimpsed from a report on what had happened to a cross-section of British manufacturing companies during the 1980s. Nearly all of the companies whose progress was reviewed in this enquiry had made drastic cuts in their labour forces. When labour productivity is mentioned in these reports it is also nearly always claimed to have increased, sometimes in association with increased mechanisation. But, quite apart from the glaring fact that some of these companies had experienced a great deal of trouble from two fluctuations that were quite outside either their control or that of their workforces – namely high interest rates and, in earlier years, high exchange rates – the most obvious conclusion to be drawn from these accounts is that there have been 'substantial improvements in productivity *and management performance*' (Owen, *et al.*, 1984, p. 1, my emphasis).

One token of the changes that have taken place within management is that Head Office staffs have often been cut, a certain amount of decentralisation having accompanied this in some cases, also the renting out of now surplus office space, with cuts also having been made at intermediate management levels. But these are only some of the most visible signs of change, and there are clear indications that since 1980 at least *some* corporate managements have been wrestling successfully with problems other than those caused by organised British labour. As judged by these accounts a general tightening up on working capital has occurred. Stock-turn has been reduced. Suppliers have been squeezed to get better credit terms. Management information and control systems have been improved, through the introduction of weekly profit and loss figures, for example. There has been better market analysis, and sales forecasting, and costing. The effects of such improvements in basic management practice are masked in the official labour productivity figures, but they contribute to them none the less – a further contribution doubtless having also been made by product rationalisation and a shift from low to higher value added operations that are also featured in these accounts.

It is worth noting here that such improvements in the internal organisation of management have probably been a feature of much greenfield site development as well. Whether impelled by a desire to outflank the entrenched battalions of the curmudgeonly British worker or not, such relocation also provides an opportunity to reconsider the management structure. For example, Rothman's 'mini-factories', in which supervisors have responsibility for personnel, disputes, ordering stock, and the meeting of production targets, have received a good deal of publicity – but at Rothman's, and at Trebor too, the tiers of management have been reduced. It seems highly likely that greenfield site development has sometimes facilitated other changes on the management side – in information and control systems, costing and the scheduling of work, plant layout, etc. – and there is indeed some evidence that the gains in productivity achieved following relocation tend to be associated with newness of plant (McKersie and Klein, 1982).

Most British manufacturing operations did *not* relocate in the 1980s, of course. But then again, physical relocation is not a staple requirement for the transformation of management control systems. In fact one of the most startling transformations on record was put through on an existing site that is part of a company which, in Britain, is a household name, Wilkinson Sword, and the changes that were introduced in this firm are worth detailing here.

According to its manufacturing director, the recession induced the realisation that this company's old practice of putting up prices to cope with inflation would eventually lead to its product (on the site in question, garden tools) being priced out of the market. To compete the better on price 'a total greenfield approach' was therefore adopted to the reorganisation of the company's plant at Bridgend, Wales. Unremarkably enough, redundancies and revised manning levels followed. But these were only part of the programme of change, and it is the *other* changes that were put in motion that are of interest here – such as the fact that the product range was rationalised; that products which had simply gone on being made before were subject to scrutiny, some being scrapped or redesigned; and that some machines in the factory, which had hitherto run for just one day a month, and this in order to turn out fifteen-year-old products, and which were also difficult to maintain, were got rid of as well.

Four million pounds was invested at Bridgend. Fewer more adaptable machines were imported from Germany. Factory space was slashed by half. Overheads dropped by no less than 30 per cent. The use of storage areas was abandoned, as were ancient booking-in and booking-out procedures. As part of a drive on quality, a new system of relations was instituted with suppliers. Reliability improved. Inside the factory, the materials throughput cycle was cut from months to nearly a fortnight. Quality control was improved by introducing manuals that listed the checks necessary to ensure that products conformed to specifications at all stages of manufacture. In short, the whole plan, launched in 1982, made for changes, not only in manning levels and machinery, but in the use of working capital, in physical layout, in asset disposal, and in products and quality control. As a harbinger of the new level of management efficiency and improved co-ordination, the plan's progress was monitored on a weekly basis against set targets. The savings that came from speeding up warehouse distribution and the introduction of a new twenty-four-hour turn-around on orders are themselves reported to have been sufficient to cover the cost of the investment programme (Reeves, 1984).

Deciding what can be made profitably and competitively, setting clear objectives, monitoring progress, getting down to detailed planning and costing, matching machine capacities and factory layout to production requirements, designing and redesigning products, actually checking out thoroughly that product quality is up to spec – some companies have recently made remarkable advances in the way they perform such tasks. But no less remarkable is what the need to introduce such changes suggests about the depth of the deficiency in the fundamentals of good management practice that existed before. Within the broad context of this book this matters. It matters because it further underlines the marked deficiency that characterised the approach to management in 1970s productivity research: it can now be seen that 'if anything were wrong we surely would have heard' is a very bad rule indeed to apply to the evaluation of that research. In retrospect, it is quite clear that a good deal was wrong on the management side, and that we did not hear about it – certainly not in any detail – because those who conducted this research either did not look and see, or having seen did not tell. But of course these changes in management are also important in another way. According to the 'common-sense' view, the improvement in productivity during the 1980s – when three million and more really did become unemployed – is the final piece of confirmatory evidence which clinches the argument that it was British workers who were at the bottom of the difficulty all along, both during the 1970s and long before that. That British management was itself characterised by substantial deficiencies, and that there has sometimes been substantial improvement in the 1980s (no doubt aided in part by CAM and other more rudimentary computer techniques), helps to underline the fact that no such simple formula will do, either historically, or in the contemporary period.

In Chapter 9 it was argued that the early productivity 'break-through' was to an important extent a statistical illusion. The attempt has been made in this chapter to examine how changes and continuities amongst workers (and managers), and in the organisation of work, may have contributed to whatever increase in labour productivity has occurred in the 1980s. It is now necessary to consider the Thatcher record on manufacturing productivity in a rather wider context.

# 11 Productivity, productiveness and myopia in Britain today

In the last two chapters it was claimed that manufacturing productivity had not undergone a 'dramatic' improvement under the Thatcher governments. The early 'breakthrough' was seen to be largely a statistical illusion and little evidence was found to support the view that widespread and radical changes had taken place in the working practices of those who continued in employment thereafter. However, it was also noted that an underclass is coming into being in Britain and that a general and continuing trend towards rationalisation and 'slimming' has been accompanied in at least some companies by efficiency-enhancing changes on the management side. Much more work needs to be done on each of these developments. The point is, though, that each of them could be interpreted as evidence that the new regime has had some measure of 'success'.

The ingredients that go to make such a 'success' story out of Thatcherism are not difficult to sketch out. Of key importance is the idea that whereas the Thatcherites are a mutation of the species *Tory vulgaris* and display a number of atavistic traits, they remain distinctive in that they see it as their historic mission to act on Britain as a determinedly bourgeois force. Their God Mammon, their sacred rite the market, it is to this end that they place such stress on individualism, competition and enterprise. And, so the argument runs, since these bearers of a long incomplete British bourgeois revolution see the degree of inertia in Britain as exceptional, so are they convinced that exceptional measures are required in order for it to be overcome. On this particular interpretation, then, not only is an improvement in management efficiency all to the good, so via the mechanism of unemployment is the creation of an underclass. End of story.

*Is* this the end of the story, though? To go back to the previous chapter: is it really satisfactory to conclude that *some* 'progress' has been made in sorting out 'the difficulty' but that it is all too easy to exaggerate the extent of this, especially with respect to the established relations of the on-going core (adding, of course, that more needs to be done)? Is it really satisfactory, either, having noted that some 'progress' has been made towards the creation of an underclass, to merely note further that the Thatcherites must do even 'better' in future if British manufacturing is not to continue to lag behind America in this respect? In short, should we accept the often implicit assumption that the worse Thatcherite policies made the recession, the louder the plaudits should be? There are those who would answer 'Yes' to all of these questions. But at various points in this book it has been urged that the determination of the productivity outcome and the success or otherwise of manufacturing economies cannot be reduced to the often all too ugly simplifications of the fear and anxiety brigade. For this and other reasons it is now necessary to go beyond the treatment of the Thatcher productivity record that was offered in Chapters 9 and 10.

The evaluation of the Thatcher record is a more difficult project than it is often thought to be. For example, it is undeniable that manufacturing was in decline throughout the advanced capitalist world before the Thatcherites came to power. It is also the case that Thatcherite exchange and interest rate policies made the recession worse in Britain. But a view that is often associated with these two observations, namely that the economy of the future will be a 'service economy', and that in driving de-industrialisation further the Thatcherites can therefore be seen to have played a 'progressive' role, is a less than convincing one. The term 'services' most certainly fails to distinguish a whole variety of different activities. None the less it remains the case that manufacturing is on the whole more likely to produce goods that can be sold abroad. This is by no means of trivial importance for an economy which, as we have been told so often, must 'export or die'. In any case the fortunes of some 'services' (banking and insurance, for example) are in part bound up with manufacturing and, looking at matters the other way round, it has to be remembered that even a 'service economy' would need its increasingly microelectronic technology to be produced somewhere. Then again, to the extent that it can be assumed that the Thatcherites really have been vitally concerned with the interests of *manufacturing* rather than of financial capital (and it is as well to remember that monetarism is about *money*), there are certain conditions that have to be met before that most perverse of all postulates, 'the worse the better', can be invoked as the basis for applauding their performance in the manufacturing sector.

For a start, it needs to be established that the Thatcherites actually did know what they were doing and that they chose their policy instruments wisely. For many years now the mystique of Thatcherism, and above all the super-confident and super-competent image projected by Mrs Thatcher herself, has seen to it that questions of this type have not figured at all prominently. The secrecy that shrouds so many important matters of public policy in Britain may see to it that it is some time, decades even, before they can be answered decisively. But it can now be seen that back in March 1980 government policy was informed by a forecast for unemployment in 1981/82 that was 700,000 too low. On anybody's reckoning that was some mistake. And although it is plain enough that the Thatcherites have been keen to squeeze as much advantage as possible out of mass unemployment, it seems possible that, right at the outset, they failed to understand where their monetarist fetish would lead. In fact, it now transpires that as early as 1981 at least one 'insider' had stumbled on the horrendous possibility that 'an awful lot of good companies [have] gone to the wall for nothing' (Sachs, 1984, p. 377; Bleaney, 1983, pp. 140–1; Keegan, 1984, pp. 160–1).

Rather than speculate on what part of the Thatcher 'success story' can be put down to deliberate intention, what part to miscalculation and what part to sheer incompetence, it is far more important to consider another issue. At the nub of this is the fact that no matter what history will tell us about the Thatcherites' technical competence, in order to deem their record on manufacturing productivity a 'success' it is necessary to view 'success' itself myopically – that is, with little regard to what has happened to some *other important determinants of productivity* that were not reviewed in the last two chapters, with little regard to what has happened in *other countries*, and with little regard to UK prospects in the *long term*. By way of conclusion it is these matters that are taken up below, an assumption being implicit in the discussion throughout – that whether these 'new Victorians' *think* they are acting *on behalf of* manufacturing capital or not, their actions (and inactions) have in fact perpetuated and in some cases added to the drag-effect on British manufacturing productivity that stemmed from some of the key determinants of poor performance reviewed in the context of the 1970s in Parts Two and Three, some of which, by a supreme irony, had their origin in the first Victorian era, and even before that.

Of course the Thatcherites have a long-term view. Whether their anti-Keynesianism goes so far as to require the best-known dictum in the whole of economics to be recast in a new and quite alien form – 'In the long run many of us will still be unemployed' – is something they have never made crystal clear, and seem less eager to spell out with every passing year. But even though that other famous dictum – about economics being the 'dismal' science – has itself become ever more appropriate during their years in office they also have a certain vision. What they have asserted over and over again is that, as far as the manufacturing economy is concerned, this will go into the future leaner and fitter, a fundamental up-turn in the world and British economy thus bringing with it the bonus of yet greater productivity when firms increase their level of investment. This, so the argument goes, is when the new 'realistic' attitudes will really pay off, and, for the moment, it is too early to make judgments.

Several clouds hang over this golden vision. One of them, the first to be considered here, is British labour. The truth is of course that British trade unionists have never been highly political nor, outside of some particular groups, highly militant. Even the miners, an apparent modern-day exception, went nearly half a century without a national strike after 1926. What British workers have been – or so it is commonly claimed – is less than fully co-operative. Easily exaggerated as this claim can be, as noted in earlier chapters it has something to recommend it. A consideration of the sort of managements that British workers have had to work with over several generations adds to its plausibility. Badly designed jobs and products, and poor workflows and factory layouts, make those who have to produce under such conditions less than enthusiastic. *Laissez-faire* management has as its complement a greater reliance on workers themselves, in order to get the job out. Workers whose experience leads them to think that 'management doesn't know what it's doing' may be less than keen to make good for management what they think management should have done already, etc., etc. However, this less than co-operative view of British workers is made the more credible when a particular historical consideration is taken into account: that the transformation of British manufacturing labour processes, which was attempted belatedly in the inter-war period, took place within the context of 'a culture of casualism and job insecurity' (Littler, 1982, p. 194) In Mrs Thatcher's brave new world this has a familar ring, doesn't it? And if in the inter-war period these were the very cirumstances that are commonly held to have fuelled British working-class resentment and to have had long-lasting effects, to consider the not dissimilar context in which the Thatcherite transformation has been attempted is most certainly to render problematic the notion that the 'scope for co-operation' brought into being by the new 'realist' Toryism will prove any better guarantee of anything that deserves to be called 'co-operation' in the longer term.

This time round some possible effects of the welfare state have to be taken into the reckoning as well. Forty per cent of the unemployed – *nearly half* – have been out of work for over a year as I write. The number of those under twenty-five who have been out of work for more than a year increased three-fold between 1981 and 1984. This does not bode well for the inculcation of 'good work motivation', and the attractions of low-wage work are also probably somewhat less compelling than half a century ago.

True enough, British workers' wages remain low by international standards. This might therefore be construed – amongst those who construe things oddly – as itself a measure of Thatcherite 'success'. But what matters for international competitiveness on the labour side is not wages as such, or even total labour costs (including employers' social security payments, etc.), but unit labour costs. In 1983, for example, total labour costs were 60 per cent higher in West German manufacturing and 86 per cent higher in the US. In Canada they were 72 per cent higher, in Norway they were 60 per cent higher, and in the Netherlands the difference was 50 per cent. In fact, a whole number of countries had higher total labour costs than the UK. Even in Japan they were 4 per cent higher. In Austria, Finland, France and Italy they were 15 per cent or so higher, with total labour costs in Belgium, Denmark and Sweden all being 40 per cent ahead. In Britain women's average earnings as a percentage of men's are also lower than in other countries, being on a par with the situation in Switzerland, and better only than in Japan. In 1983, though, it was still the case that labour productivity was half as high again in West Germany than it was in this country, and it was still about three times higher in the US. As a consequence of this, Germany – with higher wages and higher productivity – had unit labour costs that were only slightly higher than in Britain, and US labour costs were almost 40 per cent lower (Ray, 1984, pp. 63–4). Moreover, whereas British wages and salaries per unit of manufacturing output *rose* by 4½ per cent between the first quarters of 1983 and 1984, they remained steady in West Germany, and even declined by 3 per cent and 5 per cent in the US and Japan. The same trend appears to have continued since, with increases in British manufacturing labour costs rising faster than in the US or in France, and with Japan and West Germany experiencing decreases.

The alarm bells were sounding about British unit labour costs as early as April 1984, when CBI Director-General Sir Terence Becket took the unusual step of urging chief executives to adopt a unit labour cost target – with a zero increase for the next ten years and, where possible, reductions of 3 per cent. Speaking in Liverpool, he referred to a looming 'productivity crisis' and claimed that the fact that Britain's manufacturing companies had slipped in the productivity league over the past year was a problem of the 'greatest seriousness' – a theme taken up by Employment Secretary King in September, when he declared that the 'continuing yawning gap between us and our major competitors' was 'a most serious warning for the future of this country'. By October the CBI was releasing figures from its pay data-bank (which are not usually disclosed) that showed that one in twelve pay negotiations involved industrial action, compared to one in eighteen two years earlier, and the *Financial Times* was running a leader headed 'Old Habits Return to the Shop Floor'. This did not, it should be noted, point the finger exclusively at British *workers*. Fully alive to the fact that the CBI figures seemed to confirm what 'some pessimists' had always feared about a recovery, it made plain that there had been some changes on the labour side, as evidenced by 'more flexible working practices'. It also noted some of the developments to which attention was drawn in Chapter 10 ('companies are making greater use of part-time and temporary workers and are sub-contracting more of their work'). But, in addition, it stated plainly that 'management have often been as unwilling to change their ways as unions', that 'strikes and pay disputes are not always the fault of intransigent workers' and that 'shopfloor attitudes will not change without incentives' (*Financial Times*, 6 April, 20 September, 26 October 1984).

Expressions of disquiet about unit labour costs were also forthcoming from the Bank of England. It is worth considering what the Bank had to say for two reasons. Firstly, because it suggests (like the other rumblings reported above) that whether the Thatcherites think they are acting on behalf of capital or not, those who overlook the interests of capital may be somewhat lacking in conviction about the long-term success of Mrs Thatcher's policies. No doubt they would not favour a Labour government. But they have reason to suppose that all is not what it is proclaimed to be and that the wheel of British manufacturing history has not turned all that much. The Bank of England suggested, in fact, that it might prove 'difficult to sustain productivity growth' at the rate of the previous few years. Secondly, the Bank drew attention to an important factor that has helped to obscure the true extent of the problem that British manufacturing industry continues to experience with productivity – that 'UK manufacturing industry would have steadily lost cost competitiveness over the past year had it not been for the decline in sterling's effective rate' (*Bank of England Quarterly*, September 1984, pp. 302, 312). The decline against the dollar continued into 1985 of course.

Now, if the wages of those who work in British manufacturing continue to outstrip productivity gains – as they did in 1984, with the rate of increase in productivity being both down on 1983 and below that in Japan, France, West Germany and the US – this will confront the Thatcherites with an economic problem. But political problems may arise too. For the Thatcherites to concede that the much-vaunted success – the 'dramatic' improvement in productivity under their first administration – was not what it was originally claimed to be might prove difficult. To institute a private sector wage freeze would be seen for what it was, a massive 'U-turn'. To make it quite explicit how deeply the Thatcherites' own thinking is predicated on an American model – it being from a particular version of this that their insistence on greater 'mobility of labour' (and greater 'flexibility' in work) stems[1] – might not go down well at the ballot box either. This would run the danger of making quite clear what – from the standpoint of their myopic market model – the next step must logically be: to create an underclass that really is as vulnerable as the American one.

Confronted with this difficulty, one possible tactic is to attack wage earners. Indeed, this is the tactic that has been resorted to. It was pursued with renewed vigour at the 1984 Tory Conference. Since then, conscious (at last) of the need to minimise the responsibility of their government for still increasing unemployment, and no doubt thoroughly convinced of the necessity to further split the working class – not least during the long continuing miners' strike – ministers have had increased resort to the rhetoric of 'divide and rule'. Unemployment, those out of work have been told, is being caused by the wages of those in employment being too high. Those who now, once again, take centre stage as the villains of the piece – those in employment who are allegedly preventing their fellow citizens from 'pricing themselves into work' – are unlikely to be shamed into cutting their throats by this sort of thing, however. The economic theorems in which the message is now packaged do nothing to change its meaning, and it is after all the birthright of British workers to be told that they are greedy. But that the tactic has been resorted to at all is a grave indication of the Thatcherites' own desperation, which is frightening, especially since it is perfectly clear what the next steps could be. To repeat: a further move towards an unfettered market in labour to get the price of wages 'right', with the progressive dismantling of those protective barriers that are seen to interfere with this end – wages councils, unfair dismissal procedures, safety legislation and, in one way or the other, cuts in the dole. All this to make labour truly 'free': free to work even more cheaply and free to be yet poorer when out of work. And this when Britain already stands high in the league tables of the advanced industrial world for *low* wages and *high* unemployment.

The new – and yet so familiar – politics of excoriation have, however, all too neatly deflected attention from a very real problem that the Thatcherites still have to resolve in relation to wages: that those in work are tempted to take what they can in the form of wages precisely because they have no faith that, if they don't, Mrs Thatcher will stand on her head, increase demand, and provide them with some reason to suppose that they will be able to benefit from such self-denial in the longer term. A nifty little phrase coined by Chancellor Lawson in 1984 – about a 'low wage: no tech' future – is unlikely to have done much to inspire their abstinence either.

In any case, abstract economic theorems shorn of social considerations can prove an inadequate guide to reality. The fact is that unemployment is not an infallible recipe for lower wages, nor for the 'compliance' of those in work. Those in employment are not an undifferentiated mass; they experience different opportunities and different constraints and – whatever the Thatcherites think about how unemployment 'works' – those who are working are most likely to feel threatened by unemployment when it is their own jobs that are endangered. A sudden burst of redundancies among workmates, family or friends is one thing. Their enduring unemployment is another. After a year or so it becomes all to easy to regard even close associates as simply 'unemployed' – a fact of their lives, not yours. And by a final sickening twist the unemployed themselves can come to believe that as far as jobs are concerned, 'the longer you are out the more difficult it is to get back in', that 'after a year employers think there's something wrong with you', and can begin to think also that there really is something wrong with them. No government since the war has done more than the Thatcher governments to stress the idea that each and every individual is responsible for his or her life-fate. But those who are unemployed, and who see themselves as 'failures' because of this, will not necessarily continue to knock hard on employers' doors.


The notion that Thatcherism is a Europe-wide phenomenon is an important part of the justification advanced for this government's policies on welfare, unemployment and, in one form or another, the attempt to cut real wages. But this would also fail to convince British workers, in work or out of it, if only they knew what the situation was in some other countries. That the same policies are being pursued with equal commitment everywhere else in Europe is specious. True enough, Italy, Denmark, the Netherlands and Belgium have all modified or suspended their systems of wage indexation, but in all these countries pay negotiations continue to be subject to extensive national agreements and government guidelines. Belgium has recently passed a law to set pay scales for domestic servants. The Thatcherites, by contrast, are into abolishing wages councils. Then again, whereas minimum wages have been frozen or reduced in many countries, a 3 per cent cut in the Netherlands still leaves national minimum wages at over £110 a week. Cuts and reforms in social security benefits have taken place in the Netherlands, France, Denmark and Germany, but, by British standards, some of these levels of provision still remain generous. On average, single people who lose their jobs in

Germany can expect 65 per cent of their income to be replaced by benefit in the first year of unemployment, and by just under 60 per cent in the second. It is well said that 'the Thatcher government might contemplate the social upheavals required to bring Britain's labour market institutions in line with America's, but Continental governments do not appear to have the stomach for this kind of radicalism' (Kaletsky, 1984b). Moreover, whereas the relative absence of migrant labour can be seen to have contributed to British manufacturing capital's comparative disadvantage in earlier decades, it is becoming ever more likely that the Thatcherite project is to go beyond the 'correction' of this, and is beginning to be seen as such in other European countries. 'Maybe Mrs Thatcher would follow the logic of her arguments and cut wages to the level of the Filipinos', an official told Kaletsky. 'The Germans would not consider this for a moment.'

Of course it has been a staple of Tory economic analysis that high taxation, caused by high welfare expenditure, is a major reason for slow growth in Britain. In fact, Sir John Hoskyns, now Director General of the Institute of Directors, and the head of Mrs Thatcher's Policy Unit during 1979–82, was still glibly rehearsing this theme in a number of articles he wrote in 1985 to mark the tenth anniversary of Mrs Thatcher's party leadership (*The Times*, 12 February). Choosing his ground carefully, and concentrating on Japan and the US, he failed to note, however, that Britain actually has one of the lowest burdens of taxation – and the lowest levels of public expenditure in relation to GDP – of all industrial countries. As for social welfare expenditure, as Kaldor and Ward (1985) have noted, in Britain in 1981 this stood at about 23 per cent (pretty much the same as in Ireland) – but in Italy it stood at nearly 25 per cent, in France at 27, in Denmark and Germany at 29, and in Belgium and the Netherlands it was 30 per cent or more.

Whatever the material benefits that do or do not accrue to the British workers, and whatever the vulnerabilities and subjective dispositions that make them (or the unemployed) more or less compliant, it remains the case, however, that labour-power, in the sense of the workers' capacity to produce, is an important factor in the relation between labour and productivity. With the number of working days lost by strikes having risen in 1984 (irrespective of the miners' strike), and with British manufacturing's unit labour costs rising disproportionately, but with British wages being amongst the lowest in the advanced industrialised world –

which does, of course, have implications for the readiness with which employers in Britain will find it advantageous to invest in technology and so drive productivity forward on a qualitatively different basis – it is to the question of how labour-power has been developed under Thatcher that we turn now.

The most recent research underlines the gravity of the handicap under which British capital continues to operate with respect to labour-power. In round terms, for example, the percentage of workers with a recognised qualification in the US, West Germany and Japan now stands at 78, 66 and 60 per cent. In Britain it stands at about 50 per cent, a figure that flatters British educational performance for various reasons, including the fact that the minimum British qualification is represented by one pass at the CSE level (NEDO, 1984a, p. 83, Table 6.b.). As for apprenticeships: in round terms in 1979, 100,000 apprentices were recruited in Britain compared to less than 40,000 in 1983. That is a drop of 60 per cent, and between 1981 and 1984 at least 15,000 apprentices had their training disrupted, or worse, by cutbacks made by their employers (NEDO, 1984a, p. 70, para 5.45; *Employment Gazette*, March 1984, p. 128). Such is the situation within engineering that whereas manpower forecasts by Warwick University's Institute for Employment Research suggest that the industry needs an annual intake of between 5,000 and 6,000 new technicians, only 8,000 apprentices were recruited in 1983–4, fewer than half of them being technicians. In future, of course, the option of upgrading craftsmen will also prove difficult because of the drop in the number of those who are newly qualified (Pike, 1984). At this rate, as a management writer concluded after a review of some of the consequences of the 1982 Employment and Training Act: 'We'll run out of skilled labour about the same time we run out of North Sea Oil' ('Training up a Blind Alley', *Works Management*, January 1984).

It is true enough that it has for long been the case in the UK that fifteen- and sixteen-year-olds have tried to enter the labour market directly, whereas in Japan and West Germany only about 5 per cent have done so, with most young people in the US taking the High School Diploma (NEDO, 1984a, p. 6, para 1.61). But not only has the relative paucity of British vocational and technical education and the lack of skill training within industry continued into the 1980s, with the situation clearly having worsened in some respects, today there is absolutely no excuse for overlooking the implications of this for manufacturing productivity. It was seen in Parts Two and Three that in the 1970s far too much of the research into manufacturing productivity relied on price rather than physical measures, that it failed to thoroughly examine the means of production in its 'physical' aspect, that it relied too much on management opinion, that it followed the easy course of invoking 'attitudes' and 'culture', and (Prais excepted) that it generally failed altogether to examine international variations in production organisation and in the quality of labour-power. Recently, though, research has been conducted (Daly, Hitchens and Wagner, 1985) that goes a whole lot further towards meeting the rudimentary ABC of requirements that was set down for international productivity research into labour productivity in Chapter 2. It amply confirms that quality of labour-power can make an important contribution to international differences in labour productivity, and it strongly suggests that a lack of adequately qualified manpower has made an enduring contribution to the particular British 'difficulty'.

Taking the form of a comparison of forty-five matched manufacturing firms in Britain and West Germany, this research is based on firms that make relatively simple products (screws, springs, drill bits, etc.). It is possible that a comparison which concentrated on less simple manufacturing products and processes, or which considered the importance of skill and technical knowledge in a wider context than that of direct production work, might have demonstrated that differences in the quality of labour-power in these two countries have yet greater significance. But even on the basis of the products sampled in this research, German firms were found to have an average productivity differential of 63 per cent, it being quite clear that the technical competence of those directly involved in production made an important contribution to this.

Interestingly enough, this recent (and better) comparative research found no clear difference in direct manning levels. It reported that machine running speeds were much the same in both countries. It also reported that the machinery was of much the same vintage. Even so, and no less interestingly, some differences were detected on the 'physical' side. For example, careful inspection revealed that the British and German machinery was *not* 'identical'. In Germany it was more common to feed machines automatically rather than by hand. As judged by the use of numerical control machine tools, the German machinery was also more advanced technically. German products, too, tended to be more advanced technically and to be of higher quality. It was also found, however, that maintenance was poorer in the British factories and that breakdowns proved more serious in this country – and it is the different *linkages* that this research reveals between the physical plant and the technical capacities of management, foremen and workers in Britain and Germany that are relevant here.

Two-thirds of the German workforces had passed examinations to the level of a trained fitter, more than twice the proportion in Britain. Senior staff in the German factories were very nearly all qualified engineers, which was also far from the case in Britain. All the German production foremen had passed examinations as craftsmen, which once again was very far from the case in Britain. And these differences had important consequences, both for technical advance and for factory organisation. That the researchers found 'an air of complacency and despondency' in British plants (and also the owner of an old-established family firm who declared bluntly, 'We are not interested in productivity') is of importance in its own right. It reminds us that the entirety of British management had not been 'shook-up', even by 1983. But what is also important is that this research found that those who made decisions in Britain 'often seemed not to appreciate the full potential of the new technology'; that they 'could not see a payback over a longer period'; and that a far from trivial reason why breakdowns were a more serious problem in Britain was that there was 'frequently no in-house ability to carry out a repair, or even to diagnose the fault', especially on modern machinery. It is in fact all of a piece with this that an NC machine manufacturer who had investigated British repair problems should have estimated that 70 per cent of them could have been dealt with by the British users themselves if only they had employed properly skilled fitters.

As Daly *et al.* themselves conclude: 'Although there was a relative lack of NC machinery in the British plants in our sample, in our judgement the greater part of the productivity gap came from other sources: a lack of feeding devices, frequent machine breakdowns, poor maintenance procedures, inadequate control of the quality of raw materials, and similar deficiencies in basic production techniques.' Quoting a Stuttgart plant manager – who explained to them in a matter-of-fact way that 'three-quarters of all improvements in productivity are achieved through ensuring an adequate documentation of exact machine-settings; ensuring that all parts are available and are of the right dimensions; that all drawings and measuring devices are available; that all involved know how to do their jobs; that the product-design is appropriate', etc., etc., etc. – they note that 'in a British factory things are different'.

In particular, this research points to the limited technical training of British foremen. It suggests that it is this, and the relative scarcity of trained persons in Britain – and not merely general ' "cultural" preferences' – that makes for a greater division of responsibilities in Britain, with maintenance men, production controllers, and quality controllers all working more or less in parallel to the foreman. But of more importance in the specific context of the 1980s, Daly *et al.* also echo an observation that has been made in these pages already: that not only has it been the case in Germany that a broad net of craft training has provided a basis for the rapid mastery of new skills, but that in Britain in 1983 the number of craft and technician trainees in engineering under the supervision of the Engineering Industry Training Board (EITB) had actually fallen to less than a third of that in 1967. This, as they put it, must seem 'very puzzling to anyone taking a long term view of the future of British manufacturing'. So indeed it must. And, as if this were not enough, in 1984 the EITB was arguing that it should no longer seek to augment the industry's intake. In Britain, it would seem, what individual capitals will not do for themselves they are also reluctant to do collectively, and, under Thatcher, they can expect little support from the state. That the above investigation suggests the majority of NC machines installed in Germany were German but that most of those in Britain were Japanese does not bode well for the future of manufacturing capital in Britain either.

Labour that is in short supply is now traded on a world-wide market, of course, and countries can be simultaneously involved in importing and exporting it. But a small indication of the way things have been going in Britain is forthcoming from a statement made by Tom King, the Employment Secretary, in 1984. 'My Department issues work permits to people from overseas and one criterion is that the skills are not available here', he told a Commons Select Committee on Employment on 23 May. Confessing himself 'astonished' that this was necessary in the midst of high unemployment, he revealed that in 1982 alone 5,000 work permits had been issued, about 2,000 involving people who were needed for their computing or electronic skills. Perhaps Mr King had not read a letter that workers at Linotype Paul's Cheltenham plant had been driven to write to the Prime Minister over a year earlier? He would certainly have had no right to be surprised had he done so. At Cheltenham a labour force that had developed a computerised typesetting system capable of handling the large numbers of characters and symbols in the Japanese language (yes, Japanese) had been told that the company was going to shift to Germany – to tie in with R & D considerations, as assessed by the American parent company, Allied Corporation (Pike, 1983). As the workforce put it in their letter to Mrs Thatcher: 'The highly-skilled workforce at Linotype Paul will join the British dole queue while recruitment and training for these same positions is conducted in the US and Germany.' It is not difficult to imagine what such workers would feel if they were to hear about the Employment Secretary's surprise at having to import specialist labour from abroad, especially 'in the midst of high unemployment'.

There are those who would have us believe that YTS will transform the situation. It seems highly improbable that it will, either on a one- or two-yearly basis. Just look back at Figure 10.1 in the previous chapter. The entry for 'Public Subsidy Trainees' makes it quite clear what role is envisaged for this cheap labour supply in advanced thinking about the new 'flexi-firm'. And as Daly *et al.* emphasise, a combination of YTS with an increased technological element in schooling (through the so-called Technical and Vocational Initiative) would only 'raise the proficiency of the *unskilled* section of the labourforce' (1985, p. 60). The problems that exist in the implementation and development of technology in Britain are such that they cannot be remedied by these measures. They arise from the long-standing inadequacy in British manufacturing's R & D record, and from the related and again long-standing failure to develop technical manpower at all levels. Despite the passage of half a decade the Thatcher governments have done little to make a dent in these problems, and they are as much in evidence whether British manufacturing management is considered on an across-the-board basis, or whether the new technology industries are considered in particular.

In 1982, for instance, an enquiry from Salford University (one of those 'technological universities', incidentally, that were most harshly affected by the Thatcher cuts in higher education) reported that senior managements lacked sufficient knowledge to make judgments on applying microelectronics to their companies, or the confidence to seek outside advice; and that the application of microelectronics technology, to both production methods and products, was being hindered by lack of technicians and professional engineers (Hampshire, 1982). A major survey of manufacturing industry in 1984 tells the same tale. Nearly a quarter of respondents rated the fact that they lacked sufficient technical expertise as a barrier to computerisation and more automated technology. The importance attributed to the lack of technical expertise was only a few per cent less than that attributed to lack of funds (23 per cent compared to 27), and was clearly more important than any difficulties associated with 'shopfloor resistance' (10 per cent), the latter figure itself making a weak showing as compared to other difficulties – insufficient management support at the top or middle levels, and the limitations of capital justification techniques being cited in a further 30 per cent of cases (Wyles, 1984).

As for Britain's information technology industry, if this is looked to for Britain's future salvation the situation is, if anything, yet more serious. In 1984 a survey of 900 electronics companies reported that most smaller companies did not provide in-house training, and that skill shortages were a problem, particularly in the South-East (ELF, 1984). Other research on the UK computer software and services industry also points to the growth of business being limited by the shortage of qualified staff (CSA, 1984). According to a recent NEDO Report the information technology industry is facing a 'crisis of survival'. Despite its own relatively fast growth, the supply industry for communicating systems is losing out internationally. The UK's share in the aggregate output of the five market leaders (the others being France and Germany, and Japan and the US who are clearly ahead of the field) has fallen from 9 per cent in 1970 to 5 per cent, and the average annual growth rate in all these countries has exceeded that in the UK. In 1983 import penetration had reached a record 54 per cent, compared to 29 per cent in 1970. Imports have penetrated even further in semi-conductors, where the figure stands at more like 75 per cent (NEDO, 1984b, pp. 3, 4, 6; Ashworth, 1984). To read what *Crisis Facing UK Information Technology* has to say on R & D, long-term planning, finance, and marketing is in fact to experience a sense of *déjà vu*. Since information technology can be depicted as the machine tool industry of the future it is worth reporting what a few of these uncanny echoes are:

*On R & D*: 'The UK Government spends the same proportion of GDP on R and D as its main competitors but, because of the different sizes of the economies, the success of others in "levering" greater industrial contributions and the higher proportion of defence R and D in the UK budget, the actual sum spent on civil industrial R and D is very much less in the UK than in our major competitors.' 'Much more pre-competitive collaborative R and D is required to ensure that the industry has a competitive technology base.'

*On finance and long-term planning*: 'Lack of long-term strategic horizons has resulted in the UK failing to anticipate some of the most critical developments . . . One of the main reasons for short industrial horizons is the need to satisfy a financial community anxiously watching each quarter's figures.'

*On marketing* (this repeating a view already expressed in an earlier IT Report): 'UK companies needed to exhibit a higher commitment to and professionalism in marketing.'

*On education and training* – which, so to speak, is where we came in, though no apology is made for the detour, since R & D, investment and training can all form part of a virtuous circle – the Report is no less unequivocal, and no less familiar. 'Too often', it tells us, 'contracts are being lost, and employment opportunities for the less skilled are being lost with them, because of the lack of a few key engineers. Competition for these people is increasing from users and from overseas companies established in the UK, neither of which, for the most part, have shared the costs of training and development.' And again: 'One of the most critical issues of all is that of the availability of suitably skilled manpower. Shortages occur at all skill levels.'

This enquiry into IT also says something about *the unions*: that trade unions have not only been positive towards IT, but that they have been 'more positive than anyone had a right to expect' (NEDO, 1984b, pp. 9, 10, 13).

A major British survey of 1,200 factories covering the full range of manufacturing industry similarly reports that shopfloor and trade union resistance has seldom been an important problem, but lack of expertise, and the recession itself, have (Northcott and

Rogers, 1984). An international comparison of the situation in Britain, West Germany and France confirms this interpretation, for whereas this enquiry into nearly 4,000 factories in these three countries found a lack of technical expertise to have been a common problem (after all, new technology is 'new'), it also found that in Britain 43 per cent of respondents blamed the economic situation as an obstacle to the introduction of microelectronics – twice as many as in Germany and France – *and* that complaints about shop floor and trade union resistance ranged downwards from 16 per cent in France, to 14 per cent in Germany to 7 per cent in Britain (the printing industry, upon which, as we have seen, productivity researchers have been apt to dwell, contributed disproportionately to even this smaller total: see Northcott and Rogers, 1985, pp. 7, 8, 34, 37; on printing and research into British productivity see p. 62 above).

In the light of such evidence the argument that it is British workers and their unions who are putting a drag on the third technological revolution most certainly looks thin.[2]

That there are yet other dark clouds on the horizon is something that some industrialists have seen already. In the words of the managing director of a medium-sized engineering company: 'It's been 40 per cent shrinkage against a 15 per cent increase in efficiency, the infrastructure is being whittled away' (cited in Owen *et al.*, 1984, p. 1). A similar theme figured prominently at the 1984 CBI Conference, with only one speaker voicing dissent (a merchant banker, who was presumably indifferent whether his share of the surplus came from manufacturing or services). Moving a motion on the regeneration of manufacturing, Roland Long on International Harvester declared that the burdens that people in the older manufacturing areas had been made to carry would have been excessive even in some noble cause, but that 'To ask them to carry those burdens in order that the Milton Friedman economic theory of monetarism might eventually, possibly, succeed, is an outrage.' The chairman of Unilever also reminded his fellow employers that the world's high-growth economies had remained strong in manufacturing, the choice between services and manufacturing thus being a bogus one. That there is a need to spend more on infrastructure projects is not in doubt. On one estimate an additional £3.5 billion a year needs to be spent for the next ten years on housing and the road and motorway network alone to prevent further deterioration (Cowie, Harlow and Emerson, 1984) – and this with getting on for half a million building workers unemployed.

Recent years have seen no repetition of the call for a 'bare-knuckled fight' with the Government that the CBI Director General made in 1980. None the less there are clear signs of tension amongst the manufacturing employers. The longer-term danger is clear enough too. The lack of an infrastructure may itself obstruct any sustained recovery. Even Britain's *successful* companies are being driven abroad because of the collapse of the industrial base. For example, ICI, Britain's biggest industrial profit-maker, has a long-established record of technological advance behind it, and it cannot be said to lack technically qualified managers either. But it sells the vast majority of its output to other industrial companies. Since 1979, its UK workforce has been cut by a third. Sixty per cent of its assets are now located abroad, and in the wake of cuts in research in this country moves are underway to strengthen its links with universities overseas. In the words of ICI's John Harvey Jones: 'When the UK industrial base collapsed what could we do?' (Erlichman, 1985).

Within the ranks of British management Thatcherite policies have given a further lease of life to an all too familiar deficiency. For whereas high interest rates and earlier on a high exchange rate may well have done much to concentrate industrialists' minds, the one thing which they are most unlikely to have concentrated them upon is planning in the longer term. The consequences of this were of course noted in the NEDO Report on IT that was referred to above. But faced with an uncertain future, and in many cases the uncertainty that their companies would have a future, in the early 1980s cost-cutting, not planning, became the order of the day more generally. Long-standing as the planning deficiency in British industry is, the new virus that has compounded the 'British disease' – the Thatcher disease – has only served to set back the time when the patient can recover.

What new investment has been put in may well have helped to increase productivity, especially if this has been in conjunction with a decrease in manning levels. But the cost-cutting solution adopted by many companies – the replacement of existing machinery with that which is more efficient for the manufacture of the same products – does not bode well for the longer term. 'Staying in the present product area may be the easiest course in the short term', warned the Governor of the Bank of England in 1984, 'but also the riskiest course in the longer term . . . For many companies the luxury of choice between longer-term objectives has not existed during the recent phase of concentration and short-term survival . . . The skills that are required to make strategic choices, looking five and more years ahead, are quite different, wider-ranging and in many respects more difficult than those required for pruning and rationalisation' (*Bank of England Quarterly*, September 1984). It is difficult to quibble with this.

As far as management is concerned, there is little reason to suppose that the improvement in British management practice has put it ahead of the field either. As we saw in Chapter 10, one of the most important changes in British management has been the heightened attention it has given to how goods and services are *actually produced*. But this is just how a leading American business journal described what was happening in America in 1981 (*Fortune*, 15 June 1981, p. 68). 'Working smarter' is what they call it in the States, and, as *Fortune* described the situation in 1981, 'corporations in the US are pressed as never before to lift productivity and turn out higher-quality goods and services'. So too in Western Europe. In 1984 a survey of over 150 large manufacturing companies in Western Europe concluded that their common underlying concern was for consistent and reliable quality – 85 per cent thought this a key factor for success, 80 per cent adding that making dependable delivery promises and providing high performance products was of equal significance (INSEAD, 1984). In short, if changes on the management side are considered, the notion that, comparatively speaking, Thatcherism has met with success has to reckon with the awkward fact that much of the rest of the field, some of which had a clear head start, is running faster as well, and that in recent years productivity has increased throughout the industrialised world (NIESR, 1984, p. 43, Table 5). No doubt manning levels have been tightened up elsewhere as well.

Typically, of course, very few discussions of British workers, management and productivity have avoided some reference or other to 'attitudes'. Enough warnings about what for the most part has been speculation, unsupported by evidence, have been made in these pages to justify no further repetition here. But in so far as what is at issue is how British workers' attitudes differ from those of workers in other nations, and bearing in mind that in no case do workers' attitudes exist in a vacuum, it is instructive to see what the most recent international survey research on employee perceptions has to say. And whereas it indicates that UK managements are seen as no less competent in 'people-management skills' than their counterparts in many competing countries, the fact is that this most recent research suggests that more employees in the UK (still) perceive communications within their organisations to be less effective than in any of the other countries surveyed (i.e. Japan, Canada, West Germany, France, the US and the Netherlands). Indeed, UK employees would seem to be the least likely to hear things first through official channels – hardly the best basis, it might be thought, for a high degree of trust and collective endeavour. By no means less suggestive, however, is what this research indicates to be the case with respect to attitudes about *work organisation and operating efficiency.* When it comes to questions about whether employees have a clear idea of what is expected to them in their jobs, whether they think the work of their departments is well organised, whether they think their department operates efficiently and produces good quality work, UK employees (still) rate their companies less favourably than those in most other countries (ISR, 1984). Suffice it to note that these particular attitudes all relate, as the Thatcherites might themselves say, to what goes on in 'the wealth-producing process'.

There are those who have talked about 'recovery' already, and there is some justification for this as judged by profit rates. But here again both historical and comparative aspects of the British performance have to be taken into account. Not only are profit rates up in much of the advanced capitalist world, but it cannot be emphasised too strongly that in Britain such recovery as there has been has started from a very low base. In 1982 new manufacturing investment fell below the normal level for the scrapping of old equipment (Armstrong, Glyn and Harrison, 1984, p. 424). Between the end of 1979 and the middle of 1983 investment in manufacturing fell by 41 per cent, and the rate at which manufacturing industry has been acquiring fixed assets is lower than in previous recoveries (OECD, *United Kingdom Survey,* January 1984, p. 44; *Bank of England Quarterly,* September 1984, p. 309). The situation is such that even if estimates for 1984 prove correct this will still leave the 1984 figure about £2 billion short of that for 1979 (see Table 11.1) – in round terms still 25

**Table 11.1   Manufacturing investment, 1979–84**

| | Fixed capital expenditure[a] (£ billion[b]) |
|---|---|
| 1979 | 8.2 |
| 1980 | 7.3 |
| 1981 | 5.7 |
| 1982 | 5.6 |
| 1983 | 5.4 |
| 1984 | 6.2[c] |

*Source*: CSO, *Monthly Digest of Statistics*, August, 1984, Table 1.7; NIESR (1984), Table 6, p. 11.
*Notes*:
[a]  Fixed capital expenditure includes leased assets.
[b]  Revalued at 1980 prices.
[c]Estimate.

per cent lower – and the rate of increase may itself decline if, as seems quite probable as I write, the economic cycle turns down and the rate of growth begins to slacken in 1985/86. The fact that at the beginning of 1985 interest rates once again shot up – so that real interest rates were the highest they had ever been in recorded history – does nothing to make the future look less bleak, with respect to investment, new product development or long-term planning.

It has been suggested already that any judgment about the future success or otherwise of Thatcherism has to take into account the entire infrastructure. So far as the 'social' dimension of the infrastructure is concerned, it is as well to recall a point made earlier, that in their pursuit of the 'American model' the Thatcherites have done more to move towards the creation of an underclass than to develop its complement, a technically advanced stratum of sufficient quality. That the expression of governmental concern about the extent of the latter problem was long delayed tells us something about Thatcherite priorities, and about the important extent to which the Thatcherites' own peculiar vision has led them to focus on the individual enterprise *sans* infrastructure as the unit of economic analysis (this being an almost coterminous concept in their ideology to that of the enterprising individual). Of course, the household/enterprise/

British economy idea is a useful rhetorical device. It deflects attention from the actual and potential role of the state. It is through such distorted conceptions of reality that the Thatcherite pretence is maintained that what matters is what is done in households (enterprises). But what the state does do – or does not do – can be crucial for the deployment of national resources, and once we lift our eyes from the *individual enterprise* a further deficiency in the Thatcher record on productivity comes into full view. Indeed, when viewed in this larger frame it is perfectly plain that the productive deployment of national resources under Thatcher has been a *disaster*. No other word will do.

On current estimates, for example, the tax revenue from North Sea Oil is scheduled to peak at around £11 or £12 billion per year in the mid to late 1980s. This represents about twice the fixed capital expenditure that went into British manufacturing in 1984. A sobering comparison, perhaps, but not one whit as sobering as the situation underlined by another comparison. For the amazing windfall that has come from North Sea Oil is in round terms equivalent to the cost that the Exchequer has incurred through higher unemployment. Each unemployed person costs about £5,000 a year, taking into account the benefits paid and the loss of revenue from tax (Winchester, 1984). This, more or less, is where the revenue from North Sea Oil has *gone*.

Nor is this all. Following the abolition of exchange controls, an early Thatcher initiative, a whole mass of potential productivity-enhancing capital has gone abroad as well. Although the rush has now abated somewhat, direct overseas investment by British firms rose from just over £30,000 million in 1979 to more like £50,000 million in 1982. Overseas portfolio investment (mostly by the big pension and insurance funds) rose yet faster in the same period, from £12,000 million to over £37,000 million. Of course, there is another side to these developments. Over this same period, for example, inward direct overseas investment rose from about £21,000 million to about £31,000 million, so too private portfolio investment, from about £4,500 million to £6,700 million, and outward British investment also brought in profits and dividends. As against this, though, inward investment means that dividends and profits flow *outwards*, which in the period under review largely cancelled the above advantage (Lipsey, 1984). An outflow of funds through British overseas investment also reduces what is available for loans at home, and can do nothing to ease interest rates. But complex as the full ramifications of international investment are, what is quite clear is that thousands of millions of pounds have gone abroad, in large part for good; that millions of people are unemployed at home – under Thatcher, probably in considerable part for good too – and that, in 1983, for the first time in its entire history, Britain imported more manufactured goods than it exported.

For some people, there have been benefits, of course. That the rich soon got richer under Thatcher – and the poor poorer – is suggested by the latest available data on both wealth and income. Since 1979 the share of marketable wealth owned by the top quarter of people has increased from 77 per cent to 81 per cent (*Inland Revenue Statistics*, 1984, p. 50, Table 4.8). As for income, between 1978/79 and 1981/82 the top 1 per cent experienced a real increase in average income after tax of nearly 17 per cent, and the next 9 per cent benefited by nearly 5 per cent. By contrast, the bottom 20 per cent experienced a real fall in after tax average income of over 10 per cent (*Economic Trends*, July 1984). Both the high salary earners and the overlapping category of those who receive dividends have pulled away from the rest. In 1979 the twenty highest paid directors received as much as 454 'average' male manual workers; by 1983 they received as much as 722 workers.[3] Such a comparison would be the more startling if based on average women manual workers or on young workers. In 1979 male under-eighteen-year-olds received 40 per cent of adult average earnings; by 1984 this was down to 35 per cent. Earnings for young females also dropped, from 58 to 50 per cent (*Labour Research*, November 1984; December 1984). On every count Thatcher's stripped-down capitalism has made for a divided society. A decrease in income tax, with much made of the advantages of this for the lower-paid, might do something to make the situation sound better and thus provide the Tories with electoral fodder for their skilled working-class (and other) support. But should such a reform be launched in the name of 'growth' (enterprising individualism, etc.) it will be, at best, a circuitous way of achieving this particular objective.

Meanwhile, a yawning gap of another type has opened up as well. The sheer extent of this can be judged at a glance from Figure 11.1. That the massive wedge of unemployment is darkly shaded is highly appropriate, given both the human misery that so much of it represents, and the fact that a significant portion of it stems from a mixture of Thatcherite miscalculation and the deliberate priority accorded to other policy objectives to the

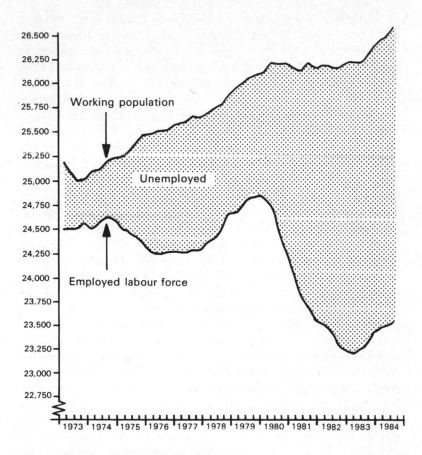

*Souroo: Employment Gazette*, January 1985.
*Note*: Seasonally adjusted. Numbers in thousands.

**Figure 11.1** Working population and employed labour force, 1973–84

detriment of employment. But with special reference to productivity the yawning abyss of unemployment spells productive waste.

Early on, the Thatcherites were full of noise about their 'dramatic' achievements with productivity. Some Tory politicians are still given to making inflated claims about their productivity record today. But what has actually been achieved on this relatively narrow front is historically unexceptional, and the rate of growth of manufacturing productivity is in any case unlikely to be sustained. This much was admitted by Chancellor Lawson in his March 1985 Budget statement. After having prefaced his comments on what had happened to the rate of growth in manufacturing productivity by reporting that revisions had been made to both the employment and the output data, the best he could come up with was the claim that there has been '*some* improvement in underlying productivity growth' (my emphasis). What Nigel Lawson had to say about the future course of underlying productivity growth was similarly muted – that it was 'expected to remain above the rate achieved between the two "oil shocks" of 1973 and 1979, but below that of the 1960s'. On the Chancellor's own data the annual average change in manufacturing output per head in 1973–9 had been a meagre ¾ per cent, as compared to 3¾ per cent in 1964–73. For the Thatcherite years, 1979–84, Lawson put the annual rate of increase at 3½ per cent. A far cry from the vision once held out by Mrs Thatcher herself of rates of change 'reminiscent of Germany or Japan'.[4] It is in fact patently obvious that the truly 'dramatic' achievement of the Thatcher regime is the economic and social devastation it has brought in its train. The Thatcherites have not only failed to develop British labour's productive potential – and what other time could have been better suited for a concerted and determined improvement of this? – they have presided over such a waste of productive potential, on both the capital and the labour side, that in order to believe that the nation's resources have been efficiently and productively deployed it would be necessary to be not just myopic but blind. For them, of all people, to repeat the words of that old, old refrain – the one about British workers and productivity – would be impertinent indeed.

# Three commentaries on productivity and the conventional wisdom

# A On the magic roundabout: A note on the production and re-production of knowledge about British workers and labour productivity

Economists have produced relatively few detailed empirical investigations into the immediate determinants of UK labour productivity. But it is important to appreciate that the productivity studies which economists have produced are not simply part of the subject-matter of economics as a specialised academic discipline. They have a wider social significance in that they contribute to the way in which British society is explained and interpreted more generally. They are, in short, one of the means by which society – and not least, even though indirectly, the working class – is 'told about itself'. Special in their wider social significance, however, such studies also tend to be socially constructed in a rather special way. Whereas all spheres of intellectual activity are subjected to processes of collective validation by fellow specialists, in the case of the specialist knowledge that is produced about productivity a further referent also tends to enter into the process of validation – management opinion. For example, economists are apt to cite managers' opinions; when they conduct empirical investigations they are apt to formulate them in the light of this received wisdom; and the validating process comes full circle when yet other economists make further reference to the opinion of managers in order to add credibility to the (often tentative) conclusions of particular pieces of empirical research. The danger is clear enough: that in this way society comes to know about itself, apparently scientifically, but in practice through a process that may be unduly influenced by the opinion of those who form only a tiny part of that society.

Such considerations make it all the more important that outsiders should intrude into the circle of opinion that economists inhabit. What follows is one such intrusion. It seeks to explore in

243

detail how evidence is presented within this circle of opinion – which clues and loose ends are followed up, and how rigorously; which are merely inferred or cited with undue selectivity, and so on. In short, it seeks to explore critically, and in detail, how evidence has been cited, presented and reproduced about British workers and productivity. Since detail is of the essence it takes as its point of entry just one particular claim, which was commonly advanced in the 1970s – that British managements incur excess costs in dealing with 'labour relations'. Yet, more particularly, it considers the manner in which Caves marshalled the evidence for this claim in the 1980 Brookings Institution study.

Among the excess costs to UK management that Caves holds to result in a productivity shortfall are included both those costs which take the form of an outright drain on resources and, more subtly, 'decreases in the effectiveness [of companies] caused by increased uncertainty about the rate of output'. He informs us that 'numerous types of such losses have been identified' (1980, p. 146), and indeed that these alleged results of UK labour practices have been 'quantified and subjected to some international comparisons' (1980, p. 143). Since Caves' work has been influential it is important to consider systematically the evidence he puts forward to support these views. It is to this end that five claims that Caves advances (1980, pp. 146–8) are considered, one by one, below.

(1) *In the UK strikes and disruptions at supplier companies make it necessary for British managements to hold larger inventories.* Caves' evidence for the view that strikes and disruptions are the *cause* of higher British inventories is (i) that 'on an average day in 1973, fifteen suppliers of Chrysler UK were on strike' (this in fact a word-for-word repetition of what was said by the CPRS (1975), p. 84, para. 42ii); (ii) that 'executives' Caves talked to 'speculated' that 'inventory holdings in the United Kingdom might be inflated 15 to 20 per cent'; (iii) what the CPRS 1975 study on the British car industry said about the effect of labour disputes on product availability; and (iv) what was said in a Price Commission report on Metal Box Ltd.

Let's just consider at a little more length what this evidence amounts to. Item (i) of Caves' evidence, about what happened on 'an average day' at Chrysler in 1973, stands or falls on the adequacy of the information supplied by the management of this particular company. Item (ii), as Caves says, rests on what executives 'speculated'. So far, then, not so good. But to track down the source for item (iii) of Caves' evidence in the CPRS Report (1975, pp. 26, 75) is not to vanquish a real element of doubt either. For to do this is to find only the statement that 'in one plant on the continent which depends on British supplies, 20 days stock is normally maintained, while in Japan stock levels of a few hours are common for many items'. This creates a distortion of the wider reality. The Japanese Kanban system has been the envy of industrialists world-wide. Even by 1983 American car manufacturers were themselves still considering JIT, the 'Just-in-Time' system that keeps stocks to an absolute minimum (Gooding, 1983). As evidence for the view that strikes and disruptions in Britain have a widespread effect on inventories Caves' evidence therefore remains slender.

As for item (iv) of Caves' evidence, an examination of what the Price Commission on Metal Box actually said reveals a situation a good deal more complex than is suggested by Caves' assertion 'Because of strikes and disruptions at suppliers companies . . . British managements find it necessary to hold larger inventories.' Sure enough, the Price Commission did report that it was 'Metal Box's policy to keep about six to eight weeks supply of tinplate as a working stock'. It also thought this practice undesirable (in the words of the Price Commission, 'the maintenance of the buffer stock is undoubtedly expensive'). Then again, the Price Commission also expressed the opinion that 'shortage may . . . be caused by industrial action at BSC' (BSC being Metal Box's tinplate supplier). But to quote the Price Commission more fully than Caves does is to cast a different light on Metal Box's supply problems. For the Commission regarded the stock as 'a buffer against both the inability at times of BSC to deliver the required specification of tinplate and the variability of customer demand'. Shortage, it added, '*may also* be caused by industrial action at BSC'. The Commission did not slate industrial action as the primary cause of Metal Box's supply problem, however. Indeed, to have done so would have meant overlooking a, quite literally, sizeable fact. For as the Commission reported – though Caves did not – BSC produced a large number of different tinplate specifications. In fact, an *enormous* number. Over 2,000, with 'probably 300 to 350' different specifications for open top cans *alone* (presumably the Price Commission and/or BSC boggled at the task of counting these accurately: Price Commission (1978b),

p. 28 para. 3.31, my emphasis). Caves cites Metal Box's supply problems as evidence of the excess costs of British labour relations without mention of this important fact about the multiplicity of tinplate specifications, which itself, one might have thought, had consequences for the size of inventory. Go back to Caves' evidence about strikes and the size of the inventories in the car industry (iii), and a similar difficulty arises. For Caves' account leaves the reader unaware that the CPRS Report *also* pointed to the existence of a large number of product variants. Elsewhere in his analysis Caves himself conceded that a mounting body of recent evidence indicates that British industry does indeed 'offer a particularly large number of product variants' (1980, p. 156). But there too he signally fails to relate this to size of inventories. The casual reader is therefore left with the clear impression that it really is terribly obvious that British inventories are higher *because of strikes*. It isn't. Not even on the basis of a fuller inspection of the evidence that Caves himself cites.

(2) *Uncertainties about output rates leave UK companies unsure how much output they will have to sell, 'thereby reducing the effectiveness of the resources ... allocated(d) to marketing activities'.* Caves tells us that 'the automobile industry supplies the most striking evidence'. He cites the CPRS Report, which says that monthly production in 'continental' plants 'seldom' varies from planned output by more than 5 per cent, with variance of 20 per cent or more being 'common in British plants'.

It has to be remarked that this 'most striking evidence' does come – once again – from the automobile industry. This, moreover, is the *only* evidence Caves supplies. (Quite apart from this, as noted in Chapter 5, no consideration is given to whether UK managements are up to scratch on marketing activities anyway.)

(3) *Companies bringing new equipment on stream face demands that the resulting productivity gains be shared with the workforce.* Caves is of the opinion that the reduction in the rate of return on investment when these demands are successful may be less costly than the uncertainty about how long newly installed equipment may be kept idle by disputes over manning. This could be so. Clearly, manning demands that lead to delays in the installation of new machinery and in modification, and other effective opposition to such installation and modification, *could* affect both the level and the rate of change of productivity. It will be remembered also that manning and controls over machine

installation were two practices that came to light in the review of Pratten's (1976a) study in Chapter 3. But what is Caves' evidence?

Two pieces of evidence are put forward. First, Caves refers to what the managers of some UK/German companies told Pratten – this is the very same evidence that we have come across before (Pratten, 1976a, pp. 55–6; and pp. 66–7 above). It takes us no further forward. Second, Caves refers – again – to the Price Commission Report on Metal Box. As he puts it: 'a metal container company reported that a new line producing two-piece cans was running at 40 to 50 per cent of capacity, largely because of difficulties in labour relations'. This might sound a relatively good piece of evidence – and certainly the Metal Box case is well on the way to becoming a staple reference for students of British labour productivity (see, for example, apart from Caves, 1980, p. 147, also Wagner 1980, p. 33; Carter (ed.), 1981, p. 36; and Prais, 1981a, p. 255). Just because of this, however, it is worth considering this case at a little more length, and indeed from a different vantage point. To this end, in 1983, I visited workers at one of Metal Box's two-piece can lines in Glasgow.

Glasgow had been one of the first sites to have two-piece production installed about ten years earlier. By 1983 it had shut. Two Metal Box workers I talked to at that time were particularly upset because, after being told over and over again they would 'be all right' (on the grounds that Scottish and Newcastle 'liked' the aluminium cans Glasgow produced), Metal Box had shifted production to Carlisle, using tinplate. They were also rather surprised about something else, however. Now out of work – one had just applied for a dumper truck job, unsuccessfully, and along with 600 others – they reported that they 'felt better'. 'It was so hard at the time, I didn't realise', one of them said, referring to the shift-work. 'I'd got to think that was how I was. But now I can see that I felt woozy all the time.' Given what they had been through (reductions in manning, as well as increased shift-working – with 'everything being cut' – the 'toilets were a right mess at the end – no soap – no towels' – 'if a man came off the line it was panic stations' – and all this in the context of production having shot from 300,000 to a million cans) they had good cause to be angry, and to distort the situation to management's disadvantage. But when I asked them about the production process they left me in no doubt that the two-piece line had experienced real technical difficulties. They had chapter and verse on this. The line had been legendary in the factory. They even talked about 'the Wooden line'. 'The Wooden line?' I asked (not used to Glasgow accents). 'The *Wooden* line', they said. 'What do you mean?' I asked. 'We used to call it the Wooden line', they said, 'because it wouldna' run.'

In Caves' account, the onus for the difficulties at Metal Box was put on 'labour relations.' But even the Price Commission referred to 'teething difficulties associated with a new technology', and not simply to 'industrial relations problems' (Price Commission, 1978b, p. 24, para. 3.20, p. 7, para. 1.2a). Suffice it to say that the workers – with whom Caves had no contact – and who, as far as one can see, made no mark on the Price Commission Report either – would strongly endorse this interpretation.

Two further comments are in order. First, since the economists seem bent on extruding as much use from Metal Box's two-piece can as possible, it is to be hoped that in future, and unlike Caves, more of them will also make plain that the most glaring 'restrictive practices' at Metal Box have been on the side of management. Until quite recently competition between the British and US industries was restricted by various non-entry agreements with the consequence, in the opinion of Wagner, that these 'lower competitive pressures in Britain' seem to some extent themselves to have 'delayed the introduction of new techniques and held back productivity' (1980, p. 32). Second, to the extent that the delayed introduction of the two-piece can at Metal Box is an instance, at least in part, of a UK workforce resisting the introduction of new technology, it remains one instance only. Clearly, most of us can think of others. The real question is, however, whether such resistance can be considered to be a significant drag on UK labour productivity more generally, and whether it can account for a significant part of the difference between UK productivity and that elsewhere. Caves, as we have seen, culls his evidence disproportionately from the car industry, Metal Box and the research by Pratten. Pratten, for his part, probably relies overmuch on printing and cars. And to consider another researcher, Prais, is also to see, if the detailed case studies in his book are consulted, that he in turn refers to industrial relations problems as significant influences on productivity in only two industries, again the predictable ones of printing and motor vehicles (as other writers have also noted: Edwards and Nolan, 1983, p. 5). It is in this manner – through an initial selectivity, and then sometimes in addition through selective re-reporting – that general views about 'the British worker' have been given currency. But on to Caves' fourth and fifth claims.

(4) *UK managements may sacrifice economies of scale because, with UK workers, big plants are a recipe for trouble.* This point needs a little spelling out. What is at issue, notice, is not the contention that big plants *are* a recipe for 'trouble', nor that big plants in the UK make for *greater* trouble than is the case elsewhere – but that UK managers are actually more reluctant than US ones even to build such plants, and accordingly do so less frequently.

The only evidence that Caves adduces is (1), that 'business executives' *told* him that 'to construct a plant employing more than 1,000 workers is to invite disaster'; and (2), a reference to the work of Prais. No information is provided about who the 'business executives' were, how many of them there were, or whether any one of them had ever made a decision not to build such a plant on these grounds. Upon inspection, the reference to Prais also constitutes an odd sort of evidence. In the work cited (1978, p. 368) Prais asks the relevant question: 'Is it possible that plants of large dimensions . . . tend not to be constructed in Britain because the risk of strikes in large plants is particularly great in Britain?' But he is referring to very large plants indeed ('say in the region of 30,000 employees'). Moreover, the question Prais asks remains just that, for he does not *answer* it in the paper referred to. Here again, then, the evidence is not good. (For further comments see Chapter 3, pp. 64–6).

(5) *Problems of labour relations in the UK take managers' time away from other tasks.* Two authorities are cited in this context. First – and yet again – the CPRS Report. From the CPRS Caves reports the 'claim by UK managers to spend about half their time dealing with labour disputes' compared with 'a figure of 5–10 per cent quoted by plant managers in Belgium and West Germany'. Other writers are also fond of citing this (e.g. Clutterbuck, 1984, pp. 65, 189). However, no reference is made to the preceding CPRS paragraph, which emphasises that '*The extent of labour relations problems varied widely among plants within the same company*' – against which the 'half their time' estimate sits awkwardly. And of course it simply isn't the case that each and every stoppage in each and every section of a car factory affects each and every other section every time.

The second authority cited is, again, Pratten, from whom the opinion is taken that 'the fact British managers must be more in evidence on the plant floor, to deal with the problems that arise, is itself a source of friction'. Ask where Pratten says this, and back we go again to the very same place (already cited by Caves in (3) above) where Pratten reports what (some) managers of UK-German operations say. As 'evidence' this is, again, slim – and it can hardly be accepted as a reasonable basis for a 'vicious circle' theory of UK labour productivity – one according to which it is UK *workers* who initiate 'trouble', and then, when poor old UK managers go down to the shop floor to sort things out, perpetuate and intensify it. In any case, this argument strikes an odd chord – if, that is, one bears in mind the number of times it has also been said that 'what is wrong with British managers' is that they *don't* 'get their hands dirty', that they are *not* 'accessible to workers like Japanese managers are', or that 'the trouble with British managers' is that they are *not* like the 'open door', 'non-status-conscious' Americans. Then again, though this doesn't firmly meet the Caves/Pratten point (such as it is), one does wonder whether the practice of consulting employees about 'plans and schemes for the development of a company's operations' – which Pratten suggests as a policy for increasing labour productivity in the UK (Pratten, 1976a, pp. 56, 66) – might not take up some time too.

Caves has a further idea: that if the uncertainty of UK labour relations is such as to affect the criteria for evaluating the plant manager's performance – thus, as he puts it, 'marking for success the resourceful improvisor who can scramble to keep things going on a day-to-day basis' – this would bode ill for the long-range planning abilities of British top management. But this opinion would seem to owe more to Caves' own powers of imagination than to any evidence. Typically, any investigation into the composition and actual basis of recruitment of UK top management is entirely lacking.

It remains to comment on a statistical analysis by Caves of UK/US inventories. Briefly, Caves developed a measure of finished good inventories relative to sales in both the UK industries and their US counterparts. Finding that this correlated positively with measures he developed to indicate 'poor labour relations', he concluded that excessive inventories were caused by uncertainty about output rates, which was in turn attributable to strikes and related measures (1980, p. 173). This positive correlation merits close scrutiny simply because it is Caves' one, original, piece of evidence that might be thought to bear on the question of whether UK managements do incur 'excess costs' relative to US managements because of the nature of UK workforces.

Statistically the result looks impressive. Caves is clearly pleased with it: 'The variable', he tells us, 'in fact has positive correlations statistically significant at the 1 per cent level with all of my variables indicating poor labour relations, for example, WDLB (0.578), STRKB (0.505), LAB1 (0.663), and FLAB1 (0.678).' But there are difficulties. For one thing, Caves' analysis does little to weaken the impression to be gained from Pratten (1976a) – that the most significant UK/North American differences relate to those in length of production runs and mixes, etc. It is certainly not outlandish to entertain the possibility that *these* might have some effect on finished goods inventories, and, as already suggested above, that they might lead UK managements to incur 'excess costs' of other than a labour-induced kind. If it was the case that an uneven or limited production flow was more in evidence in the UK, it is even possible that UK workers, being messed about more, might be more likely to experience more irritation, and maybe even strike more. Although Caves makes nothing of Pratten's managers' opinions on US/UK differences in the length of production runs, etc. – preferring as has been seen to pick out what the managers of UK-German operations told Pratten – such a possibility cannot be ruled out, even from Caves' own evidence.

However, it might appear from the way this particular statistical evidence on finished goods inventories has been reported thus far that Caves claims to have demonstrated that UK managements incurred excess costs because of the peculiar militancy of UK *workers*. But Caves himself introduced his 'test' in a way that casts doubt even on this. In fact, Caves initially presented this test as an attempt 'to investigate some of the channels through which ... interacting forces operate to depress productivity' – these 'interacting forces' being '*both* poor labour-management relations, *and* deficiencies in British management' (1980, p. 173, my emphasis). The idea that the results of the test indicate that it is UK workers who are at the bottom of the difficulty can only be sustained by a further assumption, that 'poor labour-management relations' in the UK are themselves the exclusive product of *labour*. To the extent that Caves did not assume this, we can only conclude that his test cannot be cited, with his approval, as evidence that it is UK *labour* that is at the bottom of 'the difficulty'. Rather, its results must of necessity be open to the interpretation that they reflect 'interacting forces'. But if this *is* the interpretation that Caves would like to see put on his work – and if he really is so aware of the importance of interactions – it must be remarked that he has presented his evidence in a very odd way. He does not take account of product variants when he discusses the effects of strikes on inventory holdings. He does not say anything about the marketing competence of British management when he discusses worker-induced uncertainty reducing the effectiveness of the resources allocated to marketing activities. And he does not discuss the record on, or strength of interest in, technical innovation on the part of British management (or the significance of low British wages) when he points to workers delaying the introduction of new machinery.

Caves' analysis as a whole is inevitably coloured by the manner in which he has chosen to juxtapose some relevant sources of information, to follow up possible interactions and pieces of evidence in some contexts but not in others, and to take some things more readily for granted than others. And, taken as a whole, the evidence that Caves puts forward about the contribution of labour-induced 'excess costs' to the UK productivity shortfall is neither extensive nor systematic. For the most part an illustrative pastiche, it raises very real questions about the extent of the practices cited in UK manufacturing generally, and even the particular cases cited sometimes lack the backing of adequate evidence. The car industry figures disproportionately as an example, especially as mediated through the CPRS Report. Pratten's evidence is made to carry an undue weight, given the particular uses that Caves makes of it. So too the Price Commission Report on Metal Box. Frequent references by Caves to the say-so of managers do not always serve to convince the reader either, at least not this one. Indeed, when Caves does make an attempt to test the hypothesis that any 'managerial disadvantage' of British industry is 'compounded by the need to deal with difficult labour-management relations' his analysis does not bear this out, and he remarks, a little lamely, that this 'suggests that UK management has made some headway in dealing with its labour-management relations' (cf. Caves, 1980, pp. 165 and 170). With respect to this, therefore, as well as other matters, there is much to recommend the view of Edwards and Nolan (1983): 'Caves seems to be determined to find a labour relations problem in Britain.' Quite so, and this would seem to be helped considerably by his location within a self-reinforcing circle of managerial and intellectual opinion. It is high time that someone got off the 'magic roundabout'. In this book I have tried to do so.

# B Some pitfalls in the denigration and the celebration of 'worker control'

That managements may have had a more equivocal view of restrictive practices than the term 'restrictive' (or many economists) would suggest is forthcoming from survey evidence which relates to a classic example of craft control, the 'closed shop'. A study of a sample of engineering establishments in 1971 reported that 44 per cent of them saw *advantages* in union shops (Marsh, *et al.*, 1971, pp. 159–60). By 1978, when the closed shop had spread more widely, so that somewhere between 30 and 40 per cent of the manufacturing workforce was covered, further research also indicated that whereas 14 per cent of the managements of manufacturing establishments saw only disadvantages in the arrangement, 37 per cent saw it as having disadvantages *and* advantages, and a further 35 per cent still believed it to have advantages only (Brown, 1981, p. 58). It is quite in line with this that a study of the Industrial Relations Act of 1971 should also have demonstrated widespread connivance by managements in the maintenance of the closed shop, even in the face of legislation against it (Weekes *et al.*, 1975).

Yet other researchers have come to the opinion that 'many managers actually welcomed the closed shop as a step toward stability and control'; also the 'check off' system for the deduction of union dues; also convenors, who in many studies have been 'seen as working closely with, and even for, management' (Storey, 1981). In a survey of British industrial relations that was conducted as late as 1980 managers reported that problems had arisen with closed shops in only 4 per cent of workplaces in the previous three years, the proportion of places where issues had arisen because a union had withdrawn membership from an employee being too small to measure (Daniel and Millward, 1983, pp. 80–1). Such observations have in fact been commonly made by those who have conducted thorough fieldwork. For example, Edwards and Scullion provide examples of 'restrictive' practices intended to assist production (1982, p. 287n and *passim*), and Zweig, writing in an earlier period, actually reported a steel industry manager describing seniority rules as 'the finest thing in our industry' (1951, p. 17). Not only is all this well known amongst professional students of British industrial relations, it is of course one reason why most of them do not favour legislative intervention.

Sometimes, though, ideas have surfaced in progressive liberal circles in which 'worker control' has been celebrated just as much as it has been denigrated by the political right – but without always giving full recognition to its possible advantages to *management*. The Coventry 'gang system', which existed, amongst other places, at Triumph in the 1950s, is a particularly interesting case in point. Sometimes associated with a collective swelling up of pride in craft, and an apparently clear example of the usurpation of management prerogative by workers, accounts of it are apt to add for good measure a further claim that is of special interest in the context of this book – that the higher degree of control achieved by these workers led to productivity being higher too (see the various pseudonymous publications of Reg Glover – Wright, 1961, 1962, Rayton, 1972; also Higgs, 1969).

It is possible to read the major account of this system, by Melman (1958), in a rather different way, however. Briefly, Melman reports that in the early 1950s fifteen gangs operated in the motor vehicle plant with 'very little managerial supervision'; that production labour was hired through the union office; that the workers' organisation had a substantial voice in the movement of workers between jobs; that only the electrician could alter the speed controls that governed the assembly conveyor; that there was a guaranteed weekly minimum wage; and that wages were relatively high. But on my reading – and despite the celebration it has attracted in some circles – Melman's account does not depict the gang system as something necessarily at odds with the interests of management. He notes, for example, that at one time during the 1959 contract negotiations it was *management* who pressed for very large groups, in fact for the whole factory to constitute one gang; that for the workers to establish large groups (and the entire tractor plant with 3,000 men was counted as one gang) craft union interests in particular jobs had to be overridden; that, for the employer, the gang system offered the advantage of a simplified supervisory, track-keeping and wage accounting system, and that, in fact, it was 'perfectly clear that the management of this company is profit-oriented and market expansion oriented like the management of any other . . . the methods being used towards these ends, however, [being] different in character' (1958, p. 117). Moreover, not only was Melman careful to distance himself from the idea that the gang system either was, or should have been, anything to do with socialist organisation and sentiment, he also stressed the lack of what he called 'any evidence of a formal ideology of worker behaviour'. Reporting that 'at no time was any discussion heard about "worker control"', he appears to have believed that what *went wrong* at Standard, in 1956, was that in the face of redundancy, 'a worker mutual decision system' was in part superseded by 'a policy line of competition for managerial control', a line that was symbolised by the slogan 'No Redundancy' which, in his view, resulted from a non-benign 'political' influence (1958, pp. 88, 180).

All this, it is hoped, should make some of those who are wont to cite such cases uncritically as examples of 'worker control' (or of pre-figurative socialist organisation) a little more cautious. As Melman observed, under the gang system management 'relied on the disciplinary effect of the workers' own organisation, at the production level, to maintain co-operative effort' (1958, p. 125). And not only was the control of plant – and of each other – by workers not necessarily inimical to the interests of management at Standard Triumph in the 1950s; other researchers, who like Melman actually got into the factories and had a look-and-see, were led to make very much this point about the role of shop stewards in the British car industry in the 1960s (Turner *et al.*, 1967, p. 212).

To turn to the 1970s, and to consider a worker's account of the residue of gang working at BL, is to underline the need for further caution. This suggests both that something else was involved than the unfettered *release* of 'human effort' by workers, and that the consequences of this were sometimes far from worthy of celebration either. According to Boulter (1979), for example (who it would seem was thoroughly disenchanted with the organisational botch-up that BL made when it put in measured day work), the 'secret' of gang working, or more precisely what was left of it at BL, was in fact quite mundane. It had, he reports, been 'a dog-eat-dog environment', 'a jungle', and if 'under piecework, it was the men who really ran the track' other pressures also stemmed from this. So, 'if in a gang of six men, four reckoned they could handle the job, then two were "squeezed out"', and if 'when the tracks stopped you were shouting . . . to get it going', this was because 'you were losing money'.

The observation of another Coventry worker that 'it is a myth that management manages on the shopfloor, when it comes down to detail they don't, they give instructions, and hope somehow they will be implemented' (Higgs, 1969, pp. 115–16) is one that is quite consistent with much that is said in the body of this book about British management and its leaning towards a *laissez faire* approach. Theoretically speaking, a point that some other social scientists have made – that workers' job controls, and particular payment systems, can serve capital by reinforcing their commitment to profitable production – also commands respect (Burawoy, 1978, pp. 273–4; Hyman and Elger, 1982, p. 119). But to make clear that workers' job controls *can* make for profitable production is one thing. To demonstrate that they actually *do* have this effect is quite another, and it is well worth considering the (positive) appreciation that has sometimes been accorded to the Coventry gang system for precisely this reason. As we have noted, there is a view which holds that increased 'worker control' at Standard made for *higher* productivity. But, in practice, there is reason to doubt how far Melman's research bears out this interpretation.

Back in 1958 Melman was certainly saying something which a later generation of social scientists have had to learn all by themselves as they have worked out a position *vis-à-vis* Braverman (1974), namely that there is not 'one best way' of industrial organisation and that it is not necessarily the case that management's *direct* control must rise with mechanisation. A claim made by Melman – 'it is possible to operate large industrial plants under other than unilateral, managerial control' (1958, p. 197) – *was* quite consistent with this. All the same, Melman's evidence on productivity is not quite what it is sometimes assumed to be. In his book Melman showed that net output per production worker at Standard was comparable to that for the industry as a whole. He also found that net output per employee was 10 per cent higher (there having been fewer supervisory and administrative staff at Triumph). Against this, though – and here we get to the bit that is rarely reported – Melman also tells us that Standard was more mechanised than the rest of the industry (1958, pp. 167,

152–7). Indeed, in what Melman himself regarded as 'a more critical analysis of the relative productivity level in the Coventry plants' – which took the form of a comparison of tractor production in Detroit and Coventry (half the units produced at Coventry were tractors made for Massey-Harris-Ferguson on a long-term contract) – labour productivity was found to be 15 per cent *lower* (1958, pp. 170, 174–5). True enough, Detroit was yet more highly mechanised than Coventry, but this, like the higher mechanisation of Coventry in Britain, is far from clear testimony that its higher 'worker control' contributed to higher productivity. By contrast, the lesson to be learnt from this is clear enough: that if there is no warrant to automatically accept the mainline interpretation of the relation between British workers and productivity, whereby low productivity is of course inferred from supposedly high job control, there is no warrant to stand on our heads and make the same mistake the other way round either, by inferring high productivity from high job control.

# C Unreported mysteries of the three-day week

In 1974 the Heath government restricted work in manufacturing industry to a three-day week. The State of Emergency, which had been induced by the miners' strike, low stocks of coal at the power stations and a four-fold hike in the price of oil, lasted for six weeks. What happened in this period – or what is commonly thought to have happened – has gone into the folklore as a key example of what is possible when (to invert Jack Jones' phrase: see pp. 18–19 above) 'The Buggers *Do* Work'. Amongst serious commentators, Clutterbuck, a former major-general turned political scientist and writer, has persistently claimed that the three-day week has 'deep implications for British industry' because 'though working hours fell by 40 per cent output fell by only 25 per cent' (1980, p. 110; and again 1984, pp. 105, 204n). Such an interpretation has also been advanced by some of those on the political left. Hodgson, for example, has gone so far as to claim that 'the Heath government reduced the working week by 40 per cent, but output remained at about 90 per cent of its normal level, indicating an immediate jump of labour productivity per hour of about 50 per cent' – and he is clearly just as impressed by this as Clutterbuck (and just as persistent: see Hodgson, 1981, p. 156; and again 1982c, p. 214).

Of course, to the extent that what happened in the three-day week was that labour was *intensified*, it is pertinent to ask – though it rarely is asked – whether it is desirable for workers to work so much harder, not for six weeks but forever after. As far as left-wing politics is concerned, it is also worth considering that it is rather difficult to envisage mass support for the promise of a Stakhanovite socialism at the ballot boxes of this or any other country. It can be seen from the present book, however, that there was a good deal of room for improvement in British manufacturing in the 1970s, over and above any slack that might be laid at the door of the British working class – to be counted amongst which are technical deficiencies in the composition of the labour force, and of management, and a lack of co-ordination and productive integration at a whole number of levels. Shortly, and remarkable as this may sound on first hearing, the 1974 Emergency will be examined to see whether even this – an occasion that has been widely regarded as testimony to what British workers could do, if they wanted – might provide yet further evidence of such deficiencies. Before we get into this, though, it is as well to be clear about the extent to which productivity actually did increase during the three-day week. Fortunately, this need not detain us long.

Clutterbuck's figures indicate a massive jump of 25 per cent in productivity, Hodgson's a yet more dramatic one of 50 per cent. Yet to read the enquiry into the three-day week that was commissioned by the Department of Industry is to conclude that even Clutterbuck's figure is an exaggeration. In fact, on the basis of this systematic survey evidence, it is a very considerable exaggeration indeed. As the Report itself plainly states: 'The evidence supporting the somewhat euphoric suggestion that three-days' enthusiastic work produced almost as much output as in a normal week was not forthcoming.' True enough, there was *some* improvement in output per direct labour hour, but this was nothing like 25 per cent let alone 50 per cent. Generally, it was a whole ten-fold less than this – 'about 5 per cent'. Why? Because whereas output per week had averaged around 83 per cent of normal, 79 per cent of normal hours had actually been worked (through early starts, late finishing, etc.), not the 60 per cent that so many commentators have slipped into assuming. Even the 5 per cent increase had carried a 'small labour cost penalty' (Department of Industry, 1976, p. 4).

A 5 per cent improvement in productivity is important, of course, but those who would attribute even this much less significant increase to British workers might also benefit from a close reading of the officially sponsored enquiry.

In the Report's view, 'the inescapable conclusion' to be drawn from this episode was that 'fear, lack of resources or lack of understanding limits the ability of a high proportion of managements to communicate effectively except under the influence of a common threat to survival'. Whereas the reference to 'fear' has implications for how British managements may sometimes view trade unions, other facets brought to light by this investigation also merit notice. For example, it is reported that the two most frequently and consistently given explanations for the rise in the rate of production were *esprit de corps* and the need to maintain earnings (Department of Industry, 1976, p. 9). As the investigators note, it is difficult to judge 'how much the former was conditioned by successfully achieving the latter' – this being a necessary qualification to any view that would accord pride of place to a new-found 'morale' rather than to the material need to avoid a drop in wages. But the third reason that was advanced for the improvement in the rate of production – 'keener management' – is itself particularly interesting in view of the sort of evidence presented in Chapter 8. So is the finding that not only 'better communications' but 'better planning and control' (as well as 'eating into stocks') were also thought to have had some influence on the rate of output.

In these abnormal six weeks it is highly probable that managements were helped to an unusual degree by trade unionists and by workers generally, who had a definite interest in temporarily disturbing the rhythm of their domestic routines, in cutting corners, and in getting the job out in order to stay afloat financially. But though it would be foolish to make too much of this – for the six weeks were abnormal and thus made for abnormal demands on management – it is rather interesting that the research reports that 'management and supervision were more conscious of fatigue during the three-day week than employees' (Department of Industry, 1976, p. 14). This does not quite square with what might have been expected, at least from one particular point of view – from which the productivity shortfall has so often been viewed in Britain. On this view, once British workers had stopped hindering management and worked hard to jack up the rate of production, one might have expected not so much fatigue (from managers, that is) but exhilaration. A productivity study which – quite untypically – systematically samples both managers and workers is always likely to provide at least some snippets of information that rarely surface in other accounts and to suggest different lines of interpretation, however, and the information reported so far is quite consistent with the view that in 'normal' times, and even with a sample of what we are told are probably 'above average' British companies, some British managers may *not* have been 'keen', and may *not* have communicated or planned very well. In addition to the need for managers to work harder and longer because of the emergency, it could therefore have been the case that they were also fatigued by the now urgent need to rectify long-standing deficiencies in manufacturing costs and resource control, which arose from a lack of budgets and planning objectives – indeed, the Report tells us that these were areas of deficiency that the emergency itself sometimes highlighted.

After the three-day week was over, an in-depth analysis was conducted on a structured sample of employee opinion at all levels. It concluded: 'The most powerful message that we have received . . . is the importance of consistently sound management, both [with respect to] personnel policy and its interpretation by line management, in fostering good industrial relations.' It continued, 'when *management effort* in this direction relaxes, however, so does the employee's response – and quickly' (Department of Industry, 1976, p. 13, my emphasis). As was stated in Chapter 2, the concept of 'effort' is a slippery one – but it is certainly highly unusual in productivity studies for employees' comments to be reported on the magnitude or consistency of *management* 'effort'. When they are reported, we begin to glimpse a different picture – one which brings into focus what managements do or not do rather than what workers do to obstruct them or will not do for them.

Other conclusions arrived at in this research are no less unfamiliar, at least as judged against the specialist productivity literature reviewed in the body of this book. For instance: 'There seems to be no great resistance to change if it is skilfully contrived and with good reason – rather it is welcomed' (Department of Industry, 1976, p. 13).

The idea that 'more participation' would improve British productivity is of course a commonplace. Clutterbuck argues, for example, that other nations would not have become so successful unless 'their whole team had been playing to win', and to this end he seems to favour more participation (1984, p. xxi). Hodgson, who comes out of a rather different political stable, also assumes that more participation would make for greater productivity, as well as being of importance in its own right. On theoretical grounds, and also on the basis of an inspection of the empirical social science literature, it is in fact doubtful that more participation or better communication is the universal panacea for higher productivity that it is sometimes held out to be. However, what happened in the three-day week is once again instructive in that it helps to point up the importance of a related consideration. For not only did the authors of the enquiry that was conducted into the three-day week feel 'bound to say' that on the evidence of their survey 'the [then] current trend to industrial democracy, or participative management will severely stretch the available skills in communications and industrial relations in the middle ranks of industry' – they also noted that, in some companies, the fact that 'the unions gained confidence, and benefit, from the enforced increase in communications and subsequently wanted more' was 'to the embarrassment of management' (Department of Industry 1976, p. 17). Rather than build on employee involvement, they were eager to choke it.

In Britain an awful lot is heard about how 'the trade unions have too much power'. The three-day week has entered the folklore as a crucial piece of evidence that shows what was possible when they chose 'to get on with the job' and 'took the blockers off'. As against this conventional interpretation, it has to be said that upon closer examination the three-day week may tell us as much about British management, its blockages, and in some cases its refusal to 'take the blockers off', as it does about British workers and their trade unions. But then, the whole subject of the three-day week is open to misunderstanding, not the least part of which, as we saw at the outset, is that it was not really a three-day week at all.

# Notes

## 1 Labour productivity, ideological divisions and the division of labour in the social sciences

1 This first article appeared in *The Times* on 18 November 1901. Other articles appeared on 21 November, 3, 14, 16, 24, 26, 27 and 30 December, and on 4 and 16 January 1902. The letter from the Webbs appeared on 6 December 1901. See also the book by Pratt, *Trade Unionism and British Industry* (Pratt, 1904).

2 Those referred to above as 'employers' are the chief executives of seventy-three companies selected systematically from *The Times 1,000*, who were interviewed in January–February 1981. The term 'employee' is used with reference to a nationally representative quota sample of 540 employees interviewed in December 1980. Quotas were controlled by age, sex, social class and employment sector, but the analysis is presented in such a way that specific account is not taken of this diversity, or of whether employees were union members (Sentry, 1981a, p. 24).

3 Mandel's figures are part of his resurrection of the analysis of long waves in capitalist development. The very mention of 'long waves' is likely to meet with a dusty reception from many professional economists, and perhaps most particularly from economic historians – though in recent years increased interest in them has been evident (which no doubt owes much to the very fact that the prospect of relatively untroubled growth in capitalist economies, so readily assumed by so many people in the midst of an expansionary period, is now held with less certainty).

   This extended note is appended here for four reasons. First, to state what Mandel's long waves are. Second, to defend Mandel against certain criticisms that seem to lack solid foundation. Third, to note some technical problems. Fourth, to make a point that should be borne in mind throughout this book, much of which is concerned with very short-range considerations. Since this last point can be briefly stated, it will be dealt with first. It is simply this: that try as we may to track down the role of British workers in the determination of British productivity, and to inspect the evidence put forward by others – to check how well, for example, other 'variables', as researchers in this field are apt to call them, have been 'held constant' or 'controlled for' in their investigations – the fact remains that the performance of all national economies is to some degree determined by the world capitalist system, which is more than the sum of its parts, and that the strength of its relative undulation is such as to minimise what workers, or managers, or governments, can achieve, no matter how 'hard' they work.

As to Mandel's long waves, these are four in number, each of which has two parts – an initial one, characterised by an increased rate of profit, and a subsequent one in which the rate of profit falls (the rate of profit, as he nicely puts it, being the 'seismograph' of capitalist history). The first long wave is that of the Industrial Revolution. It spans the long period from the end of the eighteenth century up to the crisis of 1847, and features the gradual spread of the handicraft-made or manufacture-made steam engine. Its initial expansionary period, 1793–1825, gives way to a stagnating one, 1826–47. The second long wave is the wave of the first *technological* revolution. Stretching from the late 1840s to the early 1890s, it features the machine-made steam engine. Its initial expansionary period, 1848–73, gives way to a stagnating one, 1874–93. The third long wave is the long wave of the second technological revolution, and is marked by the generalised application of electric and combustion engines, covering the long period from the mid-1890s up to the Second World War. Its initial expansionary part, 1894–1913, gives way to a stagnating one, 1914–39. The fourth long wave, that of the third technological revolution, starts after the Second World War (1940 in North America). Characterised by the generalised control of machines by means of electronic apparatuses, and also the gradual introduction of another energy force, nuclear power, its expansionary part gave way to a period of decelerating growth (1966 onwards).

In some quarters, any self-declared marxist analysis is likely to spark off a number of standard reactions – that it is 'abstract', 'determinist', 'mechanical' and so on. With respect to Mandel's long waves, such criticisms are not as well placed as is sometimes thought. For one thing Mandel does not claim that the long waves are, or must be, of regular duration, and his analysis is not predicated on the assumption that they can be explained adequately simply on the basis of an abstract understanding of the capitalist mode of production, no matter what. Fundamentally, long wave theories are always likely to be open to one of two criticisms. For either they posit that a self-generating cyclical pattern can be derived from a theoretical knowledge of the capitalist mode of production, in which case they encounter difficulties in taking account of real-world events (e.g. wars, and their consequences) or they concede that 'external shocks' play a part in capitalist development, in which case those critics for whom 'theory' is a plane of reason that floats untrammelled by the messy business of socio-political reality, will deem them not to be 'theories' at all. This second sort of criticism seems to rest on a peculiar conception of what theory is for, but

whatever position is taken on this, it is important to see that Mandel is
not vulnerable to criticism of the first sort. Whereas, for example, he
does claim that the internal logic of capitalist laws of motion explains
the cumulative nature of each long wave, once it is initiated, and the
transition from the initial expansion to the later stagnation (after all,
marxist political economy is in part a theory of crisis), he does not hold
that the turn from stagnation, at the end of one long wave, to
expansion, at the start of another, can be adequately explained in this
way. To explain this, a whole number of historical specifics must be
considered – like expansions and contractions in the area of capitalist
operation, inter-capitalist competition, wars of conquest, class struggle,
revolutions, counter-revolutions, etc. In fact, Mandel sees extra-
economic factors as playing a key role.

Given the above, it follows that a more specific charge – of
technological determination – is not easy to substantiate either.
Ironically, this is a criticism that many social scientists had to learn
from marxists, and in particular from post-war criticism, by marxists,
of much popular and social scientific thought. But when bent back on
Mandel's analysis of long waves, such criticism does not find its mark
for two reasons.

The first, which should be apparent already, is that Mandel does not
see 'technology' as governing the course of capitalist development, but
technology in the context of the scope and intensity of class struggle,
etc. The second is that Mandel treats technology in relation to the
search for profit. He claims, in fact, that his is a 'rate of profit theory'
(1980, p. 9).

All criticism of Mandel is far from pre-empted by the above remarks.
It is even open to question whether, in practice, the theory does live up
to Mandel's concept of it as a rate of profit theory. On its first
appearance, in *Late Capitalism*, little adequate data was provided on
the rate of profit. In the case of Britain over the last four decades of the
nineteenth century, for instance, figures were cited despite the fact that
they related to the share of profits, interest, and 'mixed income' in
national income, and even though, on Mandel's own admission, these
were 'by no means congruent with the marxist concept of the rate of
profit' and had to be treated with 'great caution' (1975, pp. 81n, 83n,
citing Deane and Cole, 1962, p. 247). In the later book, *Long Waves of
Capitalist Development*, which is wholly given over to the subject of its
title, the firm question 'Can empirical evidence for such long waves in
the average rate of profit be produced?' meets its answer by proxy
only, in resort to interest rates, the variations of which are themselves
sometimes only very broadly sketched (1980, p. 17). In these and other
respects Mandel's work invites technical criticism. For instance, in
deriving rate of production figures for Britain from the Hoffman
production index (see Table 1.1) Mandel takes no cognizance of the
revision of this by Lewis (1978, Appendix 1). As noted with reference
to Table 1.1 in the text, he also makes an arithmetical mistake. The
manner in which Mandel invokes supporting academic opinion also
sometimes leaves something to be desired. Thus his claim that data
produced by Maddison (1977) on 'phases' of capitalist development in

all sixteen OECD countries supports his own 'long waves' can only be made at the cost of a list of exceptions: namely that Maddison's analysis starts at a later point (in 1870); that it excludes the Second World War years; that it loses the Great Depression of 1837–93 within a postulated phase of 1870–1913 (whereas the 1890s mark the divide between one of Mandel's long waves and another).

Mandel's further supporting claim that 'economic historians [would] certainly not follow' Maddison when he 'lumped together the 1870–1913 period into a single wave' (1980, p. 5) is also less than accurate. Lewis' assertion – 'the growth rate of British industrial production fell after 1873 and declined till 1913. This is now generally accepted' (1978, p. 112) – flies in the face of this. Moreover, at least one economic historian of Britain has claimed that 'the major outcome of modern research has been to destroy once and for all the idea of such a period [as the Grant Depression] in any unified sense' (Saul, 1969, pp. 54, 55). Mandel, for his part, might well want to respond to this that it is in the nature of capitalist development that it will not occur evenly, either internationally or within national economies. But if Saul's stress on a lack of a 'unified sense' need not trouble him, a further opinion expressed by Saul – that 'the sooner the "Great Depression" is banished from the literature, the better' – does not auger well for Mandel's generalisation about 'economic historians'.

However, there remain things to be said in Mandel's support. His claim that 'Maddison's data do not differ essentially from ours' takes on some credibility from his own reworking of it to conform with what he calls 'the real historical movement' (i.e. the Great Depression). Mandel is able to show that if Maddison's analysis is restricted to the UK, US, Germany, France, Belgium, Japan, Italy and Holland (the rest of the sixteen OECD countries, which were less industrialised prior to the First World War being excluded), the average compound rate of growth of these countries was 2.2 per cent up till 1893 and 3.2 per cent thereafter, this being conformable with the separate upturns that Mandel himself found for Britain, for Germany and for the US. Then again if, instead of criticising Mandel for not using Lewis' revision of the Hoffman index, we actually do use it, this does not result in any substantial damage to his case. As indicated by the British figures introduced in brackets in Table 1.1 the rise from 1876–93 to 1894–1913 remains, although the rates at each period are rather higher than in Mandel's estimate. The adverse comparisons between the rates of growth for Britain *vis-à-vis* Germany and the US also remain at each period.

A recent response to Mandel's *Late Capitalism* by Maddison (1982, pp. 80–3), which deals with his British, American and German comparisons, and also Mandel's figures for the volume of world trade, all with reference to the years 1870–1913, would also seem to leave the main bones of Mandel's analysis intact. And Eklund, even though he tends to apply a slightly peculiar conception of 'theory' to the evaluation of Mandel's long waves, still concludes: 'the following facts remain, accepted by practically all economic historians: the rapid expansion from 1848 until 1873; the long depression from 1873 to

1896; the tremendous increase of economic activity from 1896 until
1914; . . . the slow economic development from 1920 until 1939; and
the fantastic expansion from 1945 until the early 1970s (Eklund, 1980,
pp. 412–13). Doubts may be in order about whether the increase from
1896 to 1914 truly was 'tremendous'. (Maddison's reworking of
Lewis' data for the UK (including construction), but using the same
periods as Mandel, yields: 1876–93, 1.4 per cent; 1874–1913, 2.4 per
cent (1982, p. 82, Table 4.6).) Doubts may be in order anyway
whenever claims are advanced about 'practically all economic
historians'. Upon practically nothing, as far as I can see, do practically
all economic historians agree. But, it is accepted here, as it is by
Eklund, that these trend periods have empirically informed capitalist
economic history. As such they constitute part of the context within
which any discussion of British retardation must be situated.

4  This holds as much for trade union leaders as for Labour politicians.
At a time that marked a high point of instability in post-war Britain –
about which *The Times* had editorialised: 'The quadrilateral of full
employment, free collective bargaining, free elections and reasonably
stable prices, has become a figure of unstable forces' – Jack Jones was
to reflect, for example, that 'Colonel this and Captain that' had wanted
to 'keep the workers down'. 'We could have easily faced a coup in
Britain', he said, but 'the trade unions and progressive management
understood the needs of the hour, and there was a response' (as quoted
in *The Guardian*, 22 January 1977; for the Editorial see *The Times*, 10
October 1974). Jones has devoted his whole life to the British labour
movement: to appreciate this, and the pride he felt looking back to
1974, is also to appreciate his anger that despite what trade unionists
did for Britain, 'The Bastards' *still* would not back them (see pp.
18–19).

5  Economists employ a number of concepts of 'productivity'. There is,
for instance, 'total factor' productivity: a measure of the ratio of all
output to a composite of all inputs. This is not merely a measure of
output per unit of labour, or of capital – or of any other *one* input
alone: hence, clearly enough, the 'total' in its name. But, for the layman
at least, the term 'labour productivity' can be confusing. The problem
is that economists, who generally use 'productivity' to refer to the
output per unit of *any* input (classically, land, labour or capital) –
hence 'labour productivity' or 'capital productivity', etc. – do not
always mean what they seem to mean when they refer to *labour
productivity*. As a specialist in the field once put it: 'Sometimes "labour
productivity" is misunderstood, it is believed that wage-earners (or
"labour" as a whole) are wholly responsible for [the differences
measured] in output per manhour' (Fabricant, 1968, p. 529). But of
course data on output per man, per man-hour or any similar measure,
does not *necessarily* take into account differences in other inputs, like
how much capital different workers may have at their elbow. The
concept of productivity that perhaps comes closest to paring down
'labour productivity', so that it means something more akin to what
the layman thinks it means, is that of the *efficiency of labour*, and it is
this which will be of central concern in the text below. Where it might

not otherwise be clear, labour productivity in this efficiency of labour
sense will sometimes be referred to as 'common-or-garden labour
productivity' or reference will be made to 'labour productivity as
narrowly conceived', etc.

This much established, however, further complications abound.
Suffice it to say here that (a) mainstream (neo-classical) economic
theory tends to regard the factors of production as given, in the sense
that so much labour, allied to so much capital, is assumed to combine
in production, and to yield an output. In short, the output itself is seen
to be determined by the particular combination of given inputs. On the
face of it, such a profoundly a-social view differs from the staple
marxist assumptions, (b), that capital is not 'a thing', that labour and
capital are not sociological equivalents – and that labour-power is
'variable' (an important role thereby being accorded, for example, to
the production of relative surplus value, which is, in part, a function of
the intensity with which workers labour). It also flies in the face of the
observations industrial sociologists have made of workers restricting
their output. But then again, some economists, following Leibenstein
(1966, 1976) refer to 'X-efficiency' or 'X-inefficiency'. 'X-efficiency'
theorists stress the importance of motivation, and that this can make
for variable outputs from the same inputs.

Note, though, that the above comments are made here in only a
provisional way. Later on, more will be said about industrial
sociologists, and the way they typically study productivity; about the
limitations of 'X-efficiency' theory, and how this differs from marxist
theory; also about how all economists, even if they do not formally
adhere to 'X-efficiency' theory, do not, in practice, necessarily
subscribe to position (a). As if all this were not enough we shall also
have cause to note that even the term 'labour efficiency' is far from
unproblematic.

6  Other writers have noted the oddity whereby 'some radicals' stress
'resistance' by workers, but do not the consider the possible 'impact on
industrial efficiency or wage inflation' (Edwards and Scullion, 1982,
pp. 286–7) – a point that ties in with the more general one made above
that marxist students of the labour process have too often neglected the
productivity outcome. However, as is made clear in the text below,
with reference to the work of Glyn and Sutcliffe, it is also possible that
some analyses may come to neglect some of the sociological influences
on productivity, despite initial appearances to the contrary. It is also
possible, of course, by stressing that students of the labour process
should not neglect the productivity outcome – but without investigating the evidence for this in particular cases (e.g. Britain) – to convey the
impression that workers actually do substantially affect the productivity outcome. The view taken in this book is that such a conclusion
has to be based on evidence, and the whole point of some of the
following chapters is to seek to determine how good the available
evidence for such a conclusion is.

## 2 British workers, 'attitudes', 'effort' and the economists

1 To find an exception it is necessary to move on to 1981, the year that saw the publication of Prais' *Productivity and Industrial Structure* (Prais, 1981a). One of the notable features of this work is that it does *not* invoke 'attitudes' in the way that so many other studies of labour productivity are apt to do. References to this research will be made later in the text, but Prais has to be excluded from the remarks made in this chapter.

2 Two British economists, Smith-Gavine and Bennett, have produced a productivity index that derives from work measurement techniques. However, popular accounts of this are misleading in so far as they imply that Smith-Gavine and Bennett's index, which is sometimes referred to as an 'elbow grease' index, measures effort in the 'X-efficiency' sense – workers making more effort, getting down to work, rolling their sleeves up, etc. In fact, this index is designed to measure the 'percentage utilisation of labour'. Based on the assumption that output is in part a function of the throughput of work (the volume of work put behind an operative's machine), it is primarily a measure of 'economic temperature' as its authors make plain (Smith-Gavine and Bennett, 1979).

3 Bruce and Kaldor both cite an enquiry by Maynard and Barry as showing that 'where workers are engaged by US firms their productivity is just as high as that of American workers using the same equipment', which sounds impressive. More specifically, they cite it to demonstrate that output per person in Wales (where the eighty US subsidiaries studied by Maynard and Barry were located) was at least as high as in the US in 63 per cent of cases, no less than 91 per cent of companies recording higher output per unit wage cost than obtained in the US (Bruce, 1982; Kaldor, 1982). Given lower British wages, the second claim is quite consistent with the first. But to go back to Maynard and Barry's original report is to discover that they only conducted interviews in 'some thirty companies' and that 'the remainder [i.e. the clear majority of the companies] were covered by telephone calls' (Maynard and Barry, 1980, p. 2). Of course, Bruce and Kaldor may well be right: the productivity of workers employed by American companies in Wales may be just as high as that of the workers they employ in America when they are using the same equipment. But in the present context it is necessary to note that 'evidence' of this ilk really is all too easy to discredit, whichever way it points.

4 In 1982, provisional results of the 1981 census of employment revealed the existence of over half a million people in employment who had previously eluded government statisticians. Further analysis in 1983 led to the discovery of getting on for another fifth of a million, and also of nearly an extra quarter of a million people who were self-employed. Suffice it to say that by the end of 1983 it was being debated within the Treasury whether the discovery of 900,000 extra people in work might mean that national output was also considerably larger than had been thought (Wilkinson, 1983).

### 3 British workers in the world of comparative statics (1)

1 Out of those managements that *did* reply to Pratten's enquiry, up to 30 per cent were deemed by him to have 'insufficient information on which to base really reliable explanations of productivity differentials'. Another 40 per cent were deemed to have 'a good knowledge of overseas and UK factories'. But only about 30 per cent *had actually made* 'detailed comparisons of labour productivity by, for example, comparing productivity for groups of operations at factories in the UK and overseas, and basing their assessments of the causes of productivity differentials on these comparisons' (1976a, pp. 24–5). Pratten tells us that the exclusion of the not 'really reliable' 30 per cent would not materially alter his conclusions, but given the possibility of bias in the response rate to begin with, and that he had no independent basis upon which to judge how 'good knowledge' of the 40 per cent of respondents was, all this further underlines the need for extreme caution in citing his evidence.

2 According to a 1982 report by the government's Business Statistics Office (*The Merseyside Economy, Performance and Prospects to 1986*) productivity in Merseyside's manufacturing industries grew by 20 per cent between 1973 and 1979, compared to 14 per cent nationally. Evidence over a ten-year period suggests that, outside the docks and the car plants, which were above-average employers on Merseyside, the strike record was not significantly different from other areas (Trafford, 1982).

3 In 'continuing the inside story of BL and its boss' for *Daily Mail* readers, Sir Michael Edwardes claimed of Speke: 'The factory was a classic example of those misguided efforts by successive governments to impose their will on the motor industry – by creating new factories and jobs in areas of high unemployment. Such areas were miles away from the traditional motor manufacturing centres, hopelessly distant from the centres of gravity as far as competitive costs were concerned.' No mention here of a decision to escape massed workforces, despite a variety of clichéd sub-heads – 'Red Robbo . . . the Spanner in the Works', 'The Women Who Defied the Pickets' and, of course, 'This "Us and Them" Nonsense' (*Daily Mail*, 22 February 1982; see also Edwardes, 1984). Academic specialists also hold to the view that it was because of government regional policy that most of the exceptionally rapid growth in the UK car industry during the 1960s led to relocation in North-West England and Scotland (Jones, 1983, p. 15).

4 Pratten's synopses for Germany in fact include five cases for Austria, Belgium, the Netherlands and Switzerland; those for North America include three for Canada. These are not always clearly identified in his synopses, and all cases have therefore been considered. More than one practice was sometimes claimed in any one of the accounts given to Pratten, and in these cases more than one has been recorded; also practices have been recorded which were said to exist in any one overseas plant of a company, even though there were sometimes several other plants.

Only comparative statements have been reported in Table 3.3, it being considered unhelpful to know, for example, that 'absenteeism in the UK was 10%' if no information is provided on the level in non-UK operations. Again, general claims about there being 'restrictive practices' or a different 'traditional standard of performance' in the UK have not been counted, and differences that were reported to Pratten (e.g. three shifts abroad but only two in the UK operation) only appear if there is any further claim that this was because of pressure from UK workers. No weighting is attributed to the practices in the table, which must be regarded only as a list of practices that Pratten's managers claimed to exist at the time that he interviewed them and which he saw fit to report. It ought to be noted that Pratten himself may have been less inclined to push for information on labour practices in those cases where UK labour productivity did not show up so badly.

The items in the table are not necessarily mutually exclusive ones, so that in many cases items that appear under one heading could appear under, or have significance for, another as well. It does not exhaust all the possibilities, for as Zweig put it (1951, p. 54): 'any practice can become restrictive if the restrictive spirit is infused into it'. Nor does it distinguish the degree of penetration by labour into the political economy of capital, which might range from influence, through to the effective imposition of veto and even, at times, control. Nor does it distinguish the level of such penetration, for though, in theory, workers might control the overall investment and accumulation process, in practice this is usually very far from being the case, as research makes clear, not just in Britain, but in Belgium, Denmark, France, Holland, Norway, Sweden, West Germany and Israel, and of course in North America (Ramsay, 1981, vol. 2, chap. 11). In addition to all this the table suggests that such practices will be restrictive to management, and that they are, in a word, unwanted. The problematic nature of this assumption (signalled by the 'Might' at the head of Table 3.3) is one that will be examined much later on, but for the present the reader is asked to accept the list for what it is – an attempt to provide a more systematic basis for the appraisal of studies of international productivity differentials than is available already, and which is designed to evaluate these studies (in this case Pratten's) on their own terms in so far as they relate to working practices.

5 For Pratten 'indirect employees' include indirect factory employees and those engaged in administration and selling. Since he regards a high proportion of indirect employees as 'primarily attributable to management rather than labour' this posed particular difficulties in constructing Table 3.3 (1976a, pp. 51–2).

6 Sometimes even these qualifications are absent from secondary references to Pratten's and other productivity research. For instance, Phelps Brown, an historian whose considerable contribution to industrial relations research testifies to an eagle-eye for detail, sets up his major analysis, *The Origins of Trade Union Power*, by reporting with reference to Pratten's breakdown of the causes of international productivity differentials (as weighted by employment) that the part of output per employee hour *'properly attributed to labour'* was 'higher

by 12 per cent or 13 per cent in North American plants than in the British, by 19 per cent in the German plants, and by 10 per cent in the French' (1983, p. 2, my emphasis). In Pratten's original report, by contrast, it was made clear that to attribute all the so-called 'behavioural effects' (to which Phelps Brown is referring here) to the labour force would be an 'extreme assumption' (1976a, p. 60), and Pratten himself was even tentative about the breakdown of 'economic' and 'behavioural' effects, of which of course labour's contribution is but one possible part. All too often in this field the 'extreme' assumptions of yesteryear get lost in the reporting and re-reporting that comes to constitute the 'what everybody knows' in the present day, and slippages of the above type are one of the mechanisms through which this occurs. Our general point is, however, that Pratten was not in a good position to reach such a conclusion anyway.

## 5 'The difficulty' reconsidered (1)

1  A more detailed exploration of the way Caves follows up clues in the literature about how British workers might contribute to lower productivity is to be found in Commentary A, pp. 243–52 below. The non-specialist reader may like to skip this, but since it also deals with the circular process through which so much knowledge in this field has been produced and re-produced it may well be of interest to those concerned with the sociology of knowledge (and ideology). It should be of interest to economists and specialist productivity researchers too.

2  Caves comments on his 'labour relations variables': 'The coefficient of UNIONB is quite insignificant and variable in size. The maximum explanatory power results when I use FLAB1 . . . It is weakly significant, . . . except when LGEB is included . . . Although in itself the coverage of employees by collective-bargaining agreements has no net influence on productivity, such an influence emerges when the product of this variable and the proportion of employment in the older industrial regions, LAB4, are used.'

   To decode the above: UNIONB = proportion of manual employees covered by collective bargaining agreements, 1973. LAB1 = WDLB.STRIKB; WDLB = ratio of working days lost by strikes during 1971–3 to actual working days of operatives, 1972; STRIKB = number of strikes reported beginning in the years 1972–5 divided by number of establishments classified to the industry, 1972; FLAB1 = WDLB.STRIKB (adjusted for the female proportion of the labour force); LGEB = proportion of employment accounted for by enterprises with 1,000 or more employees, 1968; LAB4 = REGB.UNIONB, and REGB = percentage of industry employment located (during 1972) in the West Midlands, Yorkshire and Humberside, the North-West, North Wales and Scotland (Caves, 1980, pp. 167–69; pp. 161, 162, 164).

   Caves did not report data on strikes in America; similarly other labour relations variables are exclusively British-based. As a consequence, to the extent that Caves *does* demonstrate that the more strike-prone a British industry is, it will have poor productivity compared to its American counterpart, it cannot be ruled out that the American industry is also strike-prone – a particular technical criticism that has been advanced by Edwards and Nolan (1983). Prais has also argued that Caves' analysis would have been improved technically if he had made more use of ratios, rather than some of his explanatory variables being ratios of British to American values and others relating to only British or only American absolute values (Prais, in Caves and Krause, 1980, p. 197). However, perhaps the above is sufficient to suggest that questions also arise about the validity of the variables, how they were measured in the first place, and combined.

3  Orthodox ('value') marxists have always been very much alive to the crucial importance of Marx's distinction between 'labour' and 'labour-power' – and with reason, for in Marx's own account this related directly to the question of how surplus value originated. A subsequent and more contemporary generation, whose marxism has not always been predicated on the labour theory of value, has latched on to the concept of 'labour-power' in order to express the ideas that what the capitalist buys from workers is, in Braverman's words, 'infinite in *potential*' and that 'in its *realization* it is limited by the subjective state of the workers' (Braverman, 1974, p. 57, emphasis in original). But 'labour-power' encompasses a further meaning – the (technical) capacity to labour. It is the possible consequences of the differential distribution of such capacities that those inspired by Braverman have tended to neglect. The relative vulnerability of workers to have labour bludgeoned or cajoled out of them has remained a staple element in all marxist accounts. But neither the preoccupation of many contributors to the so-called 'labour process debate' with the question of whether capital inexorably 'de-skills' nor the inclination of some feminist radicals to question whether men's privileged position in industry really does rest on technically superior skill, has stimulated much interest in international differences in technical competence. (For further comments on labour and labour-power see Hodgson, 1981, 1982a, 1982c.)

## 6  'The difficulty' reconsidered (2)

1  The need to view the Japanese steel industry in context is underlined by the way certain assumptions were built into one of the most quoted comparative studies of the Japanese and British steel industries, which was carried out by BSC and trade union representatives in 1975. In the 1980 steel dispute top management at BSC was to claim on the basis of this that at one of the five sites visited in Japan, NKK Fukuyama, labour productivity stood at 530 tonnes per man per year, even after allowances had been made for contract labour. But as Matsuzaki demonstrates, differences between Japanese and British steel production are less dramatic if, instead of the five *sites* studied in the BSC/TUCSIC Report, the comparison is drawn with the five *largest combines* in Japan, which account for 77 per cent of Japanese steel production. As to Fukuyama as a particular point of comparison, the

validity of this is put in question once it is appreciated that Fukuyama is a huge, superbly laid out site. In the words of the ISTC: 'It is as if the entire [British Steel] Corporation were built from scratch all in one place' – the potential advantages of which are obvious enough. In fact, though, the Working Party that went to Japan as part of the BSC/TUCSIC study had a remit to look at 'manpower and industrial relations matters', not technology as such. It therefore excluded itself from looking at the contribution to productivity made by plant and materials processing. The unions were to regret this when, after they had received no communication about the report for three years, management quickly dusted it down and brought it into use in the steel dispute of 1980, in order to intimidate British steel workers with the splendid achievements of the miracle workers of Fukuyama (see ISTC, *Sense or Nonsense*; ISTC, *Steelworkers' Banner* No. 6). Given this background, it is with good reason that Manwaring should have remarked that comparisons of labour productivity in steel have often been based on figures that 'misrepresent the productivity performance of BSC', and that other writers have noted with specific reference to the BSC/TUCSIC study that when the Corporation's Chief Executive wrote in his Foreword to this Report that 'it is not easy to draw valid comparisons' this was to prove 'a classic understatement of the problem' (Manwaring, 1981, p. 64; Bryer, Brignall and Maunders, 1982).

2  To an extent Pratten's relative neglect of the possible importance of migrant labour may be a function of his particular sample. He reports that guest workers formed only a small percentage of the labour forces of his German companies (only more than 10 per cent 'at some German operations'). On assembly line operations – a much-touted site of the British 'difficulty' – there were concentrations elsewhere that were very much higher than this. It is also worth noting in the context of this chapter that Pratten devoted only a dozen lines to 'skill and qualifications of employees', and that his sample was biased towards firms that employed proportionately less skilled or specialised labour (Pratten, 1976a, pp. 48, 57n).

3  In 1977 the CFT changed its name to the Confédération des Syndicats Libres (CSL).

4  That when management does 'get away with much more', injuries can result is something that is hardly suggested by the following definition of a 'restrictive practice' by Lincoln, a free enterpriser from the Institute of Economic Affairs. Whilst admitting that ' "restrictive practices" has become an emotive and controversial term' Lincoln holds that 'without engaging in self-flattery, I claim that this Inquiry does not suffer from this weakness'. That it does suffer from this weakness becomes quite evident as he warms to his task, since, for him, a restrictive practice is 'an attempt to lessen by design, combination, conspiracy or prohibition, the effects of the superiority or greater efficiency of another person or group of persons on our own skills, investment or labour. It is a supremely paradoxical and contradictory gesture of an evolutionary species trying by every means and subterfuge, none of them noble or edifying, to evade the pressures that

attend evolution . . . restrictive practices are impractical, they are uneconomic and, in the final analysis, they are socially evil' (Lincoln, 1967, pp. 20, 19, 21).

However, even Lincoln makes an exception for 'such degrees of intended inefficiency or uneconomic practices as are justified in order to maintain legally or generally required and recognised standards of health and safety'. An earlier official report entitled *Practices Impeding the Full and Efficient Use of Manpower* had followed this same tack (Ministry of Labour and National Service, 1959, pp. 6–7); so did the Donovan Report, which excluded arrangements that were 'justifiable on social grounds'. Most other definitions have also entered such a qualification (see Aldridge, 1976, p. 35). But the problem is: what *is* 'justifiable', and who is to say? It can hardly be workers if they are 'told what to do'. It is just this sort of moral and political issue that all too often gets lost in the specialist literature about 'the problem of productivity'. That by 'labour costs' economists mean the costs *of* labour *to* capital, and that a high 'quality of labour' can refer to a low quality of life and poor conditions of labour, is equally symptomatic.

5  The 'strong work ethic' percentages for each of the countries surveyed in this research were: the UK 17, West Germany 26, US 52, Japan 50 and Sweden 45. This appears to more or less confirm the conventional wisdom, save in the West German case – though the contents of another league table, for 'bad jobs', might be thought to fly in the face of it. Britain led this particular league table – the percentages being the UK 24, West Germany 21, Sweden 14 and the US 8 – with a 'bad job' being defined as one with low pay, little job security, little chance for advancement, and one where workers were 'ashamed of the place where they work'.

What these statistics actually mean is open to doubt, however. The method of investigation differed between countries, and the data is of an aggregate kind, unweighted by type of work: thus 55 per cent of the UK sample consisted of 'blue collar' workers compared to 34 per cent of the West German one; 'management and professionals' only accounted for 2 per cent of the UK sample but for 26 per cent in the US. On the other hand such research does serve to caution against the easily made assumption that a strong work ethic will mean greater 'effort' at work (even US respondents, who were more likely to have a 'strong work ethic', did not, on their own admission, put a great deal of effort into their jobs over and above what was required of them). It is of course a long step from establishing a strong or weak 'work ethic' (which is itself difficult) to concluding that these will lead to great and little 'effort' respectively.

Whatever national differences exist, work ethics cannot be assumed to remain constant over time. It is therefore perhaps interesting to note that according to other survey evidence the people of *most* industrial-ised nations thought they worked 'not as hard' at the end of the last decade as they had ten years earlier – the 69 per cent who said this in the UK were only just ahead of the Australians and Americans, at 67 and 63 per cent, with over half of West German and Japanese respondents saying the same thing. (For further details, see

Yankelovich *et al.*, 1984; Sparrow, 1983; and on the apparent across-
the-board decline in hard work, Sentry, 1981b.)

6  By 1983, as a function of unemployment, demand for apprenticeships
   in West Germany outstripped supply, 43,000 missing out on a place.
   However, the number of apprenticeships still increased, to 678,000
   from 631,000 the previous year. In Switzerland, the apprenticeship
   scheme continued in full force, 60 per cent of all school-leavers still
   entering some kind of apprenticeship in 1984. The recession of the
   mid-1970s and early 1980s led to virtually no loss of apprenticeship
   openings, the total having risen almost continuously through the last
   two decades (Davies, 1984; Wicks, 1984).

7  Between 1971 and 1976 the numbers in part-time work increased by
   nearly 1 million, only 2 per cent of this increase going to
   manufacturing and 95 per cent to services (Dex and Perry, 1984, p.
   152).

8  The assumption made here, that a *vulnerable* workforce will be more
   'compliant', is far from being an immutable sociological law, but it still
   has much to recommend it. That in Britain, as compared to Germany
   and France, the position and influence of the trade unions remained
   relatively unchallenged in the four decades up till the end of the 1970s
   is not to be lightly dismissed, for example (a theme that is taken up
   below). Even so, it does not follow that a lack of co-operation can be
   wholly accounted for in terms of a relative absence of vulnerability.
   The possible significance of this particular point is explored further in
   Chapter 8, where attention is focused on other factors that may have
   led to a possible lack of co-operation on the part of British workers.

## 7  'The difficulty' reconsidered (3)

1  It was noted earlier that the term 'restrictive practices' implies that
   these practices are unwanted by management and that sometimes this
   may be an unwarranted assumption. But just as those who denigrate
   'worker control' (or more precisely 'job control') may fall into making
   unwarranted assumptions about its effects on capital's interests, this is
   sometimes also the case amongst those who celebrate it. A brief
   account of how it is possible to encounter much the same pitfalls from
   both sides of the fence is provided in Commentary B, pp. 253–7
   below.

2  Pollard seems to have a distaste for 'the City' that is rivalled only by his
   hostility to some alleged features of contemporary British trade
   unionism (as illustrated at pp. 7–8 above). At an ideological level
   this relatively rare coupling of political sentiment would seem to be
   given a unity only by an underlying 'productivism'. I have remarked
   elsewhere that, within marxism, and *even* (as it is perhaps still
   necessary to say) within the thought of Gramsci, a stress on the positive
   aspects of the development of the productive forces fits awkwardly
   with ideas of a humanist kind (Nichols, 1980, p. 273). In the 1970s
   this dilemma was side-stepped by students of the labour process, who
   tended to take the humanist path, or who devoted their energies to

casting doubt on whether scientific management really was efficient, even in capitalist terms. With few exceptions (e.g. Cohen, 1978), in this period Western marxism as a whole also eschewed a stress on the development of the productive forces. To the extent that Pollard's thinking has been influenced by marxism, it would seem therefore that any such influence dates back to an earlier period.

## 8 'The difficulty' reconsidered (4)

1 Whereas the number of British trade unions is high by international standards, the domestic significance of this is often exaggerated. In 1980 one-quarter of those establishments that recognised manual trade unions had three or more unions which had members in the workplace. At establishments employing 2,000 or more, over three-quarters had three or more manual unions, and 38 per cent had six or more. However, the number of bargaining units was much lower: 43 per cent of the large establishments dealt with only one bargaining group, a further 31 per cent with only two, management being only slightly more in favour of jointly negotiating in one bargaining unit than their trade union counterparts (Daniel and Millward, 1983, pp. 46–49).

2 Commentary A, pp. 243–52 below.

3 It is Colchester's account that has been relied upon here. Urwick Orr felt unable to provide me with a copy of their full report.

4 Generalisations about the three-day week have often been less well founded than they might have been. For this reason further consideration is given to this in Commentary C, pp. 258–62 below. A number of facets of British manufacturing industry that have been discussed in this chapter are also to be glimpsed there.

5 As Franko observes, Japanese management has often 'been identified with labour and human relations'. That references to the Japanese having jobs for life, good team spirit, etc., are often made – to the exclusion of any recognition of the fact that Japanese management has a good record on long-term planning, R & D, and other features of operational management – is symptomatic of this. Yet the much-publicised Japanese 'quality circles' were first introduced to Japan from America. The equally famed 'life-time employment', which is also of recent origin, is available to less than 20 per cent of the managers and employees who work in large enterprises, and it is not available to the tens of thousands of small sub-contractors upon which a large firm like Toyota depends, nor to the multitude of part-time women who assemble Japan's highly successful consumer electronics products (Franko, 1983, pp. 50–1). Recently, the other side of what went into the making of Japan's success on the labour front has been given the attention it deserves in Kamata's study of Toyota (Kamata, 1983). On the management side Franko's work also does much to direct attention to the importance of 'maintaining clarity of organizational mission and structure; keeping continuity of investment', R & D etc. In addition, most especially in America, several recent investigations have had an impact in business circles precisely because they have underlined the

fact that the Japanese pay a lot more attention to the detailed organisation and monitoring of production (Hayes, 1981; Wheelwright, 1981). It is arguable, however, that the post-war fixation with Japanese 'culture', 'spirit', etc., is but one sign of two broader tendencies that have been at work in the consideration of productivity more generally: to underplay the significance of the condition of labour in the determination of labour productivity (and in much discussion of Japan, actually giving a misleading impression of this); and to reduce the social relations of production to a discussion of 'man-management'.

## 9   Enter Mrs Thatcher

1  For more precise accounts of changes at BL see Chell (1980); Fryer (1982a); Scarborough (1982); Scarborough and Moran (1985; Willman *et al.* (1985).
2  Keegan argues that Callaghan's speech was more of a tactical move than evidence of a serious and full policy reappraisal. Part of the speech was drafted by Callaghan's son-in-law, Peter Jay, an early monetarist convert for whom this accomplishment seems to have remained a matter for huge delight. In Keegan's opinion, 'It is not difficult to assess who was using whom most.' This seems about right. (See Keegan, 1984, p. 91).
3  In addition to imperfections in the official labour productivity data, which relate to cyclical differences in labour utilisation, there are also problems with the CSO *output* figures. There are no reliable indices of export prices to deflate output sold abroad. The CSO uses domestic price indices instead, and these can diverge significantly from export prices when the real exchange rate changes sharply. Muellbauer has estimated that in the first quarter of 1983, following the sharp depreciation of sterling, true output grew by only about 1 per cent, but as measured on the above basis, it supposedly grew by 2 per cent. The domestic price indices the CSO uses to deflate sterling measures of output may also fail to reflect the prices at which goods are traded, as opposed to listed. Muellbauer also suggests that the *capital stock* figures are subject to large measurement errors, since it is assumed that the efficiency of assets in use is constant as they age and that the ages at which capital assets are scrapped are independent of economic conditions. Such deficiencies do not bode well for the image of econometrics as an exact science. As we have seen, the data on numbers *employed* has sometimes also been wide of the mark (see Muellbauer, 1984, pp. 6–7, and n. 4, p. 269 above.
4  On the basis of data from Shaun Stewart. See also his letter to *Financial Times*, 22 August 1983.

## 10   The new 'realism' and reality

1  In their review of current trends in industrial relations Brown and Sisson claim: 'There can be no doubt that major changes have been

occurring in working practices during the past two years . . . the weight of evidence is of widespread abandonment of restrictions.'
Unfortunately, the strength and clarity of their opinion is not matched by their evidence, which is not presented. Even these writers do not break with the dominant view of industrial relations experts on another point however – that 'any "new realism" is likely to be as ephemeral in the face of an economic recovery as were the attitudes of the 1930s when wartime restored job security' (Brown and Sisson 1984, p. 37). Moreover, although Edwards echoes Brown and Sisson in his preliminary report of the 1984 Warwick IRRU survey of firms with 250 or more full-time workers (the 'evidence is overwhelming that changes in working practices have been widespread and substantial'), he is in fact critical of what he terms 'the myth of the macho manager'. He points out that managements' attempts to improve labour utilisation 'have not, in general, concentrated on union restrictions'; that 'the evidence does not support the view that the reported changes in working practices have removed [hitherto existing] specific labour-relations constraints'; and that 'only three per cent of the sample as a whole felt that industrial relations problems, in the sense of recalcitrant unions or workers, were the main constraints on their operations'. The highest percentage of respondents mentioning changes in working practices instanced changes related to new technologies (Edwards, 1985, pp. 31, 32).

2 From the point of view of workers, five-shift systems can be regarded as a mixed blessing. They bring increased blocks of time off, but they may also mean a more rigid specification of domestic routines. Such unwanted inflexibility can breed its own resistance. In the words of one of ICI's five-shift workers: 'They tried to call me in when I was off. They *made* me take it now. I didn't want it. Like I said, "If I'm bloody off, I'm bloody off". They won't let *me* take it when I want.' Just how common such 'paying-back' will become remains to be seen.

3 Evidence from a Gallup survey conducted for the CBI in 1984 would seem to suggest that large manufacturing firms are more likely than smaller ones to be considering changes in the employment relation. For instance, 36 per cent of all manufacturing employers expected to contract work out to a greater extent over the next five years, but 46 per cent of those who employed over 5,000 expected to do so. Similarly, large employers were more likely to expect to increase the proportion of part-timers (40 per cent compared to 23 per cent for all manufacturing). Large employers were also slightly more likely to expect to increase the proportion of temporary workers (34 per cent compared to 31) and to increase shift-work (37 per cent compared to 31). Data on future expectations does not, of course, tell us about present practices. It should also be noted that this survey appears to have been based on a response rate of only about 40 per cent. However, the survey most certainly underlines the need to take account of changes in the employment relation and it leaves little room for doubt about the direction of change (CBI, 1984, pp. 2, 8, 9).

4 'All reported injuries' for all manufacturing industries fell from 2,530 per 100,000 employees to 2,330 between 1981 and 1982 according to

provisional figures in the *Manufacturing and Service Industries 1982 Report*. The Health and Safety Executive interpreted this as 'a continuation of the long-term downward trend'. On the other hand, although this Report also noted that fatal injuries showed an increase, 'mainly within manufacturing industries', it held back from giving an opinion on whether this increase might mean that 'there has been any change in the pattern of underlying safety' (p. 60), and it made no comment either on changes between these two years in the incidence rate for 'fatal and major injuries'. Provisional data on 'fatal and major injuries', also presented in the above Report, did indicate an increase for 'all manufacturing industries', however.

According to the 1982 Report's own Table 2, the incidence rate for fatal and major injuries had increased for eleven of the seventeen SIC Orders that make up 'all manufacturing industries' – Food, Drink and Tobacco; Coal and Petroleum Products; Chemical and Allied; Mechanical Engineering; Electrical Engineering; Metal Goods nes; Textiles; Leather and Leather Goods; Bricks, Pottery, Glass and Cement; Timber and Furniture; and Paper and Printing (the other industries are Metal Manufacture; Instrument Engineering; Shipbuilding and Marine Engineering; Vehicles; Clothing and Footware, and 'Other Manufacturing').

To compare the (final) 1982 figures for fatal and major injuries per 100,000 employees in all manufacturing industries with the (provisional) data for 1983 is to see a further rise, from 62.4 to 81.9 (*Manufacturing and Service Industries*, 1984, Table 1). This increase again held for eleven of the seventeen SIC Orders, though these had a slightly different composition (Food, etc.; Chemicals and Allied; Metal Manufacture; Mechanical Engineering; Instrument Engineering; Electrical Engineering; Vehicles; Textiles; Clothing and Footwear; Timber and Furniture; Other Manufacturing). Decreases were reported in the remaining six (Coal and Petroleum Products; Shipbuilding and Marine; Metal Goods nes; Leather; Bricks, etc.; Paper, Printing and Publishing).

Since life and limb are at stake, there is no doubt that these figures should be cause for concern. But unfortunately the obvious questions to which these statistics give rise in the context of a discussion of the recession and 'labour efficiency' – are they evidence that unemployment provided the condition for work intensification and that corner-cutting and penny-pinching led to the neglect of safe working procedures and good housekeeping? and is the above data on industrial injuries the result of this? – have not yet been answered. A limited number of yearly comparisons is not the *only* problem. Very real difficulties now stand in the way of making any longer-term retrospective comparison as well. For quite apart from the general problems that would beset any such comparison – the need to ensure that the standard of reporting has been constant, that the numbers employed have been precisely determined, also their hours of work, etc. – it is not now possible to compare figures for 1981 (and thereafter) with those for earlier years. The incidence rates for earlier years were for 'operatives' only. The more recent data includes clerical and administrative staff.

As a letter from the Health and Safety Executive assured me (2 June 1983): 'It is no longer necessary, or practical, to separately identify operatives from other employees.' It would seem, indeed, that the HSE now knows nothing directly of what is happening to operatives as such – unless they suffer injuries which actually result in death. On top of this, figures for 'all injuries' collected under the 1981 Notification of Accidents and Dangerous Occurrences (NADO) regulations are simply not available for 1983, because the bulk of the HSE's information comes from the DHSS, whose rules for claiming industrial injury benefit changed in April of that year. But in addition to all these developments is the plan that the HSE put forward in March 1985 (*Plan of Work 1985–86 And Onwards*), for this proposed that it would withdraw further from routine inspection and enforcement work, mainly restricting its activities to setting standards and issuing guidance. It is also envisaged leaving more inspection and enforcement to local authorities, and insurance companies.

If local authorities were not overburdened already (but they are) shifting more responsibility to them for monitoring and enforcement might not prove injurious, but insurance companies for their part might not want to lose business by insisting on improvements, and it defies belief that more self-policing could be a recipe for anything other than more deaths and major injuries which, unevenly distributed as they have been, have been on the rise already.

5 The following, from a conversation with an AUEW maintenance worker, made redundant at Metal Box, Glasgow in 1983 may be but a particular expression of a more general point: 'Flexibility? I'm not against it. But . . . well, we had this manager they sent over once . . . "Why don't you get more flexible?" he said. "I don't mind at all," I said. I don't either. I'm a socialist, I believe in that. I *know* there's things we don't need to do. I don't want to stop them [other workers] doing things like that. So: "Will you guarantee our jobs for five years?" – That's what I asked him. Because . . . because I *am* a socialist *and* a good trade unionist *and* a steward and it's not part of my job to give other people's jobs away. I told him – "You put it in writing" I said. "I'll talk, I'm in favour." But he wouldn't, you know. Said it "wasn't necessary" . . . "Wasn't necessary." We're *all* finished now. But if he'd had his way we'd have been finished sooner. I was right. I *still* think so.'

## 11 Productivity, productiveness and myopia in Britain today

1 Those in Britain who favour a free market 'solution', and who take the US as their model, are not only apt to deflect attention from the existence of a sizeable underclass in America, they are also prone to oversimplify the situation of US manufacturing labour. Britain's free market ideologues are wont to suggest that American employers are free to discharge labour. It is, so the argument runs, because of this that they are more willing than British employers to hire new labour

and thus add to the level of employment. But this view all too neatly deflects attention from the inflexibilities in American manufacturing that arise from so-called 'seniority systems'. US managements' right to allocate work is often impeded by rules about who can be promoted to better-paid jobs, about who can be employed (many agreements give priority to previously discharged workers) and, in the case of redundancy, about how the jobs that remain will be distributed. In practice, the expansion and the contraction of particular labour forces can lead to a considerable amount of 'bidding' and 'bumping', so that as Burawoy (1979a, p. 132) puts it, 'a single vacancy can create a long vacancy chain', this in turn involving possible retraining and administrative costs. Whether the resultant 'cost of movement' is equal to the costs incurred by dismissals in Britain remains to be calculated. But as Piore (1985) states, it is 'very real'. It can deter employers from varying the level of employment and it gives some American workers, especially in manufacturing, a special interest in the tight specification of job definitions.

2  Despite the mounting body of research reported above, a recent international survey found that 43 per cent of people in Britain still think trade unions are the most important obstacle to the development of new technologies, a proportion which far exceeds that for other countries – 25 per cent in the US, 21 per cent in France and Italy, 14 per cent in Germany and Japan and 6 per cent in Norway and Spain (Atlantic Institute for International Affairs – Louis Harris International Poll, reported in the *Financial Times*, 30 May 1985). But further evidence which underlines the need to steer clear of labour-led explanations for Britain's manufacturing ills is forthcoming from the most recent Warwick IRRU survey. Of those chief executives who reported *internal* constraints on their levels of capacity utilisation, 64 per cent cited 'technical production problems', 34 per cent 'quality of management' and 21 per cent 'lack of labour, shortage of skills'. As against this, 'trade union restrictions' and 'overmanning' were mentioned by 33 per cent and 'lack of worker effort, absenteeism' by 29 per cent (Edwards, 1985, p. 33). 'Internal' constraints on manufacturing capacity utilisation are not the only fetters on industrial development, of course – a theme taken up below.

3  Directors and senior managers have done well out of Thatcherism as individuals. They both earn more and are better off post-tax. One of the CBI's most persistent complaints before Mrs Thatcher came to power was that its members were overtaxed and the improvement in their situation may in some small part account for the organisation's reluctance to mount a sustained and concerted campaign against the accelerated destruction of British manufacturing. In fact, though, the CBI's manufacturing membership is dominated by multi-nationals, it also includes some financial and commercial interests, and of course the many different manufacturing sectors have their own particular problems, with different degrees of reliance on the domestic and foreign markets and so on. The larger explanation for the CBI's reluctance to mount an offensive on Thatcherism probably therefore derives from the fact that 'the CBI reproduce[s] within itself the

structural peculiarities of British capital which [lie] at the heart of Britain's industrial problem' (Leys, 1983, p. 110). Historically forged company traditions and personal political connections no doubt also play a part. For example, Sir Terence Beckett's talk of a 'bare knuckled fight' with Mrs Thatcher in 1980, which has been the sharpest expression of disquiet to date, led to the resignation of five major companies, each of which had a staunch Conservative chairman (Grant, 1983, p. 72).

4 In the same month as the Chancellor made his budget statement, the CBI stressed that the growth in productivity had slowed sharply. Although employers' concessions on the length of the working week were at historically low levels, and although members had clearly taken to heart an injunction directed at them a year earlier ('You've stopped the Rot on Hours, What About Holidays?') – a great help to the unemployed this – British productivity growth in 1984 was clearly seen to lag behind that for competing countries. The CBI cited growth figures of 2.5 per cent for Britain, 3.5 per cent for the US, 6 per cent for West Germany, 7.5 per cent for France, and 10 per cent for Japan (CBI, *Employment Affairs Report*, March 1985; *Pay and Productivity*, July 1984).

# Bibliography

Aaronovitch, S. (1981), 'The Relative Decline of the UK', in S. Aaronovitch *et al.* 1981.

Aaronovitch, S., Smith, R., Gardiner, J. and Moore, R. (1981), *The Political Economy of British Capitalism*, London, Macmillan.

Abell, P., Macdonald, K. and French, E. (1983), 'Workplace Industrial Relations: A Review of Recent Studies Prepared for the Social Science Research council', University of Surrey, Department of Sociology.

ACARD (1983), *First Joint Report by the Chairman of the Advisory Council for Applied Research and Development and the Advisory Board for the Research Council*, London, HMSO, Cmnd 8957.

Ahsan, R. (1981), 'Solihull – Death of a Car Factory', *New Left Review*, 129.

Aldcroft, D.M. (1981), 'The Economy, Management and Foreign Competition', in G. Roderick and M. Stephens (eds), 1981.

Aldcroft, D.M. (1982), 'Britain's Economic Decline 1870–1980', in G. Roderick and M. Stephens (eds), 1982.

Aldridge, A. (1976), *Power, Authority and Restrictive Practices*, Oxford, Basil Blackwell.

Allen, W.W. (1964), 'Is Britain a Half-Time Country?', *Sunday Times*, 1 March.

Anderson, P. (1964), 'Origins of the Present Crisis', *New Left Review*, 23.

Anthony, P.D. (1977), *the Ideology of Work*, London, Tavistock.

Armstrong, P., Glyn, G. and Harrison, J. (1984), *Capitalism Since World War Two* London, Fontana.

Ashworth, J.M. (1984), 'Information Technology'. Letter to *Financial Times*, 17 September.

Atkinson, J. (1984), 'Manpower Strategies for Flexible Organisations', *Personnel Management*, August.

Austrin, T. (1978), 'Industrial Relations in the Construction Industry', unpublished Ph D thesis, University of Bristol.

Austrin, T. (1980), 'The "Lump" in the UK Construction Industry', in T. Nichols (ed.), 1980.

Austrin, T. and Beynon, H. (1980), *Global Outpost*, University of Durham, Department of Sociology.

284

Bacon, R.W. and Eltis, W.A. (1974), *The Age of US and UK Machinery*, London, National Economic Development Office.
Bacon, R.W. and Eltis, W.A. (1976), *Britain's Economic Problem: Too Few Producers*, London, Macmillan.
Bain, G.S. (ed.) (1983), *Industrial Relations in Britain*, Oxford, Basil Blackwell.
Baldamus, W. (1961), *Efficiency and Effort*, London, Tavistock.
Barnett, C. (1975), *The Human Factor and British Industrial Decline*, London, Working Together Campaign.
Barratt Brown, M. (1975), *The Economics of Imperialism*, Harmondsworth, Penguin.
Batstone, E. (1984), *Working Order: Workplace Industrial Relations over Two Decades*, Oxford, Basil Blackwell.
Batstone, E., Boraston, I. and Frenkel, S. (1977), *Shop Stewards in Action*, Oxford, Basil Blackwell.
Beckerman, W. (ed.) (1979), *Slow Growth in Britain*, Oxford, Clarendon Press.
Behrend, H. (1957), 'The Effort Bargain', *Industrial and Labour Relations Review*, 10.
Bell, D. (1947), 'Exploring Factory Life', *Commentary*, January.
Bell, D. (1976), *The Cultural Contradictions of Capitalism*, London Heinemann.
Berg, M. (1981), *The Machinery Question and the Making of Political Economy 1815-1848*, Cambridge University Press.
Bergen, S.A. (1983), *Productivity and the R and D/Production Interface*, Aldershot, Gower Publishing.
Beynon, H. (1973), *Working for Ford*, Harmondsworth, Penguin. (2nd edn, 1985.)
Beynon, H. (1978), *What Happened at Speke?* Liverpool, 6–612 Branch TGWU.
Bhaskar, K. (1975), *Alternatives Open to the UK Motor Industry*, Bristol, Bristol University.
Bhaskar, K. (1979), *The Future of the UK Motor Industry*, London, Kogan Page.
Blackaby, F. (ed.) (1979), *De-Industrialisation*, London, Heinemann Educational Books.
Bleaney, M. (1983), 'Conservative Economic Strategy', in S. Hall and M. Jacques (eds) (1983).
Blewitt, J.D. (1983), 'A Sociological Analysis of Labourism with Specific Reference to Port Talbot', 2 vols, unpublished Ph D thesis, University of Wales, Aberystwyth.
Bluestone, B. (1970), 'The Tripartite Economy: Labor Markets and the Working Poor', *Poverty and Human Resources*, July – August.
Boston Report (1975), *Strategy Alternatives for the British Motorcycle Industry*, London, HMSO.
Boulter, N. (1979), 'Where a Lack of Incentives is a Barrier to Increased Productivity', *Guardian*, 13 November.
Bowles, S., Gordon, D.M. and Weisskopf, T.E. (1983), *Beyond the Waste Land*, New York, Anchor Press/Doubleday.
Brainard, W.C. and Perry, G.L. (eds) (1984), *Brookings Papers on*

*Economic Activity*, 1983, 2, Washington, DC, The Brookings Institution.

Braverman, H. (1974), *Labour and Monopoly Capital*, New York and London, Monthly Review Press.

Brittan, S. (1978), 'How British is the British Sickness?', *Journal of Law and Economics*, 21, October.

Brittan, S. (1983), *The Role and Limits of Government: Essays in Political Economy*, Hounslow, Temple Smith.

Brown, J.A.C. (1954), *The Social Psychology of Industry*, Harmondsworth, Penguin.

Brown, P.C. (1973), *Smallcreep's Day*, London, Pan Books.

Brown, W. (ed.) (1981), *The Changing Contours of British Industrial Relations*, Oxford, Basil Blackwell.

Brown, W. and Sisson, K. (1984). 'Current Trends and Future Possibilities', in M. Poole *et al.*, 1984.

Bruce, D. (1982), 'Our Idle Over-Paid: The Facts', *The Times*, 12 October.

Bryer, R.A., Brignall, T.J. and Maunders, A.R. (1982), *Accounting For BSC: A Financial Analysis of the Failure of the British Steel Corporation, 1967 to 1980, and Who Was to Blame*, Farnbrough, Gower Publishing Co.

Buiter, W.H. and Miller, M.H. (1984), 'Changing the Rules: Economic Consequences of the Thatcher Regime', in W.C. Brainard and G.L. Perry (eds) (1984).

Burawoy, M. (1978), 'Toward a Marxist Theory of the Labour Process', *Politics and Society*, 8.

Burawoy, M. (1979a), *Manufacturing Consent: Changes in the Labor Process under Monopoly Capitalism*, University of Chicago Press.

Burawoy, M. (1979b), 'The Anthropology of Industrial Work', *Annual Review of Anthropology*, 8.

Burawoy, M. (1983), 'Between the Labour Process and the State: The Changing Face of Factory Regimes Under Advanced Capitalism', *American Sociological Review*, October.

Burgess, K. (1975), *The Origins of British Industrial Relations*, London, Croom Helm.

Burn, D. (1940), *The Economic History of Steelmaking, 1867–1939: A Study in Competition*, Cambridge University Press.

Burnham, T.H. and Hoskins, G.O. (1943), *Iron and Steel in Britain 1870–1930*, London, Allen & Unwin.

Business Statistics Office (1982), *The Merseyside Economy, Performance and Prospects to 1986*, London, HMSO.

Cairncross, A.K. (1953), *Home and Foreign Investment, 1870–1914*, Cambridge University Press.

Cairncross, A., Kay, J.A. and Silbertson, Z.A. (1983), 'The Regeneration of Manufacturing Industry', in R.C.O. Matthews and J.R. Sargent (eds) (1983).

Cairncross, F. (1977), 'The English Disease', *Guardian*, 19 February.

Carter, C. (ed.) (1981), *Industrial Policy and Innovation*, London, Heinemann.

Castles, S., Booth, H. and Wallace, T. (1984), *Here For Good: West*

*Europe's New Ethnic Minorities*, London, Pluto.

Castles, S. and Kosack, G. (1974), 'How Trade Unions Try to Control and Integrate Immigrant Workers in the German Federal Republic', *Race*, April.

Castles, S. and Kosack, G. (1980), 'The Function of Labour Immigration in Western European Capitalism' in T. Nichols (ed.) (1980).

Caves, R.E. (1980), 'Productivity Differences among Industries', in R.E. Caves and L.B. Krause (eds), 1980.

Caves, R.E., and Associates (1968), *Britain's Economic Prospects*, Washington D.C, The Brookings Institution.

Caves, R.E. and Krause, L.B. (eds) (1980), *Britain's Economic Performance*, Washington, DC, The Brookings Institution.

CBI (1984) *Attitudes Towards Employment*, London, CBI Social Affairs Directorate/Gallup.

Chambers, P. (1984), 'Restrictive Practices: The Job's Not Done Yet', *Works Management*, January.

Chandler, A.D. (1962), *Strategy and Structure*, Cambridge, Mass., MIT Press.

Chandler, A.D. (1977), *The Visible Hand: The Managerial Revolution in American Business*, Cambridge, Mass., MIT Press.

Chandler, A.D. and Daems, H. (eds) (1980), *Managerial Hierarchies*, Cambridge, Mass., Harvard University Press.

Channon, D.F. (1973), *The Strategy and Structure of British Enterprise*, London, Macmillan.

Chell, R. (1980), 'BL Cars Ltd – The Frontier of Control', unpublished M.A. thesis, University of Warwick.

Child, J. (1985), 'Managerial Strategies, New Technology and the Labour Process', in D. Knights, D. Collinson and H. Willmott (eds) (1985).

Cipolla, C.M. (ed.) (1973), *The Fontana Economic History of Europe*, V, London, Fontana.

CIS (nd) *The Ford Motor Company*, London, Counter Information Services, 20.

Clack, G. (1967), *Industrial Relations in a British Car Factory*, Occasional Paper, Department of Applied Economics, Cambridge University Press.

Clegg, H.A. (1979), *Trade Unions under Collective Bargaining*, Oxford, Basil Blackwell.

Cliff, T. (1970), *The Employers' Offensive: Productivity Deals and How to Fight Them*, London, Pluto.

Clutterbuck, R. (1980), *Industrial Conflict and Democracy*, London, Macmillan.

Cohen, G.A. (1978), *Karl Marx's Theory of History: A Defence*, Oxford University Press.

Colchester, N. (1977), 'Productivity Clichés Fail the Test', *Financial Times*, 20 December.

Connel, D. (1979), *The UK's Performance in Export Markets*, London, National Economic Development Office.

Coppock, D.J. (1956), 'The Climacteric of the 1890s: A Critical Note', *Manchester School of Economic and Social Studies*, 24.

Corfield, K.G. (1979), *Product Design*, London, National Economic Development Office.

Cotgrove, S., Dunham, J. and Vamplew, C. (1971), *The Nylon Spinners*, London, Allen & Unwin.

Cowie, H., Harlow, C. and Emerson, R. (1984), *Rebuilding the Infrastructure: The Needs of English Towns*, London, Policy Studies Institute.

CPRS (1975), *The Future of the British Car Industry*, London, Central Policy Review Staff.

CSA (1984), *Members Survey 1984*, London, Computer Services Association.

Cunnison, S. (1963), *Wages and Work Allocation*, London, Tavistock.

Dahrendorf, R. (1976), 'Not by Bread Alone', *Financial Times*, 30 December.

Daly, A. (1982), 'The Contribution of Education to Economic Growth in Britain: A Note on the Evidence', *National Institute Economic Review*, 101, August.

Daly, A., Hitchens, D.M.W.N. and Wagner, K. (1985), 'Productivity, Machinery and Skills in a Sample of British and German Manufacturing Plants', *National Institute Economic Review*, 111, February.

Daniel, W.W. (1970), *Beyond the Wage-Work Bargain*, London, PEP.

Daniel, W.W. and Millward, N. (1983), *Workplace Industrial Relations in Britain*, London, Heinemann Educational Books.

Davies, J. (1984), 'More Young West Germans Seek On-Job Training', *Financial Times*, 1 August.

Deane, P. (1973), 'Great Britain', in C.M. Cipolla (ed.), *The Fontana Economic History of Europe*, 1973.

Deane, P. and Cole, W.A. (1962), *British Economic Growth 1688–1959*, Cambridge University Press.

Denison, E.F. (1961), 'Measurement of Labour Output: Some Questions of Definition and the Adequacy of Data', in *Output, Imput and Productivity Measurement*, 25, National Bureau of Economic Research, Princeton University Press.

Denison, E.F. (1967), *Why Growth Rates Differ: Post War Experience in Nine Western Countries*, Washington, DC, The Brookings Institution.

Department of Industry (1976), *The Three Day Week*, London, HMSO.

Department of Industry (1977), *Industry, Education and Management*, London, HMSO.

Devlin Report (1965), *Final Report of the Committee of Inquiry under the Rt. Hon. Lord Devlin in Certain Matters Concerning the Port Transport Industry*, London, HMSO.

Dex, S. and Perry, S.M. (1984), 'Women's Employment Changes in the 1970s', *Employment Gazette*, April.

Dibblee, G.B. (1902), 'The Printing Trades and the Crisis in British Industry', *Economic Journal*, March.

Dixon, M. (1984), 'British and German Education', *Financial Times*, 10 February.

Dodsworth, T. (1984), 'GM Learns a Lesson from Japan', *Financial Times*, 1 October.

Dodwell (1983), *The Structure of the Japanese Auto Parts Industry*, Tokyo, Dodwell Marketing Consultants.

Doeringer, P. and Piore, M. (1971), *Internal Labour Markets and*

*Manpower Analysis*, Lexington, Mass., D.C. Heath.

Donovan Report (1967), *Royal Commission on Trade Unions and Employers' Associations, Research Papers, 4, Restrictive Labour Practices*, London, HMSO.

Donovan Report (1968), *Royal Commission on Trade Unions and Employers' Associations*, London, HMSO, Cmnd 3623.

Dore, R. (1973), *British Factory-Japanese Factory*, London, Allen & Unwin.

Dudley, N. (1975), 'Industrial Productivity – Scope For Improvement', *Midlands Tomorrow*, 8.

Duffey, H. (1980), 'Why Three into Two May Go', *Financial Times*, 6 August.

Dunlop, J.T. and Diatchenko, V.P. (eds) (1964), *Labor Productivity*, New York, McGraw-Hill.

Dunnett, J.S. (1980), *The Decline of the British Motor Industry*, London, Croom Helm.

Edelstein, M. (1981), 'Foreign Investment and Empire 1860–1914' in R.C. Floud and D.N. McCloskey (eds) (1981).

Edwardes, M. (1984), *Back from the Brink*, London, Pan Books.

Edwards, P.K. (1985) 'Myth of the Macho Manager', *Personnel Management*, April.

Edwards, P.K. and Nolan, P. (1983), 'Industrial Relations, Productivity, and Economic Performance: An Outline of the Connections', unpublished paper, University of Warwick, ESRC Industrial Relations Research Unit.

Edwards, P.K. and Scullion, H. (1982), *The Social Organisation of Industrial Conflict: Control and Resistance in the Workplace*, Oxford, Basil Blackwell.

Edwards, R. (1979), *Contested Terrain: The Transformation of Work in the Twentieth Century*, London, Heinemann.

Eklund, K. (1980), 'Long Waves in the Development of Capitalism', *Kyklos*, 33, 3.

Elbaum, B. and Lazonick, W. (1984), 'The Decline of the British Economy: An Institutional Perspective', *Journal of Economic History*, June.

Elbaum, B. and Wilkinson, F. (1979), 'Industrial Relations and Uneven Development: A Comparative Study of the American and British Steel Industries', *Cambridge Journal of Economics*, 3.

ELF (1984), *National Manpower Survey of the British Electronics Industry*, Richmond, Urban Publishing/Electronics Location File.

Elgin, R. (1982), 'Edwardes Bows Out', *Sunday Times*, 19 September.

Erlichman, J. (1985), 'The Imperial Imperative', *Guardian*, 19 February.

Expenditure Committee (1975), *The Motor Vehicle Industry*, Fourteenth Report Trade and Industry Sub-Committee, HMSO.

Fabricant, S. (1968), 'Productivity' in *International Encyclopedia of the Social Sciences*, New York, The Free Press.

Feinstein, C.H. (1963), 'Production and Productivity 1920–63', *London and Cambridge Economic Bulletin*, XLVIII.

Fidler, J. (1981), *The British Business Elite*, London, Routledge & Kegan Paul.

290    *Bibliography*

Finniston Report (1980), *Engineering Our Future*, London, HMSO, Cmnd. 7794.
Floud, R. and McCloskey, D.N. (eds) (1981), *The Economic History of Britain Since 1700: 1860 to the 1970s*, Cambridge University Press.
Flux, A.W. (1933), 'Industrial Productivity in Great Britain and the United States', *Quarterly Journal of Economics*, November.
Food and Drink Manufacturing EDC Report (1982), *Improving Productivity in the Food and Drink Manufacturing Industry – The Case For a Joint Approach*, London, National Economic Development Office.
Fothergill, S. and Dudgin, G. (1982), *Unequal Growth: Urban and Regional Employment Change in the UK*, London, Heinemann.
Frank, A.G. (1971), *Sociology of Development and the Underdevelopment of Sociology*, London, Pluto Press.
Frankel, M. (1957), *British and American Manufacturing Productivity*, Urbana, University of Illinois Press.
Franko, L.G. (1983), *The Threat of the Japanese Multinationals*, Chichester, John Wiley.
Frantz, R.S. (1980), 'On the Existence of X-Efficiency', *Journal of Post Keynesian Economics*, Summer.
Fraser, R. (ed.) (1969), *Work 2 – Twenty Personal Accounts*, Harmondsworth, Penguin.
Freeman, C. (1979), 'Technical Innovation and British Trade Performance', in F. Blackaby, (ed.) (1979).
Freeman, R.L. and Medoff, J.L. (1979), 'The Two Faces of Unionism', *The Public Interest*, Fall.
Friedman, A. (1977), *Industry and Labour: Class Struggles at Work and Monopoly Capitalism*, London, Macmillan.
Friedman, A.L. and Bhaskar, K.N. (1976), 'A Critique: The Central Policy Review Staff Report on the British Car Industry', in *Eighth Report from the Expenditure Committee: Public Expenditure on Chrysler UK Ltd*, 2, London, HMSO.
Fryer, J. (1982a), 'How They Worked a Miracle at Longbridge', *Sunday Times*, 21 March.
Fryer, J. (1982b), 'The Other Side of the Rising Sun', *Sunday Times*, 23 May.
Gaffikin, F. and Nickson, A. (1984), *Jobs Crisis and the Multinationals*, Nottingham, Russell Press.
Galbraith, J.K. (1967), *The New Industrial State*, London, Hamish Hamilton.
Gale, B.Y. (1980), 'Can More Capital Buy Higher Productivity?', *Harvard Business Review*, July–August.
Gallie, D. (1978), *In Search of the New Working Class*, Cambridge University Press.
Gallie, D. (1983), *Social Inequality and Class Radicalism in France and Britain*, Cambridge University Press.
Gamble, A. (1982), *Britain in Decline*, London, Macmillan.
Garnett, N., (1983a), 'How Vickers Built a More United Team', *Financial Times*, 28 September.
Garnett, N. (1983b), 'Pilkington's Model for Improving Productivity', *Financial Times*, 7 October.

Garnett, N. (1983c), 'Demarcation in British Shipyards', *Financial Times*, 19 December.
Garnett, N. (1984), 'How Flexibility Bore Fruit at Leyland', *Financial Times*, 9 January.
Gennard, J., and Dunn, S. (1984), *The Closed Shop in British Industry*, London, Macmillan.
Gennard, J., Dunn, S. and Wright, M. (1980), 'The Extent of Closed Shop Arrangements in British Industry', *Employment Gazette*, January.
Giddens, A. and Mackenzie, G. (eds) (1982), *Social Class and the Division of Labour*, Cambridge University Press.
Glyn, A. (1982), 'The Productivity Slow-down: A Marxist View', in R.C.O. Matthews (ed.) (1982).
Glyn, A., and Sutcliffe, B. (1972), *British Capitalism, Workers and the Profits Squeeze*, Harmondsworth, Penguin.
Gomulka, S. (1979), 'Britain's Slow Industrial Growth – Increasing Efficiency versus Low Rate of Technical Change', in W. Beckerman (ed.) (1979).
Goodhart, D., (1982), 'It Cuts Down on Industrial Relations Agony', *Financial Times*, 17 December.
Gooding, K. (1983), 'Detroit Faces Up to the Technological Challenge', *Financial Times*, 25 August.
Gorz, A. (1967), *Strategy for Labour*, Boston, Mass., Beacon Press.
Gorz, A. (1976), *The Division of Labour: The Labour Process and Class Struggle in Modern Capitalism*, Brighton, Harvester Press.
Gospel, H. and Littler, C. (eds) (1983), *Managerial Strategies and Industrial Relations*, London, Heinemann Educational Books.
Grant, W. (1983) 'Representing Capital' in R. King (ed.), *Capital and Politics*, London, Routledge & Kegan Paul.
Groom, B. (1983), ' "Jack of all Trades" Steel Plan', *Financial Times*, 26 September.
Groom, B. (1984a), 'Why Pay Bargaining Is Becoming a Local Matter', *Financial Times*, 13 February.
Groom, B. (1984b), ' "No Strike" Agreements in Britain', *Financial Times*, 22 May.
Groom, B. (1984c), 'Flexibility: A Cause Célèbre of the 1980s', *Financial Times*, 25 June.
Grunberg, L. (1983), 'The Effects of the Social Relations of Production on Productivity and Workers' Safety: An Ignored Set of Relationships', *International Journal of Health Services*, 13, 4.
Gwyn, W.B. (1980), 'Jeremiahs and Pragmatists: Perceptions of British Decline', in W.B. Gwyn and R. Rose (eds) (1980).
Gwyn, W.B. and Rose, R. (eds) (1980), *Britain: Progress and Decline*, London, Macmillan.
Hall, S. and Jacques, M. (eds) (1983), *The Politics of Thatcherism*, London, Lawrence & Wishart.
Hampshire, M.J. (1982), *Calderdale Microprocessor Applications Project*, University of Salford Electronic and Electrical Engineering Dept.
Harris, N. (1980), 'The New Untouchables: The International Migration of Labour', *International Socialism*, 8.
Harris, N. (1983), *Of Bread and Guns*, Harmondsworth, Penguin.

Hartmann, G., Nicholas, I., Sorge, A. and Warner, M. (1983), 'Computerised Machine Tools, Manpower Consequences and Skill Utilisation: A Study of British and West German Manufacturing Firms, *British Journal of Industrial Relations*, July.

Hayes, R.H. (1981), 'Why Japanese Factories Work', *Harvard Business Review*, July–August.

Heller, F. (1983), 'Involvement in Decision Making'. Letter to the *Financial Times*, 21 September.

Hennessey, J. (1984), 'A British Miracle?' in *Rebirth of Britain; A Symposium*, London, Pan Books/Institute of Economic Affairs.

Henwood, F. and Thomas, G. (1984), *The Economics of Industry and Technical Change*, Brighton, Wheatsheaf Books.

Herding, R. (1972), *Job Control and Union Structure*, Rotterdam University Press.

Hickson, D.J. (1961), 'Motives of Workpeople Who Restrict Their Output', *Occupational Psychology*, 25, 3.

Higgs, P. (1969), 'The Convenor', in R. Fraser (ed.) (1969).

Hilferding, R. (1981), *Finance Capital*, London, Routledge & Kegan Paul.

Hobsbawm, E.J. (1964), *Labouring Men*, London, Weidenfeld & Nicolson.

Hobsbawm, E.J. (1969), *Industry and Empire*, Harmondsworth, Penguin.

Hodgson, G. (1981), *Labour at the Crossroads*, Oxford, Martin Robertson.

Hodgson, G. (1982a), *Capitalism, Value and Exploitation*, Oxford, Martin Robertson.

Hodgson, G. (1982b), 'Marx Without the Labour Theory of Value', *Review of Radical Political Economics*, 14, 2.

Hodgson, G. (1982c), 'Theoretical and Policy Implications of Variable Productivity', *Cambridge Journal of Economics*, 6, 3.

Hoffman, W.G. (1955), *British Industry 1700–1950*, trans. W.O. Henderson and W.H. Chaloner, Oxford, Basil Blackwell.

Hogan, W.T. (1972), *The 1970s: Critical Years for Steel*, Lexington, Mass., D.C. Health.

Holbrook-Jones, M. (1982), *Supremacy and Subordination of Labour: The Hierarchy of Work in the Early Labour Movement*, London Heinemann Educational Books.

Hu, Yao-Su, (1975), *National Attitudes and the Financing of Industry*, London, PEP.

Hutchinson, K. (1950), *The Decline and Fall of British Capitalism*, New York, Charles Scribner's.

Hutton, G. (1953), *We Too Can Prosper: The Promise of Productivity*, London, Allen & Unwin.

Hutton, G. and Hennessy J. (1966), *Source book on Restrictive Practices in Britain*, London, Institute of Economic Affairs, Research Paper 7.

Hyman, R. (1977), *Strikes*, London, Fontana.

Hyman, R. and Elger, T. (1982), 'Job Controls, The Employer's Offensive and Alternative Strategies', *Capital and Class*, 15.

IDS (1981), *Productivity Improvements: Study 245*, London, Incomes Data Services.

IDS (1982), *Harmonisation: Study 273*, London, Incomes Data Services.
IDS (1983), *Report 298*, London, Incomes Data Services, September.
IDS (1984a), *Supervisors and Manual Workers: Study 307*, London, Incomes Data Services.
IDS (1984b), *Productivity and Working Time: Study 312*, London, Incomes Data Services.
IDS (1984c), *Group Working and Greenfield Sites: Study 314*, London, Incomes Data Services.
IDS (1984d), *Craft Flexibility: Study 322*, London, Incomes Data Services.
IDS (1984e), *Report 418*, London, Incomes Data Services, February.
IDS (1984f), *Report 429*, London, Incomes Data Services, July.
IDS (1984g), *Collective Bargaining Report 4*, London, Income Data Services, December.
ILO (1984), *1984 Year Book of Statistics*, Geneva, International Labour Organisation.
Ingham, G. (1982), 'Divisions Within the Dominant Class and British Exceptionalism', in A. Giddens and G. Mackenzie (eds) (1983).
Ingham, G. (1984), *Capitalism Divided? The City and Industry in British Social Development*, London, Macmillan.
INSEAD (1984), *The State of Large Manufacturers in Europe*, Fontaine-bleau, Cedex, INSEAD.
ISR (1984), *Employee Attitudes Towards Their Employers: An International Perspective*, London, International Survey Research.
Jamieson, I. (1980), *Capitalism and Culture*, Farnborough, Gower Publishing Co.
Jay Consultancy Services (1981), *BL – Where Does the Future Lie?*, Seer Green, Bucks, Jay Consultancy Services.
Jeffreys, J.B. (1946), *The Story of the Engineers 1800–1945*, London, Lawrence & Wishart.
JFCC (1982), *The Control of New Technology: Trade Union Strategies in the Workplace*, Dagenham, NELP Centre for Alternative Industrial and Technological Systems/Joint Forum of Combine Committees.
Jones, D.I.H. (1983), 'Productivity and the Thatcher Experiment', in M. Sawyer and K. Schott, (eds), *Socialist Economic Reiew 1983*, London, Merlin Press.
Jones, D.T. (1976), 'Output, Employment and Labour Productivity in Europe Since 1955', *National Institute Economic Review*, 77, August.
Jones, D.T. (1983), 'Technology and the UK Automobile Industry', *Lloyds Bank Review*, April.
Jones, J. (1977), 'The Bastards Won't Back Us', *New Statesman*, 9 September.
Jowell, R. and Airey, C. (1984), *British Social Attitudes, 1984*, Aldershot, Gower Publishing Co.
Kaldor, M. (1980), 'Technical Change in the Defence Industry', in K. Pavitt, (ed.) (1980).
Kaldor, N. (1966), *Causes of the Slow Rate of Growth of the United Kingdom*, Cambridge University Press.
Kaldor, N. (1982), 'Viability of the State'. Letter to *The Times*, 21 October.

Kaldor, N. and Ward, T. (1985), 'Reasons for Britain's Economic Decline'. Letter to *The Times*, 15 February.

Kaletsky, A. (1984a), 'UK Capital Investment', *Financial Times*, 11 April.

Kaletsky, A. (1984b), 'Taking a Flamethrower to an Iceberg', *Financial Times*, 16 November.

Kamata, S. (1983), *Japan in the Passing Lane*, London, Allen & Unwin.

Katrak, H. (1982), 'Labour-Skills, R and D and Capital Requirements in the International Trade and Investment of the United Kingdom 1968–78', *National Institute Economic Review*, 101, August.

Keegan, V. (1983), 'That Economic Miracle Was Really a Productivity Mirage', *Guardian*, 27 August.

Keegan, W. (1984), *Mrs Thatcher's Economic Experiment*, Harmondsworth, Penguin.

Keesing, D.B. (1971), 'Different Countries' Labour Skill Coefficients and the Skill Intensity of International Trade Flows', *Journal of International Economics*, November.

Kellner, P. (1982a), 'Exposed: The Great Productivity Myth', *New Statesman*, 30 July.

Kellner, P. (1982b), 'Thatcherism: The Miracle That Never Happened', *New Statesman*, 10 December.

Kelly, J. (1984), 'Management's Redesign of Work: Labour Process, Labour Markets and Product Markets', unpublished paper, London School of Economics, Department of Industrial Relations.

Kendrick, J.W. (1977), *Understanding Productivity*, Baltimore, Johns Hopkins, University Press.

Kerr, C. and Fisher, L. (1957), 'Plant Sociology: The Elite and The Aborigines', in M. Komarovsky (ed.), *Common Frontiers of the Social Sciences*, Glencoe, The Free Press.

Kilpatrick, A. and Lawson, T. (1980), 'On the Nature of Industrial Decline in the UK', *Cambridge Journal of Economics*, March.

King, R. (ed.) (1983) *Capital and Politics*, London, Routledge & Kegan Paul.

King, W.T.C. (1936), *History of the London Discount Market*, London, G. Routledge & Sons.

Kirby, M.W. (1981), *The Decline of British Economic Power Since 1870*, London, Allen & Unwin.

Klein, L. (1963), *The Meaning of Work*, London, Fabian Society Tract 349.

Knights, D., Collinson, D. and Willmott, H. (eds) (1985), *Job Redesign: Organisation and Control in the Labour Process*, Aldershot, Gower Publishing Co.

Kolka, J. (1978), 'Entrepreneurs and Managers in German Industrialization', in P. Mathias and H.M. Postan (eds) (1978).

Kolko, G. (1961), 'Max Weber on America: Theory and Evidence', *History and Theory*, 1.

Kransdorf, A. (1984), 'A Minor Revolution in Stock Control', *Financial Times*, 16 May.

Labour Research (1976), 'Cars: Following the Wrong Signs', *Labour Research*, February.

Labour Research (1983), 'Robots', *Labour Research*, November.

Landes, D.S. (1969), *The Unbound Prometheus*, Cambridge University Press.

Lane, T. (1982), 'The Unions: Caught on the Ebb Tide', *Marxism Today*, September.

Lash, S. (1984), *The Militant Worker: Class and Radicalism in France and America*, London, Heinemann Educational Books.

Lazonick, W.H. (1979), 'Industrial Relations and Technical Change: The Case of the Self-Acting Mule' *Cambridge Journal of Economics*, 3.

Lazonick, W.H. (1981), 'Production Relations, Labour Productivity and Choice of Technique: British and US Cotton Spinning', *Journal of Economic History*, 41.

Lazonick, W.H. (1982), 'Production, Productivity, and Development: Theoretical Implications of some Historical Research', unpublished paper, Harvard University, Department of Economics.

Leibenstein, H. (1966), 'Allocative Efficiency vs X-Efficiency', *American Economic Review*, June.

Leibenstein, H. (1976), *Beyond Economic Man*, Cambridge, Mass., Harvard University Press.

Leigh-Pemberton, R. (1980), 'Don't Blame the Banks', *Sunday Times*, 16 November.

Leslie, D. (1976), 'Hours and Overtime in British and United States Manufacturing Industries: A Comparison', *British Journal of Industrial Relations*, July.

Lever, H. and Edwards, G. (1980a), 'Why Germany Beats Britain', *Sunday Times*, 2 November.

Lever, H. and Edwards, G. (1980b), 'How to Bank on Britain', *Sunday Times*, 9 November.

Levine, A.L. (1967), *Industrial Retardation in Britain 1880–1914*, New York, Basic Books.

Lewis, W.A. (1978), *Growth and Fluctuations: 1870–1913*, London, Allen & Unwin.

Leys, C. (1983) *Politics in Britain*, London, Heinemann Educational Books.

Lincoln, J.A. (1967), *The Restrictive Society: A Report on Restrictive Practices*, London, Allen & Unwin.

Linhart, R. (1981), *The Assembly Line*, London, John Calder.

Lipsey, D. (1984), 'The World is Britain's Oyster . . . But Will We Get the Pearl?', *Sunday Times*, 5 February.

Littler, C.R. (1982), *The Development of the Labour Process in Capitalist Societies*, London, Heinemann Educational Books.

Littler, C. and Salaman G. (1984), *Class At Work*, London, Batsford.

Loasby, G.J. (1976), (Review of Leibenstein, 1976), *Economic Journal*, December.

Lomax, K.S. (1959), 'Production and Productivity Movements in the UK Since 1900', *Journal of the Royal Statistical Society*, Series A, CXXII.

Lomax, K.S. (1964), 'Growth and Productivity in the UK', *Productivity Measurement Review*, XXXVII.

Lomax, K.S. (1970), 'Growth and Productivity in the UK' in D. Aldcroft and P. Fearnon (eds), *Economic Growth in Twentieth-Century Britain*, New York, Humanities Press.

London and Cambridge Economic Service (1967), *The British Economy:
Key Statistics 1900–1970*, University of Cambridge, Department of
Applied Economics.
Lupton, T. (1963), *On the Shop Floor*, London, Pergamon.
Macarov, D. (1982), *Worker Productivity: Myths and Realities*, Beverly
Hills, Calif., Sage Publications.
McCarthy, W.E.J. (1970), 'The Nature of Britain's Strike Problem',
*British Journal of Industrial Relations*, 8.
McClelland, D.C. (1961), *The Achieving Society*, London, Van Nostrand.
McCloskey, D.N. (1973), *Economic Maturity and Entrepreneurial
Decline: British Iron and Steel, 1870–1913*, Cambridge, Mass.,
Harvard University Press.
McDaid, M. (1983), 'Debates on Finance Capital', unpublished paper,
Department of Sociology, Bristol University.
McKersie, R. and Klein, J. (1982), *Productivity: The Industrial Relations
Connection*, MIT, Sloan School of Management Working Paper.
Maddison, A. (1962), 'Growth and Fluctuation in the World Economy'
*Banca Nazionale del Lavoro Quarterly Review*, June.
Maddison, A. (1964), *Economic Growth in the West*, New York,
Twentieth Century.
Maddison, A. (1967a), *Economic Growth in the West*, New York, W.W.
Norton.
Maddison, A. (1967b), 'Comparative Productivity Levels in Developed
Countries', *Banca Nazionale del Lavoro Quarterly Review*, December.
Maddison, A. (1972), 'Explaining Economic Growth', *Banca Nazionale
del Lavoro Quarterly Review*, September.
Maddison, A. (1973), 'Economic Policy and Performance in Europe
1913–70', in C.M. Cipolla (ed.) (1973).
Maddison, A. (1977), 'Phases of Capitalist Development', *Banca
Nazionale del Lavoro Quarterly Review*, June.
Maddison, A. (1982), *Phases of Capitalist Development*, Oxford
University Press.
Maier, C.S. (1970), 'Between Taylorism and Technocracy: European
Ideas and the Vision of Industrial Productivity in the 1920s', *Journal of
Contemporary History*, 2.
Maitland I. (1983), *The Causes of Industrial Disorder: A Comparison of
a British and a German Factory*, London, Routledge & Kegan Paul.
Mallet, S. (1975), *The New Working Class*, Nottingham, Spokesman
Books.
Mandel, E. (1975), *Late Capitalism*, London, New Left Books.
Mandel, E. (1980), *Long Waves of Capitalist Development*, Cambridge
University Press.
Mann, M. (1976), 'The Working Class', *New Society*, 4 November.
Mant, A. (1977), *The Rise and Fall of the British Manager*, London,
Macmillan.
Manufacturing and Service Industries (1983a), *Health and Safety 1981*,
London, HMSO.
Manufacturing and Service Industries (1983b), *Health and Safety 1982*,
London, HMSO.
Manufacturing and Service Industries (1984), *Health and Safety 1983*,
London, HMSO.

Manwaring, T. (1981), 'Labour Productivity and the Crisis at BSC', *Capital and Class*, 14.

Marsh, A. (1982), *Employee Relations Policy and Decision Making*, Farnborough, Gower Publishing Co.

Marsh, A.I., Evans, E.O. and Garcia, P. (1971), *Workplace Industrial Relations in Engineering*, London, Engineering Employers Association and Kogan Page.

Marx, K. (1972), *Capital*, vol. 3, London, Lawrence & Wishart.

Mass Observation (1942), *People in Production: An Enquiry Into British War Production*, Part I, London, John Murray.

Mass Observation (1943), *War Factory*, London, Gollancz.

Massey, D. (1984), *Spatial Divisions of Labour*, London, Macmillan.

Massey, D. and Meegan, R. (1982), *The Anatomy of Job Loss*, London, Methuen.

Mathias, P. and Postan, H.M. (eds) (1978), *The Cambridge Economic History of Europe*, VII, Part I, Cambridge University Press.

Matsuzaki, T. (1980), 'The Japanese Steel Industry and its Labour-Management Relations', University of Tokyo, *Annals of the Institute of Social Science*, 21.

Matthews, R.C.O. (ed.) (1982), *Slower Growth in the Western World*, London, Heinemann.

Matthews, R.C.O. and Sargent, J.R. (eds) (1983), *Contemporary Problems of Economic Policy*, London, Methuen.

Matthewson, S.B. (1959), *Restriction of Output Among Unorganised Workers*, Carbondale, Southern Illinois University Press (1st. pub. 1931).

Maunder, P. (ed.) (1979), *Government Intervention in the Developed Economy*, London, Croom Helm.

Maxcy, G. and Silberston, A. (1959), *The Motor Industry*, London, Allen & Unwin.

Maynard (1978), *A Survey of Operating Conditions in Europe Experienced by US Owned Companies*, London, H. B. Maynard and Co.

Maynard and Barry (1980), *A Second Survey of Operating Conditions in Europe Experienced by US Owned Companies – Wales*, London, Maynard and Barry.

Mclman, S. (1956), *Dynamic Factors in Industrial Productivity*, Oxford, Basil Blackwell.

Melman, S. (1958), *Decision Making and Productivity*, Oxford, Basil Blackwell.

Mendis, L. and Muellbauer, J. (1983), *Has There Been a Productivity Breakthrough? Evidence From An Aggregate Production Function For Manufacturing*, Centre for Labour Economics Discussion Paper 170, London, London School of Economics.

Miliband, R. and Saville, J. (eds) (1965), *The Socialist Register*, London, Merlin Press.

Miller, J. (1979), *British Management vs German Management*, Farnborough, Saxon House.

Mills, C.W. (1959), *The Sociological Imagination*, New York, OUP.

Minchinton, W.E. (1957), *The British Tinplate Industry: A History*, Oxford, Basil Blackwell.

Ministry of Labour and National Service (1959), *Practices Impeding the Full and Efficient Use of Manpower, Report of an Inquiry Undertaken by the National Joint Advisory Council*, London, HMSO.

Ministry of Labour (1965), *Written Evidence to the [Donovan] Royal Commission*, London, HMSO.

Mitchell, B.R. and Deane, P. (1962), *Abstract of British Historical Statistics*, Cambridge University Press.

Mitchell Board of Trade Report (1960), *The Machine Tool Industry*, London, HMSO.

Montgomery, D. (1979), *Workers' Control in America: Studies in the History of Work, Technology, and Labor Struggles*, Cambridge University Press.

Moorhouse, H.F. (1978), 'The Marxist Theory of the Labour Aristocracy', *Social History*, 3, 1.

More, C. (1980), *Skill and the English Working Class, 1870–1914*, London, Croom Helm.

MORI (1980), Survey, *Sunday Times*, 31 August.

MORI (1982), Survey, *Daily Star*, 3 September.

Muellbauer, J. (1984), 'Has There Been a British Productivity Breakthrough?' Paper to Centre for Economic Policy Research, Chatham House, London, 3 December.

Murray, F.M. (1983), 'The Decentralisation of Production', *Capital and Class*, Spring.

Murray, F.M. (1985), 'Industrial Restructuring and Class Politics in Italy: A Study in the Decentralisation of Production in the Bologna Engineering Industry', unpublished Ph D thesis, University of Bristol.

NEDO (1973), *Chemicals Manpower in Europe*, London, National Economic Development Office.

NEDO (1981), *Industrial Performance: R and D and Innovation*, London, National Economic Development Office.

NEDO (1982a), *Innovation in the UK*, London, National Economic Development Office.

NEDO (1982b), *Transferable Factors in Japan's Economic Success*, London, National Economic Development Office.

NEDO (1983), *British Industrial Performance*, London, National Economic Development Office.

NEDO (1984a), *Competence and Competition: Training and Education in the Federal Republic of Germany, the United States and Japan*, London, National Economic Development Office.

NEDO (1984b), *Crisis Facing UK Information Technology*, London, National Economic Development Office.

Nelson, E.R. (1968), 'International Productivity Differences', *American Economic Review*, December.

Nelson, R.R. (1981), 'Research on Productivity Growth and Productivity Differences: Dead Ends and New Departures', *Journal of Economic Literature*, 19.

Nichols, T. (1969), *Ownership, Control and Ideology*, London, Allen & Unwin.

Nichols, T. (1979), 'Social Class: Official, Sociological and Marxist', in J. Irvine, I. Miles and J. Evans (eds), *Demystifying Social Statistics*, London, Pluto.

Nichols, T. (ed.) (1980), *Capital and Labour*, London, Fontana.

Nichols, T. (1984) (Review of Holbrook Jones 1982 and Littler 1982), *Sociological Review*, May.

Nichols, T. and Armstrong, P. (1976), *Workers Divided*, London, Fontana.

Nichols, T. and Beynon, H. (1977), *Living with Captialism*, London, Routledge & Kegan Paul.

NIESR (1984), *National Institute Economic Review*, 110, November.

Nightingale, M. (ed.), (1980), *Merseyside in Crisis*, Liverpool, Merseyside Socialist Research Group.

Northcott, J. and Rogers, P. (1984), *Microelectronics in British Industry: The Pattern of Change*, London, Policy Studies Institute.

Northcott, J. and Rogers, P. (1985), *Microelectronics in Industry: An International Comparison*, London, Policy Studies Institute/Anglo German Foundation.

Northrup, H.R. (1967), *Restrictive Labour Practices in the Supermarket Industry*, University of Philadelphia Press.

Nossiter, B.D. (1978), *Britain: A Future That Works*, London, André Deutsch.

OECD (1979), *Economic Surveys – United Kingdom*, Paris, Organisation for Economic Co-operation and Development.

OECD (1985), *Economic Surveys – United Kingdom 1984/5*, Paris, Organisation for Economic Co-operation and Development.

Office of Population Censuses and Surveys (1973), *Workplace Industrial Relations*, London, HMSO.

Owen, G., *et al.* (1984), *Wrestling with Recovery*, London, Financial Times.

Paige, D. and Bombach, G. (1959), *A Comparison of Output and National Productivity of the United Kingdom and the United States*, Paris, Organisation for Economic Co-operation and Development.

Panic, M. (1978), *Capacity Utilisation in UK Manufacturing Industry*, London, National Economic Development Office.

Pascale, R.T. and Athos, A.G. (1981) *The Art of Japanese Management*, New York, Simon & Schuster.

Pavitt, K. (ed.) (1980), *Technical Innovation and British Economic Performance*, London, Macmillan.

Payne, P.L. (1974), *British Entrepreneurship in the Nineteenth Century*, London, Macmillan.

Penn, R. (1982), 'Skilled Manual Workers in the Labour Process, 1856–1964', in S. Wood (ed.) (1982).

Phelps Brown, H. (1977), 'What is the British Predicament?', *Three Banks Review*, December.

Phelps Brown, H. (1983), *The Origins of Trade Union Power*, Oxford, Clarendon Press.

Phelps Brown, E.H. and Browne, M.H. (1968), *A Century of Pay*, London, Macmillan.

Phelps Brown, E.H. and Handfield-Jones, S.J. (1952), 'The Climacteric of the 1890's', *Oxford Economic Papers*, October.

Phelps Brown, E.H. and Webber, B. (1953), 'Accommodation Productivity and Distribution in the British Economy 1870–1938', *Economic Journal*, LXIII.

Pignon, D. and Querzola, J. (1976), 'Dictatorship and Democracy in Production', in A. Gorz (ed.) (1976).

Pigou, A.C. (ed.) (1925), *Memorials of Alfred Marshall*, London, Macmillan.

Pike, A. (1983), 'Why a Highly-Skilled Workforce Will Be Joining the Dole Queue', *Financial Times*, 14 February.

Pike, A. (1984), 'Skill Shortages Affecting Output', *Financial Times*, 13 November.

Piore, M.J. (1985) 'Labour Mobility: The US Can Be Inflexible, Too', *Financial Times*, 8 May.

Pollard, S. (1982), *The Wasting of the British Economy*, London, Croom Helm.

Pollard, S. (1983), *The Development of the British Economy, 1914–1980*, London, Edward Arnold.

Poole, M.J.F., Mansfield, R., Blyton, P.R., and Frost, P.E. (1981), *Managers in Focus: the British Manager in the Early 1980s*, Aldershot, Gower Publishing Co.

Poole, M.J.F., Brown, W., Rubery, J., Sisson, K., Tarling, R. and Wilkinson, F. (1984) *Industrial Relations in the Future*, London, Routledge & Kegan Paul.

Prais, S.J. (1976), *The Evolution of Giant Firms in Britain, 1909–70*, Cambridge University Press.

Prais, S.J. (1978), 'The Strike-proneness of Large Plants in Britain', *Journal of the Royal Statistical Society*, Series A (General), 141, 3.

Prais, S.J. (1981a), *Productivity and Industrial Structure: A Statistical Study of Manufacturing Industry in Britain, Germany and the United States*, Cambridge University Press.

Prais, S.J. (1981b), 'Vocational Qualifications of the Labour Force in Britain and Germany', *National Institute Economic Review*, 98, November.

Prais, S.J. and Wagner, K. (1983), 'Some Practical Aspects of Human Capital Investment: Training Standards in Five Occupations in Britain and Germany', *National Institute Economic Review*, 105, August.

Pratt, E.A. (1904), *Trade Unionism and British Industry*, London, John Murray.

Pratten, C.F. (1976a), *Labour Productivity Differentials Within International Companies*, Cambridge University Press.

Pratten, C.F. (1976b), *A Comparison of the Performance of Swedish and UK Companies*, Cambridge University Press.

Pratten, C.F. (1977), 'The Efficiency of British Industry', *Lloyds Bank Review*, January.

Pratten, C.F. and Atkinson, A.G. (1976), 'The Use of Manpower in British Manufacturing Industry', *Employment Gazette*, June.

Pratten, C.F. and Silberston, A. (1967), 'International Comparisons of Labour Productivity in the Auto-Industry 1950–65', *Bulletin of the Oxford Institute of Economics and Statistics*, November.

Price Commission (1978a), *Allied Breweries (UK) Limited – Brewing and Wholesaling of Beer and Sales in Managed Houses*, London, HMSO.

Price Commission (1978b), *Metal Box Ltd – Open Top Food and Beverage and Aerosol Cans*, London, HMSO.

Price Commission (1978c), *Prices, Costs and Margins in the Production and Distribution of Compound Feeding Stuff for Cattle, Pigs and Poultry*, London, HMSO.

Price Commission (1979a), *Prices, Costs and Margins in the Manufacture and Distribution of Car Parts*, London, HMSO.

Price Commission (1979b), *Perkins Engine Company, Diesel, Gasoline, Reconditioned and Short Engines*, London, HMSO.

Raimon, R.L. and Stoikov, V. (1967), 'The Quality of the Labour Force', *Industrial and Labour Relations Review*, 20, April.

Ramsay, H. (1981), 'Participation for Whom? A Critical Study of Worker Participation in Theory and Practice, 2 vols, unpublished Ph D thesis, University of Durham.

Ray, G.F. (1984), 'Industrial Labour Costs, 1971–83', *National Institute Economic Review*, 110, November.

Rayton, D. (1972), *Shop Floor Democracy in Action: A Personal Account of the Coventry Gang System*, London, Industrial Common Ownership Movement.

Rees, R. (1984), 'A New Location, A New Philosophy', *Works Management*, September.

Reeves, R. (1984), 'Wilkinson Goes on the Attack', *Financial Times*, 19 September.

Report of the National Joint Advisory Council to the Ministry of Labour and National Service (1959), *Practices Impeding the Full and Efficient Use of Manpower*, HMSO.

Riddell, P. (1983), *The Thatcher Government*, Oxford, Martin Robertson.

Roberts, B.C. (1984), 'Recent Trends in Collective Bargaining in the United Kingdom', *International Labour Review*, 3.

Roderick, G. and Stephens, M. (eds) (1981), *Where Did We Go Wrong? Industrial Performance, Education and the Economy in Victorian Britain*, Lewes, Falmer Press.

Roderick G. and Stephens, M. (eds) (1982), *The British Malaise: Industrial Performance, Education and Training in Britain Today*, Lewes, Falmer Press.

Rodger, I. (1984), 'UK Engineering: Renaissance by Computer for the Small Man', *Financial Times*, 12 June.

Rose, M. (1975), *Industrial Behaviour*, London, Allen Lane.

Rose, M. and Jones, B. (1983), 'Managerial Strategy and Trade Union Response in Plant-Level Reorganisation of Work', unpublished paper, Bath University, Centre for European Industrial Studies.

Rostas, L. (1948), *Comparative Productivity in British and American Industry*, Cambridge University Press.

Rostow, W.W. (1953), *The Process of Economic Growth*, Oxford, Basil Blackwell.

Roy, A.D. (1982), 'Labour Productivity in 1980: An International Comparison', *National Institute Economic Review*, 101, August.

Roy, D. (1952), 'Quota Restriction and Goldbricking in a Machine Shop', *American Journal of Sociology*, 57, 5.

Roy, D. (1953), 'Work Satisfaction and Social Reward in Quota Achievement', *American Sociological Review*, 18.

Roy, D. (1954), 'Efficiency and the Fix', *American Journal of Sociology*, 60, 3.

Roy, D. (1959), Introduction to S.B. Matthewson, (1959).

Rubery, J., Tarling, R. and Wilkinson, F. (1984), 'Industrial Relations Issues in the 1980s: an Economic Analysis', in M. Poole *et al.*, (1984).

Ryder Report (1975), *British Leyland: The Next Decade*, London, HMSO.

Sachs, J.D. (1984), 'Comments on Discussion' (on Buiter and Miller), in W.C. Brainard and G.L. Perry, (eds) (1984).

Salter, W.E.G. (1969), *Productivity and Technical Change*, Cambridge University Press.

Sampson, A. (1982), *The Changing Anatomy of Britain*, London, Hodder & Stoughton.

Saul, S.B. (1960), 'The American Impact on British Industry 1895–1914', *Business History*, 3.

Saul, S.B. (1969), *The Myth of the Great Depression, 1873–1896*, London, Macmillan.

Saville, J. (1961), 'Some Retarding Factors in the British Economy Before 1914', *Yorkshire Bulletin of Economic and Social Research*, 13, May.

Scarborough, H. (1982), 'The Control of Technological Change in the Motor Industry: A Case Study', unpublished Ph D thesis, University of Aston.

Scarborough, H. and Moran, P. (1985), 'How New Tech Won at Longbridge', *New Society*, 7 February.

Schott, K. (1981), *Industrial Innovation in the United Kingdom, Canada and the United States*, London, British-North American Committee.

Sentry (1981a), *Productivity: The British Perspective*, Milton Keynes, Louis Harris and Associates for Sentry Insurance.

Sentry (1981b), *Perspectives on Productivity: A Global View*, Milton Keynes, Louis Harris and Associates for Sentry Insurance.

Shadwell, A. (1913), *Industrial Efficiency: A Comparative Study of Industrial Life In England, Germany and America*, London, Longmans (1st pub. 1905).

Shimmin, S. (1959), *Payment By Results*, London, Staples Press.

Shonfield, A. (1965), *Modern Capitalism*, Oxford University Press.

Silberston, A. (1964), 'Problems Involved in International Comparisons of Labour Productivity in the Automobile Industry', in J.T. Dunlop and V.P. Diatchenko (eds) (1964).

Sloan, A.P. (1967), *My Years with General Motors*, London, Pan Books.

Smith, A.D., Hitchens, D.M.W.M., Davies, S.W. (1982), *International Industrial Productivity: A Comparison of Britain, America and Germany*, Cambridge University Press.

Smith, C. (1983) 'Japanese Car Components – A Maze or a Pyramid?', *Financial Times*, 9 November.

Smith, C.T.B. *et al* (1978), *Strikes in Britain: Department of Employment Manpower Paper 15*, London, HMSO.

Smith, K. (1984), *The British Economic Crisis*, Harmondsworth, Penguin.

Smith, R. (1981), 'The Historical Decline of the UK', in S. Aaronovitch *et al.* (1981).

Smith-Gavine, S.A.N. and Bennett, A.J. (1979), *Index of Percentage*

*Utilisation of Labour: A Description*, Leicester Polytechnic, Autumn.

Smith-Gavine, S.A.N. and Bennett, A.J. (1982), *Index of Percentage Utilisation of Labour*, Bulletin 42, Leicester Polytechnic.

Snoddy, R. (1983), 'Manufacturers Key Up for Future', *Financial Times*, 4 November.

Soskice, D. (1984), 'Industrial Relations and the British Economy 1979–1983', *Industrial Relations*, Fall.

Sparrow, P. (1983), *An Analysis of British Work Values*, Draft Document, London, Work and Society.

Spurrell, D. (1980), 'Business Strategy in the United Kingdom', *National Westminster Bank Quarterly Review*, August.

Stafford G.B. (1981), *The End of Economic Growth?* Oxford, Martin Robertson

Steer, P. and Cable, J. (1978), 'Internal Organization and Profit: An Empirical Analysis of Large UK Companies', *Journal of Industrial Economics*, September.

Stephens, J.D. (1979), 'Class Formation and Class Consciousness: Theoretical and Empirical Analysis with Reference to Britain and Sweden', *British Journal of Sociology*, December.

Storey, J. (1981), *The Challenge to Management Control*, London, Business Books.

Storey, J. (1983), *Managerial Prerogative and the Question of Control*, London, Routledge & Kegan Paul.

Sutermeister, R.A. (1963), *People and Productivity*, New York, McGraw-Hill.

Svennilson, I. (1954), *Growth and Stagnation in the European Economy*, Geneva, United Nations Economic Commission for Europe.

Sweezy, P. (1942), *The Theory of Capitalist Development*, New York, Oxford University Press.

TASS (1976), *A Policy for the British Motor Industry*, Richmond, Surrey, TASS Section of the AUEW.

Taylor, R. (1982), *Workers and the New Depression*, London, Macmillan.

Teece, D.J. (1981), 'Internal Organisation and Economic Performance: An Empirical Analysis of the Profitability of Principal Firms', *Journal of Industrial Economics*, December.

Terry, M. (1983), 'Shop Steward Development and Managerial Strategies', in G. S. Bain (ed.) (1983).

Thomas, D. (1984), 'The Strike-Free Zone', *New Society*, 30 August.

Thompson, E.P. (1965), 'The Peculiarities of the English', in R. Miliband and J. Saville (eds) (1965).

Trafford, G. (1982), 'Merseyside', *Guardian*, 11 October.

Trehel, J. (1982), *Un Homme de Poissy*, Paris, Messidor.

Trist, E.L. and Bamforth, K.W. (1951), 'Some Social and Psychological Consequences of the Longwall Method of Coal-getting', *Human Relations*, February.

Turner, H.A., Clack, G., and Roberts, G. (1967), *Labour Relations in the Motor Industry*, London, allen & Unwin.

Upham, M. (1980), 'British Steel: Retrospect and Prospect', *Industrial Journal*, July/August.

Upton, R. (1984), 'The "Home Office" and the New Homeworkers', *Personnel Management*, September.

US Bureau of Labour, Commissioner of Labour (1904), *Regulation and Restriction of Output*, 11th Special Report, 10.

US Bureau of Labour Statistics, (1968), *An International Comparison of Unit Labour Cost in the Iron and Steel Industry, 1964: United States, France, Germany, United Kingdom*, Washington DC.

Wagner, K. (1980), 'Competition and Productivity: A Study of the Metal Can Industry in Britain, Germany and the United States', *Journal of Industrial Economics*, September.

Watson, T.J. (1980), *Sociology, Work and Industry*, London, Routledge & Kegan Paul.

Weekes, B., Mellish, M., Dickens, L. and Lloyd, J. (1975), *Industrial Relations and the Limits of Law*, Oxford, Basil Blackwell.

Weinstein, P.A. (ed.) (1965), *Featherbedding and Technical Change*, Boston, D.C. Heath.

Wenban-Smith, G.C. (1982), 'Factors Influencing Recent Productivity Growth – Report on a Survey of Companies', *National Institute Economic Review*, 101, August.

Wheelwright, S.C. (1981), 'Japan – Where Operations Really are Strategic', *Harvard Business Review*, July–August.

White, M. and Trevor, M. (1983), *Under Japanese Management: The Experience of British Workers*, London, Heinemann.

Whyte, W.F. *et al.* (1955), *Money and Motivation: An Analysis of Incentives in Industry*, New York, Harper.

Wicks, J. (1983), 'Switzerland: Foreign Labour', *Financial Times*, 6 September.

Wicks, J. (1984), 'Swiss On-Job Training is Best in the West', *Financial Times*, 3 August.

Wiener, M.J. (1981), *English Culture and the Decline of the Industrial Spirit, 1850–1980*, Cambridge University Press.

Wigham, E. (1973), *The Power to Manage: A History of the Engineering Employers' Federation*, London, Macmillan.

Wiles, P.J.D. (1951), 'Notes on the Efficiency of Labour', *Oxford Economic Papers*, New Series, June.

Wilkinson, M. (1983), 'DoE Finds 900,000 Extra Workers', *Financial Times*, 29 December.

Wilkinson, M. (1984), 'Unemployment in Britain', *Financial Times*, 29 October.

Williams, F. (1982), 'The Cost of Higher Productivity', *The Times*, 20 October.

Williams, K., Williams, J. and Thomas, D. (1983), *Why are the British Bad at Manufacturing?* London, Routledge & Kegan Paul.

Williamson, O.E. (1964), *The Economics of Discretionary Behaviour*, Englewood Cliffs, N.J., Prentice-Hall.

Williamson, O.E. (1970), *Corporate Control and Business Behaviour*, Englewood Cliifs, N.J, Prentice-Hall.

Williamson, O.E. (1975), *Markets and Hierarchies*, New York, Macmillan.

Willman, P. and Winch, G. in collaboration with Francis, A. and Snell,

M. (1985), *Innovation and Management Control: Labour Relations at BL Cars*, Cambridge University Press.

Winchester, M. (1984), 'Growth Moves Into the Spotlight', *Financial Times*, 17 September.

Wood, S. (ed.) (1982), *The Degradation of Work*, London, Hutchinson.

Woodward, J. (1958), *Management and Technology*, London, HMSO.

Worswick, G.D.N. (1969) (Review of Caves *et al.*, 1968), *The Economic Journal*, March.

Wright, R. (1961), 'The Gang System in Coventry', *Anarchy*, 2.

Wright, R. (1962), 'Erosion Inside Capitalism', *Anarchy*, 8.

Wyles, C. (1984), 'Factory of the Future Survey 2', *Works Management*, July/August.

Yankelovich, D., Zetterberg, H., Burkhard, S. and Shanks, M. (1984), *Work and Human Values: An International Report on Jobs in the 1980s and 1990s*, Draft Document, New York, The Public Agenda Foundation.

Zeitlin, J. (1983), 'The Labour Strategies of British Engineering Employers, 1890–1922', in H. Gospel and C. Littler (eds) (1983).

Zweig, F. (1951), *Productivity and Trade Unions*, Oxford, Basil Blackwell.

# Author index

Aaronovitch, S., 125
Abell, P., 61
Ahsan, R., 178
Airey, C., 15
Aldcroft, D.M., 87
Aldridge, A., 274
Allen, W.W., 12–13
Anderson, P., 160
Anthony, P.D., 11
Armstrong, Peter, 15
Armstrong, Philip, 208, 235
Ashworth, J.M., 230
Athos, A.G., 169
Atkinson, A.G., 45–7, 49, 55
Atkinson, J., 201
Austrin, T., 196, 197

Bacon, R.W., 100–1
Baldamus, W., 43–4
Bamforth, K.W., 32
Barnett, C., 106, 160
Batstone, E., 189, 190–1, 197
Behrend, H., 43
Bell, D., 26
Bennett, A.J., 184–5, 269
Bergen, S.A., 159
Beynon, H., 47, 50, 120, 197, 203
Bhaskar, K.N., 82–3
Bleaney, M., 217
Blewitt, J.D., 113
Bluestone, B., 32

Bombach, G., 3
Boulter, N., 255–6
Bowles, S., 34
Braverman, H., 29–32, 35, 256, 273
Brignall, T.J., 35, 113, 274
Brittan, S., 181
Brown, J.A.C., 24–6
Brown, W., 189, 253, 278
Browne, M.H., 3
Bruce, D., 269
Bryer, R.A., 35, 113, 274
Buiter, W.H., 173, 183
Burawoy, M., 27, 29, 256, 282
Burn, D., 144

Cable, J., 150
Cairncross, A., 72, 101
Cairncross, F., 20, 21
Carter, C., 160, 247
Castles, S., 116
Caves, R.E., 22, 40, 64, 72, 98–105, 110, 114, 243–52, 272
Chambers, P., 177, 180
Chandler, A.D., 147, 148–9
Channon, D.F., 150
Chell, R., 278
Child, J., 204
Clack, G., 47, 50
Cliff, T., 32, 43

Clutterbuck, R., 249, 258, 259, 261
Cohen, G.A., 35, 277
Cole, W.A., 265
Colchester, N., 156, 277
Connel, D., 100
Coppock, D.J., 15
Corfield, K.G., 159
Cotgrove, S., 203
Cowie, H., 233
Cunnison, S., 166

Dahrendorf, R., 11
Daly, A., 226–8
Daniel, W.W., 43, 162, 253, 277
Davies, J., 276
Deane, P., 17, 265
Denison, E.F., 42–3, 45, 97, 106
Dex, S., 276
Dodsworth, T., 205
Doeringer, P., 32
Dudley, N., 154
Dunham, J., 203
Dunn, S., 189, 190
Dunnett, J.S., 117

Edwards, G., 129, 161
Edwards, P.K., 62, 248, 252, 254, 268, 273, 279, 282
Edwards, R., 33–4
Eklund, K., 266, 267
Elbaum, B., 136
Elger, T., 15, 35, 36, 256
Elgin, R., 83
Eltis, W.A., 100–1
Emerson, R., 233
Engels, F., 16–18
Erlichman, J., 233

Fabricant, S., 267
Fidler, J., 92
Fisher, L., 26
Frank, A.G., 164
Franko, L.G., 159, 277

Frantz, R.S., 164
Friedman, A.L., 32–3, 34
Fryer, J., 112, 179, 209–10, 278

Gaffikin, F., 195
Galbraith, J.K., xiv–xv, 104
Gallie, D., 29, 124, 167–8, 170
Garnett, N., 161, 203, 204, 210
Gennard, J., 189, 190
Glover, R., 254
Glyn, A., 35, 36, 127–8, 141, 208, 235, 268
Goodhard, D., 190
Gooding, K., 245
Gorz, A., 31
Gramsci, A., 276
Grant, W., 283
Groom, B., 190, 201, 203, 205
Grunberg, L., 118
Gwyn, W.B., 10

Hampshire, M.J., 230
Handfield-Jones, S.J., 16
Harlow, C., 233
Harris, N., 51
Harrison, J., 208, 235
Hartmann, G., 157
Hayes, R.H., 278
Heller, F., 163
Henwood, F., 159
Hickson, D.J., 26–7
Higgs, P., 254, 256
Hitchens, D.M.W.N., 226–8
Hobsbawm, E.J., 135, 146
Hodgson, G., 35, 36, 258, 259, 261, 273
Hoffman, W.G., 17
Hogan, W.T., 113
Holbrook-Jones, M., 137
Hu, Y.-S., 130
Hutton, G., 19–20
Hyman, R., 15, 35, 36, 256

Ingham, G., 129

Jones, B., 190
Jones, D.T., 270
Jowell, R., 15

Kaldor, M., 131
Kaldor, N., 224, 269
Kaletsky, A., 224
Kamata, S., 277
Katrak, H., 110
Keegan, W., 217, 278
Kellner, P., 186
Kelly, J., 190
Kerr, C., 26
Kilpatrick, A., 35, 36, 125
King, W.T.C., 129
Kirby, M.W., 129, 147
Klein, J., 212
Klein, L., 11
Kolko, G., 145
Kosack, G., 116
Kransdorff, A., 153
Krause, L.B., 22

Landes, D.S., 131, 135
Lane, T., 193
Lash, S., 124
Lawson, T., 35, 36, 125
Lazonick, W.H., 35, 136
Leibenstein, H., 23, 34, 169,
    267–8
Leigh-Pemberton, R., 129
Lever, H., 129
Levine, A.L., 18
Lewis, W.A., 17, 135, 265, 266
Leys, C., 283
Lincoln, J.A., 274–5
Linhart, R., 118
Lipsey, D., 237
Littler, C.R., 34, 123, 151, 177,
    196, 219
Lupton, T., 25, 26, 27–8, 166

Macarov, D., 24
McClelland, D.C., 164

McDaid, M., 129
McKersie, R., 212
Maddison, A., 97, 265, 266, 267
Maier, C.S., 123
Maitland, I., 29, 123
Mallet, S., 31
Mandel, E., 17, 31, 263–7
Mann, M., 13–14
Manwaring, T., 35, 113, 274
Marsh, A., 190, 253
Marshall, A., 133
Marx, K., 16, 29, 30, 35, 127, 141
Massey, D., 181, 197
Matsuzaki, T., 113, 273
Matthewson, S.B., 25
Maunder, P., 87
Maunders, A.R., 35, 113, 274
Maxcy, G., 47, 48
Meegan, R., 181
Melman, S., 254–7
Mendis, L., 183–4
Miller, M.H., 173, 183
Mills, C.W., 26
Millward, N., 162, 253, 277
Minchinton, W.E., 145
Mitchell, B.R., 17
Montgomery, D., 32
Moorhouse, H.F., 135
Moran, P., 278
Muellbauer, J., 183–4, 186, 278
Murray, F.M., 123

Nichols, T., 15, 30, 160, 203, 276
Nickson, A., 195
Nightingale, M., 64
Nolan, P., 62, 248, 252, 273
Northcott, J., 231
Nossiter, B.D., 12–13

Owen, G., 206, 232

Paige, D., 3
Pascale, R.T., 169
Pavitt, K., 159

Payne, P.L., 144, 145
Perry, S.M., 276
Phelps Brown, E.H., 3, 16, 132, 133, 134, 136, 143, 271, 272
Pignon, D., 206
Pigou, A.C., 133
Pike, A., 225, 229
Piore, M.J., 32, 282
Pollard, S., 8, 139, 276
Poole, M.J.F., 108
Prais, S.J., 3, 64–5, 109, 110, 114, 121, 147, 151, 154, 226, 247, 248, 249, 273
Pratt, E.A., 4, 15, 263
Pratten, C.F., 3, 22, 40, 41, 45–7, 49, 52, 55ff, 88, 90–1, 93, 101, 104, 110, 115, 247, 248, 249, 250, 251, 252, 272, 274

Querzola, J., 206

Raimon, R.L., 106
Ramsay, H., 271
Ray, G.F., 220
Rayton, D., 254
Rebhan, H., 82
Rees, R., 193
Reeves, R., 213
Riddell, P., 181
Roderick, G., 160
Rodgers, P., 232
Rose, M., 29, 190
Rostas, L., 3
Roy, D., 25
Rubery, J., 191

Sachs, J.D., 186, 217
Salaman, G., 177
Sampson, A., 106, 108
Saul, S.B., 266
Saville, J., 147
Scarborough, H., 278
Schott, K., 107
Scullion, H., 254, 268

Shadwell, A., 18, 106
Shimmin, S., 166
Silbertson, A., 47, 48
Sisson, K., 189, 278
Sloan, A.P., 149
Smith, A.D., 3, 115
Smith, C., 83
Smith, C.T.B., 90
Smith, R., 139
Smith-Gavine, S.A.N., 184–5, 269
Soskice, D., 189, 190
Sparrow, P., 275–6
Spurrell, D., 129
Steer, P., 150
Stephens, J.D., 123
Stephens, M., 160
Stoikov, V., 106
Storey, J., 165, 177, 253
Sutcliffe, B., 35, 36, 268
Sutermeister, R.A., 24

Tarling, R., 191
Taylor, R., 114
Teece, D.J., 150
Terry, M., 190
Thomas, D., 147, 148, 151
Thomas, G., 159, 205
Thompson, E.P., 160
Trafford, G., 270
Trehel, J., 118
Trevor, M., 165–6
Trist, E.L., 32
Turner, H.A., 254, 255

Upham, M., 113
Upton, R., 196

Vamplew, C., 203
Veblen, T., 145, 146

Wagner, K., 154, 226–8, 247, 248
Watson, T.J., 28
Weber, M., 23, 145

Webb, S. and B., 5–6, 16, 18
Weekes, B., 253
Wenban-Smith, G.C., 176
Wheelwright, S.C., 278
White, M., 165–6
Whyte, W.F., 29
Wicks, J., 115, 276
Wiener, M.J., 10, 160
Wigham, E., 134
Wiles, P.J.D., 39
Wilkinson, F., 136, 191
Wilkinson, M., 269
Williams, J., 147, 148, 151

Williams, K., 147, 148, 151
Williamson, O.E., 104, 149
Willman, P., 177, 278
Winchester, M., 237
Worswick, G.D.N., 40
Wright, R., 254
Wyles, C., 211, 230

Yankelovich, D., 120, 168, 275–6

Zeitlin, J., 134, 136
Zweig, F., 254, 271

# Subject index

absenteeism, 173
accountants, 86, 92
Anglo-American Productivity
  Council, 19–20
apprenticeship, 109, 225
atomism (of industrial structure):
  early, 135, 144–6, 147, 148,
  149–50; more recent, 150–1
attitudes, 40–4, 98, 115, 117, 143,
  155, 168–9; origin of, 161–2
AUEW, 193, 194
Austria, 219, 270
automation/mechanisation, 47, 71,
  82–3, 154, 176, 179, 195, 204,
  210–11, 216, 226–7, 228, 230,
  279; CAM, 214; CNC, 157–8,
  195, 226

ballots, 181, 188, 190
bargaining units, 178, 277
batch size, 71
Becket, Sir Terence, 220, 283
Belgium, 81, 116, 185, 219, 223,
  224, 249, 271
BL, 21, 49, 74–93, 106, 112, 118,
  148, 161, 177–80, 181, 182,
  191, 204, 206, 208–10, 255–6
'born again' workers, 197
Boston Report, 137
bourgeois revolution, incomplete,
  11, 160, 215

BP, 51
British Leyland, see BL
British Shipbuilders, 206
British Telecom, 188
BSC, 106, 182, 203, 206, 245,
  273–4
Brazil, 117

ca'canny, 4
Callaghan, James, 181, 278
Canada, 219, 235, 270
CAM, see automation
canny curmudgeonly worker, 14
capacity utilisation, 82, 101, 153,
  282
capital export, 237
capital-led theory, 149
capital substitution, 48; see also
  wages
casualism, 196, 197, 198, 199,
  207, 219
CBI, see employers' organisations
CFT, 118, 123, 274
CGT, 123, 124
check-off system, 253
chemicals, 57, 114, 280
Chloride Group, 21, 106
Chrysler/Rootes, 66, 86, 117–18,
  244
citizenship, 116, 133
civil service, 160

closed shop, 186, 188, 189, 190, 253
clothing, 121, 185, 280
CNC, *see* automation
Cobden, Richard, 105
Collinson, Len, 177, 180
construction, 196
co-ordination of production, 105, 136, 142–3, 152ff, 210, 213, 231; *see also* planning
cost plus, 137
Courtauld, 206
CSL, 274
culture: and British education, 160; explanation in terms of, xii–xiv; and 'spirit', 23, 106, 117, 160, 169, 278

Daimler Benz, 119
defence, 158, 161, 231
de-industrialisation, 216
demarcation, 176, 178–9, 203, 204
Denmark, 219, 223, 224, 271
domestic appliance industry, 57
Donovan Report, 90, 275
Dunlop, 106, 206
Du Pont, 149

early start, thesis of, 135ff, 144, 147
economics, xii, xiv–xv, 22, 24, 34, 50, 268; and comparative statics, 41, 53–93, 97; language of, 275
Edwardes, Sir Michael, 21, 83, 92, 106, 178, 181, 208, 270
EEF, *see* employers' organisations
EETPU, 123, 193, 194, 204
efficiency of labour, 268
effort: concept of, 42–5; international comparisons, 155; and management, 261; and work ethic, 120, 275

electronics, 57, 189, 194, 196, 203, 204–5, 228–9, 229–32, 277
employers' organisations, 143, 146, 189; CBI, 189, 194, 220, 232, 279, 282–3; EEF, 162, 178, 189; Institute of Directors, 224
employment concentration, 151
employment relation, restructuring of, 196–201: *see also* casualism
engineering industry, 57, 134, 145, 146, 153–5, 178, 225, 253, 280
engineers, 107–8, 110, 160, 227, 231
English disease, 160
entrepreneurial ability, 144–5
Esso, 203
exchange control, 237
exchange rate, 185, 211, 216, 221, 233

fascism, 122, 132
Fiat, 49
financial capital, 121, 136, 138–9, 148, 216, 231, 232, 282; quality of, 129–30; and industrial capital, 130
Finland, 219
Finniston Report, 108
Fisher Body, 193
flexibility, 178–9, 201–6, 281; flexible firm, 201, 202, 229
food, drink and tobacco, 57, 62, 113, 121, 195, 280
footwear, 185, 280
Ford, 47, 66, 80, 81, 82, 83, 112, 116, 119, 120, 205
foremen, 157–8, 227–8
France, 3, 14, 20, 55ff, 110, 116, 117, 118, 119, 121, 122, 130, 140, 144, 147, 158–9, 167–8, 219, 220, 221, 223, 224, 230, 232, 235, 271, 272, 276, 282, 283
Franklin, Benjamin, 144–5

Friedman, Milton, 232

gang system, 253–7
GEC, 207
General Motors, 149, 205
GKN, 206
GMBATU, 193
greenfield sites, 193–5, 203, 212
group working, 193

Harvey Jones, Sir John, 233
Healey, Denis, 20, 21, 55, 181
health and safety, 118–20,
    199–201, 222, 274, 279–81
Heath, Edward, 259, 275
Hitachi, 194
holidays, 19, 177, 283
Hoskyns, Sir John, 224
hours of work, 19; overtime, 99,
    176, 177, 195
Howe, Sir Geoffrey, 175, 186
'human relations industry', 26, 32

ICI, 21, 195, 206, 233, 279
ICL, 106
ideology: anti-productivist, 10, 13;
    liberal humanist, 10–15, 37,
    134; nature of, 8, 91;
    productivist, 276; reproduction
    of, 243–51, 271–2; and social
    classes, 10–11; trade union
    reaction to, 5, 18–19, 20; and
    truth, xiii
indirect workers, 62, 70, 71, 77–8,
    80, 110, 113; see also
    maintenance
individualism, 145, 151, 215
industrial capital: circuit of, 127ff;
    concentration of, 146–7; and
    state/financial nexus, 129,
    138–9, 148; and Thatcherism,
    189, 282–3
industrial relations: changes in
    Britain, 189–91; legislation, 3–4,

25, 186–9, 190, 253–4;
    specialist study of, 11, 143, 254
industrial specialisation, 146–7
inflation, 174
Institute of Directors, *see*
    employers' organisations
Institute of Economic Affairs, 274
interest rates, 211, 216, 233, 236
International Harvester, 232
investment, 20, 41, 71, 74, 82–7,
    105, 129, 138–40, 152, 179,
    184–5, 218, 231, 232–3, 235–6,
    237
Ireland, 224
iron and steel, 13, 112–13, 144,
    196, 254, 273–4
Israel, 271
ISTC, 113, 274
Italy, 117, 122, 219, 223, 224, 282

Japan, 107, 112–13, 117, 122,
    130, 136, 137, 153, 158–9,
    165–6, 169, 175, 185, 193, 197,
    205, 219, 220, 221, 224, 225,
    230, 235, 240, 245, 273–4, 275,
    277–8, 282, 283
Jay, Peter, 278
job control, and productivity,
    253–7
job enrichment, 201
job expectations, 168
job security, 6, 122, 205, 219, 275,
    277, 281
jobs, bad, 218, 275
Jones, Jack, 18–19, 258, 267

kanban system, 245
Karno, Fred, 169
King, Tom, 220, 228–9
KME, 177

labour aristocracy, 135
labour intensification, 31, 181,
    206, 209, 258, 268, 280

labour-led theory, 70, 149, 282
labour market segmentation:
  theories of, 32–4; in Britain
  today, 200–2; *see also* casualism
Labour Party, 19–20, 37, 55, 188
labour-power, 141, 273
labour productivity: definition, 20,
  267–8
labour utilisation, 183–4, 278
Lawson, Nigel, 222, 240
Liberal Party, 133
Linotype Paul, 229
long-term contracts, 189
long waves, 263–7
Lucas, 206

MacGregor, Ian, 106
machine tool industry, 57
maintenance, 87, 112–13, 167,
  197–8, 199, 201, 203, 204, 227;
  *see also* indirect workers
management: changes in, 209–13,
  215; culture and habituation,
  159–60; demarcation within,
  152ff, 228; knowledge of
  productivity, 62–3, 92–3;
  'laissez faire', 136, 156, 218;
  'macho', 191, 279; motivation,
  164; neglect of, 60–1, 91, 97,
  104; organisational/technical
  capacity, 98, 101–2, 103, 104,
  161–2, 192, 230, 234–5; and
  relocation, 205; social origin, 6,
  160–1; and social science,
  164–5, 243ff; and vengeance,
  177–8, 180; workers' views of,
  166–70, 234–5
'man-management', 278
marketing, 87, 99–100, 105, 137,
  138, 211, 230–1, 246; and
  empire, 137, 146–7
marxism: and capacity to labour,
  141, 273; and co-ordination,
  164; and economics, 32, 37,
  127, 267–8; and productivity,

34–7, 163–4; and productivism,
  276–7; and study of labour
  process, xv, 29–34, 37, 142
Marshall Aid Plan, 19–20
Massey Ferguson, 206, 257
mergers, 146, 147, 150, 185
Metal Box, 195, 244, 245–6,
  247–8, 252, 281
'm-form', 149–50, 201
microelectronics, *see* automation
migrant labour, 115–26, 224, 274
Mobil Oil, 203
monetarism, 173–4, 217, 232
monopoly capitalism, 124, 132,
  135, 145, 151; and deskilling,
  31
motor bike industry, 137
mutuality, 178

National Free Labour Association,
  4
nationalisation, 146
Netherlands, 116, 121, 185, 219,
  223, 224, 235, 270, 271
new technology, *see* automation
NGA, 188
Nissan, 112, 194
Norway, 219, 282
NUM, 123

OCS, 197
oil, North Sea, 237
oil refining, 124
Opel, 119
organisation of production,
  127–70; *see also* co-ordination,
  planning
organisation of work, changes in,
  191–203
output: concentration, 146–7;
  measurement, 278; under
  Thatcher, 183
over capacity, 91
'overmanning', 76–8, 101, 113,

114, 139, 186, 226
overtime, *see* hours of work

participation, 28, 162–3, 179, 253–7, 261–2, 271
part-time work, 121, 196–7, 220, 276, 277, 279
pendulum arbitration, 193
Peugeot, 116
physical means of production, nature of, 45, 142, 152–3, 163; *see also* plant
picketing, 186
Pilkingtons, 203–4
planning, 139, 154, 156, 157, 159, 166, 167, 209, 230–1, 233, 250, 260–1
plant: age, 20, 74, 81, 84, 86, 87, 100–1, 103, 105, 154, 161, 278; interplant relations, 147–51; layout, 81, 85–6, 87, 92, 101, 154, 161, 212, 213, 218; size and ownership, 150–1
Playfair, Sir Lyon, 108
POEW, 188
'polyvalent worker', 123, 203
printing, 62, 189, 204, 232, 248, 280
Pritchard Services, 197
product design, 155–7, 159, 210, 228
product variants, 245–6
production breakdowns, 80, 227–8
profit: rate, 235, 264; short-term in Britain, 227, 231

quality circles, 277
quality faults, 79–80, 213, 234

R & D, 105, 107, 130–1, 158, 229, 230–1, 277
Raleigh, 206
'Red Robbo', *see* Robinson, Derek

regional differences, 64, 189, 193, 195
relations of production, vertical and horizontal, 141–3
relocation, 193–4, 205, 212, 237; and multinationals, 195
Renault, 116
resistance to change, 15, 40, 67, 70, 88, 90, 98, 102, 118, 204, 205, 230, 231–2, 248, 261, 279, 282
restriction of output studies, 24–7, 34, 166, 254
restrictive practices, definitions of, 274–5
Robinson, Derek ('Red Robbo'), 178, 270
Rothmans, 193, 212
Ryder Report, 46, 47, 49, 74

Saunderson, Roy, 204
scale of production, 47, 48, 71
scientific management, 29, 30, 122, 135, 151, 277
Scottish and Newcastle Breweries, 203, 247
scrapping, 182, 183, 235, 278
self-certification, 206
self-employment, 196, 197, 202, 207, 269
seniority system, 254, 281–2
services, 121, 190, 196–7, 216, 232, 276
shiftwork, 195, 201, 247, 279
shipbuilding, 136, 145, 146, 203, 206, 280
single union agreements, 190, 193, 194
size effects, 64, 249
'slimming', 206–7, 215
slow work pace, 79, 88, 135
small enterprises, 199, 200, 201
social sciences, division of labour in, 22–36, 164–5; *see also*

economics, industrial relations, sociology
sociology, xiii, xv, 11, 14, 22, 23, 24–9, 268
Spain, 122, 155, 282
Stewart, Shaun, 278
stock control, 154, 156, 213
stock turn, 153, 211, 244–6, 250, 255, 260
Stone-Platt, 154–6
strikes, 19, 49, 62, 79, 90, 99, 173, 188, 224, 244ff, 270; no-strike agreements, 193
sub-contract, 111, 112, 191, 196–8, 200, 201, 202, 207, 220, 277, 279
Sweden, 121, 153, 168, 219, 271, 275
Switzerland, 67, 115, 116, 118, 119, 121, 219, 270, 276

Talbot, 206
task model, 192
TASS, 80–1
Taylor, F.W., 29
taxation, 224, 238, 282
technical education and training, 77, 106–10, 114, 121, 125, 157, 161–2, 225, 227–31, 233; and flexibility, 114
technological revolutions, 264; third, 232, 264
textiles, 57, 121, 145, 146, 195, 280
TGWU, 124, 193
Thatcherism: and American model, 221, 236, 281–2; as bourgeois force, 215, 217, 221; and 'co-operation', 175, 176, 183, 219; early claims about productivity, 175; as European phenomenon, 233–4; and fear, 173ff, 216; and investment, 218, 231, 232–3, 235–6, 237; and manufacturing decline, 173, 183; and manufacturing performance, 183–6, 240; and 'new realism', 187–214, 219; political problems of, 208, 221–2; and R & D, 229, 230–1; as 'success', 215, 219; and training, 225–30; and tunnel vision, 236; and wages, 219–20, 224; and wealth and income, 238
'Think Tank Report', 21, 40, 46, 47, 52, 74–93, 104, 118, 244, 245, 246, 249, 252
three-day week, 162, 259–62
TI, 206
tinplate, 145, 245
Tory Party, 9, 20
Toshiba, 194, 204
Toyota, 277
trade unions: craft, 114, 122, 123, 132, 136, 204, 254; decentralised in Britain, 64, 66, 123, 134, 146; and demarcation, 114; development of British, 132–7, 146; enterprise unionism, 193–4; and law, 4, 132–4, 187–9; membership, 173; number of unions, 146, 277; and politics, 19, 67, 122, 123, 124, 133, 134, 218; public opinion and, 15, 282; strength of, 122–4, 165–6, 262; Taff Vale, 132, 188
Trebor, 193, 212
Triumph, 66, 253–7
TUC, 146, 188

UAW, 205
underclass, 207–8, 215, 216, 221, 281; *see also* casualism
'underproduction', 78–84
unemployment, 122, 173, 174, 217, 238–9
Unilever, 232
Urwick-Orr, 154–5, 277

USA, 3, 5, 14, 20, 55ff, 100, 105, 107, 110, 117, 122–3, 135, 140, 144, 145, 147, 149–50, 152, 153, 154–5, 158–9, 205, 207–8, 220, 221, 223, 224, 225, 229, 230, 234, 235, 250, 251, 272, 274, 277–8, 281–2, 283

Vauxhall, 118, 206
vehicles, 45–50, 57, 62, 65–6, 74–93, 112, 116–20, 121, 246, 248, 252, 270
Vickers, 161
Volkswagen, 49, 51
vulnerability of labour: and casualism, 196, 197, 198, 207; and compliance, 276; international differences, 115–26; and marxism, 273

wages, 8, 48, 71, 83, 135, 154, 155, 224, 275; payment systems, 156–7, 205, 256; and skill, 106, 176, 208, 238; unit costs, 219–21, 224
war-time production, 6–7, 9, 122, 137
Wass, Sir Douglas, 176

welfare state, 207–8, 219, 224
Weinstock, Arnold, Lord, 207
West Germany, 3, 5, 14, 20, 55ff, 106, 107–10, 114, 115, 116, 118, 120, 121, 123, 130, 136, 140, 144, 145, 147, 152, 153, 157, 158–9, 168, 175, 219, 220, 221, 223, 224, 225, 226–8, 229, 230, 232, 235, 240, 249, 271, 272, 274, 275, 276, 282, 283
Whitbread, 193
Wilkinson Sword, 212–13
women workers, 102–3, 121, 122, 125, 196–7, 219, 238, 277
work ethic, 120, 275; Protestant, 144–5
'worker control', 253–7
working class: images of, 4–5, 7–8, 14; restructuring of, 201, 207, 215, 222, 236
working practices: Britain compared, 45–50; failure to examine, 44, 59

X-efficiency, 23, 34, 164, 169, 267–8

YTS, 229